Rupert of Deutz

Published under the auspices of the
Center for Medieval and Renaissance Studies
University of California, Los Angeles

Publications of the
UCLA Center for Medieval
and Renaissance Studies

1. Jeffrey Burton Russell, *Dissent and Reform in the Early Middle Ages* (1965)

2. C. D. O'Malley, ed., *Leonardo's Legacy: An International Symposium* (1968)

3. Richard H. Rouse, *Serial Bibliographies for Medieval Studies* (1969)

4. Speros Vryonis, Jr., *The Decline of Medieval Hellenism in Asia Minor and the Process of Islamization from the Eleventh through the Fifteenth Century* (1971)

5. Stanley Chodorow, *Christian Political Theory and Church Politics in the Mid-Twelfth Century: The Ecclesiology of Gratian's Decretum* (1972)

6. Joseph J. Duggan, *The Song of Roland: Formulaic Style and Poetic Craft* (1973)

7. Ernest A. Moody, *Studies in Medieval Philosophy, Science, and Logic: Collected Papers 1933–1969* (1975)

8. Marc Bloch, *Slavery and Serfdom in the Middle Ages: Selected Essays* (1975)

9. Michael J. B. Allen, *Marsilio Ficino: The Philebus Commentary, A Critical Edition and Translation* (1975)

10. Richard C. Dales, *Marius: On the Elements, A Critical Edition and Translation* (1976)

11. Duane J. Osheim, *An Italian Lordship: The Bishopric of Lucca in the Late Middle Ages* (1977)

12. Robert Somerville, *Pope Alexander III and the Council of Tours (1163): A Study of Ecclesiastical Politics and Institutions in the Twelfth Century* (1977)

13. Lynn White, jr., *Medieval Religion and Technology: Collected Essays* (1978)

14. Michael J. B. Allen, *Marsilio Ficino and the Phaedran Charioteer: Introduction, Texts, Translations* (1981)

15. Barnabas Bernard Hughes, O.F.M., *Jordanus de Nemore: De numeris datis, A Critical Edition and Translation* (1981)

16. Caroline Walker Bynum, *Jesus as Mother: Studies in the Spirituality of the High Middle Ages* (1982)

17. Carlo M. Cipolla, *The Monetary Policy of Fourteenth-Century Florence* (1982)

18. John H. Van Engen, *Rupert of Deutz* (1983)

Rupert of Deutz

JOHN H. VAN ENGEN

University
of California
Press

Berkeley
Los Angeles
London

The emblem of the Center
for Medieval and Renaissance Studies
reproduces the imperial eagle
of the gold *augustalis* struck
after 1231 by Emperor Frederick II;
Elvira and Vladimir Clain-Stefanelli,
The Beauty and Lore of Coins, Currency and Medals
(Croton-on-Hudson, 1974), fig. 130 and p. 106.

University of California Press
Berkeley and Los Angeles, California

University of California Press, Ltd.
London, England

© 1983 by
The Regents of the University of California

Printed in the United States of America

1 2 3 4 5 6 7 8 9

Library of Congress Cataloging in Publication Data

Van Engen, John H.
  Rupert of Deutz.

  (Publications of the UCLA Center for Medieval and
Renaissance Studies; 18)
  Revision of thesis (Ph.D.)
  Bibliography: p.
  Includes index.
  1. Rupert, of Deutz, ca. 1075–1129. 2. Theology,
Doctrinal—History—Middle Ages, 600–1500. I. Title.
II. Series.
BX4705.R73V36 1983   271'.1'024 [B] 82-40089
ISBN 0-520-04577-7

To
Gerhart B. Ladner
and
the memory of
Peter Classen

Contents

CONTENTS

Acknowledgements

MANY INSTITUTIONS and individuals have generously supported my work on this book. An award from the Deutscher Akademischer Austauschdienst made possible two years of research at Heidelberg, a Research Assistantship at UCLA's Center for Medieval and Renaissance Studies allowed me to complete the dissertation (1976), and a fellowship from the American Council of Learned Societies for Recent Recipients of the Ph.D. (1980) enabled me thoroughly to revise the dissertation. I can express only in a word, and very inadequately, my great debt to individuals: to Howard Rienstra, Edwin Van Kley, and Robert Otten at Calvin College, for introducing me to the study of the past; to Robert Benson at UCLA, for sound advice all along the way; to Giles Constable, John Benton, and Robert Brentano, for critical readings of the dissertation; to Caroline Bynum and Jaroslav Pelikan, for helpful reviews of the revised manuscript; to Hubert Silvestre at Brussels, for his supportive interest which included sending many offprints and even answering manuscript queries; to all my colleagues in the History Department at the University of Notre Dame, especially Father Marvin O'Connell, for collegial support; to Ralph McInerny, Director of the Medieval Institute at Notre Dame, for providing encouragement and excellent working conditions; to Brian Pavlac, graduate student at the University of Notre Dame, for drawing the map and the sketch of Deutz; and to Carol Lanham, senior editor at UCLA's Center for Medieval and Renaissance Studies, for her meticulous work on the final manuscript. None of this would have been possible without the continuous support of my mother and my parents-in-law. Still more, my wife Suzanne and our four sons have borne with great patience the repeated loss of husband and father to his preoccupation with a twelfth-century monk; their love sustained me throughout. This book is dedicated to two teachers, Gerhart Ladner of UCLA and the late Peter Classen of Heidelberg, who first inspired and informed my understanding of the medieval historian's task.

Abbreviations

Rupert's Works

Alt.	*Altercatio monachi et clerici, quod liceat monacho praedicare* (PL 170.537–42)
Anulus	*Anulus siue Dialogus inter Christianum et Iudaeum*, ed. R. Haacke, in M. L. Arduini, *Ruperto di Deutz e la controversia tra Cristiani ed Ebrei nel secolo XII* (Studi Storici 119–121, Rome 1979) 183–242
Apoc.	*In Apocalypsim* (PL 169.825–1214)
Cant.	*In Canticum Canticorum de incarnatione Domini*, ed. R. Haacke (CM 26)
Carm.	*Carmina exulis de calamitatibus ecclesiae Leodiensis*, ed. H. Boehmer (MGH LdL 3.622–41)
Epistola	*Epistola ad Everardum abbatem Brunwillarensem* (PL 170.541–44)
Glor.	*De glorificatione Trinitatis et processione Spiritus Sancti* (PL 169.13–202)
Herib.	*Vita Heriberti*, ed. P. Dinter (Bonn 1976)
Incendio	*De incendio*, ed. H. Grundmann, *DA* 22 (1966) 441–71
John	*In euangelium sancti Iohannis*, ed. R. Haacke (CM 9)
Laes.	*De laesione uirginitatis* (PL 170.543–60)
Matt.	*De gloria et honore Filii hominis super Matthaeum*, ed. R. Haacke (CM 29)
Medit.	*De meditatione mortis* (PL 170.357–90)

Off.	*De diuinis officiis*, ed. R. Haacke (CM 7)
Omnip.	*De omnipotentia Dei* (PL 170.453–78)
Proph.	*In XII Prophetas minores* (PL 168.9–836)
RegBen.	*Super quaedam capitula regulae Benedicti*, or *Liber de Apologeticis suis* (PL 170.477–538)
Trin.	*De sancta Trinitate et operibus eius*, ed. R. Haacke (CM 21–24), which includes *Gen., Exod., Levit., Num., Deut., Iosue, Iud., Reg., Ps., Is., Hier., Hiez., Dan., Evang.*, and *Spir.* = *De operibus Spiritus sancti*
Vict.	*De uictoria Verbi Dei*, ed. R. Haacke (MGH Geistesgeschichte 5)
Vol.	*De uoluntate Dei* (PL 170.437–54)

Secondary Works

AHDL	*Archives d'histoire doctrinale et littéraire du moyen âge*
Beinert, *Kirche*	Wolfgang Beinert, *Die Kirche—Gottes Heil in der Welt: Die Lehre von der Kirche nach den Schriften des Rupert von Deutz, Honorius Augustodunensis und Gerhoch von Reichersberg* (BGPT n.F. 13, Münster 1973)
BGPT	Beiträge zur Geschichte der Philosophie und Theologie des Mittelalters
Bischoff, *Controversy*	Guntram G. Bischoff, "The Eucharistic Controversy between Rupert of Deutz and His Anonymous Adversary: Studies in the Theology and Chronology of Rupert of Deutz (c. 1076–c. 1129) and his Earlier Literary Work" (diss. Princeton Seminary, 1965)
CC	Corpus Christianorum
CM	Corpus Christianorum, Continuatio mediaevalis

DA	*Deutsches Archiv*
Dinter, *Heribert*	P. Dinter, *Rupert von Deutz, Vita Heriberti: Kritische Edition Mit Kommentar und Untersuchungen* (Bonn 1976)
DTC	*Dictionnaire de Théologie Catholique*
Gessler, "Bibliothèque"	J. Gessler, "La bibliothèque de l'abbaye de Saint-Laurent à Liège au XIIe et XIIIe siècles," *Bulletin de la société des bibliophiles liégeois* 12 (1927) 91–135
Leclercq, *Love of Learning*	J. Leclercq, *The Love of Learning and the Desire for God*, trans. C. Misrahi (2nd ed. New York 1974)
Lottin, *Psychologie*	O. Lottin, *Problèmes d'histoire littéraire: L'école d'Anselme de Laon et de Guillaume de Champeaux*, in his *Psychologie et morale aux XIIe et XIIIe siècles*, vol. 5 (Gembloux 1959)
Magrassi, *Teologia*	M. Magrassi, *Teologia e storia nel pensiero di Ruperto di Deutz* (Studia Urbaniana 2, Rome 1959)
MGH	Monumenta Germaniae Historica
DD	Diplomata
LdL	Libelli de Lite
SS	Scriptores
Pelikan, *Theology*	J. Pelikan, *The Growth of Medieval Theology* (Chicago 1978)
PL	J. P. Migne, *Patrologia Latina*
Rauh, *Antichrist*	H. D. Rauh, *Das Bild des Antichrist im Mittelalter: Von Tyconius zum deutschen Symbolismus* (BGPT n.F. 9, Münster 1972)

RB	*Revue Bénédictine*
RBPH	*Revue Belge de philologie et d'histoire*
RHE	*Revue d'histoire ecclésiastique*
RTAM	*Recherches de théologie ancienne et médiévale*
Saint-Laurent	*Saint-Laurent de Liège* (Liège 1968)
SMBO	*Studien und Mitteilungen zur Geschichte des Benediktiner-Ordens*
Van den Gheyn	J. Van den Gheyn, *Catalogue des manuscrits de la bibliothèque royale de Belgique* (9 vols. Brussels 1901–09)

Chronology of the Life and Works of Rupert of Deutz

OTHER LISTS OF Rupert's works may be found in Magrassi, *Teologia* 23–35; Haacke, *DA* 26 (1970) 533–40; Beinert, *Kirche* 412–13; Dinter, *Vita Heriberti* 99–102; Silvestre, *RB* 88 (1978) 286–89; and the *Index Scriptorum Operumque Latino-Belgicorum Medii Aevi* 3.2.235–64.

ca. 1075	Born in or near Liège
ca. 1082	Enters St. Lawrence just outside Liège as oblate
ca. 1091	Professed as a monk of St. Lawrence
February 1092 –July 1095	In exile at priory of Evergnicourt in France
1095	*Carmina exulis*
ca. 1100–1105	St. Lawrence adopts Cluniac customary
ca. 1100–1108	Vocational crisis; visionary experiences
ca. 1105–1108	Resists ordination by Bishop Otbert
1095–1108	*Libellus* (LOST); *De diuersis scripturarum sententiis* (LOST); *De incarnatione Domini* (LOST); *Vita sancti Augustini*; *Cantus de Theodardo*

	martyre, Goare ac Seuero confessoribus (LOST)
ca. 1108	*Hymnus siue Oratio ad sanctum Spiritum*
ca. December 1108	Ordination
ca. 1108–1110	*In Iob*
1108–1119	*Contra presbyteros concubinatos* (LOST); *Contra monachum clericum factum* (LOST)
1109–1112	*De diuinis officiis*
1112–fall 1116	*De sancta Trinitate et operibus eius*
ca. 1113–1115	Eucharistic debate in Liège with Alger
1114–1116	*In euangelium sancti Iohannis* Predestinarian debate in Liège
Summer 1116	*De uoluntate Dei*
September 1116	Trial
November 1116 –spring 1117	Exile at Siegburg *Epistula ad Cunonem Sigebergensem abbatem* (dedicatory for *Trin.*); *De omnipotentia Dei* cc. 1–18; *Epistula . . . ad Cunonem . . . qua de causa hoc opus in Iohannem euangelistam aggressus sit*
ca. May 1117	Returns to Liège, and completes *Omnip.*
July –August 1117	Debates masters at Laon and Bishop William in Châlon-sur-Marne
Fall 1117–1118	His teaching on creation of angels attacked in Liège
April 1119	Departs to Cologne
1119–1120	*Vita sancti Heriberti*

1119–1121	*In Apocalypsim*
Fall 1120	Appointed abbot of Deutz
ca. 1120–1122	*Altercatio monachi et clerici*
1121–1124	*In XII Prophetas minores*
ca. 1121–1′124	*De laesione uirginitatis*
1121–1128	*Passio beati Eliphii*
ca. 1122–1124	*Epistola ad Everardum*
1123–1124	*De uictoria Verbi Dei*
ca. 1124	Norbert charges heresy
Christmas 1124	Journeys to Rome
1125–1127	*De gloria et honore Filii hominis super Matthaeum*
1125	*Super quaedam capitula regulae Benedicti; In Canticum Canticorum de incarnatione Domini*
ca. 1125–1128	*Epistola ad F.; Quaestio utrum monachis liceat praedicare; Sermo de sancto Pantaleone*
Spring 1126	*Anulus*
Summer 1126	*Ad . . . episcopum Cunonem epistula . . . pro libro de diuinis officiis*
1126–1127	*In Samuelen et David* (LOST)
1126–1128	Strife over the castle at Deutz
January –February 1128	Journeys to Münster; debates Hermannus
March –August 1128	*De glorificatione Trinitatis et processione Spiritus sancti*
28 August 1128	Fire at Deutz
Fall 1128	*De incendio*
1129	*De meditatione mortis*
4 March 1129	Dies and is buried at Deutz

xix

Introduction

$\mathfrak{B}$ETWEEN THE YEARS 1050 and 1150 deep change affecting nearly every aspect of society and culture transformed the world of the early middle ages. Contemporaries sought words and images to distinguish their times and achievements from the world of "antiquity," and ever more frequently they struck upon the word "modern."[1] So also in this century medieval historians have invented one label after another to take account of all the startling new developments first evidenced around the year 1100: the Second Age of Feudalism (Bloch), the Commercial Revolution (Lopez and others), the Twelfth-Century Renaissance (Haskins), the Gregorian Reform (Fliche and others) or Revolution (Rosenstock-Huessy), the Origins of European Dissent, meaning heresy (Moore), and still others. Historians of every kind have analyzed these novelties and proposed in turn nearly every conceivable factor as the single most important agent of change, from better diets and population growth to individualism and increased self-awareness. The sheer magnitude

1. See W. Freund, *Modernus und andere Zeitbegriffe des Mittelalters* (Neue Münsterische Beiträge zur Geschichtsforschung 4, Münster 1957); W. Hartmann, "'Modernus' und 'antiquus': Zur Verbreitung und Bedeutung dieser Bezeichnungen in der wissenschaftlichen Literatur vom 9. bis zum 12. Jahrhundert," and E. Gossmann, "'Antiqui' und 'Moderni' im 12. Jahrhundert," both in *Antiqui und Moderni* (Miscellanea mediaevalia 9, Berlin and New York 1974) 21–39, 40–57. This perception also underlies much of Alexander Murray's *Reason and Society in the Middle Ages* (Oxford 1978). For an elegant statement by a master who lived through the invention of all the other labels listed below: E. Gilson, "Le moyen âge comme 'saeculum modernorum,'" in *Concetto, storia, miti e immagini del medio evo*, ed. V. Branca (Florence 1973) 1–10.

I

of demographic, socio-economic, and institutional change inspired Duby to label it the "take-off" of the European economy, that which modern economists long for and seek to effect in third-world countries.

But such change, dramatic though it may be in its total impact, remains difficult to trace in detail during the earlier middle ages. Consequently, the images historians have fashioned still depend very considerably upon their regard for a few leading individuals. William the Conqueror and Roger of Sicily, for instance, have come to represent the new feudal monarchies, William of Aquitaine and Chrétien of Troyes the new courtly culture, Berengar of Tours and Peter Abelard the new theology, Cardinal Humbert and Pope Gregory VII the new Church, Peter Damian and St. Bernard of Clairvaux the new religious. Sometimes, as in the oft-rewritten essay on Abelard and St. Bernard, a clash between individuals has come to stand for two diverging movements (here, "scholastic" and "monastic" theology, or the new monasteries against the new schools). Just as frequently, a single individual has given form to a widely used general category. Nearly every depiction of "wandering scholars" depends ultimately upon Abelard's description of himself in his *Historia calamitatum*; Dom Jean Leclercq's highly influential notion of "monastic theology" is founded upon and works best for the life and works of St. Bernard; Duby's argument for a new "courtly ideology" comes back ever and again to Lambert of Ardres, author of the *History of the Counts of Guines*; and Pirenne's conception of the "origins of the bourgeoisie" found its support and expression in Godric of Finchdale.

Such a close identification of whole movements with single, often extraordinary, individuals, even in matters pertaining to ecclesiastical, intellectual, or religious history, risks severe oversimplification; and historians have begun to distinguish more carefully between Pope Gregory and the new Church, Peter Abelard and the new schools, St. Bernard and the new monks. But beyond the felt need for a deeper analysis of social and institutional dimensions, another objection arises: each of these figures helped to usher in and thus came to stand for that which was distinctively new. To enrich our understanding of this transitionary age the perceptions of still other individuals, not so readily identified with the emerging new order, must also be considered. For the historian's purpose, in fact, the perspective offered by a conservative—or better still, by someone deeply rooted in the old order struggling alternately to keep up with and to resist the new—often provides far greater insight into the actual depth and extent of historical change. Such is the perspective on the early twelfth century afforded by the life and works of Rupert of Deutz.

The most prolific of all twelfth-century authors, Rupert of Deutz (ca. 1075–1129) wrote his major works during the twenty years between St. Anselm's death in 1109 and the emergence of St. Bernard, Peter Abelard, and Hugh of St. Victor late in the 1120's. Rupert's life and works are emblematic of this transitionary age. He entered the monastic life as a child oblate, yet suffered an extended vocational crisis as a young man, only to emerge an ardent defender of traditional Benedictine monasticism. A zealous supporter of papal reform, he spent nearly thirty years subject to the most loyal of all Henry IV's imperial bishops. Probably a Walloon and certainly close enough to the French border to follow developments there, he nonetheless lived all but three of his approximately fifty-five years inside the German Empire, just outside two of its leading episcopal cities. As a theologian, finally, he was scorned by the new schoolmen for irremediable ignorance of dialectic, while at the same time very nearly condemned to silence for impudent new interpretations of Scripture.

A similar ambiguity overshadows Rupert's ultimate importance and influence. He was not a religious or theological figure of the first magnitude, but neither was he the relatively minor archconservative, the token voice of protest, which much of the extant literature has made him out to be. Two independent literary histories from the generation after his death concluded their accounts with Rupert and his works.[2] In the 1140's and also in-

---

2. Honorius, *De luminaribus ecclesiae* 4.16: PL 172.232; *Anonymous Mellicensis* [Wolfger of Prüfening], ed. E. Ettlinger (Karlsruhe 1896) 96.

dependently, a Thuringian and a Bavarian labeled Rupert, together with Hugh of St. Victor, the "two modern lights" or "two modern angels."[3] In 1146/47 Arno of Reichersberg paid Rupert perhaps the most fitting compliment in describing him as the leading author among Cluniacs or traditional Benedictines, comparable to Hugh of St. Victor among canons regular and St. Bernard among Cistercians.[4] But no such testimonies have come down from anyone outside the German Empire, and none at all from after the year 1150.

The manuscript transmission of Rupert's works confirms the testimony of his contemporaries.[5] In numbers alone, with over two hundred fifty extant copies of his works, Rupert far surpassed Benedictine contemporaries such as Guibert of Nogent, Godfrey of Vendôme, and even Peter Abelard,[6] and he compared favorably with Bruno of Segni[7] and Anselm of Canterbury. But he nowhere approached the numbers (1500?) and influence of St. Bernard, whose works were distributed throughout Europe by the rapidly expanding Cistercian Order, nor indeed those of Hugh of St. Victor, whose works appealed equally to the student-clerics of Paris and the cloistered canons and monks of Bavaria.[8] Rupert had likewise no single devotional

3. Sindaldus of Reinhardsbrunn, in *Die Reinhardsbrunner Briefsammlung*, ed. F. Peeck (MGH epist. sel. 5, Weimar 1952) 32–33; Gerhoch of Reichersberg, *In Ps. 33*, in *Opera inedita*, ed. D. and O. van den Eynde and P. Rijmersdael (Rome 1955) 2.209.

4. *Scutum canonicorum*: PL 194.1519.

5. I am wholly indebted here to R. Haacke, "Die Ueberlieferung der Schriften Ruperts von Deutz," *DA* 16 (1960) 397–436, though his thesis that Rupert was a spokesman for the Siegburger Reform and his works therefore circulated largely in reformed houses is not persuasive. See also idem, "Nachlese zur Ueberlieferung Ruperts von Deutz," *DA* 26 (1970) 528–40; H. Silvestre, "La tradition manuscrite des oeuvres de Rupert de Deutz," *Scriptorium* 16 (1962) 336–45; idem, "Les manuscrits des oeuvres de Rupert," *RB* 88 (1978) 286–89.

6. N. M. Häring, "Abelard Yesterday and Today," *Pierre Abélard—Pierre le Vénérable* (Paris 1975) 341–403.

7. About 175 MSS: R. Grégoire, *Bruno de Segni* (Spoleto 1965) 59–144.

8. About 1350 extant MSS: R. Goy, *Die Ueberlieferung der Werke Hugos von St. Viktor* (Stuttgart 1976). Cf. *Speculum* 53 (1978) 574–75, and Silvestre (n. 5 above) 287–88.

"best-seller" such as Hugh's *De arrha animae* (327 extant copies!), St. Bernard's *Sermons*, or William of St. Thierry's *Golden Epistle* (276 MSS), though his *De diuinis officiis* exists still in seventy copies and his *Commentary on the Canticle of Canticles* in more than forty. Hugh and St. Bernard also had their works distributed more widely by far than any other contemporary author. Even St. Anselm, as R. W. Southern has shown, was little known at first outside England and Normandy. So also Rupert remained almost completely unknown in England, Spain, southern France, and Italy; and in northern France, apart from his widely used commentary on the divine office, only particular works reached individual houses, with no discoverable pattern of influence. Clairvaux, for instance, possibly still in St. Bernard's lifetime, possessed copies of *De diuinis officiis* and *De uictoria Verbi Dei*.

Rupert's greatest influence lay inside the German Empire north of the Alps, and more particularly in the ecclesiastical provinces of Cologne and Salzburg. War and secularization have taken a heavy toll of manuscripts in the province of Cologne, including virtually all those from Deutz and Siegburg, so that even though Rupert's two homebases were the diocese of Liège and the archdiocese of Cologne, no large numbers have survived from this region and no autographs at all. In 1126 Rupert's chief patron, Abbot Cuno of Siegburg, became bishop of Regensburg (1126–32), and in 1128 Rupert complained that Cuno had taken with him many copies (*multa exemplaria*) of his works.[9] These, with Cuno's enthusiastic support, founded a large readership throughout Bavaria (that is, the ecclesiastical province of Salzburg), so that within a generation or two the houses with the largest collections of Rupert's works outside Liège and Deutz were Prüfening, Admont, Reichersberg, Tegernsee, Salzburg, and Klosterneuburg. More than one-half the extant manuscripts date from the twelfth century; thereafter Rupert's influence declined rapidly.

De uictoria Verbi Dei was the first of his works to be printed,

9. PL 169.14. One such MS, and thus probably the closest one to Rupert now extant, was Clm 14055 (*De uictoria Verbi Dei*), on which see E. Meuthen, *DA* 28 (1974) 542–57, and Haacke's edition, p. xxx.

in 1487 at Augsburg. (A pro-Lutheran press at Nuremberg, doubtless attracted by the title, reprinted it in 1524, whence his works may have influenced the reformer Osiander.)[10] The complete edition of Rupert's works originated, however, in the combined efforts of German humanists and Benedictine reformers (Bursfelder Reform) who, led by Johannes Cochläus, managed to bring out during the 1520's at the printing house of Franz Birckmann in Cologne editions of nearly all his major works. First gathered in 1577, the *Opera omnia* published by Hermann Mylius at Mainz in 1631 provided the basis for editions at Paris in 1638 by Chastelain (dedicated to the Congregation of Cluny) and at Venice in 1748 by Pleunich. J. P. Migne reprinted Pleunich's edition in *Patrologia Latina* 167–170. In 1967 Pater Rhabanus Haacke of Siegburg began to publish a helpful critical edition in the *Corpus Christianorum* series.

Rupert of Deutz never wholly disappeared from sight after the publication of his works, but neither did he attract sufficient attention to become much more than the occasionally cited proponent of certain unusual doctrinal views. In the 1570's, Cardinal Robert Bellarmine noted in his *De scriptoribus ecclesiasticis* that after nearly four hundred years of darkness the light of Rupert's "neither bad nor unlearned" works had begun to shine again; by charging Rupert with "impanation" (meaning then, a Lutheran doctrine of the eucharist), however, he effectively snuffed out that glimmer for generations to come.[11] Bellarmine's judgement eventually provoked the first extended study of Rupert's life and works. The Maurist Gabriel Gerberon, famed as editor of St. Anselm's collected works, prepared an *Apologia pro Ruperto abbate Tuitiensi* (Paris 1669 = PL 167.23–194) to show that Rupert's eucharistic doctrine was in fact Catholic and that he was moreover a "master of great learning, humility, and piety, an ornament of the German nation, and glory of the Benedictine Order." The thorough historical-literary analysis of Rupert's works which prefaced his doctrinal argument remained

10. J. Beumer, "Rupert von Deutz und seine Einfluss auf die Kontroverstheologie der Reformationszeit," *Catholica* 22 (1968) 207–16.

11. *Roberti Bellarmini Opera omnia*, ed. J. Fevre (Paris 1874) 12.435–36; 4.231ff, 244ff.

fundamental until this century. The eighteenth-century Maurist *Histoire littéraire de la France* devoted a lengthy section to Rupert in which his works were summarized rather than analyzed.[12] The late nineteenth-century Catholic theologian Josef Bach seized upon the works of Rupert and others who had criticized the early abuse of dialectic, in order to muster historical support for his own battle against liberal, philosophizing Protestant theology. Bach considered Rupert the first in a group of thinkers such as Honorius Augustodunensis, the Victorines, and Gerhoch of Reichersberg who represented "*die speculative Systematik*" over against the "*Dialektiker*," specifically Peter Abelard and Gilbert of Poitiers.[13] A decade later Rudolf Rocholl, a Protestant theologian with deep sympathy for Rupert's scriptural commentaries, brought out the first full-length study of Rupert's life and works, in which he was interpreted as a great representative of "Platonism"—a thesis Rocholl subsequently retracted.[14]

In the twentieth century, among disparate studies of his life and work, a German Benedictine celebrated Rupert as the model and master of his monastic life;[15] and Egid Beitz, curator of the Schnütgen Museum (then located in the former abbey church at Deutz), attempted to demonstrate Rupert's considerable influence upon artistic monuments, thus raising questions which have continued to fascinate art historians.[16] From a theological perspective, Kahles used Rupert's works, which he knew well,

12. 11.422-587 (Paris 1759); reprinted in PL 170.703-804.

13. J. Bach, *Dogmengeschichte des Mittelalters* (Vienna 1873-75) 1.412-16, 2.243-97.

14. R. Rocholl, *Rupert von Deutz* (Gütersloh 1886), and in *Realenzyklopädie für protestantische Theologie und Kirche* (1906) 17.229-45.

15. O. Wolff, *Mein Meister Rupertus: Ein Mönchsleben aus dem zwölften Jahrhundert* (Freiburg 1920).

16. E. Beitz, *Rupertus von Deutz: Seine Werke und die bildende Kunst* (Veröffentlichungen des kölnischen Geschichtsvereins 4, 1930). For the large literature on Rupert and art history see Gribomont (n. 28 below) 17 nn. 5-6. Four studies deserve mention: W. Neuss, *Das Buch Ezechiel in Theologie und Kunst bis zum Ende des 12. Jahrhunderts* (Münster 1912); J. Stiennon, "La Vierge de Dom Rupert," in *Saint-Laurent* 81-92; R. Haacke, *Programme zur bildenden Kunst in den Schriften Ruperts von Deutz* (Siegburger Studien 9, Siegburg 1974); H. Silvestre, "Le retable de l'agneau mystique et Rupert de Deutz," *RB* 88 (1978) 274-86.

as a springboard from which to take on contemporary philosophical and theological issues;[17] Beinert investigated Rupert's ecclesiology, and Guntram Bischoff's unpublished dissertation his eucharistic views. But from a strictly historical perspective three brief biographical sketches,[18] Grundmann's interpretation of *De incendio*,[19] Bernards' survey of the lay world in Rupert's commentaries,[20] and Arduini's study of Rupert and the Jews[21] are very nearly all that has been done.[22]

Almost thirty years ago Beumer argued in a thoughtful article that Rupert "mediated between" the scholastic and monastic worlds, a view that may not be strictly accurate but nevertheless recognizes the difficulty of categorizing Rupert's exact place in the world of the early twelfth century.[23] Yet in most twentieth-century scholarship Rupert has been made to embody any one of three historical abstractions. For historians of scholasticism early in this century, beginning with Grabmann and his student Ott, Rupert represented one of the conservative "mystics" opposed to an excessively dialectical (*hyperdialektiker*) approach to theology;[24] much of this interpretation they based upon a single

17. W. Kahles, *Geschichte als Liturgie: Die Geschichtstheologie des Rupertus von Deutz* (Münster 1960).

18. A. Cauchie, "Rupert de Saint-Laurent," in *Biographie Nationale* 20 (Brussels 1910) 426–58; R. Haacke's introduction to *De uictoria Verbi Dei* (MGH Geistesgeschichte 5, Weimar 1970) vii–xvi; and M. L. Arduini, "Contributo alla biografia di Ruperto di Deutz," *Studi Medievali* 3rd ser. 16 (1975) 537–79.

19. H. Grundmann, "Der Brand von Deutz," *DA* 22 (1966) 385–471 (the best historical essay on Rupert).

20. M. Bernards, "Die Welt der Laien in der kölnischen Theologie des 12. Jahrhunderts: Beobachtungen zur Ekklesiologie Ruperts von Deutz," in *Festgabe für Josef Kardinal Frings* (Cologne 1960) 391–416.

21. M. L. Arduini, *Ruperto di Deutz e la controversia tra Cristiani ed Ebrei nel secolo XII* (Studi Storici 119–121, Rome 1979).

22. For a complete bibliography, see Arduini (n. 18 above) 579–82 and (n. 21 above) 171–74.

23. J. Beumer, "Rupert von Deutz und seine 'Vermittlungstheologie,'" *Münchener Theologische Zeitschrift* 4 (1953) 255–70.

24. M. Grabmann, *Die Geschichte der scholastischen Methode* (1909–11) 2.98–104. L. Ott, *Untersuchungen zur theologischen Briefliteratur der Frühscholastik* (BGPT 34, Münster 1937) 73–80.

incident in his life (chapter V in this study). Second, in the 1920's Alois Dempf produced a highly influential, positive evaluation of these "mystics" under the collective term *der deutsche Symbolismus* (which presupposed its never explicitly stated opposite *der französische Rationalismus*).[25] In German-speaking lands, "German symbolism" continues to signify a self-evident twelfth-century form of thought allegorical or "symbolic" in method, "salvation-historical" in structure, and "imperial" in orientation. This notion recently gave form to a useful investigation into Rupert's view of Antichrist and apocalyptic matters in general.[26] Third, twenty-five years ago Jean Leclercq argued for the existence of a "monastic theology" contemplative in orientation, scriptural in method, and conservative with respect to the authority of the Fathers; and he named Rupert "the source *par excellence* for traditional monastic theology."[27] In the best recent study of Rupert's thought, Magrassi interpreted his life and works as the perfect embodiment of Leclercq's "monastic theology."[28] In a volume published at virtually the same time, Chenu reiterated Ott's view of Rupert as an archconservative opposed to dialectic, but also cited him frequently and positively to exemplify "*la mentalité symbolique*" which issued in a "*théologie symbolique*."[29]

These studies, especially Magrassi's, have contributed much to our knowledge and understanding of Rupert's work, but all have forced his life and thought into preconceived historical molds. From very different points of view and with different audiences in mind, each of their formulas—Bach's "*speculative Systematik*," Grabmann's "*Mystiker*," Dempf's "*deutscher Symbolismus*," Leclercq's "monastic theology," and Chenu's "*théologie symbolique*—sought to do justice to the scriptural, allegorical, and salvation-historical character of Rupert's thought, yet always under the shadow of or in reaction to "scholastic theology" as

25. A. Dempf, *Sacrum Imperium* (Munich 1929) 233–38.
26. Rauh, *Antichrist* 178–235.
27. Leclercq, *Love of Learning* 272.
28. Magrassi, *Teologia*. In the introduction to *Rupert de Deutz, Les oeuvres du Saint-Esprit* (Sources chrétiennes 131, Paris 1967) 7–45, J. Gribomont summarized Magrassi's results in French.
29. M. D. Chenu, *La Théologie au douzième siècle* (Paris 1957).

the norm for appraising medieval thought. From the historical point of view adopted in this study that approach is simply inaccurate and misleading: in the second decade of the twelfth century Rupert's work was perceived as no less innovative and suspect than that of the schoolmen, and his form of thought—as historians of art, literature, and liturgy have learned—was to shape high medieval culture at least as much as theirs. Rupert's work must therefore be understood first of all with respect to the received tradition and only thereafter in comparison to the work of contemporary schoolmen.

This book will attempt to understand Rupert's thought and works by way of his life, and to place that life in its early twelfth-century ecclesiastical, religious, and theological setting. Such an approach has noteworthy implications for what is and especially what is not to be found here. Particular theological or religious conceptions are dealt with, normally, at that point in his life when they became prominent or controversial; consequently there is no systematic analysis or even listing of every passage in his writings relevant to a particular topic. Likewise, various aspects of Rupert's theology and spirituality not easily integrated into such a continuing narrative were necessarily left out; several of these definitely merit serious comparative consideration by historians of theology or spirituality. This book will have accomplished its primary goal if it has established a solid historical foundation upon which other studies of Rupert's thought and works can profitably build.

I

Youth
and
Formation

$\mathcal{R}$UPERT WAS BORN around the year 1075[1] in or near the city of Liège; his native tongue was probably Walloon.[2] Otherwise wont to talk about himself, he said nothing in his works about the parents or guardians who placed him at an early age in the abbey of St. Lawrence, though once he lamented that he had been the sole survivor from among three children.[3] Almost certainly of humble origins, he never hinted at noble connections but insisted instead that spiritual gifts determined nobility in the Church.[4] The abbey of St. Lawrence just outside Liège became thus his true home, his mother house and residence for nearly forty (ca. 1082–April 1119) of his roughly fifty-five years. For all but two and one-half of those years, Abbot Berengar (1077–1116) reigned, a man Rupert came to revere as his spiritual father and to rely upon as his protector. Three different times, political or theological difficulties drove Rupert into exile, first to

1. See M. L. Arduini, "Contributo alla biografia di Ruperto di Deutz," *Studi Medievali* 3rd ser. 16 (1975) 546–56; her arguments supersede those of H. Silvestre, "La date de la naissance de Rupert et la date de son départ pour Siegbourg," *Scriptorium* 16 (1962) 345–48.

2. J. Mabillon, *Annales ordinis sancti Benedicti* 568.44; and Van Engen, "Chronicon," *DA* 35 (1979) 57 n. 146. Cf. nn. 6, 154 below.

3. *Matt.* 12: CM 29.368–69.

4. Grundmann, "Deutz," *DA* 22 (1966) 419; *Exod.* 3.22: CM 22.714.

northern France (1092–95), then to Siegburg in the Rhineland (November 1116–spring 1117),[5] and finally to Cologne (April 1119).[6] Each time he sought or expected to return to Liège.[7] Late in the year 1120, however, Archbishop Frederick of Cologne appointed him to the abbacy of Deutz, a Benedictine house just across the Rhine from the cathedral, where he reigned until his death eight and one-half years later on 4 March 1129.[8]

Even as abbot of Deutz, Rupert continued to consider Liège his *patria*, to call upon St. Lawrence as his patron,[9] and to nur-

5. *Trin.* epist.: CM 21.120. The date of Abbot Berengar's death and Rupert's consequent first departure for the Rhineland is crucial to the reconstruction of his biography. Silvestre (n. 1 above) 345–48 first argued, correctly, that Berengar died on 16 November 1116 and Heribrand was consecrated abbot on Sunday, November 19. Rupert therefore spent little time and wrote very few works at Siegburg, quite unlike the reconstruction by J. Semmler, *Die Klosterreform von Siegburg* (Bonn 1959) 372–76. Objections by Bischoff, *Controversy* 128, 272–75, in behalf of the older date (November 1113) also fail: his doubts about the authenticity of a charter showing Berengar still alive in 1116 are completely groundless (see M. de Waha, "Note sur la mort de Bérengar de Saint-Laurent, la charte de Mont-Saint-Guibert et la Carta de villicatione de Gembloux," *Le Moyen Age* 87 [1981] 57–69), and his reading of *Gallia Christiana* 3.990 is textually mistaken. Similarly, the attempt by V. I. J. Flint, "The Date of the Arrival of Rupert of Deutz at Siegburg," *RB* 81 (1971) 317–19 to show that Rupert *first* went to Siegburg in 1119 fails to account for Rupert's own reference to "returning" (*reuerti*, as in n. 6 below). This was also pointed out by Arduini (n. 1 above) 569–75, Silvestre (n. 39 below) 227 n. 10, and Dinter, *Heribert* 99, all of whom likewise date Berengar's death to 16 November 1116.

6. Six years after his departure Rupert said: ". . . cum inquam patriae [Liège] tribulatio uehemens prope iam adesset, me dissimulante exire et reuerti ad te [Cuno of Siegburg] . . . secum [Frederick of Liège] huc ad Agrippinensem metropolim cum electionis testibus adduxit me. Extunc obedienter hic [Cologne] ego passus sum detineri." *RegBen.* 1: PL 170.496. "*Patria*" probably meant the diocese of Liège; see J. Lejeune, "Les notions de 'patria' et d' 'episcopatus' dans le diocèse et le pays de Liège du XIe au XIVe siècle," in *Problèmes Liégeois d'histoire médiévale* (Anciens pays et assemblées d'états 8, Louvain 1955) 3–51, esp. 11, 19.

7. Still in 1119/20 Rupert pointed out to Abbot Markward of Deutz that he was not bound to obey him because "monachicam sub tuo regimine militiam professus non fuerim." (*Herib.* prologus: ed. Dinter 31).

8. For the date, see Grundmann, "Deutz," *DA* 22 (1966) 432–36.

9. *Incendio* 18–23: *DA* 22 (1966) 463–70.

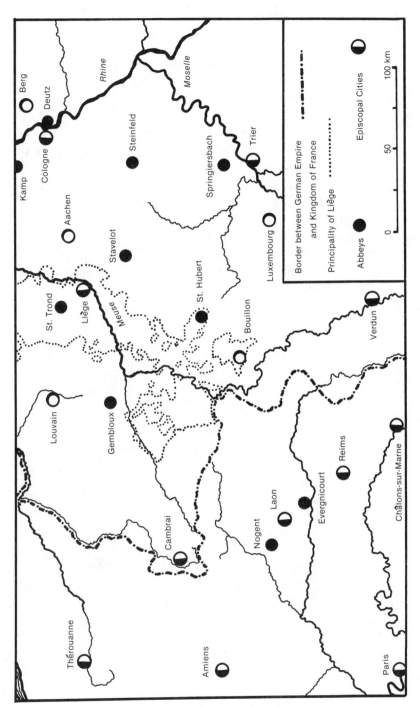

Figure 1.

ture close ties to his mother house.[10] Indeed, he once compared his lot at Deutz to Joseph's in Egypt, and around 1127 very nearly resigned his post.[11] Historians therefore might well, or perhaps even more appropriately, have called him "Robert of St. Lawrence in Liège."[12] But his last years in a Rhineland abbacy, his large following among German-speaking readers, and the edition of his works by German Benedictines and humanists in the sixteenth century conspired to make him known instead as "Rupert of Deutz."[13] This book follows that convention. To be sure, Rupert's later patrons, Abbot Cuno of Siegburg (1105–26) and Archbishop Frederick of Cologne (1100–31), also influenced his life and thought. But the determinative setting for Rupert's ecclesiological, intellectual, and spiritual formation was the Lotharingian bishopric of Liège and the Benedictine abbey of St. Lawrence.

1

The Bishopric of Liège
and Abbey of St. Lawrence
in the Eleventh Century

The medieval city of Liège owed its foundation neither to the Romans nor to the commercial revolution of the eleventh century but rather to the residence there, from about 800 on, of

10. See chapter VI, p. 234, esp. n. 46 on Deutz's confraternity book. The monks at St. Lawrence also knew about and had copies of nearly all the works Rupert wrote at Deutz: Reiner, *Inept.* 1: MGH SS 20.596–97; Gessler, "Bibliothèque" 121–23: 2.64–69, 76.

11. *Incendio* 14: *DA* 22 (1966) 458, 459.

12. In the abbey of St. Lawrence (Reiner, *Inept.* 1: MGH SS 20.596; and Adrian d'Oudenbosch's *vita Roberti*, in H. Silvestre, *Le Chronicon sancti Laurentii Leodiensis dit de Rupert de Deutz* [Recueil de travaux d'histoire et de philologie, 3ᵉ série 43, Louvain 1952] 327–29) and in the environs of Liège (see n. 154 below), his name was always "Robertus." In German-speaking lands this became "Ruotpertus," "Rodbertus," etc.; for the various forms, R. Haacke, MGH Geistesgeschichte 5, vii n. 1.

13. Gerberon and most subsequent authors considered him "Rupertum . . . Germaniae decus" (PL 167.26). The most extreme claims were made by

the bishops of Tongres-Maastricht.[14] St. Lambert's cathedral dominated the city sprung up around it on the northern bank of the river Meuse. An island and marshy lowlands stretched away to the south, while to the north and west steep, wooded hills shielded the city and its episcopal lords from the ambitious counts of Louvain. The abbey of St. Lawrence stood atop the most prominent of those hills, one called the Mons Publicanus, or Public-Mount. From the grounds of his monastery Rupert enjoyed a full view of the city.[15] Just below him and to the east stood the cathedral and episcopal palace, the center of political

---

A. Dempf, *Sacrum Imperium* (Munich 1929) 229ff. With greater attention to the evidence, H. Sproemberg in Wattenbach-Holtzmann, *Deutschlands Geschichtsquellen im Mittelalter* (3rd ed. Tübingen 1948) 658 n. 70 concluded he was of "reichsromanischer Herkunft."

14. On the history of Liège, see: A. Cauchie, *La querelle des investitures dans les diocèses de Liège et de Cambrai* (Louvain 1890–91); G. Kurth, *La cité de Liège au moyen âge* (Paris 1909) 1–52; idem, *Notger de Liège et la civilisation au Xe siècle* (Paris 1905); H. Pirenne, *Histoire de Belgique* (3rd ed. Brussels 1909) 132–36; F. Rousseau, *La Meuse et le pays mosan en Belgique* (Namur 1930); E. de Moreau, *Histoire de l'église en Belgique* (2nd ed. Brussels 1945) 2.25–52, 79–91; J. F. Niermeyer, in *Algemene Geschiedenis der Nederlanden* (Utrecht 1950) 2.20–21, 41–43, 107–10; J. Lejeune, *La Principauté de Liège* (Liège 1948) 11–47; Sproemberg (n. 13 above) 124–56, 715–50; idem, "Lüttich und das Reich im Mittelalter," in *Beiträge zur Belgischen-Niederländischen Geschichte* (Berlin 1959) 346–67; W. Reese, *Die Niederlande und das deutsche Reich* (Berlin 1941) 36–80; F. Vercauteren, "Marchands et bourgeois dans le pays mosan aux XIe et XIIe siècles," in *Mélanges Felix Rousseau* (Brussels 1958) 655–73; L.-F. Genicot, *Les églises mosanes du XI siècle* (Recueil de travaux d'histoire et de philologie 4th ser. 48, Louvain 1972) xxvi–xlvi; and Giles Constable, "Monasticism, Lordship, and Society in the Twelfth-century Hesbaye: Five Documents on the Foundation of the Cluniac Priory of Bertrée," *Traditio* 33 (1977) 159–224, esp. 206ff.

15. Good maps of Rupert's Liège in Kurth, *Notger* (n. 14 above) 2 (foldout between 28–29); J. Stiennon, *Etude sur le chartrier et la domaine de l'abbaye de Saint-Jacques de Liège (1015–1209)* (Bibliothèque de la Faculté de philosophie et lettres de l'Université de Liège 124, Paris 1951) 212; and H. E. Kubach and A. Verbeek, *Romanische Baukunst an Rhein und Maas* (Berlin 1976) 696. For a dramatic view of the abbey perched above the city, see the engraving done in 1467, reproduced in *Saint-Laurent*, pl. 28. Still in the early eighteenth century, E. Martène and U. Durand, *Voyage littéraire* (Paris 1724; repr. 1969) 186, reported: "La vue y est charmante; on y découvre toute la ville. . . ."

power in the principality of Liège, often the site of episcopal synods and judicial assemblies. There in Rupert's lifetime the future King Henry V was knighted (Easter 1101), Henry IV died and was buried (August 1106), Henry V became a canon of the cathedral chapter (Christmas 1107), and later (Easter 1110) was betrothed to the daughter of the English king. Around 1110 Rupert himself compared the festivities of *Laetare* Sunday to those celebrated at the coronation of a Christian emperor—a hint that the monks of St. Lawrence were not wholly isolated from the life of this imperial bishopric.[16] In addition to the bishop's entourage, with its prestigious clerics and powerful vassals, the city streets thronged with more than two hundred fifty canons attached to the cathedral chapter and seven other collegiate churches, numerous foreign student-clerics attracted by the fame of the schools, and a growing number of merchants resident near the riverport. By 1075, the approximate year of Rupert's birth, Liège had become, after Cologne, the leading city in northern Lotharingia and probably the entire German Empire.

Once the heartland of Charlemagne's empire, Lotharingia was permanently joined to the German monarchy in 925 without ever wholly losing its Carolingian imprint. This was particularly true for Liège, whose diocese included Charlemagne's palace and chapel at Aachen and whose city code was later popularly called the "Loi de Charlemagne." In its preference for collegiate foundations,[17] in the quality of its schools, and even in its architecture,[18] Liège managed to retain or to restore the best of Carolingian tradition. Notably, three of the theological controversies in which Rupert became most embroiled concerned issues inherited from the Carolingian era.

16. *Off.* 4.13: CM 7.122. On the other hand, he criticized religious who attended weddings: *John* 2: CM 9.101.

17. Genicot (n. 14 above) xxxiv–xxxv, estimates there were 270 canons in the city of Liège alone and 700–800 in the diocese, together with about 150 female canons. See also C. Dereine, *Les chanoines réguliers au diocèse de Liège avant Saint Norbert* (Brussels 1952) 33–52.

18. L.-F. Genicot, "Les cryptes extérieures du pays mosan au XIe siècle: reflet typologique du passé carolingien?" *Cahiers de civilisation médiévale* 22 (1979) 337–47.

At least three other traditions were also at work in eleventh-century Liège. Saxon and Salian monarchs, heirs to the Carolingian imperial tradition, now wielded the dominant political influence. It was precisely in order to master the ever rebellious Lotharingians that Archbishop Bruno of Cologne (953–65) devised the institutional arrangement known as the "imperial church system," whereby bishops came to serve as the chief agents of imperial authority and bishoprics were endowed with extensive lands and rights protected by full immunity. Bishops of Liège beginning with Notger (972–1008), in league with the German emperors, thus transformed their diocese into a powerful territorial principality. Second, throughout the middle ages Liège was suffragan to Cologne, so that ecclesiastical affairs, religious movements, and the artistic works associated with them tended to develop much in common throughout the lower Meuse and lower Rhine valleys.[19] So also Rupert was to divide his adult theological career evenly between Liège and the Rhineland. Yet Lotharingia remained, thirdly, a borderland with strong ties to neighboring French bishoprics (especially Reims, Laon, and Tournai) and adjacent French counties (Champagne and Flanders). Scholars from Liège kept up with colleagues at Chartres, Reims, and Laon; bishops of Liège addressed letters to kings of France, sometimes in behalf of the German monarch; the Peace of God movement entered the Empire by way of Liège; and Rupert too followed critically the newer intellectual and religious movements generated in northern France. This, then, was the larger setting for Rupert's life: an imperial bishopric, with deep roots in the Carolingian past, on a borderland between the "German" and the "French" worlds.

Imperial bishops, greatest among whom were Notger (972–1008), Wazo (1042–48), and Otbert (1091–1119), shaped the history of Liège throughout the eleventh century. From the time of Evraclus (959–71) to that of Otbert (d. 1119), each was

19. See now *Rhein und Maas: Kunst und Kultur 800–1400* (Cologne 1972–73); and Kubach and Verbeek (n. 15 above).

appointed by and swore fidelity to the German monarch; most gained ecclesiastical preferment after first serving in the royal chapel.[20] At Liège, unlike other bishoprics controlled by dynastic houses and their interests, imperial service came foremost. With around five hundred knights—a force equal to that of the French king—the bishop of Liège commanded the fifth largest contingent in the Empire after Mainz, Cologne, Strassburg, and Augsburg. During the rebellion of Duke Godfrey (1044–69) in the 1040's, Bishop Wazo's military leadership saved Lotharingia for the Empire, and in 1105 at Visé Otbert rescued Henry IV from certain defeat at the hands of his rebellious son, the future Henry V.

The bishops of Liège also supplied the Empire with scholars. Clerics trained in Bishop Notger's cathedral school were sent to the bishoprics of Utrecht, Cambrai, Toul, Metz, and Salzburg, and later King Henry II wished for his new foundation at Bamberg a school equal to that of Liège.[21] Henry III repeatedly sought advice from Bishop Wazo and later, from Bishop Dietwin, a master for the abbey school at Fulda. Scholars trained in Liège gained teaching posts at Speyer, the necropolis of the Salian dynasty, and Mainz, Germany's primatial see.[22] It was hardly an accident, then, that Henry IV found in Sigebert of Gembloux, adviser to the high clergy in Liège, his most eloquent pamphleteer, and that Henry V turned to scholars in Liège for the preparation of his position paper on investiture.[23]

20. J. Fleckenstein, *Die Hofkapelle der deutschen Könige* (MGH Schriften 16, Stuttgart 1966) 2.44–45 (Notger), 88–89 (Balderic), 186 (Wolbodo), 202 (Durandus), 224 (Reginald), 193 (Wazo). On their social origins, L. Genicot, "Haut clergé et noblesse dans le diocèse de Liège du XIe au XVe siècle," in *Adel und Kirche*, ed. J. Fleckenstein and K. Schmid (Freiburg 1968) 237–58.

21. *Anselmi Chronicon* 29: MGH SS 8.205; Kurth, *Notger* (n. 14 above) 251–99.

22. Adelman was master in Speyer ca. 1044–50. See H. Silvestre, "Notice sur Adelman de Liège, évêque de Brescia (d. 1061)," *RHE* 56 (1961) 855–71. Gozechin was master in Mainz ca. 1058–75. See M. Manitius, *Geschichte der lateinischen Literatur des Mittelalters* 2 (Munich 1923) 470–78.

23. See J. Beumann, *Sigebert von Gembloux und der Traktat de investitura episcoporum* (Sigmaringen 1976); idem, "Der Traktat 'de investitura episcoporum' von 1109," *DA* 33 (1977) 37–83.

The first imperial bishop of whom Rupert had personal memories was Henry (1075–91), sometimes called the "Peaceful," whose reign he described, in hindsight and from exile, as a happy and flourishing time.[24] A son of Count Frederick of Toul, a relative of the dukes of Lotharingia, and formerly an archdeacon in Verdun, Henry was appointed and invested by King Henry IV during the summer of 1075. During those tempestuous early years of the Investiture Contest, Henry concentrated upon internal affairs, chiefly the reduction of feudal violence and monastic reform. Early in his reign he acquired two more castles (Waremme and Mirwart), solidifying control over the northwestern and southern boundaries of his principality, and in 1082 he became the first imperial bishop to institute the Peace of God (actually something closer to a Truce of God), thereby at once reducing the level of private feudal violence in the diocese while increasing his own power and prestige.[25] Together with his concern for peace and stability went a genuine inclination to the monastic life. Henry spent long periods, including major feast days, in the abbey of St. Hubert, and he apparently had a personal obituary calendar prepared to guide his daily prayers.[26] In cooperation with his uncle, Bishop Herman of Metz, he forcibly reformed the monastery of St. Trond,[27] and at the very beginning of his reign the abbey of St. Lawrence—whence Rupert's admiration for him.

During the later tenth and early eleventh centuries the bish-

24. Rupert, *Carm.* 10.8: MGH LdL 3.636. On Henry, see Cauchie (n. 14 above) 1.26–65; de Moreau (n. 14 above) 2.80–86.

25. R. Deprez, "La politique castrale dans la principauté de Liège du Xᵉ au XIVᵉ siècle," *Le Moyen Age* 65 (1959) 505–06; and A. Joris, "Observations sur la proclamation de la trêve de Dieu à Liège à la fin du XIᵉ siècle," in *La Paix* (Recueils de la Société Jean Bodin 14, Brussels 1961) 503–45.

26. *Cantatorium sive Chronicon sancti Huberti* 45: ed. K. Hanquet (Brussels 1906) 112–14 (hereafter *ChronHub.*); M. Coens, "Un calendrier-obituaire de Saint-Laurent de Liège," *Analecta Bollandiana* 58 (1940) 48–78; and the interpretation in H. Wellmer, *Persönliches Memento im deutschen Mittelalter* (Monographien zur Geschichte des Mittelalters 5, Stuttgart 1973) 110–13.

27. *Rodulphi Gesta abbatum Trudonensium* 2.4ff: MGH SS 10.237ff; summary in Cauchie (n. 14 above) 1.49ff, and de Moreau (n. 14 above) 2.201–04.

ops of Liège had founded seven collegiate churches. Bishop Evraclus (959–71) founded two, one of which (St. Martin's at the base of the Public-Mount) was originally meant to become a new cathedral. He began to build a third atop the Public-Mount in an effort to render the city more defensible by moving its center up and away from the river valley; a stone collegiate church, overlooking the valleys of both the Meuse and the Legia, would have completed such a plan.[28] But Evraclus died, leaving this church unfinished, and Bishop Notger (972–1008) decided instead to fortify the old city with walls, to rebuild the cathedral and palace of St. Lambert, and to found three additional collegiate churches at strategic locations.

It was not until the second decade of the eleventh century that Bishop Balderich II (1008–18) finally established the first Benedictine house near the city, the abbey of St. James at the far southern edge of Liège on what was then an island in the Meuse.[29] A later rumor, indignantly rejected by a monk of St. James citing elderly contemporary witnesses, held that the bishop first considered using the uncompleted church of St. Lawrence.[30] The foundation there, so soon after, of a second Benedictine house must be placed in the context of the monastic reform movement in Lotharingia led by Richard of St. Vanne.

Richard (d. 1046) was trained in the cathedral school at Reims before he converted to the monastic life.[31] Dismayed by what he found at St. Vanne in Verdun, he first reformed his own house and then went on to become an apostle of reform. His

28. See F. Vercauteren, "Note sur les origines de Saint-Laurent de Liège," in Saint-Laurent 15–24; Silvestre (n. 12 above) 267.

29. Stiennon (n. 15 above) 205–32; C. Lays, Etude critique sur la Vita Balderici episcopi Leodiensis (Brussels 1948).

30. Vita Balderici 20: MGH SS 4.732.

31. On Richard, see H. Dauphin, Le bienheureux Richard, abbé de Saint-Vanne de Verdun (Louvain and Paris 1946); E. Sackur, Die Cluniacenser (1894; repr. Darmstadt 1971) 2.133–54; E. Sabbe, "Notes sur la réforme de Richard de Saint-Vannes dans les Pays-Bas," RBPH 7 (1928) 551–70; de Moreau (n. 14 above) 2.161–68; K. Hallinger, Gorze-Kluny (Studia Anselmiana 22–25, Rome 1950–51) 283–316, 473–516; and in review of Hallinger: H. Dauphin, Downside Review 70 (1952) 62–74.

career paralleled Odilo of Cluny's, but in the more stable political conditions prevailing in Flanders and Lotharingia he worked
quite differently. After assuming personal control for a year or
more, he normally moved on, leaving one of his disciples in
charge. There was, in other words, no system of priories, such
as Cluny was to develop, and no written customary, just a personal bond to Richard himself.[32] He likewise never sought immunity or exemption, but rather worked closely with the count
of Flanders and especially with the bishops of Verdun, Tournai,
Cambrai, and Liège. Around 1110 Gerard, the later bishop of
Cambrai (1012–51), entrusted him with a new foundation on
family property at Florennes in the diocese of Liège. Then in
1120 bishops Gerard of Cambrai and Wolbodo of Liège jointly
reformed the monastery of Lobbes, a possession of the bishopric of Liège located just inside the diocese of Cambrai. Abbot
Ingobrand (1007–20) was forcibly removed and Richard himself (1020–32) installed, and from Lobbes his influence radiated
out over the diocese of Liège for more than a decade. Deeply
affected by Richard's reforms, Wolbodo also brought monks
"trained in Richard's discipline" from the abbey of Gembloux
to the new house of St. James,[33] and then resolved to found
himself still another Benedictine house on the site of the uncompleted church of St. Lawrence.

The documentary evidence for the early history of St. Lawrence is very scant, and legends found in the works of Reiner
of St. Lawrence (ca. 1110–ca. 1190) and in the anonymous
compilation called the *Gesta abbatum et episcoporum*, some of
them attributable to a lost work by Rupert written around 1100,
must be treated with considerable caution.[34] Bishop Wolbodo
(d. 1021) was buried in the crypt of St. Lawrence, and already

32. Sabbe (n. 31 above); elaborated upon by Hallinger (n. 31 above) 473–
516.

33. *Gesta abbatum Gemblacensium* 35: MGH SS 8.538–39.

34. U. Berlière, *Monasticon Belge* (1929) 2.32ff (full review of sources and
literature); J. Daris, "Le Cartulaire de l'abbaye de Saint-Laurent," *Bulletin de la
Société d'art et d'histoire du diocèse de Liège* 2 (1882) 142–243; Silvestre (n. 12
above) passim; Van Engen, *DA* 35 (1979) 33–81.

by the 1050's a cult venerated him as the "holy founder."[35]
Bishop Durandus was also buried at St. Lawrence, and then,
approximately a year after assuming office, Bishop Reginald
(1025–37) installed Abbot Stephen and several monks, all apparently brought from St. Vanne in Verdun.[36] Tensions arose
somehow between Richard, still in Lobbes, and Bishop Reginald so that in 1032 Richard returned permanently to St. Vanne
in Verdun.[37] On 3 November 1034, Reginald dedicated the
church of St. Lawrence, claiming for himself full credit for its
founding and endowment. His charter granted the monastery
over three hundred manses of land scattered throughout the diocese (but with some concentration in the rich agricultural region of the Hesbaye to the northwest), together with incomes
from seventeen different churches.[38] Temporal control remained
firmly in the bishop's hands. Reginald was also buried before
the high altar, and Abbot Lambert, nephew to Abbot Stephen,
wrote his epitaph.

The church dedicated in 1034 was rebuilt in the 1580's and
then completely destroyed in 1809 following the Revolution.
But archaeological digs made in 1966–67, brief contemporary
descriptions, and later engravings have made it possible for art
historians to reconstruct, approximately, the church in which
Rupert spent a goodly part of his first forty-five years.[39] Just as

35. *Anselmi Gesta* 35: MGH SS 7.209; *Gesta abb. Trudon.* 2.4: MGH SS
10.237.

36. *Anselmi Gesta* 37: MGH SS 7.209; *Hugonis Chronicon* 2.10: MGH SS
8.376. On the date, Silvestre (n. 12 above) 363–67.

37. MGH SS 8.398. For interpretation, Dauphin (n. 31 above) 201–11.

38. P. Bonenfant, "Les chartes de Reginard, évêque de Liège, pour l'abbaye de Saint-Laurent," *Bulletin de la Commission royale d'histoire* 105 (1940)
306–66, esp. 336–44. Anselm's *Gesta* (MGH SS 7.209) reports there were 30
monks. Bishop Wazo and Abbot Stephen had the abbey's possessions confirmed in 1044: MGH DH III.123.

39. F. Ulrix, "Fouilles archéologiques récentes à l'abbatiale Saint-Laurent
de Liège," in *Saint-Laurent* 25–40; Genicot (n. 14 above) 141–43; Kubach and
Verbeek (n. 15 above) 714–15; H. Silvestre, "Trois témoignages mosans du
début du XIIᵉ siècle sur le crucifix de l'arc triomphal," *Revue des archéologues et
historiens d'art de Louvain* 9 (1976) 225–31.

the diocese of Liège proved a pacesetter for the Empire in intellectual matters, so also in architectural and artistic achievements.[40] St. Lawrence was an impressive stone church almost seventy meters in length. The massive west front had three towers, the choir was large (as one would expect for a monastic church) and almost square, and the crypt was an exterior one, that is, a low rectangular building adjoining the east end of the choir at ground level; here Wolbodo, the holy founder, was buried and his cult nurtured. At the far east end there was a small apselike chapel dedicated to the Virgin Mary.[41] From early poems we can also learn something about the interior. There was an altar dedicated to St. Benedict, a wooden cross with Christ in agony, a cross suspended from the church's triumphal arch, a wall painting of the Lamb of God in Paradise, a tapestry given by Abbot Stephen, probably another altar with a depiction of Christ as the Winnower, additional painted panels (*tabulae*), and an ambo front divided into three tiers depicting the four animals, the Gospel writers, and their christological meanings, as well as such standard items as a reliquary (for St. Lawrence), a chalice, an antiphonary prepared by the first brothers, and a great lantern. The refectory had a large picture of Christ in majesty dispensing his blessings both material (i.e. food) and spiritual (i.e. the readings).[42] These, in brief, were the spiritual themes of which Rupert was daily reminded in his church, at the altar, and in the refectory.

St. Lawrence was soon considered among Richard's most distinguished Lotharingian foundations, and Abbot Stephen gained sufficient prestige to influence Theodoric of Lobbes' ap-

40. Genicot (n. 14 above) passim, esp. 333–34; L. Grodecki, *L'architecture ottonienne* (Paris 1958) 311ff.

41. Ground plans in Genicot (n. 14 above) 143 and Kubach and Verbeek (n. 15 above) 714, with a graphic reconstruction on p. 715. On the crypt, see Genicot 141ff; idem (n. 18 above) 340; but there are important earlier references to this chapel in Rupert (CM 29.369; *Carm.* 10.50: MGH LdL 3.637) and in Rudolph (MGH SS 10.237).

42. Karl Hampe, *Neues Archiv* 22 (1897) 373–80. *Gen.* 2.28: CM 21.219 may reflect the image on the ambo.

pointment to the abbacy of the ancient house of St. Hubert.[43] Houses formed or reformed by Richard often distinguished themselves in intellectual and literary pursuits, and St. Lawrence was no exception. Already in the year 1050 its monks made lengthy additions to the mortuary roll of Count Guifred, comparing themselves atop the Public-Mount to inhabitants of the Alps and setting for themselves the norm of St. Benedict.[44] Around 1056 a canon and later provost of the cathedral named Godfrey acquired relics from San Lorenzo in Rome by way of "sacred theft," a holy adventure recounted by Louis of St. Lawrence.[45] Abbot Stephen ruled for thirty-three years (d. 12 January 1061), and was succeeded by his nephew Lambert (1061–70), who had once studied with Adelman at the cathedral school and also served as *scholasticus* at Deutz before returning to St. Lawrence.[46] Lambert wrote several poems (already noted), some going back to the 1040's: epitaphs for three noblemen who left bequests to the monastery, for a brother monk, for an uncle (a brother of Abbot Stephen) who was also a priest, and for the founding bishops. After Lambert's death, Everard of Florennes (1070–71), that is, a monk from the first house in the diocese connected to Richard, became abbot, but he died within one year.

Once Richard and his disciples had died, no steadying force such as the centralized control and written customary of Cluny prevented sudden decline under an unworthy abbot. This the house of St. Lawrence came ruefully to experience during the

43. MGH SS 8.376; *Vita Theodorici* 16: MGH SS 12.45–46.

44. L. Delisle, *Rouleaux des morts du IXe au XVe siècle* (Société de l'histoire de France 135, Paris 1866) n. 128, pp. 119–21. For interpretation, see J. Stiennon, "Le rouleau mortuaire de Guifred, comte de Cerdagne, moine de St. Martin du Canigou (d. 1049)," *Annales du Midi* 76 (1964) 305–14.

45. MGH SS 20.579–81; for interpretation, see G. Tellenbach, "Zur Translation einer Reliquie des heiligen Laurentius von Rom nach Lüttich im elften Jahrhundert," in *Storiografia e Storia: Studi in onore di Eugenio Dupré-Theseider* (Rome 1974) 2.601–15. Not treated in P. Geary, *Furta Sacra: Thefts of Relics in the Central Middle Ages* (Princeton 1978).

46. *Monasticon Belge* 2.35–36; Silvestre (n. 12 above) 363–66; Sproemberg (n. 13 above) 650–51, 725.

abbacy of Wolbodo (1071–75), a nobleman more given to squandering the abbey's goods than upholding its religious discipline. In the summer of 1075 Archbishop Anno of Cologne, the founder of Siegburg, enjoined the newly consecrated Henry of Liège to set Wolbodo straight. After private warning and a public condemnation, he was banished to St. Airy in Verdun, whence he escaped to appeal personally, though unsuccessfully, first to Pope Gregory VII and then to King Henry IV, whose party he eventually joined.[47] Bishop Henry meanwhile took the abbey back into his own possession and asked Theodoric of St. Hubert, then the most prestigious abbot in the diocese, to provide a caretaker. Theodoric sent his prior and "dearest disciple" Berengar, who proved so able a prelate that both the brothers and Bishop Henry insisted upon making him abbot. Theodoric reluctantly agreed, and Berengar was consecrated on 17 September 1077.[48]

A commoner by birth, converted from the clerical to the religious life by Theodoric of St. Hubert, Berengar was described by the contemporary chronicler of St. Hubert in almost hagiographic terms as tempering his commands and guidance to the needs of individual monks while paying no heed to social distinctions. He rekindled religious life in St. Lawrence, reclaimed and added to lands and incomes alienated by Wolbodo,[49] was charged with important diocesan missions (particularly in handling monastic affairs), had an obituary calendar prepared for Bishop Henry's personal use, and offered aid and shelter to both

47. Adrian, *Historia* 19–20: ed. Martène 4.1068–71; *ChronHub.* 29: ed. Hanquet 88–89; Gregory VII, *Reg.* 4.21: ed. E. Caspar (MGH Epist. sel. 2, 1920–23) 329–30 (6 April 1077); and *Annales S. Jacobi*: MGH SS 16.639. On Wolbodo, see *Monasticon Belge* 2.36. Adrian's *Historia* c. 19 claims he was related to bishops Wolbodo and Reginald.

48. *ChronHub.* 35–36: ed. Hanquet 96–98; Adrian, *Historia* 20: ed. Martène 4.1070; *Vita Theodorici* 30: MGH SS 12.55–56. On Berengar, see *Monasticon Belge* 2.37.

49. ". . . illius [Berengar's] labore et ingenio accreuerit interius optime religionis congregatio et exterius multiplex rerum ecclesiasticarum acquisitio." *ChronHub.* 36: ed. Hanquet 98. See the charters in Martène, *Ampl. Coll.* 4.1174–75, 1184–85, and the two noted by Berlière, *Monasticon Belge* 2.37.

clerics and monks in trouble.[50] In short, as Rupert said later, the abbey of St. Lawrence, under the direction of Abbot Berengar and in close cooperation with Bishop Henry, thrived (*floruit*) for almost fifteen years, from September 1077 until February 1092.[51]

2

Exile (1092–95):
An Early Poem

However happy the memory of his early years in the reformed abbey of St. Lawrence, Rupert was to receive his decisive ecclesiological formation by way of protracted struggle with his bishop, lasting from roughly his seventeenth to his thirty-third year and beginning with three and one-half years in exile. Bishop Henry had managed to maintain relations with both Henry IV and Gregory VII such that a poem from around the year 1090 described him as "grieving the schism."[52] In practice he associated primarily with the emperor who had appointed him, participating, for instance, in that Synod of Worms which had denounced Gregory's "abuse" of the pontifical office and himself boldly questioning Gregory's actions on two different occasions; yet at least until 1084 Pope Gregory could not tell whether he was friend or foe.[53] Whatever Henry's personal ambivalence may have been—and some at least regarded him later as a "Gregorian"[54]—the diocese itself was solidly in the imperial camp. The cathedral annals, in an unusually lengthy notice, recorded Henry IV's conquest of Rome in 1084 and subsequent installation of Wibert as Pope Clement III. That same year a scribe at Lobbes remarked in a colophon on the king's three-

50. *Gesta abb. Trudon.* 2.4–5, 12, 3.2: MGH SS 10.237, 239–40; *Chron-Hub.* 68: ed. Hanquet 153. For the obituary calendar, see n. 26 above.

51. *Carm.* 10.7–11: MGH LdL 3.636.

52. MGH LdL 2.171.

53. *Udalrici Codex* 48: ed. P. Jaffe, *Bibliotheca rerum germanicarum* (Berlin 1869) 5.103–06; Gregory VII, *Reg.* 4.6, 6.4: ed. Caspar 303–04, 396–97.

54. This in Rupert's not unbiased account, *Carm.* 10.29: MGH LdL 3.636; but see also *Gesta abb. Trudon.* 4.1: MGH SS 10.247.

year siege against "that rebel Hildebrand,"[55] and about the same time Sigebert of Gembloux, at the behest of Archdeacon Henry of Liège, rebutted two of Pope Gregory's major innovations, his attack on masses said by immoral priests and his attempt to depose the king. As one contemporary chronicler pointed out, most Lotharingian bishoprics, including the diocese of Liège, favored the imperial party and recognized its pope.[56]

Only two houses in the entire diocese mounted any active resistance on behalf of the reformed papacy. St. Hubert, hidden far away to the southeast in the Ardennes, had established firm connections to reforming circles in Rome already during the abbacy of Theodoric I (1055–86), and its persistent loyalty rested on deep conviction.[57] St. Lawrence, less than a thousand yards from the imperial bishop's palace, had in Abbot Berengar Theodoric's closest disciple. But political circumstance probably more than ideological loyalty first drove its monks, Rupert among them, into the reformers' camp.

Bishop Henry died on 31 May 1091, and Otbert (1091–1119) succeeded him.[58] Otbert's ancestry, training, and early career are unknown; slight evidence suggests he hailed from lesser nobility in the Hesbaye. He first comes into view in the 1080's as a canon of the cathedral chapter and provost of Holy Cross, a post from which Bishop Henry deposed him for "crimes" unknown. Abbot Berengar sheltered him for a time, but Otbert chose to seek his fortune at the king's court, probably early in 1090, as Henry IV campaigned in Italy against the forces of Pope Urban II.[59] When the news of Bishop Henry's death ar-

55. MGH SS 4.21, 29; and Tournai, Bibl. du Séminaire MS 1, fol. 276. See *Manuscrits datés conservés en Belgique* (Brussels 1968) 1.18, pl. 5.

56. *Hugonis Chronicon* 2: MGH SS 8.461.

57. See I. S. Robinson, "The Friendship Network of Gregory VII," *History* 63 (1978) 1–22, esp. 19–20.

58. On Otbert, see H. Pirenne, in *Biographie Nationale* 16 (Brussels 1901) 356–63; Reese (n. 14 above) 70–81; de Moreau (n. 14 above) 2.86–92; Cauchie (n. 14 above) vol. 2 passim; J.-L. Kupper, "Otbert de Liège: les manipulations monétaires d'un évêque d'Empire à l'aube du XIIᵉ siècle," *Le Moyen Age* 86 (1980) 353–85.

59. *ChronHub.* 68: ed. Hanquet 152–54; "spe adipiscendi . . . episcopa-

rived, Otbert promptly received the appointment in return for which he swore fidelity and performed homage to the excommunicated king. The reformers claimed money also changed hands, but this is unlikely.[60] When by the fall of 1091 news of Otbert's appointment reached Liège, two deposed abbots, Wolbodo of St. Lawrence and Lupo of St. Trond, also set out for Italy, where the king and bishop-elect agreed to restore them. All sources agree that simony was involved here.[61] Otbert and the abbots returned together, arriving in Liège on Christmas Eve 1091, where—at least according to one contemporary source—the new bishop was splendidly and happily received.[62]

Upon returning from his consecration in Cologne on 1 February 1092, Bishop Otbert ordered Berengar to leave St. Lawrence at once.[63] The abbot protested to diocesan officials, demanding that proper charges be brought against him, but Otbert insisted he was simply executing the orders of his lord the king. The bishop had in fact already installed abbots simoniacally at St. Trond, Florennes, and Brogne without incident; he may have waited longest to take on the prestigious Berengar, who was in the event allowed to keep his abbatial staff. The deposed abbot retired first to his mother house, St. Hubert in the Ardennes. There Abbot Theodoric II, acting without direct provocation but rather on the principles of the strict reformers, decided together with his monks to withdraw from communion with Bishop Otbert; and several of them—against Berengar's

---

tum," according to Rodulph (MGH SS 10.250). Since these sources both refer clearly to Italy, where King Henry went early in 1090, the "per decennium excommunicatus [Henry IV]" of *ChronHub*. 68 must refer to the excommunication of 1080, rather than 1076 (as in Hanquet 153 n. 1), which had been lifted at Canossa.

60. *ChronHub*. 69: ed. Hanquet 154–55; Van Engen, *DA* 35 (1979) 56 n. 138.

61. *ChronHub*. 70: ed. Hanquet 156; *Gesta abb. Trudon.* 4.11: MGH SS 10.250–51; Rupert, *Carm.* 10.31–34; MGH LdL 3.367.

62. Reimbald, *Chronicon*, vv. 399–400, 491–98: CM 4.136, 139.

63. This paragraph based on *ChronHub*. 70: ed. Hanquet 156–66; Adrian, *Historia* 24–26: ed. Martène 4.1073–74; Rupert, *Carm.* 10.30–45: MGH LdL 3.637.

more moderate advice—joined him in exile. Berengar and the monks of St. Lawrence took up residence in a priory of St. Hubert named Evergnicourt, located in the archdiocese of Reims about halfway between Reims and Laon. The monks of St. Hubert later went on to another priory named Cons-la-Grandville. Altogether there were about twenty-five monks in exile. Their religious fervor and discipline soon won them a considerable reputation as well as material support from the local populace.

Berengar gained the support of bishops Reginald of Reims and Halinard of Laon, and soon established contact with two zealous adherents of the reform party, Abbot Ierunta of St. Benigne in Dijon, who also offered refuge, and the papal legate Hugh of Die.[64] It was probably Hugh who finally brought their case to Pope Urban's attention. At the conclusion of the Council of Piacenza in March 1095, Urban addressed a letter to Berengar, announcing that Otbert had been condemned in council for simony and was now excommunicated for heretical crimes against the Church.[65] Berengar himself received high praise for upholding the truth in this otherwise desolate region, though the pope could not hide a certain pique that in the midst of this awful struggle for a pure Church the abbot should be so unduly concerned about his lost post and squandered properties. But the pope's support for the exiles was genuine, and his messenger was to give secret instructions for arranging a personal visit. Three years nevertheless had passed, and Otbert's hold upon his episcopal principality remained unshaken. Embittered especially at the monks of St. Hubert for breaking off communion with him, he excommunicated them in turn and eventually appointed one of his own followers, a monk of Lobbes named Ingobrand, to replace Theodoric II. Meanwhile the monks still at St. Lawrence grew disenchanted with Wolbodo (whom some may originally have favored)[66] and fearful of Otbert, who was

64. *ChronHub.* 71ff: ed. Hanquet 166ff. Brief summary in Cauchie (n. 14 above) 2.7–39; and de Moreau (n. 14 above) 2.204–08.

65. JL 5538: PL 151.395–97.

66. Adrian, *Historia* 23: ed. Martène 4.1072–73. This information was probably based on Rupert's lost *Libellus*: see Van Engen, *DA* 35 (1979) 52–53, 78.

apparently given to fits of rage whenever his authority was challenged. In the spring of 1095 they too fled to Berengar in France, and so the abbey of St. Lawrence stood empty.

Rupert was among those who in February 1092 had preferred, in his own words, to follow his true pastor even into exile rather than hearken to the voice of a hireling. Twenty years later he again interpreted this biblical passage (John 10:1–16), contrary to St. Augustine, to justify a shepherd's flight from the persecution of wolves unleashed by secular powers, particularly when such flight preserved the shepherd for his sheep and thus protected the flock as well.[67] As one of Berengar's disciples now,[68] Rupert spent three and one-half years in exile at a priory halfway between Reims and Laon. Near the end of that time, around his twentieth year, he first emerges from obscurity as the author of a polemical poem recounting the struggle against Bishop Otbert.

Reiner of St. Lawrence reports (ca. 1160) that Rupert wrote a small work (*Libellus*) on the history and woes of his monastery (part 3 below) and a poem in sapphic meter on the same subject. In 1841 Bethmann discovered such a poem in sapphic meter, without title or author, in a manuscript at Cambrai containing as well Rupert's *Anulus*. Its themes and its biblical imagery make ascription to Rupert a virtual certainty.[69] The date of

67. *Carm.* 10.35–38: MGH LdL 3.637; *John* 9: CM 9.525. Cf. Augustine's *Tractatus in euangelium Iohannis* 96.6–7, where there is no justification for flight.

68. "Et assumptis secum [Berengar] fratribus quos placuit sibi, secessit. . . ." *ChronHub.* 70: ed. Hanquet 157.

69. Reiner, *Inept.* 1: MGH SS 10.595. Cambrai, Bibliothèque municipale MS 410 (formerly 386); see *Catalogue générale des manuscrits des bibliothèques publiques de France* (Paris 1891) 17.151–52. For editions and commentary, see E. Dümmler, "Zur Geschichte des Investiturstreites im Bisthum Lüttich," *Neues Archiv* 11 (1886) 175–94; B. Hauréau, "Notices sur un poème dans le numéro 386 des manuscrits de Cambrai," *Notices et extraits des manuscrits de la bibliothèque nationale et autres bibliothèques* 31.2 (1886) 165–94; R. Rocholl, *Rupert of Deutz* (Gütersloh 1886) 269–87; Cauchie (n. 14 above) 2.48–64; H. Boehmer, in MGH LdL 3.622–41 (cited below by stanza and line); and Van Engen, *DA* 35 (1979) 79–81.

its composition can be narrowed to the spring of 1095: Rupert had just begun his fourth year in exile,[70] thus putting it after February 1095, and yet he saw still no prospect for return, which was to be negotiated in July 1095. Whether Pope Urban's letter (March/April) had arrived is not clear, despite similarities in the imagery.[71]

Rupert saw the Church as divided and almost destroyed. Heresy reigned everywhere: simony had penetrated to every corner of the world; each sacred office had its price.[72] And for this the king was chiefly to blame. He had captured Rome and driven out the true pope (Gregory VII), the one who alone had dared resist this evil, and set up his own puppet-pope—in fact, the only one recognized in the diocese of Liège—thereby dividing the entire Church, since the world (*orbis*) could not be in unity when the Roman see was rent in two.[73] Rupert pointed to conflict and schism at Metz, Worms, and Würzburg. Indeed, so many prelates had bowed low before this evil that the few righteous now mostly languished in exile in foreign lands and cities. But, Rupert lamented, who can help them when Nero himself holds Rome and Simon Magus is called pope?[74] In its final section Rupert addressed his *patria* (*Tu quoque modo, Leodium sedes, / quondam meus flos, dulce meum*). He clearly had a good grasp of the situation: he knew about simoniacal transactions at Florennes, St. Trond, and Brogne; he understood St. Hubert's use of its exemption against Bishop Otbert's jurisdictional claims; and he echoed Berengar's pressing concern—too pressing, in Pope Urban's view—for the properties alienated from St. Lawrence. But however much simony and division in the Church troubled him, he came back first and last to the same thing: what most grieved Mother Church was the flight and exile of her true sons, and what deeply grieved Rupert was his lengthy

70. *Carm.* 10.43–44: MGH LdL 3.637.
71. Urban receives high praise, especially as a Cluniac (4.7–12), but Otbert's excommunication is never mentioned. Cf. n. 77 below.
72. 1.21–22; 3.42–48; 9.25–32; 10.17–23.
73. 9.33–36, 58–64.   74. 1.25–28, 41–44.

stay in a poor priory (*aeda parua, casa paupere*) far from Liège and St. Lawrence.[75]

Rupert denounced all these evils in strikingly apocalyptic terms. Tyconius and St. Augustine had once successfully defused such explosive language, and early medieval commentators on the Book of Apocalypse remained content to interpret it in moral, spiritual, and historical generalities.[76] But the leading reformers, including Humbert, Pope Gregory, and Pope Urban, once again applied apocalyptic images specifically to persons and events in their own times; and Rupert's poem did so more concretely and extensively than any other eleventh-century text.[77] Thus, in the received exegetical tradition the "great red dragon" of Apoc. 12:3 was understood to refer generally to the Devil and his persecutions, especially those wrought by pagan emperors in the past; but for Rupert the dragon reigned "again" and "here and now" in the person of King Henry IV.[78] Likewise, the third part of the stars cast down by the tail of the dragon (Apoc. 12:4) had stood generally for all pagans, Jews, and false Christians, whereas in Rupert's poem they became the simoniac prelates and clerics cast out of the Church for their heresy.[79]

75. 1.33–34; 9.88; 10.40.

76. Rupert knew the commentaries of Jerome, Bede, and especially Haimo: W. Kamlah, *Apokalypse und Geschichtstheologie* (Historische Studien 285, Berlin 1935) 77ff. Library catalogues at St. Lawrence attest to Haimo (1.5: 2.79) and Autpertus (1.6–7): Gessler, "Bibliothèque" 107, 123.

77. In his letter to Berengar, Pope Urban referred to Wibert as "bestia terribili et uaria, quae ascendit de mari et fecit bellum cum sanctis" and to Otbert as "Antichristi signifer, satanae iumentum perfidiae." JL 5538: PL 151.397. Compare Rupert: "Nunc hostis antiquus ruit a mari, / Septemque uictor collibus imperat" (*Carm.* 9.21–22). On the beginnings of such "actualization," see Rauh, *Antichrist* 172ff and 185–96 on Rupert.

78. I cite Haimo as the author Rupert probably knew best: "Per draconem . . . intelligitur diabolus. . . . Per septem autem draconis capita, omnes intelliguntur reges illi subiecti, qui contra septiformem ecclesiam pugnant." Haimo, *In Apoc.* 3: PL 117.1082. Rupert says: "Nunc agit bellum draco bellicosus (1.1—the first line of the poem!) . . . Draco factus ingens / Hic modo regnat (3.35–36) . . . redivivus hostis" (12.22). Cf. nn. 77, 81. The reference is to Henry's capture of Rome in 1084—something which Goderranus of Lobbes and the annalists in Liège saw as justified (n. 55 above).

79. Haimo: PL 117.1083. Rupert, *Carm.* 1.2–4, 9, 13–16.

Again, the woman about to give birth whom the dragon seeks to devour (Apoc. 12:4) represented for Rupert much more than the general condition of the Church and her sons in a sinful world: she is the Roman Church attacked by the king and divided by heresy.[80]

Was Rupert then truly convinced that the Last Times were upon him? Certainly the ecclesiastical crisis which had caught him up far surpassed anything anyone could read about or recall, so that he made specific, unfavorable comparisons to the troubles wrought earlier by Nero and Arius, figures often cited in Apocalypse commentaries as examples of terrestrial and heretical persecution.[81] Yet Rupert should not be counted the first in a long line of medieval prophets.[82] A monk since childhood, for whom Scripture and saints' lives had become second nature, Rupert drew his imagery directly from the Bible and had the respective saints, the true possessors of monastic houses and properties, speak—poetically—for themselves. Accordingly, to depict those times in which the Church had flourished and to personify the lament of the Church to her Lord, Rupert turned naturally to the imagery and language of the Canticle of Canticles, on which he was later to write one of his better-known and more original commentaries; and to convey the gravity of the present situation, he employed the full resources of the Book of Apocalypse. That such apocalyptic language was for Rupert a kind of rhetoric in no way lessens the fearfulness of the times as he perceived them from exile, nor the novelty and daring required to name that man the "dragon" and even the "Antichrist" for whose salvation and prosperity, in more peaceful times, he was expected to offer public prayer.[83]

If the imagery of Rupert's first poem revealed his command

80. Haimo: PL 117.1083–84. Rupert, *Carm.* 1.29–32.

81. "Statim peruideo quale periculum / Nunc est ecclesie. . . . Intus turba, foris chaos" (2.24). "Symon atque Nero / Nunc reuixerunt, miseramque matrem / Rursus oppugnant. . . . Nemo tam seuus fuit antichristus, / Arrius quamuis fuerit malignus" (3.29–31, 37–38).

82. Rauh, *Antichrist* 185–235; B. McGinn, *Visions of the End* (New York 1979) 94–97.

83. *Levit.* 1.35: CM 22.847.

of Scripture, and its themes the degree to which he had made his own the convictions of the reform party, its form demonstrated the quality of his literary education. This poem may have originated as a student exercise. Rupert's teacher, Heribrand, was a firm adherent of the reform party who later wrote a *vita* (now lost) of Abbot Theodoric II, the most uncompromising follower in the event of the reformed papacy.[84] He may also be identical with that Heribrannus among the exiles whose hatred for Otbert was so great that he reportedly spit each time he even heard the bishop's name.[85] In any case, Rupert had learned from Heribrand to write competently in at least ten different meters, an unusual feat in the late eleventh century, and to make skillful use of lines from Vergil, Horace, and Ovid. Above all, Rupert made full use of the poetic sections in Boethius' *Consolation of Philosophy*, one of the standard items in any good medieval literary education.[86] Indeed, Boethius' reflections on his plight probably served as a model for Rupert's "complaint on his exile."

Rupert began with a thundering denunciation of the dragon, the modern Nero (Henry IV), for which he employed the same meter (sapphic) Boethius had used to describe the destruction wrought by the real Nero;[87] and his opening reflections on the state of the Church directly echo Boethius' first prose lines.[88]

84. MGH SS 20.594. Heribrand's may have been an apology, just as Nizo, also of St. Lawrence, was to write the life of the "martyred" pro-papal successor to Otbert, Bishop Frederick (1119–21): MGH SS 12.501–08.

85. *ChronHub.* 70: ed. Hanquet 164–65.

86. See G. Glauche, *Schullektüre im Mittelalter* (Munich 1970) passim; P. Courcelle, *La Consolation de Philosophie dans la tradition littéraire. Antécédents et posterité de Boèce* (Paris 1967); for a commentary on *Cons. Phil.* 3.9 available to Rupert, see H. Silvestre, "Le commentaire inédit de Jean Scot Erigène au mètre IX du livre III du *De consolatione philosophiae* de Boèce," *RHE* 47 (1952) 51–64, and "La Consolation de Boèce et sa tradition littéraire," *RHE* 64 (1969) 30–31.

87. *Carm.* 1; *Cons. Phil.* 2.6. Compare Rupert's citation of this verse in *Spir.* 6.10: CM 24.2021–22.

88. *Carm.* 2.1; *Cons. Phil.* 1.1. See H. Silvestre, "La Consolation" (n. 86 above) 27.

Mother Church then cries out against the evils besetting her, in the same meter as Boethius calling to God for relief from his woes,[89] whereupon the Virgin Mary intervenes, just as Philosophia had and in the same meter, to recall better days.[90] The Church's case goes before the Judgement Seat in the same meter in which Boethius is enjoined to seek truth fearlessly.[91] Christ, the Sponsus and Judge, responds in lines echoing Boethius but in a meter borrowed from Horace's ode on man's hopelessly erring ways.[92] The Sponsa answers in imagery taken from the Canticle of Canticles and in glyconic meter, often used by Boethius, at least once to describe the reign of "love,"[93] to which the Sponsus responds again in a meter taken from Horace.[94] The remaining stanzas, a description of actual events by the respective patron saints, have less direct relationship to either Boethius or Horace.

Rupert concluded his poem on a despairing note. Mother Church cries out: *Hec mala cuncta super me ceciderunt. / . . . Heu me! quanta tuli! quot mala uidi. . . .* Shortly after returning to St. Lawrence, he would take up a short work in prose on the good and evil (*quae bona uel quae mala*) his abbey had experienced.

3

Return and Resistance
(1095–ca. 1108)

Help came at last in the summer of 1095. Duke Godfrey of Bouillon, who was to die five years later as the first "Defender of the Holy Sepulchre," together with several of Bishop Otbert's vassals (*fideles*) refused to support him in the siege of a

---

89. *Carm.* 4; *Cons. Phil.* 1.5.
90. *Carm.* 5; *Cons. Phil.* 1.2. Hauréau (n. 69 above) 173 n. 2.
91. *Carm.* 6; *Cons. Phil.* 1.7. Compare *Gen.* 5.16: CM 21.349, where Rupert cited this verse from Boethius as teaching "nec dolere de aduersis huius mundi . . . nec timere mundi huius aduersa."
92. *Carm.* 7; Horace, *Carm.* I, ode 3. Hauréau (n. 69 above) 176.
93. *Carm.* 8; *Cons. Phil.* 2.8.
94. *Carm.* 9; Horace, *Carm.* II, 14. Hauréau (n. 69 above) 180.

castle (Clermont-lez-Nandrin on the Meuse near Huy) until the exiled abbots had been granted a fair hearing.[95] The lords may well have sought any excuse to halt Otbert's territorial ambitions, but there is also evidence that his excommunication in March had begun to undermine his authority.[96] The bishop was forced to relent. Wolbodo of St. Lawrence and Ingobrand of St. Hubert (1093–95) were tried before the assembled archdeacons and abbots of the diocese, found guilty of simony, and removed. Otbert still refused totally to deal with Abbot Theodoric II, the man of principle who had decided *suo instinctu* not to commune with his heretical bishop. Theodoric was forced to live out his life in exile at St. Remi in Reims, the stubborn representative of the "pure" reformers.[97] But Otbert invited Berengar to return. Rupert's abbot hesitated at first, lest he seem to betray the reform party and all the principles he had espoused so fervently over the last three years. In the end he decided that restoration of his house was more important, and he agreed to return on condition that all properties alienated by Wolbodo be restored. Sympathetic archdeacons made the arrangements with Bishop Otbert, whom Berengar publicly kissed to seal the reconciliation—a grave scandal to the zealous reformers since Otbert was still excommunicate. Berengar and his monks returned to St. Lawrence in Liège on 9 August 1095, the vigil of their patron's feastday.[98]

95. H. Dorchy, "Godefroid de Bouillon, Duc du Basse-Lotharingie," *RBPH* 26 (1948) 961–99, here 990–96; G. Despy, "La date de l'accession de Godefroid de Bouillon au duché de Basse-Lotharingie," *RBPH* 36 (1958) 1275–84; K. Reindel, "Gottfried IV.," in *Neue Deutsche Biographie* 6 (Berlin 1964) 663. Deprez (n. 25 above) 506–07 n. 20 doubted the account of these events in *ChronHub*. 77–78: ed. Hanquet 184–97, on the basis of Gilles d'Orvalles, MGH SS 24.94: "Clarimontis castellum . . . multo precio acquisiuit." But if the vassals indeed resisted, would not Otbert be forced to buy the castle at great expense? The *Chronicle of St. Hubert* was contemporary, whereas Gilles's work is a thirteenth-century compilation. See also Kupper (n. 58 above) 372–77.

96. *ChronHub*. 77, 78: ed. Hanquet 185, 195.

97. *ChronHub*. 80–95 passim; *Monasticon Belge* (Liège 1975) 5.37–38; de Moreau (n. 14 above) 2.207–10.

98. *ChronHub*. 79: ed. Hanquet 197–98. The date is reported only in Adrian's fifteenth-century *Historia* 28: ed. Martène 4.1075, which may rely

Restoration by lay lords acting against the will of their bishop made a deep impression on Rupert. Though generally conservative in matters of clerical privilege, Rupert remarked that today many sons of this world (laymen) are wiser in public affairs than the sons of light (clergy), and elsewhere—in the spirit of Pope Gregory's canon authorizing the laity to reject masses said by immoral priests—Rupert declared that laymen could rightly condemn (*non iniuria condemnat*) priests proven unworthy either in their lives (*pro merito uitae*) or in their training (*pro qualitate uel quantitate scientiae*).[99] Like Balaam's ass (Num. 22:22ff), the laity should reproach its rider, the prelate, for simony, and should rightly (*iusta licentia*) and forcibly keep him from carrying out his avaricious desires, even when he is angered to the point of whipping.[100] The reformers were eventually to create a more strictly "clerical" Church, but to do so they called upon the help of "good" laymen against "false" prelates and priests. Sigebert of Gembloux, writing for the clergy in Liège, deplored this papally sponsored revolution in the traditional and sacred order of Christendom.[101]

From the summer of 1095 until sometime after November 1106 when Otbert was reconciled to the reformed papacy, Rupert lived less than a thousand yards from his excommunicated bishop, the "wolf" of his poem, and indeed for several months of the year 1106 equally close to "Nero," the "dragon" himself, Henry IV. The combined strength of Bishop Otbert and King Henry rendered the reformed papacy completely helpless in the diocese of Liège. In November 1098 Pope Urban addressed one of his sternest letters to the clergy and people of Liège, calling upon them to cast out Otbert, or if that were impossible at least to separate themselves from communion with him lest they too

---

here on Rupert's lost *Libellus*; cf. Van Engen, *DA* 35 (1979) 53 n. 128. To schedule important public events, such as restoration of divine office, on major feastdays was the rule rather than the exception in the middle ages.

99. *Reg.* 2.15: CM 22.1259; *Exod.* 3.22: CM 22.714. *Num.* 1.8: CM 22.923. Cf. Beinert, *Kirche* 307–09.

100. *Num.* 2.17: CM 22.986–87. Cf. Van Engen, *DA* 35 (1979) 73–74.

101. ". . . totius humanae societatis confusa, christianae sanctitatis statuta conuulsa, popularis status subitam immutationem. . . ." MGH LdL 2.438.

become polluted.[102] In a still more striking act, virtually without precedent, Pope Paschal II in 1102 ordered Count Robert of Flanders to go on crusade against the rebellious bishop and clergy of Liège![103] Sigebert of Gembloux, already seventy years old, powerfully denounced this new abuse of papal power.[104] Finally in 1104 nearly all the leading clergymen in Liège, spurred on by a criminous insult to the provost of St. Lambert and the bishop's monetary policy, protested Otbert's abuse of the episcopal office to Archbishop Frederick of Cologne, who set a public hearing for shortly after Easter. But King Henry traveled to Liège and quashed it.[105] Through it all and despite their complaints, the secular clergy in Liège and all the abbots except Theodoric II continued to work routinely with Otbert in diocesan affairs, and Alger, Otbert's secretary since 1101, sought to clarify several of the canonistic issues in his *Liber de misericordia et iustitia*.[106] Only monks, if they so chose, had the luxury of avoiding communion with their bishop—except, of course, in ordination, and that became the chief sticking point.

Rupert's return to St. Lawrence in 1095 resolved nothing; it rather sharpened his focus on the principles at stake. His stance during these twelve or thirteen years prior to ordination can be reconstructed from three different kinds of evidence: his remarks on simony and similar issues in later works, his book of reflections on the history of St. Lawrence, and, above all, his refusal to receive ordination from the excommunicated Otbert. Rupert utterly condemned simony in all three forms as heresy and idolatry, that is, the worship of mammon and the Devil

102. "Auferte malum ex uobis ipsis. . . . Si quis autem deinceps eis communicare presumpserit . . . sciat se eiusdem excommunicationis uinculo innodatos." JL 5712: *ChronHub.* 92: ed. Hanquet 238.

103. JL 5889: printed in MGH LdL 2.451–52. See C. Erdmann, *Die Entstehung des Kreuzzugsgedanken* (Stuttgart 1935; repr. Darmstadt 1955) 244–45.

104. MGH LdL 2.449–64. Beumann (n. 23 above) 36–37.

105. *ChronHub.* 96–97: ed. Hanquet 247–50; cf. Kupper (n. 58 above) 365.

106. G. Le Bras, "Le *Liber de misericordia et iustitia* d'Alger de Liège," *Nouvelle revue historique de droit français et étranger* 45 (1921) 80–118; N. M. Häring, "A Study in the Sacramentology of Alger of Liège," *Mediaeval Studies* 20 (1958) 41–78.

rather than Christ (cf. Eph. 5:5; Col. 3:5). The Church is now in tumult, he complained, overrun with those seeking office for their own avaricious ends.[107] As a warning to them, Rupert pointed out the fate of Achan, who was utterly destroyed for stealing things sacred to God, and Gehazi, the servant whose greed brought upon himself the leprosy Elisha had cured.[108] He particularly despised those prelates who flattered rather than reproached their patrons precisely in order to preserve material benefits[109]—doubtless Rupert's view of most imperial bishops.

Fully in the spirit of the reformed popes cited above, and directly contrary to the thrust of Alger's argument "On Mercy," this monk of St. Lawrence insisted that all these "polluted," "leprous" heretics be cast out of the Church, since they are of one body with the Devil and threaten to pollute all others, and he cited canon law verbatim to reinforce his demand.[110] From St. Augustine Rupert knew full well that the Church was a "mixed" body, requiring the faithful sometimes to tolerate false and evil brothers among them;[111] but he consistently demanded that publicly condemned heretics, such as Simon Magus, be cast out without delay—just as Pope Urban had commanded—for all their sacramental acts were null.[112] Still more emphatically, Rupert held that lapsed clerics—he meant mostly simoniac prelates and unchaste priests—could not be restored to their ecclesiastical offices: they were to be content with lay communion,

107. *Gen.* 7.14, 46: CM 21.445, 483; *Iosue* 21: CM 22.1143; *Exod.* 3.40: CM 22.736; *Off.* 4.16: CM 7.131; *John* 6: CM 9.303, 313. Cf. Beinert, *Kirche* 378–80.
108. *Iosue* 21: CM 22.1143; *Reg.* 5.31: CM 22.1446.
109. *Levit.* 1.36: CM 22.849.
110. *Deut.* 1.22, 30: CM 22.1032, 1052. Cf. *Gen.* 4.4: CM 21.284–85.
111. *John* 7.10: CM 9.381, 573; *Evang.* 23: CM 23.1809–10.
112. ". . . statim eicienda et separanda est lepra nequissima [Simon Magus], ne corrumpantur ceteri." *Levit.* 2.18: CM 22.875. On separation from communion with them: "At ubi manifesto conuictos actu . . . iam nec ratio, nec ueritatis regula patitur, ut cum eiusmodi uel cibum sumamus." *Evang.* 23: CM 23.1809–10. "Maxime ergo uitanda est immunditia haeretica, cuius cuncta opera uel mysteria quaedam sunt morticina." *Levit.* 1.21: CM 22.830. See n. 102 above.

preferably doing penance in a monastery.[113] For this too he cited canon law and more than once argued a position directly contrary to Alger's.[114]

During those same years Rupert gave expression to the intense passions fostered by exile and continuing struggle against Otbert in a small "history" of his abbey. This work is lost, but something of its character and several of its major themes can be reconstructed.[115] As in the poem and his much later work *De incendio*, Rupert conceived of and depicted his monastery's struggle against the forces of evil wholly by way of biblical imagery. Historical material was interwoven with religious themes. In the midst of controversy with his bishop, moreover, Rupert completely reinterpreted the early history of St. Lawrence so that its entire past seemed a continuous struggle to protect rights and possessions from grasping bishops. Those bishops in turn were depicted as simoniacs almost to a man, and even Bishop Reginald's foundation became an act of penance for simoniacal entrance into the episcopal office. Finally, Rupert's lauding a certain layman, a brother of the duke of Lotharingia, as the moving force during the abbey's early days recalled the role of its recent protector and certainly removed all honor from the true founders, the early eleventh-century bishops of Liège. Rupert's little work probably was not known outside the walls of St. Lawrence, but the sentiments which shaped it came to public expression in his refusal to receive ordination from Bishop Otbert.

Political circumstances causing a lengthy exile first drove Rupert into such violent hatred of Bishop Otbert, but his continued opposition for more than a decade afterwards rested on a point of principle. From early on the strict reformers had insisted that simony was heresy and that heretics could not validly dispense any of the Church's sacraments since they were themselves outside the one true Church. On precisely these grounds

113. *Levit.* 1.18, 26: CM 22.825, 836; *Spir.* 8.5–7: CM 24.2077–82.
114. This treated in my forthcoming study of Rupert and canon law.
115. This paragraph summarizes my argument in *DA* 35 (1979) 33–79.

Theodoric II and the monks of St. Hubert had voluntarily broken off communion with their bishop.[116] Such views were so prevalent among the exiles that Rupert could not help but absorb them. His own abbot, according to contemporary witnesses, became the most eloquent spokesman for this position, and Rupert himself, upon entering the archdiocese of Reims, was absolved of the "Wibertine heresy," that is, of his "polluting" contact with Otbert and the anti-pope he recognized.[117] Abbot Ierunta also encouraged the exiles to avoid all contact with Bishop Otbert, that tool of Satan and of Antichrist, and never to stray from the narrow path of the Roman (i.e. the reformed) Church.[118] Pope Urban used similar language in his letter to Berengar and later called on the clergy of Liège to separate themselves from their bishop (see n. 102 above). Two monks named to abbacies after returning from exile, one from St. Hubert and another from St. Lawrence, agonized publicly over Otbert's power validly and effectively to consecrate them into office. Rupert's confrere later resigned his post in remorse. Likewise the new house of canons regular at Rolduc was dedicated by Otbert, but its first provost postponed consecration precisely because of the bishop's reputation for simony.[119] Most of the secular clergy, on the other hand, including, it seems, Abbot Berengar after his return, adopted a moderate, more practical position to the effect that sacraments were of Christ, not Otbert, and pollution involved consent, not contact.[120]

This issue came to a head for Rupert when he reached his thirtieth year, presumably about 1105. This is how, twenty years later, he described the stance he had taken then:

> Division, originating in the schism of the apostolic see, vexed the Church of Christ for a long time, until its authors [Henry IV and Wibert] finally died and peace slowly returned. For

116. *ChronHub.* 70: ed. Hanquet 158.
117. *ChronHub.* 70, 76–79, 90: ed. Hanquet 156–66, 181–98, 227–28.
118. *ChronHub.* 71: ed. Hanquet 169.
119. *ChronHub.* 87: ed. Hanquet 225; and MGH SS 16.697, 700.
120. *ChronHub.* 70, 89: ed. Hanquet 158, 224–25.

that and other reasons, many, especially those who seemed more religious and more devoted to ecclesiastical purity, refused to receive ordination at the hands of their bishops—with a simple eye, to be sure, but it is good to be discreet in all things. . . . For so long as any minister of the sacraments remains in the body of the whole, whatever he administers will be valid; but when he has been condemned in a legitimate judgement so that he is cut off or damned, then what he does may have the appearance of piety but it is devoid of sacramental power. And so I too, with a single eye, shunned the ordination of those who were infamous. Even though other younger men were ordained before me, I still did not receive ordination. . . .[121]

To grasp the strength of his conviction, it must be emphasized that Rupert disagreed on this point with several younger members of his own community (*praeordinatis quibusdam iunioribus*)—not to speak of the secular clergy in Liège—and also with his revered abbot, who reportedly "rejoiced" (*gratulatus*) when Rupert finally ended his resistance. This stance put Rupert permanently out of favor with Bishop Otbert,[122] and continued to affect his theology and relations with the secular clergy long after his ordination.

4

Education and Early Works

More than fifteen years of ecclesiastical crisis, extending roughly from Rupert's seventeenth to his thirty-third year, provided the context for his ecclesiological formation. His intellectual and literary formation cannot be traced in the same detail, though its general context is also clear, namely, the fine scholastic tradition maintained in Liège throughout the eleventh century. The fame of the schools in eleventh-century Liège attracted students from as far away as England, Normandy,

121. *Matt.* 12: CM 29.381.
122. *Off.* epist.: CM 7.1.

Spain, and Bohemia.[123] As late as the year 1117 Liège was still considered to have the leading schools in the German Empire.[124] Most scholars trained there, as noted earlier, served inside that Empire, but several also achieved recognition in Christendom at large. Duke Godfrey's brother Frederick, for instance, after several years in Liège as student and then archdeacon, went on to become chancellor of the Roman Church under Pope Leo IX (1049–54), abbot of Monte Cassino (1057), and finally Pope Stephen IX (1057–58); and Canon Hezilo of St. Lambert's received mathematical training which enabled him to become the chief architect of Cluny III, the greatest romanesque church in Christendom.[125]

No single master at Liège, such as Gerbert at Reims or Fulbert at Chartres, loomed above all others. The monastic school at Lobbes had flourished first: Ratherius (d. 974) proved the most learned theologian of the tenth century; Abbot Folkwin introduced a new historical genre into the Empire; and Abbot Heriger (990–1007) excelled in history, mathematics (a lost work on the abacus), and theology. With Heriger's help, Bishop

123. Basic works on the schools of Liège: S. Balau, *Les sources de l'histoire de Liège au Moyen Age. Etude critique* (Brussels 1903); Kurth, *Notger* (n. 14 above) 251–99; E. Lesne, *Histoire de la propriété ecclésiastique en France* (Lille 1940) 5.349–68; H. Sproemberg (n. 13 above) 124–52, 715–37; H. Silvestre, "Renier de St.-Laurent et le déclin des écoles liégeoises au XIIᵉ siècle," in *Miscellanea Tornacensia* (1951) 112–32; J. Stiennon, "Etudes des centres intellectuels de la Basse Lotharingie (Xᵉ–XIIᵉ siècles)," ibid. 134–45; idem, *Les écoles de Liège aux XIᵉ et XIIᵉ siècles* (Catalogue d'exposition, Liège 1967); idem, "Du Conflent au pays mosan en 1050: Une tradition séculaire des relations intellectuelles," in *Cahiers Saint-Michel de Cuxa* (1971) 2.62–75; P. Butzer, "Die Mathematiker des Aachen-Lütticher Raumes von der karolingischen bis zur spätottonischen Epoche," *Annalen des historischen Vereins für den Niederrhein* 178 (1976) 7–30; P. Riché, *Ecoles et enseignement dans le haut moyen âge* (Paris 1979) 164–67; and Christine Renardy, "Les écoles liégeoises du IXᵉ au XIIᵉ siècle: Grandes lignes de leur évolution," *RBPH* 57 (1979) 309–28.

124. Ekkehard of Corvey, *Chronicon* (Freiherr vom Stein Gedächtnis Ausgabe, Darmstadt 1972) 334; but compare local complaints of decline in Reimbald, *Chronicon* 382–96: CM 4.136.

125. J. Stiennon, "Hézélon de Liège, architecte de Cluny III," in *Mélanges René Crozet* (Poitiers 1966) 1.345–58.

Notger transferred scholastic activity to the city, where a whole series of distinguished masters taught, presumably at the cathedral school: Wazo (before 1008 to ca. 1030), Egbert, Radulph, Adelman (ca. 1030 to ca. 1044), Gozechin (ca. 1044–1058), and Franco (ca. 1058–1080's). Beyond their expertise in grammar and rhetoric, the fundamentals of early medieval education, these masters became most distinguished for their work in mathematics, so much so that a recent study (Butzer, n. 123 above) labeled Liège the center of mathematical learning in Europe during the years 1010–70.

Rupert's abbey benefited from steady contact with secular masters in Liège. Abbot Lambert (d. 1070) studied, probably in the early 1040's, with the famous Master Adelman;[126] Falchanus, *magister scholarum* in St. Lawrence roughly during the 1060's–70's, assisted Franco, the last distinguished secular master, in the composition of works on the squaring of the circle and the observance of the Ember Days; and another monk, Engelbert, did useful work in computus, a specialty of the schools in Liège.[127] During the 1080's Abbot Berengar and Master Franco also worked together on diocesan affairs.[128] Falchanus trained his successor in St. Lawrence, Heribrand, and he in turn trained Rupert.[129] Heribrand was considered an effective teacher, learned in both human and divine matters, and able to compose with ease (*promptissimum*) in verse and prose. Reiner later claimed that the schools of Liège and St. Lawrence had flourished most during the reign of Abbot Berengar (1077–1116), that is to say, precisely during Rupert's formative years.[130] Rupert deeply re-

126. Hampe (n. 42 above) 376; Sproemberg (n. 13 above) 650–51; Reiner, *Inept.* 1: MGH SS 20.593. This merits emphasis since Lambert, a nephew of Abbot Stephen, would have been a monk already when he studied with Adelman.

127. MGH SS 20.594.

128. MGH SS 10.237.

129. ". . . uir fidelis et prudens Heribrandus, qui et ipse litterarum peritus pueritiae meae magister exstitit. . . ." CM 21.121. On Heribrand, see Berlière, *Monasticon Belge* (1928) 2.37–38.

130. "Summopere apud *monachos seu clericos* urbis nostrae studia tunc uigebant scolaria. . . ." MGH SS 20.595 (my italics).

sented the sneering remarks of later detractors about his failure to travel in order to study with the new masters. Adapting a line from Horace for his purposes, he pointed out to them that learning was to be had in monasteries too and, again, that he had also read widely and studiously in the prescribed authors of the liberal arts curriculum.[131]

Indeed, so great was the impact of his education that he later devoted an entire book of *De sancta Trinitate* to an exposition of the seven liberal arts under the aegis of *scientia* as a gift of the Holy Spirit. His remarks there and elsewhere suggest the general contours of Rupert's education. His basic training in grammar was grounded in Donatus, Bede's *De schematibus et tropis* and *De arte metrica*,[132] and Isidore's *Etymologies*. Rhetoric still dominated the educational curriculum of the eleventh century, and Rupert too devoted the greatest space to it in his treatment. Beyond Isidore and Cassiodorus Rupert learned most from Ps.-Cicero's *Rhetorica ad Herennium*.[133] But in line with later eleventh-century developments Rupert gave almost equal time to dialectic, although his presentation here hardly exceeded the basic expositions of Cassiodorus[134] and Isidore. His much shorter treatment of the quadrivium also relied almost entirely upon Cassiodorus or Isidore. Rupert had no objection whatsoever to the teaching of these arts, something he quite probably did himself (see chapter III, part 1), but he deplored the failure of secular masters to apply them fruitfully to the study of Holy Scripture.[135] For each of the arts in fact Rupert provided his own scriptural illustrations.

131. *Omnip.* 22: PL 170.472; *Matt.* 12: CM 29.386.

132. *John* 1: CM 9.1. *Spir.* 7.11: CM 24.2050–51, lines 463–65 = Bede's *De schematibus et tropis:* CC 123A.142, lines 6–8; Rupert, lines 468–71 = Bede, 143, lines 25–28; etc. (missed by Haacke). On the basic disciplines in the early middle ages, see Riché (n. 123 above) 246–66.

133. *Spir.* 7.12: CM 24.2051, lines 503–04 = *Rhet. ad Heren.* 1.3.4; etc. See H. Silvestre, "L'édition R. Haacke du *De Trinitate* de Rupert de Deutz," *Sacris Erudiri* 22 (1974–75) 399.

134. *Spir.* 7.13: CM 24.2060, lines 845–47, 849, 850 = Cassiodorus, *Institutiones* 2.3, 8: ed. Mynors 112, lines 12–13, 15–16, etc.

135. "Non ergo studia condemnat [St. Paul, Rom. 1:18–20] uel scholas

In conjunction with the arts of grammar and rhetoric medieval students read prescribed "school authors," to whom they were introduced by a set form known as the *accessus ad auctores*. These authors made a lasting impression on Rupert,[136] even though his later works were not directly modeled upon them, as his poem was on Boethius. Vergil (the "*poeta*"), Horace ("*Ethnicus*"), Lucan (the "*auctor*"), Prudentius (*egregius atque orthodoxus uersificator*),[137] Boethius, Sallust, and Macrobius[138] are cited, roughly in that order of frequency, throughout Rupert's scriptural commentaries. For general knowledge about nature and chronology Rupert employed Bede's influential works *De natura rerum* and *De temporum ratione*,[139] for Jewish history Josephus, and for Christian history Jerome's *Chronicle* and Cassiodorus' *Historia tripartita*. Rupert's vast knowledge of the Church Fathers, made possible by the quality of his abbey's library, has never received systematic study, but Silvestre has recently made an interesting observation: while in his first work Rupert still frequently cited the Fathers verbatim and by name, he later integrated their thought into his own language without reference—

---

grammaticorum, dialecticorum, rhetorum, arithmeticorum, geometricorum, musicorum, astronomorum, sed hoc in eis culpat, quod non quaesierunt ex eis sapientiae fructum, propter quem artes istae a Deo datae sunt." *Spir.* 7.4: CM 24.2042.

136. H. Silvestre, "Les citations et réminiscences classiques dans l'oeuvre de Rupert de Deutz," *RHE* 45 (1950) 140–74; idem, "Rupert de Saint-Laurent et les auteurs classiques," *Mélanges Felix Rousseau* (1958) 541–51. See Rupert's own remarks in *Matt.* 5: CM 29.153–54.

137. Rupert knew a gloss on Prudentius from Brussels, Bibl. roy. MS 10066–77 fols. 85ᵛ–86ʳ, 87ᵛ: see H. Silvestre, "Aperçu sur les commentaires carolingiens de Prudence," *Sacris Erudiri* 9 (1957) 65–74, 398; idem, *Scriptorium* 11 (1957) 102–04; idem, "A propos du Bruxellensis 10066–77 et de son noyau primitif," in *Miscellanea codicologica F. Masai dicata* (Ghent 1979) 131–56.

138. H. Silvestre, "Macrobe utilisé par un Pseudo-Erigène et par Rupert de Deutz," *Classica et Mediaevalia* 19 (1958) 129–32; idem, "Une adaptation du commentaire de Macrobe sur le Songe de Scipion dans un manuscrit de Bruxelles," *AHDL* 29 (1962) 93–101.

139. Brussels, Bibl. roy. MS 9932–34. Silvestre, *Scriptorium* 6 (1952) 289.

a sign of growing independence and self-confidence.[140] Much remains to be done on Rupert's sources and the way in which he employed them, such as the materials in a tenth-century florilegium taken up into his *Commentary on Genesis*.[141]

Of Rupert's youthful works[142] only three have survived: the poem on his exile, a poem on and to the Holy Spirit written in the aftermath of his vocational crisis, and a *vita sancti Augustini*, still unedited, made up largely of excerpts from Augustine's own works.[143] In addition to the lost *Libellus* mentioned above, Rupert wrote a poem in heroic verse based on the Canticle of Canticles, a *vita sanctae Odiliae*, and various liturgical *cantus*. Such hagiographical and liturgical works met concrete needs in his monastery and could also advance the career of a scholarly monk, as evidenced by Sigebert of Gembloux who also started out with hagiographical compositions in verse. Rupert later dismissed these early works, but only after his vocational crisis and the discovery of his gift for lengthy commentary in prose on Holy Scripture.[144] From the beginning, to be sure, Rupert was interested in scriptural interpretation: Reiner and the library catalogue ascribe to him a versified collection of *sententiae* on the Scriptures.[145] Worthy of much greater attention is his abbreviation of Gregory's *Moralia on Job*.[146] Gregory's work remained

140. H. Silvestre, "La répartition des citations nominatives des Pères dans l'oeuvre de Rupert de Deutz," in *Sapientiae Doctrina: Mélanges Dom Hildebrand Bascour O.S.B.* (Louvain 1980) 271–98. I cannot agree, however, that Rupert hid his quotations purposefully to trip up adversaries (pp. 288–89); Silvestre's *post hoc ergo propter hoc* reasoning in this regard fails because the passage which later caused trouble for Norbert (see chapter IX, part 1 below) was written at a time when Rupert had as yet no adversaries. I prefer to see growing self-confidence on Rupert's part.

141. Silvestre, "Bruxellensis 10066–77" (n. 137 above) 146ff.

142. Reiner, *Inept.* 1: MGH SS 20.595. See Van Engen, *DA* 35 (1979) 38; Silvestre (n. 12 above) 37–40.

143. Brussels, Bibl. roy. MS 9368 fols. 73ᵛ–81ᵛ. The prologue in *Catalogus codicum hagiographicorum Bibliothecae Regiae Bruxellensis* (1869) 2.328.

144. CM 7.1: CM 29.381.

145. Gessler, "Bibliothèque" 122 n. 72; MGH SS 20.595.

146. Brussels, Bibl. roy. MS 9935 fols. 1–96ᵛ: van den Gheyn 2.410 (n.

fundamental for both exegesis and spirituality throughout the early middle ages; indeed, abbreviations of his work became a kind of spiritual exercise for monks.[147] Rupert's précis should be understood therefore as a kind of exegetical and theological apprenticeship.

In sum, the breadth and thoroughness of Rupert's education, hardly conceivable apart from the excellence of Liège's schools, was to serve him well. Yet it was not to his education but rather to a series of divinely inspired visions that Rupert ascribed the release of his prodigious talent.

5

Vocational Crisis

The spiritual formation of monks during the tenth and eleventh centuries can be reconstructed only indirectly.[148] Most were oblates, children bound at an early age to the monastic life by their parents' promises rather than their own volition. They learned the religious life, much as their brothers in the world

---

1521) = PL 168.961–1196. Whether this is indeed Rupert's "Commentariolum in Iob librorum decem abbreuiatum ex abundantia sensuum atque dictorum beati Gregorii . . ." (CM 7.3) remains uncertain; see Arduini (n. 1 above) 563 n. 155.

147. For Odo of Cluny, see now G. Braga, "Problemi di autenticità per Oddone di Cluny: l'Epitome dei 'Moralia' di Gregorio Magno," *Studi Medievali* 3rd ser. 18 (1977) 611–711. See also R. Wasselynck, "Les compilations des *Moralia in Iob* du VIIe au XIIe siècle," *RTAM* 29 (1962) 5–32; idem, "L'influence de l'exégèse de Gregoire le Grand sur les commentaires bibliques médiévaux," *RTAM* 32 (1965) 157–204, 177–81 on Rupert.

148. Four studies by J. Leclercq, "Deux opuscules sur la formation des jeunes moines," *Revue d'ascétique et de mystique* 33 (1957) 387–99; "Lettres de vocation à la vie monastique," *Analecta Monastica* 3 (Studia Anselmiana 37, Rome 1955) 169–97; "Pédagogie et formation spirituelle du IVe au IXe siècle," *La scuola nell'Occidente latino dell'alto medioevo* (Settimane di studio 19, Spoleto 1972) 255–90; and "Textes sur la vocation et formation des moines au moyen âge," in *Corona gratiarum* (Bruges 1975) 2.169–94; and P. Riché, "L'enfant dans la société monastique au XIIe siècle," in *Pierre Abélard—Pierre le Vénérable* (Paris 1975) 689–701.

did the seigneurial life, simply by practicing it, until as young adults they made formal profession. The novitiate was thereby reduced to a formality, particularly since oblates had no real option to leave.[149] They could flee, but only at the risk of losing their souls and often their social standing as well. The truly obstreperous sometimes got locked up in the monastery's prison, but doubtless many went through the motions of a life for which they had no "vocation" in the strict modern sense of the term. Guibert of Nogent complained that in his youth (1070's) many ancient and wealthy houses were in the keeping of uninspired monks placed there by their parents. On a higher plane, Eadmer, an oblate, and Anselm of Canterbury, a convert at age twenty-seven, debated the relative advantages and disadvantages of their respective spiritual developments. Until the last third of the eleventh century the religious life was seen first of all in functional terms: so long as monks could and did read, pray, and make intercession, it mattered little that they were essentially a "conscript army."[150]

There were always, to be sure, converts from the secular clergy, such as Abbot Berengar, and occasionally from the laity as well. But the tempo of such conversion experiences picked up dramatically during the last third of the eleventh century, to the point where whole villages in Swabia reportedly adopted the religious life *en masse*.[151] Indeed, nearly every significant religious and theological leader of the years 1075–1125 was such a

149. On oblation, and its binding character until the early twelfth century, see P. Hofmeister, "Die Klaustral-Oblaten," *SMBO* 72 (1961) 5–45, esp. 7–11; J. Orlandis, "Notas sobre la 'oblatio puerorum' en los siglos XI y XII," in *Estudios sobre instituciones monasticas medievales* (Pamplona 1971) 205–15; J. Hourlier, *Les religieux* (Histoire du droit et des institutions de l'église en Occident 10, Paris 1974) 160–63, 187–88.

150. The phrase of R. W. Southern, *The Making of the Middle Ages* (New Haven 1953) 162. See *Guibert de Nogent, Histoire de sa vie*, ed. G. Bourgin (Paris 1907) 23–24; and *Liber Anselmi de humanis moribus per similitudines* 78, ed. R. W. Southern and F. S. Schmitt, *Memorials of St. Anselm* (London 1969) 68–69.

151. There is a vast literature on this; see especially H. Grundmann, "Neue Beiträge zur Geschichte der religiösen Bewegungen im Mittelalter," and

convert.[152] Many, such as Lanfranc of Bec, Anselm of Canterbury, and Peter Abelard too,[153] poured their zeal and talent into theological endeavors; but an even larger number—St. Bruno (the Carthusian), St. Bernard, Norbert of Xanten, and many others—founded or promoted new religious orders. Most demanded exacting ascetic practices rather than a magnificent performance of the divine office, and altogether they reshaped Western spirituality to take greater account of individual religious experience, beginning with St. Anselm's prayers and meditations. The new orders eliminated the practice of oblation, while about the same time canon law gave oblates in the older orders a real choice at the moment of profession; and hence a new literary genre, the "letter of vocation," sprang into being.

Rupert was reared in the old way. He doubtless had his childish hand wrapped in the altar cloth, signifying his subjection henceforth to the altar and abbey of St. Lawrence. Later he twice described himself as "detained" or "confined" since "childhood" (*infantia, puerilibus annis*) in the "silence of the cloister."[154] Yet he underwent a conversion experience at least as dramatic as those of his better-known contemporaries. Rupert related this experience more than twenty years after the event only at the injunction of his friend and patron Cuno of Siegburg and with the express intent of commending his works to readers.[155] He

---

"Adelsbekehrungen im Hochmittelalter: Conversi und nutriti im Kloster," in *Ausgewählte Aufsätze* (MGH Schriften 25.1, Stuttgart 1976) 38–77, 125–49; and M. D. Chenu, "Moines, clercs, et laics au carrefour de la vie évangélique" and "Le reveil évangélique," in *La théologie au douzième siècle* (Paris 1957) 225–73.

152. A convenient, though by no means complete, list: L. K. Little, "Intellectual Training and Attitudes toward Reform, 1075–1150," in *Pierre Abélard-Pierre le Vénérable* (Paris 1975) 235–49.

153. For Abelard as a convert to the monastic life, see D. Luscombe, "Pierre Abelard et le monachisme," ibid. 271–78.

154. *RegBen.* 1: PL 170.480; *Omnip.* 22: PL 170.472. Cf. Reiner, MGH SS 20.593; and the report of a contemporary from St. Trond (MGH SS 10.303): "Iste Robertus Leodii nutritus fuit in coenobio sancti Laurentii. . . ."

155. *Matt.* 12: CM 29.366–86. Earlier hints in *Cant.* 5: CM 26.110–11, where he also refers to himself as being then an "*adulescentulus*"; and *RegBen.*

had kept it secret in fear that his adversaries would dismiss his cherished experience as a "childish fantasy." He insisted now upon its historicity, and cited Augustine's *Confessions* and Jerome's Letter 22 as precedents for such personal revelations.[156] Thus, while all the details in Rupert's account cannot be verified and his purpose in telling it must be kept in mind, the formative character of this experience for his spiritual vocation is beyond doubt.

Rupert, then a young man probably in his twenties and not yet ordained, feared terribly for his salvation, so much so that he had come to envy the dead as safely out of the Devil's grasp, and he began to "go around with a heavy and brooding spirit."[157] One morning at dawn Rupert sat hidden behind the altar in a Marian chapel—this must have been the crypt—where, as was his custom, he bowed before, embraced, and kissed a wooden cross with an image of the Savior. Suddenly, he says, the Lord responded to his expressions of love: Rupert saw Him with inner eyes and for the first time tasted His inexpressible sweetness. But the experience passed and when it did not return soon, in childish petulance (his own description) he skipped his early morning devotional exercises and stayed in bed. There he was visited with a dream which called him to the church, where two choirs sang antiphonally the fiftieth (*Miserere mei Dominus*) and twenty-sixth (*Dominus illuminatio mea*) psalms, but the Devil now blocked his entrance and scared him awake. The entire day he grieved and next morning the dream returned. This time he ran into the church, where a full Sunday mass seemed in progress. A young man, whom he later identified as Christ, drove away enemies who attacked him once again, and three persons, later identified as the Holy Trinity, raised him up high on an

---

1: PL 170.497–98. See now R. Haacke, "Die mystischen Visionen Ruperts von Deutz," in *Sapientiae Doctrina* (n. 140 above) 68–90.

156. CM 29.367, 384; CM 26.111.

157. What follows is condensed from the texts cited in n. 155 above. For a nearly contemporary text on fear of the Judgement, see Anselm's *Meditatio* 1: ed. Schmitt 3.76–79.

open book.[158] He awoke this time to find himself naked in the abbey church, returned to his bed, and for three days sank into an even deeper depression, only to be visited by more dreams and visions. Finally, while keeping the vigil of St. Matthew— that is, late on the evening of September 20, about the year 1100, if the account is trustworthy—Rupert learned in a vision that he would die at the end of eight years.[159]

He understood the message literally (something he later recognized as a mistake) and began to meditate upon his impending death, so that by the eighth year he had turned almost completely in upon himself (*ego fere totus et solito uigilantior in me conuersus*). Ever more intense in prayers and tears, he called upon the Holy Spirit to ward off fiendish attacks and to bring the final resolution he now anticipated. On the vigil of Ash Wednesday Rupert was caught up in a truly mystical (rather than visionary) experience. A substance like liquid gold, he says, filled his bosom to capacity in ever increasing inundations. But afterwards he reacted first with uncertainty and then disappointment since he had not died. Still full of thoughts of the Last Judgement, he went to bed, and Christ appeared to him again. Beckoned to his accustomed veneration of the crucified Savior, Rupert saw the great altar open up so that he could run to his Lord who "kissed" him intimately with opened mouth. Rupert knew he had been called to a deeper understanding of Christ's mysteries.[160]

Visionary experiences frequently accompanied spiritual cri-

---

158. Thus Rupert in 1127: "De apertione libri . . . non opus est ut interpretationem faciam tuae caritati [Cuno], cuius de me iudicium saepe audierunt et secuti sunt multi, quod uere Deus librum suum, idest Scripturam sanctam mihi aperuit, et multis sanctorum patrum sententiis . . . aliquanta meliora dixerim. . . ." CM 29.372–73.

159. Rupert himself (CM 29.374) suggested a possible source for this motif in Gregory's *Dialogi* 4.56: ed. V. Moricca (Rome 1924) 320.

160. ". . . cum ad me reuersus fuissem et infra uigilias nocturnas uisum huiusmodi suauissime retractarem, sicque interpretarer illam altaris et ipsius oris Domini Jesu apertionem, quod sacramentorum eius profunda deinceps clarius intelligere deberem. . . ." CM 29.382–83.

ses and conversions.[161] Whether Rupert could still vividly recall these dreams and visions twenty years later or was rather influenced in his account by hagiographical commonplaces may be left aside. The fact remains that he has described all the elements of a deep religious crisis: pressing concern for his salvation, fear of the Last Judgement, extraordinary devotional exercises,[162] a spiritual intensity which set him apart from his brothers, and uncertainty about his worthiness to assume the priesthood[163] (this last doubtless nurtured by the reformers' demand for a "pure" Church). Still unable to write properly (*ecclesiastico more*), he finally agreed to ordination, without explaining the circumstances to his grateful abbot. Thirty days after ordination he was blessed with another mystical experience, from which he dated his beginnings as an author.

Rupert's is among the first recorded cases of an oblate, bound to the religious life since childhood, who underwent such a vocational crisis. Otloh of St. Emmeran, Guibert of Nogent, and Peter Abelard also recounted such crises in the earliest medieval autobiographies, but these Black Monks were all converts; and Suger, an oblate, made no mention of religious crises in his *De administratione sua*. The outcome in Rupert's case was also notably different: he did not found a new religious order, move to a more ascetic house, or take to the road as a wandering preacher. Instead he wrote, and at great length, for the work appointed him was the interpretation of Holy Scripture; his "consolation," as he preferred to call it, was the spiritual gift of understanding. Directly after his ordination and culminating vision he began to write and, in his own words, could not stop thereafter even if he had wanted to.[164] This was for him a kind of breakthrough into

161. See H. Schauwecker, "Otloh von St. Emmeram: Ein Beitrag zur Bildungs-und Frömmigkeitsgeschichte des 11. Jahrhunderts," *SMBO* 74 (1963) 52–93; Otloh's *Liber visionum* (1060's) in PL 146.341–88.

162. But not *ascetic* exercises, as Cuno also noted (CM 29.366); this may well distinguish the Black Monk from many newer monks.

163. CM 29.381–382.

164. ". . . cito subsistit inundans illa uis amoris paulatimque decessit; ego autem *extunc* os meum aperui et cessare quando scriberem nequaquam potui, et *usque nunc*, etiam si uelim, tacere non possum." CM 29.384 (my italics).

the apostolate. He took up the task of interpreting Holy Scripture with the same zeal, the same inner confidence, and the same audacity which marked the new convert's approach to the religious life. Already in the prologue to his first major work—probably written soon after this last experience and before there was any need to defend himself against adversaries—Rupert announced his independence by way of a phrase adapted from Horace and Amalarius. Whatever others may have written on this subject (the divine office), he said, "it was permitted and always will be permitted for anyone to say, within the bounds of the faith, what he thinks" [or, perceives: *senserit*].[165]

Ordination in his thirty-second or thirty-third year marked the end of Rupert's youthful formation and the beginning of his theological career. It followed more than fifteen years of ecclesiastical dispute which permanently influenced his view of the Church; his first scriptural commentary (ca. 1113), however, counseled reconciliation after such struggles.[166] Ordination also divided the minor works of his early years from his major ones and quite probably composition in verse from commentary in prose.[167] And it conferred upon him the office to which he felt divinely called in the midst of spiritual crisis; he had now a mission to interpret and to preach Scripture.[168]

It is all the more unfortunate that the date of his ordination can be determined only approximately. Henry IV died in Liège

165. "Neque enim auctoritati ueterum quidquam detrahimus, Amalarii scilicet et aliorum. . . . Sed licuit semperque licebit cuique dicere salua fide quod senserit." *Off.* prologus: CM 7.6. The phrase "licuit semperque licebit" is from Horace, *Ars poetica* 58: P. Classen, *DA* 26 (1970) 514. The phrase "dicere . . . quod senserit" may have been suggested by a sentence from Amalarius' prologue: "non frenum passus sum timoris alicuius magistri, sed, ilico mente gratias agens Deo, scripsi quod sensi." *Opera Amalarii*, ed. J. M. Hanssens (Studi e Testi 139, Vatican City 1948) 2.19.

166. *Gen.* 7.47: CM 21.485.

167. "Sic incipiens [before his ordination] magnam intus uersabam materiam . . . dum metricis pedibus uerba ligando, ut in scholaribus assuetus eram, longum in paucis sermonibus laborem assumerem." CM 29.381.

168. See *Spir.* 7.9: CM 24.2048 (to be discussed in chapter III).

on 7 August 1106, and in a tremendous outpouring of grief and fidelity the people of Liège forced a reluctant clergy to bury their excommunicated king, at least temporarily, in the cathedral. So notorious was Otbert, moreover, that he was damned again when other imperial bishops were reconciled with the reformed papacy at the synod of Guastalla on 22 October 1106. But in a letter dated 10 November 1106 Pope Paschal instructed Archbishop Bruno of Trier to lift the excommunication of bishop and clergy in Liège if they swore allegiance; and that presumably happened shortly thereafter.[169] One must, however, allow at least a year for Rupert's antagonism toward Otbert to cool down and for his spiritual crisis to be resolved. He himself says that peace only slowly (*paululum*) returned after the end of the schism and that his call to the priesthood only gradually (*paulatim*) became manifest.[170] The most likely reconstruction would have the final, decisive series of mystical experiences begin on Ash Wednesday of the year 1108, and set the "next appropriate time for ordination," the only time mentioned in *De diuinis officiis*, on the fourth Sunday of Advent, 1108.[171] Rupert's first major work was completed late in 1111 or (more probably) early in the year 1112.

169. MGH SS 17.746; JL 6099. See U.-R. Blumenthal, *The Early Councils of Pope Paschal II, 1100–1110* (Studies and Texts 43, Toronto 1978) 32–73; idem, "Some notes on papal policies at Guastalla, 1106," in *Mélanges G. Fransen* (Studia Gratiana 19, 1976) 61–77.

170. CM 29.381, 383.

171. ". . . ut primum adfuit tempus ordinationis. . . ." CM 29.383. Cf. *Off.* 3.9, 11: CM 7.73–74, 76–77.

II

The
Divine Office,
Holy Scripture,
and
Triune God

IN FULFILLMENT of their religious vows eleventh-century Benedictine monks were to perform the divine office as prescribed by St. Benedict, say mass daily if they were priests, and meditate prayerfully upon Holy Scripture. Correspondingly, Rupert undertook in his first major work an exposition of the office,[1] and in his second a commentary on the whole of Scripture as revelatory of Triune God.[2] Yet his decision to write such works was hardly as self-explanatory as it might first appear. Despite the growing importance of liturgical worship in tenth-

1. *De diuinis officiis*, ed. R. Haacke (CM 7, 1967). Haacke's is a useful but not strictly critical edition; see P. Classen, *DA* 26 (1970) 513–17. Rupert was about two-thirds finished sometime after Easter 1111 (*Off.* 8.4: CM 7.268ff), and is presumed to have completed the work in 1112.

2. *De sancta Trinitate et operibus eius*, ed. R. Haacke (CM 21–24, 1971–72). See H. Silvestre, "L'édition Rh. Haacke du *De Trinitate* de Rupert de Deutz," *Sacris Erudiri* 22 (1974–75) 377–99. On the date of this work, begun probably in 1112 and brought out in the spring of 1117, see chapter III, Appendix.

and eleventh-century monasticism, no monk for two hundred and fifty years had attempted to elucidate or to reflect upon the entire divine office.[3] Monks were, to be sure, responsible for much of the creative growth in liturgy during those years, and their customaries dealt largely with liturgical matters, setting forth primarily "what to do," with its significance at least implied if not fully articulated. Monks also occasionally wrote short works on particular practices: thus, for instance, several of the treatises by Odorannus of Sens (d. ca. 1045) and Berno of Reichenau (d. 1048). But for expositions of the entire office tenth- and eleventh-century monks still relied upon Carolingian authors, chiefly Amalarius and Rhabanus Maurus.

To write a commentary on all of Scripture with a distinctively thematic approach was still more unusual. The Fathers of the Church had prepared expositions of single biblical books, such as—just to name a few with which Rupert was demonstrably familiar—Augustine on Genesis, Jerome on Isaiah, Jeremiah, Daniel, the Minor Prophets and Matthew, and Gregory on Job, and had also delivered sermons later compiled as commentaries, such as Augustine on St. John and the Psalms and Gregory on Ezechiel. In the early middle ages Bede and Carolingian commentators, especially Rhabanus Maurus, attempted to cover Scripture more thoroughly, but once again by way of individual works on particular books and often with a kind of cut and paste adaptation of the Fathers. The very few commentaries written first during the years 900–1050, such as by Odo of Cluny on Job, Atto of Vercelli on the Epistles of St. Paul, and Bruno of Würzburg on the Psalms, consisted almost entirely of texts excerpted from the Fathers.[4] Rupert, however, wrote origi-

---

3. Therefore Rupert's work is often used without historical qualification to characterize monastic attitudes toward the divine office throughout the tenth, eleventh, and early twelfth centuries: thus U. Berlière, *L'ascèse bénédictine des origines à la fin du XIIe siècle* (Paris and Maredsous 1927) 162–64; and G. Duby, *The Making of the Christian West* (Geneva 1967) 159; but see the more carefully nuanced statements in Leclercq, *Love of Learning* 289–91.

4. Useful overview of these works in C. Spicq, *Esquisse d'une histoire de l'exégèse latine au moyen âge* (Bibliothèque Thomiste 26, Paris 1944) 9–60.

nal commentaries on the whole of both the divine office and Holy Scripture during the years 1109–17, and the task here is to examine how that came about.

1

De diuinis officiis

Reform of the Church required renewal of the divine office. Or, differently put, the removal of immoral priests, the establishment wherever possible of canons regular, the making of a more "Roman" pontifical, and the effort to conform all divergent liturgies to Roman usage aimed essentially at purifying and strengthening the Church's prayer and worship. Hildebrand, for instance, fifteen years before becoming Pope Gregory VII, had insisted upon an improved version of a particular office for canons,[5] and Peter Damian wrote letter-treatises elucidating various aspects of liturgical worship.[6] Thus, just as the Carolingian reform two hundred years earlier had produced a whole series of manuals and treatises on the liturgy, then at imperial initiative, so now papal reform did likewise.[7] Some of these works, particularly Bernold's *Micrologus* (written ca. 1085), were inspired more or less directly by the reform movement,[8] while others, such as Honorius' *Gemma animae* (shortly after 1100?),

5. Gratian, *De cons.* D. 5 c. 15. But he did not write a rule for canons regular, as older literature claimed; see now C. D. Fonseca, *Medioevo canonicale* (Milan 1970) 101–09, and Reynolds (n. 7 below) 112n. 11.

6. *De horis canonicis* [commended to a layman!], PL 145.221–32; *Dominus uobiscum* [written for a hermit], PL 145.231–52.

7. Roger E. Reynolds, "Liturgical Scholarship at the Time of the Investiture Controversy: Past Research and Future Opportunities," *Harvard Theological Review* 71 (1978) 109–24; for the liturgical treatises written in the Carolingian era and the years 1050–1150, see Ludwig Eisenhofer, *Handbuch der katholischen Liturgik* (Freiburg 1932) 120–29; Adolph Franz, *Die Messe im deutschen Mittelalter* (Freiburg 1902, repr. 1963) 351–57; and Wright (n. 11 below) 5–41.

8. V. L. Kennedy, "For a New Edition of the *Micrologus* of Bernold of Constance," in *Mélanges en l'honneur de Monseigneur Michel Andrieu* (Strasbourg 1956) 229–41; and Reynolds (n. 7 above) 114–15.

reflected the general spirit of renewal.[9] Both Bernold and Honorius were Benedictine monks, but both had served earlier with the secular clergy and knew firsthand their needs. In the mid-twelfth century Johannes Beleth, a student of Gilbert of Poitiers and himself a master for a time in Paris, prepared a briefer, updated version of their works specifically designed for parish clergy.[10] All these works were taken up into the most influential of twelfth-century liturgical commentaries, Pope Innocent III's *De missarum mysteriis* (ca. 1195)[11] and Sicard of Cremona's massive *Mitrale* (ca. 1200).[12] Of Bernold's work there are about fifty extant manuscript copies, of Honorius' about thirty twelfth-century copies, of Beleth's more than one hundred thirty copies altogether, and of Pope Innocent's around two hundred copies. By way of comparison, Rupert's *De diuinis officiis* is preserved in more than seventy extant manuscripts, thirty-five of which date from the twelfth century. His influence and popularity, in other words, ranked with or excelled that of his near contemporaries.

The reformers' concern to assure purity of worship, reflected in Rupert's doubts about his own worthiness to assume the priestly office, and the interruption of divine office during exile certainly must have inspired greater thoughtfulness about the form and meaning of the monks' daily worship. But there was still another stimulus. Sometime after returning from exile, most probably in the years 1100–05, the monks of St. Lawrence adopted the Cluniac customary, taken over from the abbey of St. James where Abbot Stephen (1095–1112) first introduced it. The abbey of St. Trond did likewise on 1 March 1107; Abbot

9. Scattered, and not altogether consistent, evidence on dating and sources of the *Gemma animae* in V. I. J. Flint, "The Career of Honorius Augustodunensis," *RB* 82 (1972) 63–86, esp. 70–74, 79; idem, "The Chronology of the Works of Honorius Augustodunensis," *RB* 82 (1972) 215–42, esp. 225–26; and idem, "The Place and Purpose of the Works of Honorius Augustodunensis," *RB* 87 (1977) 97–127, esp. 122–23 (with a list of twelfth-century manuscripts).

10. *Summa de ecclesiasticis officiis,* ed. H. Douteil (CM 41, 1976).

11. See David F. Wright, "A Medieval Commentary on the Mass: Particulae 2–3 and 5–6 of the De Missarum Mysteriis (ca. 1195) of Cardinal Lothar of Segni (Pope Innocent III)" (diss. University of Notre Dame 1977).

12. PL 213.13–432.

Berengar and Abbot Stephen sent two monks each to teach the new observance.[13] Rupert had made laudatory remarks about the Cluniacs and "their pope," Urban II, already in 1095.[14] Just how and to what degree these new practices differed from those established three generations earlier by Richard of St. Vanne is not known, however, nor precisely which form of the Cluniac customary was followed.[15] Rhabanus Haacke discovered at least seven matters in Rupert's *De diuinis officiis* which Hallinger considered distinctively Cluniac.[16] Though Rupert never became polemical on these points, his commentary suggests the need for additional clarification or justification of practices probably introduced only recently. Just as important, St. Lawrence, according to a contemporary source, experienced that stir of enthusiasm and influx of new vocations which often accompanied such a reform.[17] At the very least, then, the monks of St. Lawrence must have become far more conscious of the particular form in which they carried out their divine service.

Rupert wrote his exposition of the divine office primarily for monk-priests like himself. Unlike Amalarius and his heirs who began with the Church year, and all other commentators who began with Mass, Rupert dealt first with the service monks rendered daily to God (*quotidianum nostrae seruitutis pensum*), the seven canonical hours (1.1–17), and only then with the high-point of each day's office, their ministry at the altar (1.17–2.21).

13. *Gesta abb. Trudon.* 8.16: MGH SS 10.278. See J. Stiennon, "Cluny et Saint-Trond au XII⁰ siècle," in *Problèmes Liégeois d'histoire médiévale* (Anciens pays et assemblées d'états 8, Louvain 1955) 55–86. The unknown date of adoption at St. Lawrence occurred long enough before March 1107 for Prior Rudolph to learn of it and to prevail over resistance at St. Trond. Thus, "vers 1106" (Stiennon, 61 n. 17) may be rather late; the *Gallia Christiana* 3.980 and U. Berlière, *Monasticon Belge* 2.37 suggested 1103.

14. *Carm.* 4.7–9: MGH LdL 3.628.

15. St. Trond possessed a mid-twelfth century copy (Université de Liège MS 1420) of Bernard's customary: Stiennon (n. 13 above) 67ff.

16. CM 7.xvii.

17. ". . . de saeculo tam clerici quam laici plures ad eos conuertebantur, et inualescente religione augebatur et fratrum numerus et fructus ecclesiae." *Gesta abb. Trudon.* 8.16: MGH SS 10.278.

In concluding his treatment of these "daily matters" he took a stand on several contemporary controversies. He defended, for instance, the Roman use of azymes or unleavened bread, drawing upon letters of Pope Leo IX (in fact written by Cardinal Humbert) and Humbert's own little-known treatise on this subject;[18] and he also argued in behalf of the traditionally ornate decoration of altar and church which zealots of poverty and religious reform had begun to attack (2.23; see chapter VIII, part 2). Rupert's commentary took account of laymen, particularly lay monks, who faithfully participated in the Church's divine worship even though they could not grasp its inner rationale (*causas eorum* [*mysteria uel signa*] *scire non potuerint*). But his chief concern was for those who themselves celebrated the mysteries without properly understanding them: they needed correction even as St. Paul had admonished those who spoke in tongues without comprehension. Only the truly religious and erudite, however, could in fact attain such understanding, which Rupert considered akin to prophecy, for it permitted them, through the Holy Spirit, to grasp the mysteries of Christ cloaked in the external garb of the office.[19]

Holy Scripture was to provide the interpretative yardstick (*didasculum atque symmisten*) for the divine office. All the prayers and readings for a given day were to be strictly related to the central message of its Gospel proper.[20] This emphasis was Rupert's own, but one grounded finally in the priestly status of most eleventh-century monks. Sometime during the eighth century, monasticism had ceased to be the lay movement St. Benedict still presupposed. By Rupert's time the majority of his

18. *Off.* 2.22: CM 7.52–56. (Haacke's reference at CM 7.52 should be corrected to PL 143.744ff.) The manuscript with Humbert's treatise on the azymes (and the *Collection in 74 Titles*) is now Bibl. roy. 9706–25: van den Gheyn 2.295–97; see A. Michel, *Humbert und Kerullarios* (Paderborn 1924–30) 1.88ff; and idem, *Amalfi und Jerusalem im griechischen Kirchenstreit (1054–1090)* (Orientalia Christiana Analecta 121, Rome 1939).

19. *Off.* prologus: CM 7.5–6. Of the need for understanding what is done in the office, cf. Honorius (PL 172.543) and Beleth (CM 41A.1–2).

20. *Off.* prologus, 1.36–37: CM 7.5, 29–31.

confreres were ordained, and daily mass was expected of all devout monks.[21] But since only one monk could be assigned daily or weekly to the major conventual mass each morning, most said mass privately, and it was precisely for such monk-priests that Rupert wrote his first book. Carolingian clerics had been equipped with homiliaries, collections of sermons drawn from the Fathers for each Sunday and feastday; and though originally intended to aid in the instruction of the people, these books often guided the priests' own private devotions, so that among monks a homily on the Gospel of the day eventually became the third nocturnal reading.[22] Rupert's *De diuinis officiis* offered in effect a condensed homiliary—though it still comes to four hundred printed pages—in which the prayers and readings for a given day are all shown to illuminate a particular mystery or teaching of Christ taught in its Gospel and celebrated in its office. Thus uninspired monk-priests, especially those who had entered the religious life involuntarily or even for materialistic reasons and of whom Rupert was so often critical, could be brought to grasp spiritually that which they did each day perfunctorily, even uncomprehendingly. Rupert's work was not meant, at least in the first instance, to be a "how to do it" or a "how to explain it to the people" book, but rather an edifying, even reforming, guide for the spiritual lives of other monk-priests.

Rupert believed firmly that the divine office was no accidental arrangement of prayers, scriptural readings, and Roman stations. The Holy Spirit had inspired Pope Gregory to set forth the mysteries of Christ in precisely this way, that is, in the form

21. Otto Nussbaum, *Kloster, Priestermönch und Privatmesse* (Theophaneia 14, Bonn 1961) 65–151; Angelus A. Häussling, *Mönchskonvent und Eucharistiefeier* (Liturgiewissenschaftliche Quellen und Forschungen 58, Münster 1973); J. Dubois, "Office des heures et messe dans la tradition monastique," *La maison Dieu* 135 (1978) 61–82. The Cluniac customaries of both Bernard (1.81) and Ulrich (2.30) devoted chapters to private masses.

22. On Carolingian homiliaries, see Rosamund McKitterick, *The Frankish Church and the Carolingian Reforms, 789–895* (London 1977) 80ff; and Réginald Grégoire, *Les homéliaires du moyen âge* (Rome 1966). The monastic practice noted by P. Salmon, *L'office divin au moyen âge* (Lex orandi 43, Paris 1967) 121.

of the Roman missal.[23] Rupert himself must often have meditated upon a stunning illumination, still preserved, of the Dove
whispering the Office into Pope Gregory's ear.[24] The theme
taught in each day's Gospel[25] and the way those themes related
to one another were therefore not arbitrary matters, mere "allegorizing." There was a right meaning for each office, the one
intended by the Holy Spirit. Since it might sometimes be difficult (*occultior*) to discover that meaning, Rupert twice invoked
the Spirit's aid in his search (*quaerentibus*), once in the prologue
and again at the beginning of the Church-year section.[26] But
once uncovered and linked together those meanings revealed
the whole way of salvation. The Sundays of Advent set forth
the coming of the Lord (Book III). The Sundays beginning with
Septuagesima recalled the seven ages of the world leading up to
Christ's passion (Book IV). Rupert explicitly rejected here the
traditional interpretation found, for instance, in Amalarius: mankind's sinful state prior to Christ's redemption ought to be understood through salvation-history since Adam rather than as a
spiritual metaphor (Septuagesima = Babylonian Captivity).[27]
He devoted four books to Holy Week and the octave of Easter
(V–VIII). His detailed treatment of the Passion anticipated later
medieval spirituality in its attempt to make the reader identify
personally with Christ's suffering along each stage of the way.
The days of Holy Week, which celebrate the coming of re-
creation in Christ, are made to correspond to the seven days of
creation,[28] while the octave of Easter sets out the new life made
possible by the seven gifts of the Spirit and taught in the Beati-

23. This he learned from Paul the Deacon's *Vita S. Gregorii* 28: PL 75.58,
quoted in *Off*. 3.4: CM 7.70. Additions to the ceremony of the Mass he ascribed, with the tradition, to individual popes: *Off*. 2.21: CM 7.50–52.

24. Bibl. roy. MS 9916–17 fol. 2ᵛ, reproduced in C. Gaspar and F. Lyna,
Les principaux manuscrits à peintures de la Bibliothèque Royale de Belgique (Paris
1937) I, plate 16. See the discussion by J. Stiennon in *Saint-Laurent* 144ff.

25. This thematic approach is often pronounced: "Summa igitur huius of-
ficii est. . . ." *Off*. 3.3: CM 7.67.

26. Cf. *Off*. 3.7: CM 7.72.

27. *Off*. 4.1–3: CM 7.103–04. Cf. Amalarius, *Liber officialis* 1.2–9.

28. This same theme, creation/re-creation, provided the structure a few

tudes.[29] Ascension (Book IX), Pentecost (Book X), and celebration of the Triune God (Book XI) complete the story of salvation. At each point Rupert explained how the books of the Bible prescribed for the nocturnal office also pertained to the story.

The homiletic intent of Rupert's *De diuinis officiis* becomes especially evident in Book XII, on the twenty-three Sundays after Pentecost. No previous commentator had bothered to treat this part of the office, partly because it lacked any reference point in the history of salvation and probably also because the office itself was not yet clearly fixed. The Gospel for the first Sunday, in Rupert's interpretation, taught the rejection of the Jews and conversion of the Gentiles, while that for the last (c. 23) foretold the Jews' final conversion. These were for Rupert always the first and last major events in the progress of the New Testament Church. While the twenty-one intervening Sundays do not present a chronological history of the Church, Rupert certainly interpreted them so as to address monk-priests and prelates in the context of the Church's "present" troubles. He first (c. 2) condemned those who preferred terrestrial to celestial things and thus violated their *sanctum propositum*; and after reminding them of the Lord's concern for lost sinners (cc. 3, 4), he described more precisely the present situation (c. 5): the nets of the Church have been let down, filled to overflowing, and are now torn apart by dissension and tumult. The Lord will cast out all those who buy and sell holy orders (c. 10): they make the Holy Spirit venal and their sacrifices are unacceptable to God. Each individual monk-priest must be engaged in constant renewal based on baptism (c. 6) and the eucharist (cc. 15, 16), even though he may sometimes be deceived by false brothers (c. 8) or struck a heavy blow by the Devil (c. 21). The brothers must also maintain a spirit of reconciliation and mutual love among

---

years later for Hugh of St. Victor's *De sacramentis Christianae fidei* (PL 176.183–84).

29. Suggested by Augustine's *De sermone Domini* 1.4.11, of which there was a copy in St. Lawrence: Gessler, "Bibliothèque"114, 2.19 (probably Bibl. roy. MS 10792–95; van den Gheyn no. 1106).

themselves (cc. 11, 22). Prelates, equated with the Church itself, are charged with the regeneration of lost souls (c. 16) and the preaching of the Word (c. 12). They should not be greedy for high office and power (cc. 17, 18), but rather fair in their exercise of penitential discipline (c. 9). Their chief responsibility is intercessory prayer (cc. 18, 19). Rupert's ideal was a unified Church, cleansed of heresy and division, daily offering its sacrificial praise to God (c. 14). These views, though hardly novel, clearly reflected Rupert's link to the reformers, not just because he included them, but still more because he integrated them into the history of salvation as correspondent to the Church's present needs and status.

In the context, then, of reform, both in the Church at large and in his own monastery, Rupert sought to improve the quality of the priesthood and of the Church's worship by teaching his readers, chiefly fellow monk-priests, the deeper spiritual meaning of the office they daily performed. For, as he said elsewhere, only those who comprehend spiritually what they are doing truly offer a sacrifice of praise.[30] But Rupert had still other purposes: commentary on the divine office afforded an opportunity to join in major theological discussions of his day. After all, in what better context could one consider "Why God became Man" (*Cur Deus homo*) than the feastday celebrating His incarnation? This "theologizing" tendency distinguished Rupert's work from the explanatory and devotional commentaries of his predecessors and contemporaries.

In fact, nearly all of Rupert's pronounced theological views, the ones which eventually got him into public disputes, were at least adumbrated in the devotional setting of *De diuinis officiis*. His commentary on the canon of the Mass offered an original solution to the Berengarian eucharistic controversy. The Christmas vigil led him to state his views on "*Cur Deus homo*," while the Easter vigil, following ancient tradition, occasioned lengthy reflections on baptismal theology. After the celebration of Christ's resurrection, questions arose about His glorification

30. *Levit.* 1.8: CM 22.811.

and the grace which flowed from Him. Pentecost Sunday suggested theological matters pertinent to the Holy Spirit, including the *filioque*, and Trinity Sunday produced a whole treatise on that subject. In short, already in this first work two essential aspects of Rupert's life and thought, often difficult to hold together in scholarly discussion, become manifest: his theological interests and ambitions, driving him to try his own hand at questions under discussion in the leading schools, and his instinctive presupposition that theology should be done only in the context of worship.

Rupert brought out this first work around the year 1112 without dedication and probably without identifying himself in the title. Fifteen years later Rupert explained to Cuno that the bishop at that time (Otbert) doubted he had any special gifts as an ecclesiastical writer and refused to patronize his work. Rupert professed not to have cared much about such patronage, confident that Christ rather than any bishop dispensed the necessary spiritual gifts.[31] Rupert's work nevertheless soon became known, to Otbert's secretary Alger, for instance, and to William of St. Thierry, once of Liège but presumably then in Reims. Did Rupert send out copies seeking their approval and support? Alger was then the leading master in Liège, and William apparently a friend (*charissime*), a fellow Benedictine, and budding theologian. However that may be, Rupert's *De diuinis officiis* eventually became his best-known work by far, the only one read widely outside the Empire. Thus St. Victor in Paris (possibly in Hugh's, certainly in Richard's lifetime),[32] Clairvaux (possibly in St. Bernard's lifetime), Belval (1156), Bonne Espérance (at the time of Philip of Harvengt), Corbie (1180), Tours, St. Denis, and Bec all possessed copies. Norbert of Xanten criticized one of its positions in the early 1120's, while the enthusias-

31. *Off.* epist.: CM 7.1–2.
32. Book VII of the *Miscellanea* once ascribed to Hugh contains many excerpts: see H. Silvestre, *RTAM* 45 (1978) 236. For manuscript copies at St. Victor (eventually three!) and the other abbeys mentioned, see R. Haacke's introduction, CM 7.xvii–xliii.

tic Abbot Cuno of Siegburg thought it should have been longer.[33]
It was an auspicious beginning. With the same confidence and
sense of independence Rupert next undertook a commentary on
all of Holy Scripture.

2

Scripture and
the Contemplative Life

Scriptural commentaries make up around ninety percent of
Rupert's complete works. Each is a whole and distinct literary
unit to which Rupert, alone among his contemporaries, often
gave a particular title: *De sancta Trinitate et operibus eius, De incarnatione Domini* (Canticles commentary), *De gloria et honore Filii
hominis* (Matthew commentary). His were not glosses or lectures
strung together as among schoolmen, nor were they sermons
compiled for publication, the frequent practice of monastic authors such as Bruno of Segni and St. Bernard. These scriptural
commentaries were rather the very pride and purpose of Rupert's life. Three different times he prepared complete lists of
them, once in an apologia for all interested readers (spring 1125),
again for his chief patron upon elevation to the bishopric of
Regensburg (fall 1126), and finally for Pope Honorius II (fall
1128).[34] Polemical and occasional pieces, several of them now
much more famous, received little or no mention. As the foundation therefore of all that is to follow, Rupert's general approach to Holy Scripture must be considered. Since his views
changed very little during twenty years (1109–29) as an author,
illustrative texts can be drawn from all his works.[35]

33. *RegBen.* 1: PL 170.489–92.
34. *RegBen.* 1: PL 170.489; *Off.* epist.: CM 7.3; *Glor.* epist.: PL 169.11.
See, in brief, Dinter, *Heribert* 100.
35. On Rupert's exegesis, see Spicq (n. 4 above) 114–15; Magrassi, *Teologia* 36–86; Beinert, *Kirche* 144–51; H. de Lubac, *Exégèse Medievale* (Théologie 42, Paris 1961) 2.219–38; F. Pickering, "Exegesis and Imagination," in
his *Essays on Medieval German Literature and Iconography* (Cambridge 1980)
31–45; and *DTC* 14.2.174–84.

The divine office provided the framework for Rupert's meditation upon Scripture. Particular texts received their meaning
automatically from the feastdays and Sundays for which they
were the designated reading, and whole books of the Bible
gained built-in interpretation from that point in the liturgical
year when they were read in the night office. Thus Isaiah was
linked to the Advent season, Jeremiah and Lamentations to
Lent, and the Acts and the Apocalypse to the period immediately following Easter. Rupert's interpretation of Septuagesima
as the beginning-point in the history of salvation was suggested
in part by the reading then of the Octateuch. Rupert doubtless
read the Bible through from beginning to end outside the prescribed office, though in the case of St. Bernard that was considered worthy of mention.[36] For Rupert it was simply self-evident
that one "treated" Scripture in the context of prayerful chanting
or reading.[37]

Scripture alone, on the other hand, endowed that office with
content and meaning. With little authoritative precedent Rupert
virtually identified the monastic life with meditation on Scripture: the marks (*insignia splendida*) of the contemplative life, he
declared in his pithiest summary, were to hear and ruminate on
the words of God and to proclaim with voice and pen the mysteries of Holy Scripture.[38] The "better part" which Mary chose
was nothing other than the reading, hearing, and understanding
of the Word.[39] The religious was to "sell all that he had" and "to
cast off the cares of this world" precisely in order to be the more
able (*expeditius*) to hear and to treat (*tractare*) the Word of God.[40]
Jacob's preference for Rachel, another traditional image of the
contemplative life, suggested to Rupert the attractions of scriptural study (*studiis*) and thence the contemplative life.[41] So also

36. Compare de Lubac (n. 35 above) 1.583.
37. ". . . quoties cantantes aut psallentes siue legentes sacram Scripturam
tractamus. . . ." *Gen.* 8.26: CM 21.513.
38. *Apoc.* 6: PL 169.1010–11.
39. *Apoc.* 4: PL 169.925; *Gen.* 7.31: CM 21.466; *Evang.* 31: CM 23.1822.
40. *Matt.* 6: CM 29.187; *Zach.* 2: PL 168.744; *John* 4: CM 9.221.
41. *Gen.* 7.31: CM 21.466.

meditating upon Scripture is likened to a festival, and treating Scripture to a sacrifice of praise.[42] In short, to "seek the Kingdom of God first" is to cast all else aside in order to meditate upon, to treat, and to do the Word of God.[43] While this view clearly grew out of eleventh-century monastic practice, in which scriptural meditation, as mediated by the office, pervaded the monks' activity, Rupert's close identification of the contemplative life with "treating Scripture" is not found among either the Fathers or his contemporaries, for whom total love of God, prayer, silence, and holy leisure (*otium*) recurred far more often as the distinguishing marks of the contemplative life.[44] And Rupert's emphasis upon preaching, at least written preaching, directly contradicted tradition, which had assigned this task to the secular clergy.[45] This point Rupert was later forced to defend (chapter VIII, part 4).

Meditation upon Scripture held such a privileged place in his view of the contemplative life because, as all medieval exegetes agreed, the Scriptures are filled with the mysteries of Christ.[46] To uncover those mysteries, to penetrate through terrestrial images to the underlying spiritual realities, was to transcend earthly forms and to communicate with Christ Himself.[47] True contemplatives were to feed daily on both the Body and the Word of God.[48] Such quasi-sacramental meditation on Scripture could even provide a glimpse of the eternal vision.[49] Thus

42. *Zach.* 5: PL 168.813; *Glor.* 1.14: PL 169.26.

43. *Matt.* 6: CM 29.187.

44. See "Contemplation" in *Dictionnaire de Spiritualité* 2 (Paris 1949) 1911–66; but for the importance of Holy Scripture in monastic life, see Leclercq, *Love of Learning* 87–109.

45. See, for instance, Rhabanus Maurus, *Gen.* 3.16: PL 107.596.

46. *Glor.* 6.8: PL 169.127; *John* 6: CM 9.308–09; *Apoc.* 4: PL 169.925.

47. *Spir.* 1.7: CM 24.1829; *Vict.* 1.5: ed. Haacke 10.

48. *John* 6, 7, 10: CM 9.301–02, 308, 310, 343, 375, 584; *Exod.* 4.15: CM 22.768; *Reg.* 5.28: CM 22.1442–43. On this traditional notion, see H. J. Spitz, *Die Metaphorik des geistigen Schriftsinns* (Munich 1972) 79–88.

49. "Nondum quidem dum Scripturas legimus aut intelligimus facie ad faciem Dominum uidemus? Verumtamen ipsa Dei uisio, quae quandoque perficienda est, hic iam per Scripturas inchoatur." *Apoc.* prologus: PL 169.825.

Rupert often spoke of knowing Christ *ex parte* already in this life.[50] Indeed, the more zealously someone meditated upon Scripture, the more closely he approached the "seventh age" (the present state of the faithful departed) and the higher his eventual place in the eternal choir.[51] But like all forms of grace, this understanding, this experiential communication with Christ by means of Scripture, was a gift of the Holy Spirit, first granted, in Rupert's view, at Pentecost and thereafter given only to a few devout persons, mostly monks.[52]

Rupert's approach was grounded in a fundamental presupposition about man's knowledge of the divine: while God might be known extraordinarily in Himself (*cognoscitur ex semetipso*), an experience Rupert later claimed for himself, He is known chiefly and ordinarily through His works (*cognoscitur ex operibus*).[53] And Holy Scripture, as Rupert once said, is the record of "all that God has done (*operatus*) from the beginning of creation until now."[54] It is also the *only* record of His works, making it alone the divinely authoritative source of truth.[55] Such a view must take seriously the literal-historical sense, for without that, as Rupert frequently noted, there is no reliable basis for the knowledge of God.[56] But in Rupert's interpretation the spiritual sense nearly always referred as well to *events*, acts of God in the history of salvation. All Scripture, indeed, revolved around the four great mysteries (*sacramenta*) of Christ, His incarnation, passion, resurrection, and ascension, a scheme borrowed from Gregory the Great.[57] These salvific deeds of God recur all through Rupert's works as the true spiritual sense of each scriptural book. Usually treated in strict chronological order, they are often listed at the

50. *John* 14: CM 9.782–83; *Matt.* 13: CM 29.419–21; *Glor.* 7.7: PL 169.148.

51. *Evang.* 31: CM 23.1822.

52. *John* 2: CM 9.117; *Apoc.* 2, 6: PL 169.895, 1009–10, 1015; *Spir.* 4.1–9: CM 24.1938–50.

53. *Vict.* 1.3: ed. Haacke 7.

54. *Glor.* 1.4: PL 169.17.

55. *Matt.* 7: CM 29.202; *Glor.* 1.5: PL 169.18. Additional texts cited in DTC 14.175–76; cf. de Lubac (n. 35 above) 227–29.

56. Cf. Séjourné, *DTC* 14.179–81.

57. *Matt.* 1: CM 29.7–8. Cf. Gregory, *Ezech.* 1.4.1.

outset of a commentary with reference to the verses signifying each event.[58] To make these acts of God the primary spiritual sense of Scripture brings us full circle, for they were precisely what Rupert and his fellow monks celebrated daily and annually in the divine office.

On Rupert's actual exegetical practice, one must write either very much or very little, for the subject is as vast as the works themselves. Thoroughly acquainted with the tradition, with the teachings in Augustine's *De doctrina christiana*, with Tyconius' seven rules, and with Gregory's influential pattern of division into the literal, allegorical, and moral senses, Rupert most often simply distinguished broadly between the historical and the spiritual senses. He had an unusual genius for linking scriptural images together and then to the larger history of salvation, and took insatiable delight in discovering new spiritual meanings. Beyond his astounding command of Scripture and the received exegetical tradition, what stands out most is his great sense of liberty with respect to that tradition. He took pride and joy in "going beyond the Fathers" to find better and richer meanings for a particular text, and he justified them on grounds they were "more useful."[59] From the Fathers, Gregory and Bede for instance, Rupert had learned that scriptural interpretation should be "useful" (*utilis*) to edification and ultimately to eternal life.[60] Thus, whereas St. Bernard and William of St. Thierry vigorously protested against novel interpretations of Scripture (this directed mostly at the new schoolmen),[61] Rupert constantly sought "more useful" interpretations without, as he saw it, directly impugning the authority of the Fathers.[62]

58. ". . . distinctiones operum utilium de quibus omnis Scriptura sancta consistit. . . . Primum est creatio coeli et terrae . . . [etc., until] subsequetur opus clarissimum Dominicae incarnationis, passionis, resurrectionis, atque ascensionis, et aduentus Paracleti Spiritus sancti. . . ." *Glor.* 1.4: PL 169.17. Cf. *Is.* 1.2: CM 23.1455–56; *Cant.*: CM 26.8–9.

59. *Apoc.*: PL 169.825–28; cf. chapter I above, n. 158.

60. Gregory, *Ezech.* 1.19; Bede, *De schematibus et tropis*, Intro. (quoted by Rupert, *Spir.* 7.11: CM 24.2051).

61. Bernard, *Epist.* 77 (*De baptismo*): ed. Leclercq 7.184; William, *In Rom.*: PL 180.547.

62. Very clear, for instance, in *Exod.* 1.7: CM 22.590.

In actuality these new meanings rarely represented true novelties in either theology or spirituality; they were rather old truths freshly put, always with a salvation-historical accent and often discovered in new places. There was in this style of exegesis a kind of poetic imagination at work, enormously influential in the later middle ages by way of sermons, devotional books, art, and literature. After generations of debunking by those favoring only a literal exegesis and a scholastic theology, both theologians (de Lubac, Chenu) and historians of literature (Ohly, Robertson) have come to recognize and to appreciate this style of thought, even if it still lacks a proper name.[63] Rupert's sensibilities and imagination, moreover, seem to have been particularly well attuned to this mode of thought, for his commentaries often yield, if not the first, at least one of the clearest and most forceful, statements of a given spiritual meaning widely adopted in the later middle ages.

3

The New Dialecticians
and the Trinity

For the elucidation of Holy Scripture, early medieval scholars—in keeping with the program first outlined by St. Augustine and instrumental still in shaping Rupert's outlook—drew upon the resources not only of the Fathers but also of the liberal

---

63. The word "symbolism" (Dempf's *Der deutsche Symbolismus* and Chenu's *La mentalité symbolique*) has gained the greatest following. But this term has, in my judgement, two serious drawbacks. In the middle ages the word was linked chiefly with Ps.-Dionysian thought rather than exegesis: see now G. B. Ladner, "Medieval and Modern Understanding of Symbolism: A Comparison," *Speculum* 54 (1979) 223–56. Secondly, in the modern literary movement which doubtless suggested or at least fostered the use of this term, symbols are highly arbitrary and their meaning capricious, when intelligible at all. But for medieval exegetes—without denying the playfulness and the poetic qualities found in an author like Rupert—the "figures" of Christ were utterly true and important sources of knowledge about Him. "Figural Thought," though much blander, would at least suggest the exegetical base, as well as the multivalent imagery which was its chief tool and means of expression.

arts. Those arts they viewed as subordinate to the study of Scripture. In the course of the eleventh century that subordination was forever cast off, in practice if not altogether in theory. The study of rhetoric, for instance, now produced two independent disciplines, law and *dictamen*, imparting precisely the administrative skills required in this new age. Dialectic too assumed ever greater importance until it became virtually an independent discipline akin to the modern study of philosophy and prerequisite for all higher studies, especially in theology. By the middle of the eleventh century, leading masters in northern France were no longer content to rehearse logical principles and ancient philosophical problems; they began to investigate dialectically propositions crucial to the Christian faith.

This bold exploration of sacred dogma by reason alone, apart from Scripture and the Fathers, was greatly facilitated by Boethius' theological tractates, the source in many respects of Western speculative theology, commentary on which soon became standard for all teachers of dialectic with theological interests and ambitions.[64] Many students responded enthusiastically to the challenge of constructing a logical exposition of the faith, on grounds that man's image-likeness to God resides in his rationality. Others rejected as outrageous any attempt to make scriptural language and sacred truths conform to the rules of logic.[65] Neither side had a monopoly on sanctity: Peter Damian, a severe critic of dialectic, himself enlisted the tools of rhetoric to an unprecedented degree, whereas Anselm of Bec sought to discover the inner rationale of the faith by reason alone. Monks as well as secular clerics shared initially in this new-found enthusiasm for dialectic. Otloh of St. Emmeran clearly kept up

64. See G. R. Evans, *Old Arts and New Theology* (Oxford 1980) 27–46, 91–136.

65. For the large literature on this subject, see André Cantin, ed., *Pierre Damien, Lettre sur la toute-puissance divine* (Sources chrétiennes 191, Paris 1972); still helpful are J. de Ghellinck, "Dialectique et dogme aux X⁰–XII⁰ siècles," in *Festgabe Cl. Baeumker* (Münster 1913) 79–99, and the essays of J. A. Endres, *Forschungen zur Geschichte der frühmittelalterlichen Philosophie* (BGPT 17, 1915); good now on the general context is P. Riché, *Ecoles et enseignement dans le haut moyen âge* (Paris 1979) 335–44.

with developments from a distance; Anselm of Bec allowed at least one of his monks to study at a cathedral school with Master Roscellin;[66] and Damian's oft-cited attack on the new dialecticians arose out of conversation and disagreement with none other than Abbot Desiderius of Monte Cassino (later Pope Victor III).[67] Dialectic's first real assault, testing the limits of its applicability to sacred dogma, was directed at the mystery of the Trinity, the problem of reconciling the Three and the One, the subject too of one of Boethius's best-known tractates.

Early medieval theological handbooks summarized Trinitarian theology very briefly and in language borrowed preponderantly from St. Augustine's *De Trinitate*. This held true still for most of those early twelfth-century sentence collections lumped together as belonging to the "School of Laon."[68] The new dialecticians, however, could not pass up the challenge this doctrine posed, and thus Trinitarian theology became a major item of debate from around 1090; in the 1150's Lombard's textbook codified it as the first major subject in a theological education.[69] Early in the 1080's Master Roscellin, a canon of Compiègne whose career and irascible character drove him through several French and English schools,[70] began to argue that '*per-*

66. Anselm, *Epist.* 128: ed. Schmitt 3.270–71.

67. Damian, *De diuina omnipotentia*: ed. Cantin (n. 65 above) 384–88.

68. See, for instance, Gennadius, *De ecclesiasticis dogmatibus* 1–2: PL 58.979–81; Honorius, *Elucidarium* 1.1–9: ed. Y. Lefèvre 361–62. For the influential *Sententiae Magistri A.*, see H. J. F. Reinhardt, "Literarkritische und theologiegeschichtliche Studien zu den Sententiae Magistri A. und deren Prolog 'Ad iustitiam credere debemus,'" *AHDL* 36 (1969) 23–56, esp. 35; and for the scarcity of Trinitarian matters in texts associated with the "School of Laon," see Hofmeier (n. 69 below) 101–54.

69. Overviews of early twelfth-century Trinitarian theology in: *DTC* 15.1702–30; J. Hofmeier, *Die Trinitätslehre des Hugo von St. Viktor* (Münchner Theologische Studien 25, Munich 1963); Walter Simonis, *Trinität und Vernunft* (Frankfurter Theologische Studien 12, Frankfurt 1972); Pelikan, *Theology* 262–67.

70. On Roscellin, see F. Picavet, *Roscellin philosophe et théologien* (Paris 1911), with a useful collection of texts, 112–43; J. Reiners, *Der Nominalismus in der Frühscholastik* (BGPT 8, Münster 1910), with a critical edition of Roscel-

sona' should be defined with Boethius as '*substantia rationalis*' and that common or universal terms were merely "*flatus uocis*." This tended to create three '*res*' in the Trinity—he actually made comparisons to three angels or three spirits—held together only by a unity of will and power. All this was necessary, Roscellin claimed, in order to defend the incarnation of the Son without involving incarnations as well of the Father and the Spirit.[71] To lend authority to these views he claimed that Lanfranc had agreed with them and that Anselm of Bec surely would too, given a chance to hear his arguments. Anselm and others protested vigorously, whereupon Roscellin's views were condemned at a council held in Soissons sometime during 1092.[72] But Roscellin soon took up his old views again and elicited a series of rebuttals: Anselm's *De incarnatione Domini* in the later 1090's;[73] probably the teaching ascribed to William of Champeaux;[74] and the first major work by Peter Abelard, a former student of Roscellin, which was itself condemned at a later council of Soissons.[75] To these rebuttals must be added Book XI of Rupert's *De diuinis officiis*, written in 1111 or 1112.

Rupert was probably already in exile near Reims when Archbishop Reginald, the exiled monks' new-found protector, presided over the council in 1092 which condemned these suspect views. When Roscellin defiantly returned to his old views and to France, word spread through all the northern French schools impelling masters everywhere, such as Odo of Tournai, later bishop of Cambrai (1103–13), to take up the logical and doctri-

---

lin's only known work, a letter to Abelard, 63–80; Endres (n. 65 above) 131–49; R. W. Southern, *St. Anselm and His Biographer* (Cambridge 1963) 77–82.

71. Reiners (n. 70 above) 68ff; Anselm, *Epist. de incarn.* 2: ed. Schmitt 1.282; Abelard, *Theologia christiana* 3.89–93: CM 12.230–31.

72. Hefele-Leclercq, *Histoire des conciles* (2nd ed. Paris 1912) 5.365–67.

73. Southern (n. 70 above) 77–82. Ed. Schmitt 1.281–90, 2.3–35.

74. Lottin, *Psychologie* 5.190–94.

75. H. Ostlender, *Peter Abaelards Theologia 'summi boni'* (BGPT 35, Münster 1939); see E. M. Buytaert, "Abelard's Trinitarian Doctrine," in *Peter Abelard*, ed. idem (Louvain 1974) 127–52.

nal issues involved.[76] Like Anselm of Bec, Rupert, whether still near Reims and Laon or back in Liège, would have had only secondhand accounts of Roscellin's position, since the wandering master wrote virtually nothing down. But when his commentary on the divine office reached Trinity Sunday, Rupert devoted to the subject a whole book in which only the first and last chapters interpreted the prescribed office; the rest is a doctrinal treatise. At the end of chapter one Rupert announced that he too, coming last (but also most recently, *nouissimi*) like a grape-picker after the Fathers had already filled the winepresses, wished to set forth the Catholic faith on this matter.[77]

Rupert began with a definition of the Trinity which made extensive use of the category of relations, then refuted the notion that three persons implied three gods, rejected any predication of accidents to the Godhead, discussed the generation of the Son without diminution to the substance of the Father, and finally argued that the incarnation would not make of the Trinity a "quaternity." The questions dealt with and their order of treatment betray Rupert's keen interest in the debate generated by Roscellin, a debate he had effectively joined in, for most of his argumentation was in philosophical language learned, it seems, from the Boethian corpus.[78] Rupert quoted Aristotle at the outset, to the effect that the words imposed are the expression (*notae passionum*) of things (*res*) already understood,[79] and he "conceded" to the philosophers that all things could be divided into "substances" and "accidents."[80] One had also to distinguish between the "substantial names" applied commonly to the God-

76. *Hermanni Liber de restauratione S. Martini Tornacensis* 1–2: MGH SS 14.275.

77. *Off.* 11.1: CM 7.370.

78. The twelfth-century library catalogue from St. Lawrence lists the following works: 1.27: Topice differentie, in quo et alia opuscula Boetii, 1.38: Item topice differentie, 1.39: Corpus dialectice. Gessler, "Bibliothèque" 110–11.

79. *Off.* 11.2: CM 7.371. The phrase is from Aristotle's *De interpretatione* 1, which Rupert probably knew from a Boethian commentary: PL 64.297, 405.

80. *Off.* 11.7: CM 7.376. This doctrine stands at the beginning of Boethius' commentary on Porphyry: PL 64.10.

head and the "relative names" used of the three Persons.[81] But the pagan philosophers never knew God's "proper [Trinitarian] name" and Triune God could not be subjected to such a logical description, for, as Boethius also taught, God is pure form[82] and not a substance of which accidents can be predicated, because Scripture attributes to Him contrary things.[83] Because therefore number or individuation arises from a multitude of accidents and no accidents can be predicated of the persons of the Trinity, number cannot be ascribed to the Triune God, that is, Roscellin cannot speak of the Trinity as having three 'res'.[84] Drawing upon a distinction suggested by Augustine, and anticipating thereby Abelard's famous ternary of 'potentia', 'sapientia', and 'benignitas', Rupert contended nevertheless that the Father is substantively (substantialiter) 'uita', the Son 'sapientia', and the Holy Spirit 'amor'.[85] Rupert argued, finally, that the Son was generated without change in the substance of the Father; debate on this matter was associated later with a suspect position charged to Master Alberic of Reims.[86]

Rupert employed all this philosophical language, he tells us, not because he judged Triune God in any way subject to the vanity of the philosophers, but rather in order to express the matter better and more briefly (melius et compendiosius).[87] He clearly appreciated the resources of dialectic and knew reasonably well the Boethian tractates which had emboldened teachers of dialectic to become speculative theologians. But he insisted

81. Off. 11.4: CM 7.372–73. This distinction stemmed from Augustine, Trin. 5.11ff: CC 50.218ff, whence it entered the mainstream of Western theology: Isidore, Etymologies 7.1.18ff; and Peter Lombard, Sent. 1.22.

82. Off. 11.6–7: CM 7.374, 376. Cf. Boethius, De Trinitate 2.

83. Off. 11.7: CM 7.376; cf. Boethius, De Trin. 4. Even Anselm (De incarn. 4: ed. Schmitt, 1.282–83) was tempted briefly by the language of 'accidents'; cf. Abelard, Theologia Christiana 3.78ff: CM 12.226ff.

84. Off. 11.5: CM 7.373. Cf. Boethius, De Trin. 3.

85. Off. 11.7: CM 7.375–78.

86. Known from Abelard, Theologia Christiana 4.78: CM 12.301–02. See John R. Williams, "The Cathedral School of Reims in the time of Master Alberic, 1118–36," Traditio 20 (1964) 93–114.

87. Off. 11.7: CM 7.376.

that the "proper name" or "true definition" of Triune God came from Scripture alone.[88] Just as important, this "treatise" and the debate which had provoked it started him thinking about a contribution to Trinitarian theology more in keeping with his own convictions, talents, and piety. Indeed, the last chapters of Book XI read like a first draft of his prologue to *De sancta Trinitate et operibus eius.*[89]

Rupert believed that God could be known either in Himself (i.e. mystically) or through His works (see n. 53 above). After summarizing briefly Augustine's psychological analogies (c. 12), he explained how the Trinity is commended to us in creation (c. 16), how the particular work of each Person is discernible especially in the creation of man (c. 17), and why the work of incarnation and redemption pertained to the Son alone (c. 18). That Triune God manifested Himself in the creation of the world and of man was an exegetical commonplace. It was another matter, however, to make those deeds of God revealed in Scripture the primary and virtually the exclusive source of knowledge about His being, in effect to replace the mirror of man's mind (as in Augustine) with the mirror (*speculum*) of God's work in salvation-history. This was the program Rupert set for himself in his massive volume (2125 pages) *On the Holy Trinity and Its Works:* to seek an understanding of the Three in One by way of the works distinctive to each Person.[90] The majestic being of Triune God dazzles man's mortal and infirm eyes, but His deeds can be observed and followed "to some degree with-

88. *Off.* 11.2: CM 7.371–72.

89. Compare especially *Off.* 11.17: CM 7.389–91 with *Trin.* prologus: CM 21.126–27. The striking similarities, and hence the connection between the Trinitarian debate and Rupert's original plan for his *magnum opus*, seem to have escaped previous scholars.

90. "Quid enim propositum est nisi sanctae Trinitatis gloriam per ipsius opera quasi per speculum contemplari, et cuiusque personae proprietatem agnoscere ex proprii qualitate operis?" *Gen.* 2.1: CM 21.185. See Leo Scheffczyk, "Die heilsökonomische Trinitätslehre des Rupert von Deutz und ihre dogmatische Bedeutung," in *Kirche und Überlieferung*, ed. J. Betz and H. Fries (Freiburg 1960) 90–118; and G. R. Evans, *Anselm and a New Generation* (Oxford 1980) 18–20 on Rupert's new approach to Trinitarian theology.

out error,"[91] a point aimed perhaps at those seeking to grasp God's being by means of speculative philosophy.

There is, Rupert argued, a particular work (*actio propria*) which corresponds to the distinguishing property (*proprietas*) of each Person, namely, creation, redemption, and renovation.[92] Rupert knew very well that the word *proprium* normally referred to the terms "Unbegotten, Begotten, and Proceeding," the approved way of describing relations within the *being* of eternal and indivisible God, but he regularly applied it instead to the distinguishing *work* of each Person. Although it was common enough to see the Son in the "*principium*" of Gen. 1:1 and the Spirit in Gen. 1:2, Rupert claimed as a result that the "*Dixitque Deus*" of Gen. 1:3 referred to the generation of the Son which occurred *actualiter* when God, through Him, made the heavens and the earth.[93] If Rupert seems here to confuse inner-Trinitarian relations with a Person's *missio* or work *ad extra*, that is precisely the point: he meant to grasp the former by means of the latter.[94] Thus he could say that the Book of Genesis "contained," that is, set forth, both the eternal and the human generation of the Son.[95] More strikingly, he stated several times that the generation of the Son ceased at creation or the incarnation, whereas the procession of the Spirit continues as long as the work of sanctification.[96] Likewise, the full equality of Father and Son, which Anselm of Bec had just argued by way of the Supreme Being's full identity with His "Speech," Rupert found revealed in the equality between the Father's work of creation in seven days and the Son's work of redemption in seven world-

---

91. *Trin.* prologus: CM 21.126.

92. Ibid.

93. "Verbum tunc actualiter generauit, quando caelum et terram creauit, quando lucem et cetera fecit." *Gen.* 1.10: CM 21.136. Cf. Bede, CC 118A.7–8.

94. The Western tradition tended at times to blur the distinction (Pelikan, *Theology* 278); Abelard, for instance, noted this particularly in the language of the Church's prayers and was more careful in his theology: *Theologia summi boni* 3.1: ed. Ostlender 85ff; *Theologia Christiana* 4.65–69: CM 12.293–97.

95. *Gen.* 1.2: CM 21.130.

96. *Spir.* 1.4: CM 24.1826; *Glor.* 1.16: PL 169.28–29.

ages.[97] Or yet again, on unity of substance and distinction of persons, Rupert held that while the totality of their work was inseparable, their actual effects nevertheless manifested distinction (*distantia*) in their processions.[98] So also the grace of God the Father and of Jesus Christ could refer to the double procession of the Holy Spirit.[99] This was no product of mere ignorance or exegetical playfulness on Rupert's part, though the latter should not be discounted. In the midst of debate and dissent on Trinitarian theology Rupert attempted to comprehend and to elucidate the ineffable inner being of Triune God anew by way of meditation on Scripture, that is, on the acts of God, alone. Or, as he put it once in terms of his own experience, just as the "Love" of God comes to us through reading the "Word" of God, so the Holy Spirit proceeds also from the Son.[100]

A decade before Roscellin was charged with heresy, Anselm of Bec had set aside the testimony of Scripture and attempted in his first major work to penetrate the mysteries of the Trinity by sheer force of reason alone. His *Monologion* or *Meditation upon the Faith* argued the necessary existence of a Supreme Being and the need for such a Being to express Himself (*Verbum*) and to love Himself (*Amor*), hence the divine Three in One. For Anselm reason was the preferred instrument because it made man among all creatures most nearly like God,[101] whereas for Rupert the record of divine deeds in Holy Scripture constituted God's most direct revelation of Himself to man—both, age-old principles here given a new, perhaps somewhat one-sided emphasis in order to attain a fresh grasp of the faith. Anselm recognized the difference between God Himself and the language used about Him in a reasoned argument;[102] so also Rupert frequently noted that knowledge of God by way of Scripture remained partial and inchoate. Both were Benedictine monks removed from and yet fully aware of the new schools, driven in their

97. *Monologion* 29: ed. Schmitt 1.47–48; *Gen.* 3.36: CM 21.279–80.
98. *Glor.* 1.16: PL 169.28.   99. *Spir.* 1.28: CM 24.1855.
100. *Spir.* 1.6: CM 24.1827.
101. *Monologion* 66–68: ed. Schmitt 1.77–79.
102. Ibid. 65: 75–77.

own spiritual and intellectual quests to work out from within the framework of monastic contemplation new approaches to problems first raised outside the cloister. But while Anselm's work is still widely read, Rupert's is barely known. What therefore it became, apart from the contribution to Trinitarian theology it set out to be, requires closer examination.

4

De sancta Trinitate
et operibus eius

Immediately upon completing *De diuinis officiis*, probably still in the year 1112, Rupert outlined the plan of his proposed work in a brief prologue: it was to be divided into three parts corresponding to the "proper" work of each person in the Trinity, God the Father revealed in the seven days of creation (I–III), God the Son in seven world-ages from the fall to His passion (IV–XXXIII), and God the Holy Spirit active through His seven gifts from the incarnation to the Last Judgement (XXXIV–XLII). Rupert's dedicatory epistle, written in the spring of 1117, reviewed what he had actually accomplished.[103] Preoccupation with public disputes and other works had prevented him from commenting upon the whole of Scripture in a single thematic work, and he was forced to curtail the expansive style in which he had begun: nine books on Genesis, four on Exodus, two each on Leviticus, Numbers, and Deuteronomy, one each on Joshua and Judges, and so on. Rupert also lacked finally the sustained intellectual power to rewrite Trinitarian theology, that is, to describe the being of Triune God and the inner relations of the Persons wholly by means of their acts. Yet his work became the largest ever of its kind, requiring division into six parts for manuscript transmission. Only four abbeys—St. Lawrence in Liège, Deutz, Corbie (dated 1182), and Prüfening—and later,

---

103. CM 21.122, 125–27 (note his careful use of tenses). For a schematic overview of his divisions, themes, and scriptural texts, see Haacke's introduction: CM 21.x–xvi.

interestingly, the University of Cologne possessed all six parts.[104]

The work of Triune God across the span of salvation-history represents perforce the whole of divine truth. Otherwise stated, Rupert's work was also a kind of theological *summa* cast in the only form he considered authoritative, a thematic treatment of the Sacred Page. This theological orientation emerged very clearly in his opening interpretation of the Father's work. Gen. 1:1–2 (cc. 1–9) teach, in Rupert's view, the generation of the Son, the procession of the Spirit, and in unity with the Father their creation of all things visible and invisible. Gen. 1:3–4 (*Fiat lux*, etc.) teach the creation and fall of the angels, whereby Rupert included formal questions on God's predestinating will (cc. 10–19). On the foundation of Christ (= *dies primus*), the one in whom and through whom all things were made (cc. 20–21), Rupert took up the six days of creation (cc. 22–58), culminating in the creation of the animals and the implanting in them of the power and the desire to reproduce themselves. Book II (Gen. 1:25–2:25) turned to the creation of man. Rupert first discussed man's image-likeness to God, especially his rationality (cc. 2–7), then interpreted the Sabbath as a foretaste of the eternal rest originally intended for all mankind (cc. 13–19), and continued into a description of Paradise (cc. 23–29), introduced by the question as to whether man was created or placed there. He concluded with the creation of woman, the institution of marriage, and man's status and obligations in the paradisiac state. Book III (Gen. 3:1–4:2) then concentrated wholly upon man's fall and its consequences.

Rupert's order of topics, suggested for the most part by Scripture itself, followed almost exactly that found in early twelfth-century sentence collections and theological handbooks, including, eventually, Lombard's. But whereas those books abstracted from Scripture topics around which relevant and often contradictory authorities were assembled, Rupert integrated his theological exposition into a biblical commentary. His systematic orientation nevertheless stands out, especially in comparison

104. CM 21.xvii–li.

to the *Glossa ordinaria* then in preparation at nearby Laon: made up almost entirely of excerpts from the Fathers, it offered only raw material for, rarely direct initiation into, theological questions. At St. Lawrence, moreover, Rupert had access to virtually all the texts which went into the making of the Gloss on Genesis and the sentence literature on man's creation and fall: Augustine's *Literal Commentary on Genesis*, probably Ps.-Bede on the Pentateuch and Remigius of Auxerre on Genesis,[105] together with Ambrose's hexaemeral commentary, Jerome's *Questions on Genesis*, and Bede's influential commentary.[106] Rupert read all these works, and carefully; but he was not content merely to string together excerpts, as many of his Carolingian predecessors had done and the masters at Laon, in more systematic fashion, were still doing.

Summarizing first in his own words Ambrose's critique of Platonic cosmology (c. 1 = Ambrose 1.1) and Jerome's definition of "*genesis*" and "*principium*," Rupert then posed a question, in fact the first major question in Augustine's commentary and consequently also in the *Ordinary Gloss*:[107] why does the text read "God created heaven and earth" rather than, as it would in succeeding verses, "God said, Let there be heaven and earth"? Rupert gave three answers (*Ad quod tripliciter respondendum est*), the basic thrust of which was to obviate any possible notion of pre-existing material. Augustine, by contrast, saw here the making of "formless material" given form later on by the "*fiat*" of the Son.[108] Rupert's first three books on Genesis posed such questions, found implicitly in the Gloss and explicitly in the sentence collections, for nearly every important verse. Many

105. Bibl. roy. MS 10791: van den Gheyn no. 1051 (Augustine); Bibl. roy. MS 9327–28: van den Gheyn no. 1354 (Remigius and Ps.-Bede).

106. Gessler, "Bibliothèque" 113, 116, 118: 2.9: Ieronimus hebraicarum questionum, in quo exameron Basilii; 2.29: Exameron Ambrosii; 2.42: Beda super Genesim.

107. There is no evidence Rupert knew the Gloss. Many short excerpts from Rupert's commentary appear in its printed editions—probably, like several from Hugh of St. Victor, later additions.

108. *Gen.* 1.4: CM 21.132. Cf. Augustine, *Gen.* 1.3–4: CSEL 28.7–8.

deal with the creation and fall of man and angels, then much discussed in the schools (separately treated below in chapter V), and most were suggested either by the Fathers themselves, as in this first example,[109] or by an obvious contradiction between them. Especially in such instances Rupert could not pass up the opportunity to offer his own solution.

He preferred, for instance, a literal account of creation. In the controversy between Augustine and Bede as to whether creation was instantaneous or at intervals in time, Rupert struck a kind of compromise: it was instantaneous in the mind of the Creator, but took place in time, culminating in the sixth day—the same position Abelard would later adopt.[110] He knew the Fathers also disagreed on the "waters above the firmament." Rejecting the spiritual interpretation of those waters as angels, he criticized as "conjectural rather than rational" the argument by Ambrose and others that these were solidified waters (*acquas congelatas*) and finally settled on just plain water; but to avoid the physical problem involved he argued for a kind of water still in its primeval state.[111] Rupert also objected vigorously to those who interpreted Paradise only in terms of spiritual and moral allegories, again a problem raised already by St. Augustine. To prove its physical existence Rupert mustered geographical lore from pagan authors.[112] Finally, he held that the Tree of Life was a real tree, not just a symbol, and he drew on medical lore regarding Asclepius and the mandragora to substantiate the power of certain herbs to extend or even restore life—a kind of proof the tree should be understood literally.[113] To these exegetical

109. The schoolmen did not invent these "questions": G. Bardy, "La littérature patristique des *Quaestiones et responsiones* sur l'écriture sainte," *Revue Biblique* 41 (1932) 210–36, 341–69, 515–37 (just on St. Augustine, who may have been the most influential) and 42 (1933) 14–30, 211–29, 328–52.

110. *Gen.* 1.37, 2.18: CM 21.165–66, 203–05. Abelard: PL 178.740, 745. The contradictory positions of the Fathers reported in Lombard, *Sent.* 2.12.2.

111. *Gen.* 1.22–25: CM 21.151–54. Abelard: PL 178.742ff.

112. *Gen.* 2.24–25, 29: CM 21.212–14, 219–21. Cf. Augustine, *Gen.* 8.1: CSEL 28.229. On the spiritual interpretations of Paradise, see G. Lodolo, "Il tema simbolico del paradiso nella tradizione monastica dell'Occidente latino (secoli VI–XII)," *Aevum* 51 (1977) 252–88.

113. *Gen.* 3.29–30: CM 21.269–71.

matters might be added passages which suggest Rupert's sensitivity to mountains, birds, and the changing seasons. The fact is, Rupert's work of about 1112 appears to be the earliest commentary on Genesis to reflect a newly revived interest in nature and cosmology.

In the early twelfth century a new orientation to "natural" forms of life is evident, for instance in art and poetry, sprung at least in part from the sheer vitality and prosperity of material life.[114] Schoolmen became fascinated with creation and cosmology. Already in 1085 Manegold of Lautenbach had felt compelled to warn Abbot Wolfhelm of Brauweiler (just west of Cologne) against an uncritical reading of pagan cosmologists, especially Macrobius;[115] and during the first decade of the twelfth-century Adelard of Bath was lecturing on "natural" scientific topics at Laon.[116] In the 1120's and 1130's Honorius, Peter Abelard, Thierry of Chartres, and Hugh of Amiens, among others, revived the ancient hexaemeral tradition with new commentaries on the account of creation in Genesis, and William of Conches and Bernard Silvester produced independent treatises on cosmology based on Platonic sources, chiefly Chalcidius and Macrobius' *In Somnium Scipionis*.[117] Rupert's Genesis commentary of about 1112 also made relatively extensive reference to Macrobius, whose work was found in the abbey's library.[118] Utterly

114. G. B. Ladner, "Erneuerung," in *Reallexikon für Antike und Christentum* 6 (1964) 246–47 (with large bibliography). The most influential essay is that by M. D. Chenu, "La nature et l'homme: La Renaissance du XIIᵉ siècle," in *Théologie* 19–51. See also G. Post, "The Naturalness of Society and the State," in his *Studies in Medieval Legal Thought* (Princeton 1964) 494–561.

115. Wilfred Hartmann, "Manegold von Lautenbach und die Anfänge der Frühscholastik," *DA* 26 (1970) 47–149; and his edition, *Manegold von Lautenbach, Liber contra Wolfelmum* (MGH Geistesgeschichte 8, Weimar 1972).

116. C. H. Haskins, *Studies in the History of Mediaeval Science* (Cambridge, Mass. 1927) 20–42. See Adelard's *De eodem et diverso*, ed. H. Willner (BGPT 4.1, Munich 1906), and his *Quaestiones naturales*, ed. M. Müller (BGPT 31.2, Münster 1934).

117. Brian Stock, *Myth and Science in the Twelfth Century* (Princeton 1972), with additional literature and sources; Richard C. Dales, "A Twelfth-Century Concept of the Natural Order," *Viator* 9 (1978) 179–92; and Evans (n. 64 above) 167–92.

118. Gessler, "Bibliothèque" 109: 1.25.

rejecting any notion that would seem to make form or matter co-eternal with God—a fiction "concocted" by pagan philosophers—he insisted that Triune God Himself rather than 'ideas' or 'forms' served as the 'exemplar' for creation.[119] Rupert likewise repudiated the notion of certain "*Platonici*" that men have souls fallen from heaven.[120] On the other hand, he, like Abbot Wolfhelm, had no fear of drawing upon the "*physici*" to explain various aspects of God's creation. That the sun is the source of fire and warmth, that the firmament revolves at a fixed speed, that the sun is larger than the earth or moon—these and other ideas Rupert took over directly from Macrobius.[121] He also affirmed, against patristic tradition, the possible existence of *Antipodes*, one of the items specifically rebutted by Manegold.[122] In sum, Rupert's exposition of the Father's creative work shared in this new fascination with creation and cosmology, but tested the "Platonists" and their enthusiastic expositors against Holy Scripture.

Still another area in which the early twelfth century saw much learned discussion was the Church's position on marriage. The reformers' zeal to put the Church in right order and to improve the clergy reached the laity in the form of a new concern to codify and to enforce marriage legislation.[123] Follow-

119. *Gen.* 1.1: CM 21.129. Cf. Ambrose, *Hex.* 1.1: CSEL 32.3–4.

120. *Gen.* 2.21: CM 21.208. Cf. Macrobius, *In Somn. Scip.* 1.11.11–12: ed. Willis 47.

121. *Gen.* 1.8, 41: CM 21.136, 168 (cf. Macrobius 1.20.7–8: ed. Willis 79–80); *Gen.* 1.26: CM 21.155–56 (cf. Macrobius 1.19.11: ed. Willis 75); *Gen.* 1.42: CM 21.169–70 (cf. Macrobius 1.20.32: ed. Willis 84). See H. Silvestre, "Macrobe utilisé . . . par Rupert de Deutz," *Classica et Mediaevalia* 19 (1958) 131–32.

122. *Gen.* 1.33: CM 21.162. Macrobius, 2.5.25–26. Silvestre (n. 2 above) 383–84 cites as another possible source an anonymous commentary on Boethius' *Consolation of Philosophy* 3.9 also known to Rupert. Cf. Manegold, *Liber contra Wolfelmum* 4: ed. Hartmann 51. The position of the Fathers on the "Antipodes" in T. Gregory, *Platonismo medievale* (Rome 1958) 26 n. 1.

123. Best orientation: G. Le Bras, "Mariage," *DTC* 9.2133–2317. See also Heinrich J. F. Reinhardt, *Die Ehelehre der Schule des Anselm von Laon* (BGPT n.F. 14, Münster 1974); and H. Zeimentz, *Ehe nach der Frühscholastik* (Düsseldorf 1973). A perceptive account of the reformers' impact by P. Toubert, *Les structures du Latium médiéval* (Rome 1973) 738–49.

ing the order of Scripture, twelfth-century theologians frequently treated marriage early, as an institution founded at creation, and Rupert did too. Elaborating upon an idea found in St. Augustine, he emphasized that human sexuality was present already in Paradise, since God had meant it as the means for procreating heirs to eternal beatitude.[124] Rupert conceded that after the fall lust (*libido*) had become almost impossible to extinguish for both the married and the continent, but he rejected specifically any idea that human sexuality as such resulted from the fall.[125] Eve was made from Adam's rib, Rupert declared emphatically, in order to establish the bond of love and marriage already in Paradise, a union to be sundered only by reason of adultery or if both agreed to join the religious life.[126] Beyond this last point, for which he referred specifically to canon law, Rupert did not concern himself with the intricacies of marriage legislation. But neither did he ever consider the position, proposed by William of Champeaux,[127] that marriage was only permitted in Paradise, not commanded, nor did he view marriage chiefly as a remedy for the wayward flesh, an argument increasingly deployed by schoolmen. Rupert actually warned monks not to look down upon the married as an "inferior grade" of Christian.[128] His aim was essentially that of a preacher—he addressed the laity directly (*O coniuges*) when he condemned divorce—determined to establish the divine institution and permanence of marriage. This too linked him to the reform party, and his Genesis commentary to a major theme in twelfth-century theological and canonistic discussion.

Whatever its larger ambitions, Rupert's work was nevertheless written in a monastery and for other monks. He spoke re-

124. *Gen.* 2.8–9: CM 21.191–94. Cf. Augustine, *Gen.* 9.3ff: CSEL 28.271ff; *De civitate Dei* 14.21–22. See M. Müller, *Die Lehre des hl. Augustinus von der Paradiesehe und ihre Auswirkung in der Sexualethik des 12. und 13. Jahrhunderts bis Thomas von Aquin* (Regensburg 1954): Zeimentz (n. 123 above) 36–44; Reinhardt (n. 123 above) 41–46.

125. *Gen.* 2.9, 3.10–11: CM 21.193, 245–47. Was this an ancient error known to Rupert from Augustine, or had he learned of John Scot Eriugena's position, as in his *Periphyseon* 4.13.16? Cf. Silvestre (n. 1 above) 384.

126. *Gen.* 2.34–36: CM 21.228–31.

127. Lottin, *Psychologie* 5.286 no. 402.   128. *John* 2: CM 9.101.

peatedly of "contemplating" rather than "demonstrating" the glory of Triune God as revealed in His works. Monastic exegesis had in general a predilection for the moral sense of Scripture, for interpretations which spoke to the monk's continuing battle against the vices of the old nature.[129] So too Rupert pointed out that Adam never thanked God for His original blessings, that he sought to hide rather than to confess his sin, and so on. All monks stood to one degree or another in the shadow of Gregory the Great, whose notion of the moral sense encompassed in practice the whole of the spiritual life. Yet distinctions must be made among different persons and eras. Guibert of Nogent, writing twenty years before Rupert, explained that while he dared not rival Augustine's literal commentary on Genesis (Rupert was not nearly so obsequious toward the Father's authority) he would attempt a new moral commentary. For although everyone's familiarity with the faith made it unnecessary to dwell further on the allegorical sense, all still suffered temptation in the ongoing struggle between virtue and vice.[130] Thus Gen. 1:1, for Rupert and the Fathers the creation of all things visible and invisible, suggested to Guibert the fierce struggle between the spirit and the flesh at the beginning of conversion (*in principio conuersionis nostrae inter nosmetipsos*). Likewise the "light" of Gen. 1:3, for Rupert the creation of angels and the resultant first steps in the history of salvation, meant to Guibert the first good (*primum bonum*) given a convert, namely, the fear of God which is the beginning of wisdom, whereas the text which inspired Rupert to preach about marriage (Gen. 2:23) led Guibert only to brief remarks on the weakness of the flesh.[131] In sum, these two Benedictine monks independently took it upon themselves to reinterpret Genesis, the one with a view to uncovering the Father's creative work in salvation-history and the other its teachings on the whole of the spiritual life. Guibert's work (of which an autograph survives, B.N. Lat 2500) reflected that heightened inward-looking spirituality characteristic of twelfth-century religious life, and Rupert's the new directions in theology and cosmol-

129. De Lubac (n. 35 above) 1.571–86.
130. PL 156.20; Guibert, *De vita sua* 1.17: ed. Bourgin 66–69.
131. PL 156.31–34, 37–38, 70.

ogy. Though trained in part by St. Anselm and resident near Laon, Guibert remained little known. Excerpts from Rupert's commentary entered the *Ordinary Gloss* and in greater compass Arno of Reichersberg's hexaemeral commentary.[132]

In the great central portion of *De sancta Trinitate*, almost three-fourths of the total work, Rupert expounded the redemptive work of God the Son. So also contemporary theological handbooks took up the person and work of Christ immediately after the creation and fall (Book III, for instance, of Lombard's textbook).[133] Rupert concentrated on the *work* of Christ, and he taught it by way of the types and figures (*mysteriis*) of Him found in the Old Testament rather than by analysis of the Gospels, summarized in a single book, or of the Pauline Epistles.[134] Dividing the period of Christ's work into seven world-ages, a scheme familiar from Augustine and Bede,[135] he saw Christ prefigured in the first age, from Adam to Noah, only in deeds; in the second, from Noah to Abraham, in deeds and words (*sermones*); in the third, from Abraham to David, through direct promises; and so forth. Thus where the six days of creation had concerned "*naturalia*" and pertained to the Father, the six world-ages dealt with "*doctrinalia*" and pertained to the Person of the Son.[136] This presupposed an allegorical, that is to say, christo-

132. Israel Peri, "Das Hexaemeron Arnos von Reichersberg: Eine Exegese aus dem 12. Jahrhundert," *Jahrbuch des Stiftes Klosterneuburg*, n.F. 10 (1976) 9–115.

133. Compare H. Cloes, "La systématisation théologique pendant la première moitié du XIIᵉ siècle," *Ephemerides theologicae Lovanienses* 34 (1958) 277–329; Evans (n. 64 above) 192–214.

134. Rupert was very conscious of his thematic approach, as evidenced by his own later summary of this work: "de operibus caeteris, de creatura mundi, de mysteriis huius uerbi legalibus, propheticis atque euangelicis et de gratia spiritus sancti iamdudum dixi uel egi quod potui. . . ." *Vict.* 1.5: ed. Haacke 10.

135. Rupert's teaching that the sixth and seventh ages, the latter representing the present state of the faithful departed, run parallel (see *Evang.* 29–31: CM 23.1820–22) amplifies and sharpens something he probably learned from Bede, *De temporum ratione* 66: CC 123B.463ff.

136. *Gen.* 3.35–36: CM 21.278–80. Additional references to his scheme in *Gen.* 5.1: CM 21.332; *Reg.* 22.1: CM 22.1193; *Hier.* 1–2: CM 23.1572–74; *Evang.* 1–2: CM 23.1782–83.

logical reading of all Scripture. Just a decade later, Hugh of St. Victor described his work *On the Mysteries of the Christian Faith* as a compendium of that to be learned from an *allegorical* reading of Scripture, and he also divided all things between the works (*opera*) of creation and restoration; but secular books, he believed, taught creation, whereas Scripture concentrated upon restoration which, unlike Rupert's Part III, he ascribed wholly to Christ.[137] Hugh nevertheless also began with an abbreviated hexaemeral commentary setting forth the work of creation.

Rupert's Part II became in practice an extended meditation on Christ and His salvific work, carried out in virtually separable commentaries on individual books of the Old Testament written over two or three years' time. They are therefore best analyzed with respect to the exegetical tradition for a given book, Ezechiel,[138] for instance, or indeed the whole Pentateuch.[139] Most reveal that same inclination to reconsider, or at the very least to reorganize, the received tradition so evident in his first three books on Genesis. In general, however, a contemplative orientation, very close to the heart of Rupert's religious life, pre-dominated over more theological or scholarly concerns. His christology, for instance, would come through much more crisply in his contemporaneous *Commentary on St. John*.

Part III of Rupert's *De sancta Trinitate*, on the work of the Holy Spirit from the incarnation to the Last Judgement, was by contrast completely innovative; and to shape it he drew upon several traditions. From Augustine's *City of God* he borrowed his external framework, the resurrection first of man's soul in baptism and then of his body at the end of time.[140] Augustine, however, had hesitated to proceed concretely into the New Testament age, persuaded in any case that the world was slowly

137. Hugh, *De sacramentis* prologus: PL 176.183.

138. W. Neuss, *Das Buch Ezechiel in Theologie und Kunst bis zum Ende des XII. Jahrhunderts* (Beiträge zur Geschichte des alten Mönchtums und des Benediktinerordens 1–2, Münster 1912).

139. A formal ending to the Deuteronomy commentary (CM 22.1117–18) and a fresh schematic start on Joshua (CM 22.1119) suggest Rupert may have considered his first nineteen books a complete commentary on the Pentateuch.

140. *Spir.* 1.1, 9.24: CM 24.1823, 2125. Compare *De civitate Dei* 20.6–7.

growing old (*senescens*). So Rupert turned to the tradition of Apocalypse commentary for his basic structure (apostles, martyrs, confessors/heretics, false brothers, and Antichrist), even though it too, in reaction to millenarian movements, had become vague and moralistic. Rupert "historicized" this tradition,[141] as he had already in his poem, and thus was the first in the twelfth century to carry the history of salvation directly down to the "present age."[142] Rupert's Age of the Spirit corresponded to the period *"sub gratia"* in Augustine's influential tripartite division of salvation-history (*ante legem, sub lege, sub gratia*). During this third age, as Rupert explained it, the seven gifts of the Spirit, possessed in plenitude by the incarnate Christ, flow (*manare*) from Him in reverse order, each dominant in consecutive ages of the Church.[143] By way of comparison, in neighboring Flanders and at almost the same time (ca. 1109) Franco of Afflighem prepared an overview of salvation-history entitled *De gratia Dei* with seven short books on the New Testament era in honor of the seven gifts, but unlike Rupert he made no attempt to continue the story into the present.[144] Apart from polemics on the *filioque*, Rupert's was in fact the first such separate treatment of the Holy Spirit in the West, and thus represented an important early witness to a new form of piety singling out the Spirit's work in Christian life, comparable to the new cult of Christ's humanity. Five years or so after the completion of Ru-

141. See W. Kamlah, *Apokalypse und Geschichtstheologie* (Berlin 1935) 57–74 (for the received tradition), 75–104 (Rupert).

142. See J. Spörl, *Grundformen hochmittelalterlicher Geschichtsanschauung* (Munich 1935; repr. 1968) 18–21; and Amos Funkenstein, *Heilsplan und natürliche Entwicklung: Formen der Gegenwartsbestimmung im Geschichtsdenken des hohen Mittelalters* (Berlin 1965), who accorded little attention to Rupert because his view seemed too religious and unpolitical. That is to miss the chronological concreteness which distinguishes his approach from the vagueness of early medieval thought: see M. Bernards, "Geschichtsperiodisches Denken in der Theologie des 12. Jahrhunderts," *Kölner Domblatt* 27 (1967) 115–24; J. Ratzinger, *The Theology of History in St. Bonaventure* (Chicago 1971) 98–103; B. McGinn, *Visions of the End* (New York 1979) 108–10; and n. 148 below.

143. *Spir.* 1.22–25, 31: CM 24.1848–52, 1860–61. A similar idea with a nonchronological formulation in Hugh, *De sacramentis* 2.2.1: PL 176.415.

144. *De gratia* 6 prologus: PL 166.744.

pert's work, Abelard was accused of still another heresy when he dedicated his oratory to the Paraclete (rather than to Christ or the Trinity); yet within decades numerous churches and an influential hospitaller order would adopt the Holy Spirit as their patron.[145]

To order the Spirit's work of sanctification in the Church and the Christian life, Rupert had no clear precedents to follow. Contemporary handbooks and sentence collections amassed texts on the sacraments, the virtues and vices, the problems of the current age (especially simony), and the Last Judgement in seemingly helter-skelter fashion. Hugh of St. Victor ascribed all of it to Christ's work of restoration, and organized it so far as possible around the sacraments He had instituted. Lombard's textbook took up the gifts of the Spirit and the virtues in Book III, immediately after Christ's person and work, and reserved for Book IV the seven sacraments and the Last Things. Rupert of St. Lawrence integrated into a single progressive account three different matters: the continuing work of the Spirit in the Church, the history of salvation to the end of time, and six topics relevant to the work of sanctification (the sacraments, Scripture and its interpretation, the virtues and counsels, preaching, education, and "current affairs"), each placed at a particular moment in salvation-history under the aegis of a particular gift. Book I expounded the Spirit's role in the incarnation by reinterpreting Genesis with reference to the New Man. The gift of "wisdom" then manifested itself supremely in Christ's passion (Book II) and in the sacraments (Book III) instituted thereby. The gift of "understanding" (Book IV) became manifest historically in the apostles at Pentecost; it referred topically to the Scriptures, the authoritative source of truth in the Church. The Spirit's "counsel" (Book V) worked the awful rejection of the Jews and conversion of the Gentiles, culminating in the destruction of Jerusalem in 70 A.D.; so now the counsels of perfection must

145. *Historia calamitatum*: ed. Monfrin 95. Cf. Classen, *Gerhoch* 113. There is still no study of this shift in piety which, it seems to me, is prerequisite to understanding later medieval millenarian movements.

supersede the precepts, evoking from Rupert a brief treatise on the religious life. "Fortitude" (Book VI) once inspired the martyrs, and must now inspire the clergy to courageous preaching; the book concludes with a homily on St. Lawrence, the patron saint of Rupert's house. "Knowledge" (Book VII) enabled the doctors or confessors to combat heresies raised by the Devil; here Rupert explained and defended the role of the liberal arts in divine learning and the service of the Church. "Fear" (Book IX), finally, refers to the coming Last Judgement, though Rupert generally, after his early poem, placed much greater stress on the vision of God anticipated in monastic contemplation than on the horrors of Antichrist.[146]

Between the confessors and the Last Judgement comes the "present age," to which Rupert assigned the gift of "piety" (Book VIII). True piety, he quoted from Augustine's *City of God*, is true religion, or the worship of God in meekness and penitence.[147] Otherwise stated, monks have now replaced apostles, martyrs, and confessors as the forward troops in the advancing history of salvation.[148] Although other twelfth-century authors added a contemporary "monastic age" to the traditional scheme of apostles, martyrs, and confessors,[149] Rupert's account was apparently the first, and was also unusually concrete. In it he charged certain theological adversaries with impiety for wanting, in his judgement, to ascribe evil to God rather than man and blaspheming against the Spirit by impugning Holy Scripture and His other works (cc. 3–4). He reaffirmed the reality of penance and forgiveness in this life, but argued again that publicly condemned prelates and clerics be restricted to lay com-

146. See Rauh, *Antichrist* 196–235.

147. *Spir.* 8.2: CM 24.2075. *De civitate Dei* 10.1.

148. "Sanctum pietatis Spiritum, qui *deinde ordine sequitur*, nos maxime pauperes . . . adoramus, confitentes illi, quia qui neque sapientes fuimus neque intelligentes, neque consulti aut consultores, neque fortes, neque multam scientiam habentes, *nunc* uiuimus ex abundantia huius gratiae. . . . Ista enim illa est gratia, quae *hodie*, cum domus Dei uocatorum ex diversis conditionibus atque ordinibus uenientium multitudine impleta est. . . ." *Spir.* 8.1: CM 24.2074 (my italics).

149. See de Lubac (n. 35 above) 1.574.

munion, preferably in the monastic life (cc. 5–9). He urged his brothers in the religious life to humble and contrite confession (cc. 10–13), and he admonished priests and prelates to a just and discreet use of the power of binding and loosing (cc. 20–21). Finally he reproached the Jews for their blindness, while reminding his readers of their promised final conversion. In short, though he issued no prophecies or dramatic calls for reform, he made monks like himself the leaders of the "present age" and assigned matters of demonstrable urgency in his own life to a particular place in salvation-history. About twenty years later Gerhoch of Reichersberg appropriated Rupert's scheme wholesale, and transformed his own ages of piety and fear into a fiery treatise on the need for continued reform in the spirit of Gregory VII.[150]

In sum: The lengthiest account of salvation-history since Augustine's *City of God* and perhaps the first to carry the story down to the present age, the earliest theological *summa* extant from the twelfth century, an attempted new approach to Trinitarian theology, and the first attempt ever to prepare a meditation upon all of Scripture in a single work—such was Rupert's *De sancta Trinitate et operibus eius*, written between 1112 and late 1116.

150. Classen, *Gerhoch* 108–14.

III

Scriptural
Theologian

ROUND 1114 Rupert interrupted work on *De sancta Trini-*
tate to take up a *Commentary on the Gospel of St. John*, which he
completed in fourteen books and nearly eight hundred pages by
the summer of 1116.[1] To comment at such length on a single
Gospel rather than to concentrate wholly upon his contemplative *summa* strongly suggests changed circumstances and new
theological concerns. Indeed, the eighteenth-century Maurists
found in its first seven books "a kind of survey-course in theology."[2] It is striking, however, that Rupert should resolve to deal
with new issues by way of the Gospel rather than the Psalter or
the Epistles, and doubly so that he should choose to comment
on St. John's Gospel, for Augustine's *Sermons on John* had gained
such authority that in nearly seven hundred years no author had
bothered or dared to reconsider this Gospel's teachings.[3] In a
"*praefatio apologetica*" designed in part to deal with this very

1. See Appendix to this chapter.
2. *Histoire littéraire* 11.523. Compare M. Bernards, in *Zeitschrift für Kirchengeschichte 84* (1973) 112.
3. The commentaries by Ps.-Bede (PL 92.633–938) and Alcuin (PL
100.725–1008) were compiled from Augustine's work. St. Lawrence possessed Augustine and Ps.-Bede on John (Gessler, "Bibliothèque" 107, 114:
1.10, 2.13). On sources, see also H. Silvestre, "Emprunts non repérés à Jérome et à Bède dans l'*In Iohannem* de Rupert de Deutz," *RB* 84 (1974) 372–82.

problem Rupert acknowledged the authority of "Doctor Augustine," whose "way rather than footsteps he would try to follow": where Augustine had soared at the mountaintops, he would remain in the foothills; and since Augustine had plucked all the great mysteries from the top of the tree, he would pick only the lesser fruit of the letter.[4] But like his comments in the prologue to *De diuinis officiis* about the "old wine" of Amalarius, this was nothing other than a declaration of independence.

1

Black Monks and
the Study of Theology

When Rupert began his *Commentary on John* the scholarly study of theology, soon to become the queen of medieval sciences, was still in its infancy. When the Fathers treated Scripture in sermon or commentary and composed treatises on doctrinal issues, they presupposed for basic training in the arts Roman secular education. In his influential work *On Christian Learning* Augustine argued that Christians should take over so much of secular education as would aid them in the understanding of Scripture. When the Western Roman Empire collapsed and with it eventually its educational system, Augustine's program together with Cassiodorus' *On Divine and Human Learning* became in practice the whole of Western education, or more accurately, the distant ideal of educational reformers. Thus Carolingian scholars, true to their Augustinian heritage, reformed education with a view to improving divine learning and ecclesiastical service. Their efforts produced numerous biblical commentaries and doctrinal disputes, but with the singular exception of John Scotus Eriugena rarely got beyond gathering up the tradition and "correcting" inadequacies and difficulties which emerged, for instance, in Augustine's views on the eucharist and predestination.[5]

4. See H. Silvestre, "*Diversi sed non adversi,*" *RTAM* 31 (1964) 124–32 for related formulas and additional literature.

5. P. E. Schramm, "Karl der Grosse: Denkart und Grundauffassungen. Die von ihm bewirkte 'Correctio,'" in his *Kaiser, Könige und Päpste* I (Stuttgart 1968) 302–41 (with additional literature). Pelikan, *Theology* 50–105.

Divine matters remained for the most part still sacrosanct.[6] With the collapse of the Carolingian Empire came yet again a steep decline in learning, especially learning applied to divine matters, so that for almost one hundred fifty years, or more than five human generations, prelates, teachers, and monks produced virtually no new scriptural commentaries or theological treatises and likewise no theological disputes of any consequence.

To discover the origins of theology as a school discipline one must trace just how, when, and where Holy Scripture came to be taught by masters, as distinguished from preached by prelates, chanted by priests, and meditated upon by monks. These new masters applied the arts systematically to the study of Scripture, speculated logically on dogma, and responded apologetically to heretics and infidels: taken together their work founded the new scholarly discipline of theology.[7] While a certain dialectic between reason and authority permeated this development, becoming especially prominent in public doctrinal controversies, the most fundamental change, overlooked in much of the older literature and still to some degree by Evans, was that which transformed Holy Scripture, the divine repository of sacred dogma kissed, incensed, and invoked each day at mass, into a textbook routinely lectured upon in the schools and haggled over in public disputes. The handbooks, culminating in Peter Lombard's *Sentences*, state clearly, almost without exception, that they were not themselves the chief object of theological study. The *Sententiae diuinae paginae* (formerly ascribed to Anselm of Laon), Hugh of St. Victor's *De sacramentis christianae fidei*, Peter Abelard's *Theologia 'scholarium'*, and the *Summa sententiarum* all were written to serve as introductions or guides to

6. Briefly but well put by P. Riché, *Ecoles et enseignement dans le haut moyen âge* (Paris 1979) 280–84.

7. G. R. Evans, *Old Arts and New Theology* (Oxford 1980), which reinterprets some of the older literature: M. Grabmann, *Die Geschichte der scholastischen Methode* (1909–11); J. de Ghellinck, *Le mouvement théologique du XIIe siècle* (2nd ed. Brussels 1948); G. Paré, A. Brunet, and P. Tremblay, *La renaissance du XIIe siècle: Les écoles et l'enseignement* (Paris and Ottawa 1933) 213–312; M. D. Chenu, "Les *Magistri:* la 'science' théologique," *Théologie* 323–50; Leclercq, *Love of Learning* 233–86.

the study of Scripture.[8] So also later, commenting upon Lombard's textbook marked the first step, not the endpoint, in the making of a theological career. Full professors of theology in medieval universities lectured *ordinarily* upon Scripture.

Rupert wrote his *Commentary on John* between 1114 and 1116, and in 1117 the first master of the Sacred Page to gain a Europe-wide reputation, Anselm of Laon, died just as Rupert entered the city to debate him.[9] About 1060 a German abbot and former *scholasticus* in Bamberg still complained that most teachers studied the arts alone and neglected Scripture, the true end of education, except now for Master Lanfranc in France whose lectures on the Psalter and Epistles had attracted many German students.[10] Fifteen years later a German student wrote encouraging his friend to forget the wars at home and join him in study; the master had just finished with the Psalms and was about to begin the Epistles.[11] Manuscript evidence confirms what these remarks suggest: masters normally taught the Psalter and the Epistles, and French masters enjoyed the greatest fame as scriptural teachers.[12] Commentaries on St. Paul can safely be attrib-

8. Abelard may speak for the others: "Scholarium nostrorum petitioni prout possumus satisfacientes, aliquam sacrae eruditionis summam, quasi diuinae Scripturae introductionem, conscripsemus." CM 12.401.

9. B. Smalley, *The Study of the Bible in the Middle Ages* [read: in the schools] (2nd ed. Oxford 1952) is still basic. For the state of affairs ca. 1050: Riché (n. 6 above) 335–44.

10. Martène-Durand, *Vet. Script. Amplissima Collectio* (Paris 1724) 1.507. M. Gibson, *Lanfranc of Bec* (Oxford 1978) 39, 204.

11. Ed. C. Erdmann and N. Fickermann (MGH Briefe der deutschen Kaiserzeit 5, Weimar 1950) 95. B. Smalley, "Some Gospel Commentaries of the Early Twelfth Century," *RTAM* 45 (1978) 148.

12. But the first commentaries known at all from this era are by Bruno of Würzburg (d. 1045) on the Psalms (PL 142.39–530) and Herman of Reichenau (d. 1054) on the Epistles (St. Gall Stiftsbibl. MS 64): see Gibson (n. 10 above) 52–54. This probably reflects the general predominance of German imperial civilization down to about the mid-eleventh century. According to R. W. Southern, "Master Vacarius and the Beginning of an English Academic Tradition," in *Medieval Learning and Literature: Essays presented to Richard William Hunt* (Oxford 1976) 267–70, the teaching of Scripture was practically unknown in England before the 1130's.

uted to Drogo of Paris, Berengar of Tours, Lanfranc of Bec (1055–70), Master Bruno of Reims (before 1086), Manegold, Master Lambert of Utrecht (ca. 1100), and Anselm of Laon (both a gloss, the basis of the *Ordinary Gloss*, and lost lectures).[13] Commentaries on the Psalter are attested for nearly all the same authors.[14] Although many more remain anonymous,[15] two masters were to become famous. About the time Rupert began work on his Johannine commentary, Gilbert of Poitiers lectured as a young student before Master Anselm in Laon.[16] Peter Abelard also came to study with Anselm, found that venerable old master all smoke and no fire, and began on a dare to lecture himself on that most difficult (*obscurissima*) book, the prophet Ezechiel.[17] Lectures on the Gospels were far less common and seem to have originated at Laon under Anselm and his brother Ralph.[18] All around Rupert, then, at Utrecht, Reims, and above all Laon, masters had begun to lecture on Holy Scripture as well as the arts.

This activity hardly escaped a monk resident just outside a

13. B. Smalley, "La Glossa Ordinaria: Quelques prédécesseurs d'Anselme de Laon," *RTAM* 8 (1936) 24–60 and 9 (1937) 365–99; M. Gibson, "Lanfranc's *Commentary on the Pauline Epistles*," *Journal of Theological Studies* 22 (1971) 86–112; A. Stoelen, "Les commentaires scripturaires attribués à Bruno le Chartreux," *RTAM* 25 (1958) 177–247; J. M. De Smet, "L'exégète Lambert, écolâtre d'Utrecht," *RHE* 42 (1947) 103–10.

14. D. van den Eynde, "Literary Note on the Earliest Scholastic *Commentarii in Psalmos*," *Franciscan Studies* 14 (1954) 121–54 and 17 (1957) 149–72; W. Hartmann, "Psalmenkommentare aus der Zeit der Reform und der Frühscholastik," *Studi Gregoriani* 9 (1972) 313–66; and V. I. J. Flint, "Some Notes on the Early Twelfth Century Commentaries on the Psalms," *RB* 38 (1971) 80–88.

15. A. Stoelen, "Bruno le Chartreux, Jean Gratiadei et la lettre de S. Anselme sur l'eucharistie," *RTAM* 34 (1967) 18–83; B. Smalley, "Les commentaires bibliques de l'époque romane," *Cahiers de civilisation médiévale* 4 (1961) 15–22.

16. R. A. B. Mynors, *Catalogue of the MSS of Balliol College, Oxford* (Oxford 1963) 26. Smalley (n. 11 above) 153.

17. *Historia calamitatum*: ed. J. Monfrin (Paris 1959) 68–69.

18. Smalley (n. 11 above) 147–80; idem, "Peter Comester on the Gospels and His Sources," *RTAM* 46 (1979) 84–129.

city with its own distinguished intellectual tradition. Tenth- and eleventh-century Benedictines, set apart from the world and pledged to the contemplative life, continued perforce to take part in worldly affairs as long as they also found themselves the wealthiest landowners and generally the best-educated churchmen. Their monasteries—models of estate management, nuclei of new population centers, training sites for growing numbers of the secular clergy, and much more—were decidedly in the world, even if they were not supposed to be of it. Contemplatives "living among men in cities, towns, and villages," as the author of the *Libellus de diuersis ordinibus* described Black Monks, frequently responded favorably to the people's demand for intercessory, advisory, and homiletic services.[19] The tension may be seen in the contrast, for instance, between Abbot Odilo of Cluny appearing before the king as a great prince escorted by dozens of knights and Abbot John of Fécamp yearning to free himself of the legal wrangles incurred by his ducal monastery in order to return to the eremitical life he had learned as a young man in Italy.[20] Between 1050 and about 1130, moreover, the Black Monks' involvement in medieval society increased naturally and correlatively, so to speak, with the concurrent dramatic expansion of the economy, culture, and Church. Black Monks supplied the major reform popes down to 1120, built the greatest church in Christendom (Cluny, 1090), invented a new architectural ideal (Suger at St. Denis), took over numerous parish churches given up by lay owners in the wake of the reform movement, wrote the first medieval "autobiographies" (Otloh, Guibert, Rupert, Abelard), and much more. Theirs was, in short, an almost unconscious assumption of leadership such as they had exercized in a much more primitive world for nearly two centuries.

19. *Libellus de diuersis ordinibus* 2: ed. Constable and Smith 18–45; cf. Jacques Dubois, "Les moines dans la société du moyen âge," *Revue d'histoire de l'église en France* 60 (1974) 5–37.

20. Adalbero of Laon's *Carmen ad Rotbertum regem*, in *Recueil des Historiens de la France* 10.67ff; and J. Leclercq and J. P. Bonnes, *Un maître de la vie spirituelle au XIe siècle* (Etudes de théologie et d'histoire de la spiritualité 9, Paris 1946) 195.

The same held true *a fortiori* for monastic involvement in intellectual life. In Italy, where the newer trends in economy and culture first became evident, Peter Damian complained that monks (not just clerics!) were now learning law in the public courts.[21] An Italian monk (Gratian) was to prepare the standard textbook on canon law in the 1130's, and an English monk a generation later one of the first "case-books of a common lawyer."[22] Likewise, the *Sententiae magistri A.*, a most influential early theological handbook, originated with an English monk; Dom Abelard incorporated numerous theological "questions" into his *Commentary on the Epistle to the Romans*; and another religious wrote the first scholastic commentary on a Gospel (the *Enarrationes in Matthaeum* formerly ascribed to Anselm of Laon).[23] Indeed, both Anselm and Abelard, the two intellectual giants of the new theology, wrote all their important works as Black Monks.

Rupert never attended one of the new schools, but he followed the development of scriptural study and fully endorsed the older Augustinian program. Learning (*scientia*) he considered a divine blessing, one of the seven gifts of the Spirit, though it was not to be confused with the true wisdom (*sapientia*) found in Christ alone. The seven maidens representative of the liberal arts were wanton and garrulous until brought under the severe *magisterium* of the Word and compelled to focus upon elucidating the Creator and his creation. Wanton maidens chasing about after their own self-indulgent interests—such was Rupert's view of arts teachers (such as dialecticians) not bound by Holy Scripture. But the arts could and should be applied to the understanding of Scripture; his own description of how that might be done proved among the most elaborate and progressive of the early twelfth century, anticipating the later work of the schools.[24]

21. *Epist.* 1.15: PL 144.227.

22. Thus Eleanor Searle, ed., *The Chronicle of Battle Abbey* (Oxford 1980) 1. Cf. Southern (n. 12 above) 271.

23. Reinhardt, *AHDL* 36 (1969) 33; Smalley, *RTAM* 45 (n. 11 above) 166–75 and 46 (n. 18 above) 95–105.

24. *Spir.* 7.2–6, 8, 10: CM 24.2039–44, 2046–47, 2048–49. See Evans (n. 7 above) 57–79 for an extended treatment of this matter in Rupert.

Moreover, if those learned in the liberal arts, here compared to the woman at the well, offered what they had to Christ, that is, used it to repel heretics and to edify the faithful, He in turn would give them living water, that is, an ever deeper understanding of Holy Scripture so that after amusing instruction (*leuioribus*) in the arts they might not only read and comprehend the received tradition but also become themselves a fountain pouring forth things profitable for others.[25]

Rupert's vision of his role as a churchman, a "defender of the ecclesiastical faith, whose tongue was worthy to rebut heretics and edify the Church," was at once traditional and progressive. His defense of the arts and his expectation to write commentaries of his own (*ab aliis utiliter legenda ipsi scriberent*) upset his monastic brethren, who held that learning merely puffed up while charity alone edified (I Cor. 8:1). Rupert responded to his "simpler brethren" that charity and learning must be combined for true wisdom and as such applied to the service of the Church.[26] On the other hand, Rupert's sense that the arts should be bound by the teachings of Scripture and that new interpretations be edifying (*utiliter*) met scornful reproach from student-clerics. In one of his most revelatory remarks, Rupert noted that "today" when someone rises from the bottom and attains sufficient learning to go up to the temple with Christ and speak to the Church, others vex him because he has not traveled hither and yon to study with great masters. They ask, "Who is this?" and "How can this man know anything when he has never been taught?" In response Rupert insisted his teaching was not his own but rested on both Scripture and his divine call to interpret it.[27] With

25. ". . . quos ecclesiasticae fidei defensores habere, quorum lingua contra haereticos uel ad eruditionem ecclesiae suae uti dignaretur, ipse [Christ] egit, ipse prouidit, ut prius artibus liberalibus instruerentur, et in maris periculum ad pugnandum descensuri in nauibus prius quasi circa litora leuioribus ludis exercerentur. Sic etenim acceperunt, sic acquam uiuam biberunt, ut fieret in eis fons . . . idest ut non solum aliorum scripta legerent et intelligerent, sed et ab aliis utiliter legenda ipsi scriberent." *Spir.* 7.9: CM 24.2048.

26. *Spir.* 7.6: CM 24.2043–44. For such suspicion of learning in monasteries, see also Otloh, PL 146.29, 51.

27. *John* 7: CM 9.394. Cf. *RegBen.* 1: PL 170.480.

such adversaries in mind he stated elsewhere that the church-man (*uir ecclesiasticus*) should avoid contentious debate as far as possible, defending the truth of Scripture with moderating reason and in such a way as not to fuel the flames of controversy still further.[28]

This magisterial calling, to defend truth and to refute heretics, required ordination to the priesthood (so much is clear from Rupert's account of his own life) and in some sense the teaching of Scripture. Reiner reported around 1160 that Rupert had taught at St. Lawrence and he named Abbot Wazelinus as one of his former students.[29] Alger referred to Rupert as leading himself and others into ruin by "teaching" and defending false doctrine on the eucharist.[30] Wibald of Corvey came to Liège for schooling, and there met Rupert and read his works.[31] The likelihood is great, in short, that Rupert succeeded his teacher Heribrand, now made prior, as *scholasticus* in the abbey of St. Lawrence.

Rupert would have taught, first of all, the liberal arts, this probably reflected in his elaborate exposition of them in *De sancta Trinitate* as the Spirit's gift of *scientia*. Is it conceivable that he also taught Scripture to brothers in the abbey? His *Commentary on John* certainly bears some marks of a teaching format. The prologue in effect offers an *accessus ad auctorem*: it names the author (*Discipulus quem diligebat Iesus*), the title (*in euangelio suo*), material context (christological heresy and persecution), intent (to bear witness to Christ's divinity), and utility (to help meditate on Christ's divinity) of this book.[32] Book I on the "Word made flesh" reviewed and refuted all ancient christological heresies. At the beginning of Book II Rupert proposed that "three separate matters be considered here" and twenty pages later noted that he had concluded them.[33] The first several books par-

28. *John* 8: CM 9.467.
29. MGH SS 20.595, 597.
30. PL 180.739.
31. Wibald, *Epist.* 1, 295: ed. Jaffé 77, 526.
32. Thus on its central theme, Christ's divinity: "sed huius maxime hoc propositum esse tam causa quam et ipse textus operis manifeste defendit. Causa uidelicet quia. . . . Textus uero operis quia. . . ." CM 9.5.
33. *John* 2: CM 9.57, 75. Again in Book 3: CM 9.128.

ticularly contain numerous such "questions" on theological topics.[34] But his audience was clearly monastic, and the questions
often devotional in cast. At least twice, for instance, he enjoined
readers to "ask themselves" questions which bore on the true
followership of Christ; he discussed whether the continent ought
to attend weddings; and he reminded his brothers that they
should be so intent on heavenly meditation as to forget the terrestrial harvest (a major item of "small talk" in an agrarian
economy).[35]

To conceive of Rupert's *Commentary on John* as theological
exposition in a monastic setting offers several advantages. It explains why he started a large commentary midway through his
major project, something he never did again except once under
duress, and why too he included so many theological matters
expressly, as he had first in the opening books of *De sancta Trinitate*. It might also indicate why this particular commentary immediately attracted attention, and at least in part why Rupert's
pupil Wazelinus later excerpted from this work and no other.[36]
Historically speaking, Rupert's commentary would then represent a transitional stage between monastic efforts to pass on the
Fathers and those full-fledged scholastic commentaries replete
with theological questions which emerged in the early twelfth
century. Rupert himself blurred the distinction between preaching and teaching (*praedicando uel instruendo*),[37] but the first books
of his *Commentary on Genesis*, much of the *Commentary on John*,
and his treatment of the Spirit's works came (in my reconstruction of their chronological order) much closer to the latter.
However that may be, Rupert's desire and vocation to "teach"
the Church, taken either in a general or a more specific sense,

34. He also had a notion of treating them in particular places: "De Spiritu
sancto uel eius operatione propria dicendum erit in aliis huius euangelii locis."
John 5: CM 9.277–78. Cf. Bernards (n. 2 above).

35. *John* 2, 3, 4: CM 9.84, 100, 126, 221.

36. H. Silvestre, "Le *De Concordia et expositione quattuor evangeliorum* inédit
de Wazelin II, abbé de Saint-Laurent, à Liège (ca. 1150–ca. 1157)," *RB* 63
(1953) 310–25.

37. *Is.* 2.27: CM 23.1560.

must be recognized in order to understand the purpose and theme of his Gospel commentary.

Since all theological issues were at base scriptural problems, new disputes should drive would-be theologians to a fresh examination of Scripture; and since in Rupert's view the Spirit's gift of counsel also compelled those who understood the truth of such matters to rouse themselves in behalf of others,[38] he had, given his vocation, little choice. But why, especially given a theological purpose, should he choose to comment on a Gospel rather than the Psalter or Epistles? Just a few years earlier Anselm of Laon had glossed this same Gospel and then together with his brother Ralph had worked on Matthew and Mark; otherwise teaching of the Gospels was unknown.[39] Rupert's thought and piety were always strongly christocentric, but more importantly St. John's Gospel afforded him the opportunity to confront directly false teachings on christology and the eucharist. Indeed, as he had learned elsewhere and stated plainly in the first sentence of his commentary, this Gospel was written specifically to "contend against every heretical depravity."[40]

2

Christ, the Son of God and the Son of Man

The theme of Rupert's *Commentary on John*, from its opening lines (*Itaque non recentem adoramus Deum*) to its very last sentence (*beneuolis auditoribus satis factum est: Iesum esse Christum Filium Dei*) and emphasized everywhere in between, is the full divinity of Christ, at once the Son of God and the Son of Man.[41] From a Bedan sermon for the feastday of the Evangelist, proba-

38. *Spir.* 5.18: CM 24.1998.

39. Smalley (n. 11 above) passim; see also H. Weisweiler, "Paschasius Radbertus als Vermittler des Gedankengutes der karolingischen Renaissance in den Matthäus-Kommentaren des Kreises um Anselm von Laon," *Scholastik* 35 (1960) 363–402, 503–36.

40. *John* 1: CM 9.9.

41. "Tota summa est unum eundemque Christum et ante omnia saecula

bly read in the night office from Paul the Deacon's homiliary, Rupert learned that St. John had written his Gospel to rebut heretics "who denied Christ existed before Mary."[42] This served to describe historical context, as required by *accessus ad auctorem*; but Rupert went on to reassert Christ's divinity again and again, in many traditional ways such as the miracle at Cana and also with new interpretations. Thus the cleansing of the temple, he argued, testified not only to the rejection of the Jews (a traditional view) but also and supremely to the power of Christ's divinity.[43] These reassertions and his vehement attack upon "ancient" christological heresies were aimed in fact at more recent views on Christ's person.

The first dogmatic dispute of the Carolingian era involved a form of adoptionism. Scholars have not yet pursued the echoes of that debate down through the tenth and eleventh centuries, nor have they investigated the degree to which Carolingian formulations may have set the stage for questions hotly debated in the twelfth century. From the later 1120's controversy raged on nearly all matters pertaining to the hypostatic union, so that at mid-century Peter Lombard could summarize three distinct views in his textbook (*Sent.* 3.6). About 1135 Gerhoch of Reichersberg seized upon several of Rupert's ideas in order to join battle with Gilbert of Poitiers and others. But to discover Rupert's likely adversaries and thus to provide a context for the major theme of his *Commentary on John* requires the examination of texts and arguments from the later eleventh century, thus pushing back the known christological debates at least two decades. The views Rupert held suspect, all of which appeared to impugn the full divinity of Christ's person, reached him from at least three distinguishable directions.

Deum uerum exstitisse et uere Filium hominis in fine saeculorum factum esse." *John* 8: CM 9.449.

42. *John* praefatio: CM 9.5. Cf. Bede, *Hom.* 1.9: CC 122.66; see Silvestre (n. 3 above) 372–75, and for the homiliary (not noted by Silvestre), R. Grégoire, *Les homéliaires du moyen âge* (Rome 1966) 81.

43. *John* 3: CM 9.124.

The first source—and the easiest to uncover—had already provoked his work on the Trinity. The dialecticians' assault upon Trinitarian doctrine necessarily affected christology as well, since the concept of a Triune God had been worked out, historically speaking, precisely in order to encompass the conviction that Jesus Christ was also fully God. Indeed, Roscellin claimed he had originally posited three "*res*" in the Trinity just in order to explain and to protect the unique incarnation of the Son; and so also in the 1090's St. Anselm's critique of Roscellin was entitled *De incarnatione Domini*, not *De sancta Trinitate*. Moreover, teachers of dialectic, working their way through the Boethian corpus, would come upon his *Contra Eutychen et Nestorium*, requiring them to comment on the union of Christ's two natures in a way that was at once doctrinal and logical. Thus the same nominalist logic which had divided the Trinity into "three things," when applied to the God-Man would tend to make of Him "two." That St. Anselm, Hugh of St. Victor, the Gilbertine *Sententiae diuinitatis*, and later commentaries on Boethius' tractate all refer to precisely this teaching[44] means it was commonly discussed in the schools from at least 1090 onwards, even though it is not certainly attributable to any known teacher of dialectic except possibly Roscellin.

Near the end of his Trinitarian treatise in *De diuinis officiis* and then early on in his *Commentary on John*, Rupert attacked directly and personally (*tu*) someone who wished to predicate

---

44. Anselm, *De incarnatione Domini* 11: ed. Schmitt 2.28, with a citation of John 1:14; cf. Rupert, *John* 1: CM 9.26–27 (also attacking heretics). Hugh, *De sacramentis* 2.1.9: PL 176.394, quoting John 3:13; cf. Rupert, *John* 3: CM 9.154–55, attacking "Nestorians." What Rupert criticized is very close to that described in *Sent. diuinitatis* 4: ed. Geyer 68 (and sometimes ascribed to Abelard): "Tales hodie multi conantes diuidere Christum et duos Christos ostendere, unum de Deo natum, alterum de uirgine, subtilius Nestorio considerant et dicunt Christum personam esse, sed nec Verbum quod erat in constitutione, nec aliquam de tribus, nec aliam a tribus. Unde colligitur quod Christus nec est persona, nec est Christus. Item si non est Verbum uel Pater aut Spiritus sanctus, ergo non est Deus."

"two" of the God-Man Christ.[45] Echoing Boethius' tractate,[46] he indignantly rejected this as impossible on both theological and dialectical grounds. Even boys, he declared, and especially dialecticians, ought to know that an adjective wants a substantive in agreement and that predication is possible only of a common substance. Yet the only common name in the God-Man is "Christ" or His unique "substance." But one cannot predicate "two" of the God and man in Christ because they are wholly different substances, like a horse and his rider, nor can one have "two Christs," "two substances," or "two persons." This argument followed Boethius quite closely, and yet it is couched in such personal and vehement terms that one is tempted to imagine Rupert addressing his adversary directly, whether he be Roscellin or some local dialectician holding similar views.

Rupert battled these dialecticians on their own ground, but he also—silently—drew upon authorities from the tradition. He paraphrased a text from Ambrose, known to him through Bede or Hincmar and found also in Hugh's *De sacramentis*, which stated clearly that there were not two sons but one and therefore the incarnation did not make a "quaternity" of the Trinity.[47] From Paschasius Radbertus, or a Matthew commentary in that tradition, Rupert also learned that "Christ" is the name of an "office"; therefore, he concluded, it is not a substantial name and nothing can be predicated of it—least of all "two."[48] But Rupert's basic and instinctive response was simply to affirm the absolute unity of Christ, the Son of God and the Son of Man. In so doing he came close to Hugh's position but expressed it less

45. "Cum ergo masculino genere de Christo Deo et homine praedicaueris duos, quod substantiuum huic adiectiuo appones? . . . Quid ergo subicies, cum in Christo Deo et homine praedicaueris duos? Numquid Christos subicies?" *John* 2: CM 9.77. Cf. the very similar *Off.* 11.13: CM 7.384–85.

46. See *Contra Eutychen* 4.34–43: ed. Rand 94ff.

47. *Off.* 11.13: CM 7.384. Cf. Bede's *Commentary on Luke* (CC 120.32), and Hincmar's *De una et non trina deitate* 9: PL 125.553. Hugh, *De sacramentis* 2.1.4: PL 176.380.

48. *Off.* 11.13: CM 7.385; *John* 2: CM 9.77. Cf. Paschasius, *In Matt.* 1: PL 120.44.

cautiously, for more than once he spoke of the "person" of Christ's deity assuming or absorbing (*absorbet uel absumit*) totally the "person" of His humanity.[49]

Many people today, Rupert noted, find this hard and murmur about it. They seek to distinguish between the eternal Word and the incarnate Christ, and so renew the ancient heresy which denied Christ's existence before Mary. Peter Abelard raised precisely this point in a relatively longer distinction of *Sic et Non*,[50] and his school was later to be charged with such a teaching, which, doctrinally speaking, overlooked or simply denied the "communication of idioms." Repeatedly, but especially on the strength of John 3:13, Rupert insisted that the "Son of Man who descended from heaven" was one and the same person as the "Son of God born of the Virgin Mary."[51] Here, as the texts Abelard collected also make clear, Rupert had most of the tradition behind him. But the point at issue was no abstraction; it touched upon the very reality of salvation. For if these "Nestorians" succeeded in dividing the Son of God from the Son of Man, what possible hope of "ascending into heaven" and "becoming like gods" (Ps. 51:6) had any of us lesser sons?[52] And if the Son of Man were actually separated from the Son of God and made to originate in Mary, how could he possibly be worshipped as the equal of, or rather as, God Himself?[53] This last question was not peculiar to the dialecticians: the new masters of the Sacred Page explicitly and the proponents of a new piety implicitly raised this very same issue.

In an apologia written from exile during the spring of 1117, Rupert charged his critics with at least as many heresies as they claimed to have found in his *Commentary on John*. Three of his charges appear to have had specific adversaries in mind (*Ille* . . .

49. *John* 2: CM 9.77. Cf. *De sacramentis* 2.1.9 and Pelikan, *Theology* 61–63.

50. Quaestio 75: ed. Boyer and McKeon 269–73.

51. *John* 3, 7, 9: CM 9.154–55, 403, 516.

52. *John* prologus 3: CM 9.6, 154.

53. See also Abelard, *Sic et Non* 89: "Quod creatura [Christ the man] sit adoranda et non," ed. Boyer and McKeon 311–13. Cf. Lombard, *Sent.* 3.9.

hic . . . Alius . . .), and indeed the circumstances at least, sometimes also the persons, are still discoverable (see chapters IV and
V). His fourth charge, concerning christology, is less specific:
still others (*alii nonnulli*), he reports, contend that Christ's human nature, made a little lower than the angels in His incarnation and passion, never in any way (*nullo modo*) attained equality
with the Godhead.[54] It was evidently this particular teaching,
even more than the unmentioned dialecticians, which elicited
Rupert's ardent defense of Christ's divinity in the form of a new
commentary on St. John's Gospel.

Contrary to Rupert's emphasis upon mere human perver-
sity, however, these christological questions sprang rather from
basic shifts in the intellectual life and piety of Latin Christendom. The new teachers of Scripture insisted upon a good grasp
of the letter, including that of the Gospels, before taking up the
spiritual sense, and laboriously compiled the sometimes contradictory teachings of the Fathers as the basis for their own lectures. The new religious began at the same time to move per-
ceptibly away from the transcendent and victorious image of
Christ, the Lord and Judge depicted on so many abbey churches,
toward a more human Christ, one whose life, passion, and
death they could imitate, identify with, and worship.[55] Rupert
himself was an early witness to this transformation: Christ's
passion had become the focal point of his theology (as we shall
soon see), and his devotion to Christ's cross matched or exceeded the earlier development of that cult in Cluniac monasticism.[56] But there came the rub both for the religious and for
the masters of the Sacred Page. How could the Son of God actu-

54. ". . . alii nonnulli hominem Christum, hominem nouum qui secundum Deum creatus (Eph. 4:24), *et in unitatem personae cum Deo Verbo as-
sumptus* est, quique ante passionem non solum Patre uerum etiam angelis suis
secundum humanitatem minor erat, nullo modo ad *aequalitatem* Dei peruenisse
contendebat [sic!]." CM 9.2–3. Italicized words taken from Ps.-Athanasian
creed: see H. Silvestre, *RHE* 65 (1970) 893.

55. See Pelikan, *Theology* 106–57.

56. *Off.* 6.21: CM 7.202–04; and of his youthful devotions: "complecterer
crucem ligneam et in ea imaginem eiusdem salvatoris." *Matt.* 12: CM 29.369.
On Cluniac devotion to the Holy Cross, see R. G. Heath, *Crux imperatorum
philosophia* (Pittsburgh 1976) 126–43.

ally increase in wisdom, suffer, and finally die?[57] And, most crucially (see n. 53 above), was it permissible to worship Christ the man? Whatever the impact upon Rupert of the monks' new way of perceiving the Lord they worshipped and followed, the teachings of the new masters certainly roused his ire and drove him to set forth the true teachings of the Gospel.

The notion Rupert charged to his adversaries, that the Son of Man in no way attained equality with the Godhead, arose precisely out of the masters' reconsideration of Christ's humanity, especially his mortality.[58] The key texts were Ps. 8:6, Phil. 2:6–10, and Hebr. 2:9–10. Hugh of St. Victor affirmed the absolute unity of God and man in Christ, like Rupert on the basis of John 3:13, and then took up an objection: But you say, how then was God able to die?[59] Two decades earlier Rupert likewise criticized the "fool" who had become so conscious of Christ's suffering humanity as to object "God could not die."[60] The adversaries of Christ, Rupert reports, take as their major proof that He was not God the fact that He suffered death. So also those heretics who contend that Christ originated in Mary and divide Him into "two" attempted thus to explain the obvious "creatureliness" of the Son of Man.[61]

---

57. Abelard's *Sic et Non*, out of a total of 158, has fully twenty questions of this sort (60–82). For instance, Q. 76: "Quod humanitas Christi ignorauerit diem iudicii et non" (see Mk. 13:32); or, perhaps more peculiarly Abelardian, Q. 82: "Quod in Christo suggestio etiam delectationis fuerit et non."

58. A. M. Landgraf, *Dogmengeschichte der Frühscholastik* (Regensburg 1952–56) distinguished four questions which make up basically a single problem for Rupert: "Die Stellungnahme zur Frage, ob Christus ein Geschöpf sei" (2.1.172–98), "Die Sterblichkeit Christi" (2.1.199–272), "Die Stellungnahme zum Adoptianismus" (2.2.7–43), and "Der Kult der menschlichen Natur Christi" (2.2.132–69).

59. "Sed dicis, Quomodo Deus mori potuit?" *De sacramentis* 2.1.9: PL 176.395.

60. ". . . quia solam attendit tribulationem, qua cingi uel constringi potuit uera eius humanitas, et hoc habet scutum cordis, ut uere insipiens dum dicit quia non Deus qui mori potuit [cf. Hugh, n. 59 above!] . . . catholica fides confitetur, quia passibilis quidem homo, sed impassibilis erat, ut semper est, Deus unus idemque Christus." *John* 14: CM 9.759.

61. *John* 10: CM 9.540, 605.

The received tradition down through the Carolingian era had insisted that the Son of Man who suffered and died was the equal of God and therefore fully deserving of worship.[62] But the teachers of Scripture at Laon drew attention to a gloss on Phil. 2, falsely ascribed to Ambrose, which denied to Christ's human nature the "name above every name" and adoration on "bended knee."[63] A gloss on Phil. 2:10 ascribed to Master Bruno of Reims or to the circle of Ralph of Laon (by Landgraf) states very nearly the exact position Rupert criticized: it implies that while Christ's humanity is now king over creation, it is nevertheless not equal to His divinity.[64] And the paraphrase of Ambrosiaster used by Gilbert and others began in a way Rupert may even have echoed, though St. Lawrence apparently also possessed a copy of Ambrosiaster's commentary.[65] The exact text and the particular master or student Rupert had in mind will probably never be identified. It suffices to show that masters of the Sacred Page all around him had, from Rupert's perspective, erred in their attempt to reconcile Christ's passion with His divinity.

Rupert, who had bowed before and embraced a "wooden cross with an image of the Savior" and whose mystical experiences began when the "adored One" on the cross acknowledged His "adorer," reacted instinctively against any thought that the suffering Savior was not also fully God. But as in his treatment of Trinitarian doctrine, so here Rupert sought a solution which em-

62. Texts gathered by Landgraf, "Kult" (n. 58 above) 132–34.

63. Landgraf, "Stellungnahme" (n. 58 above) 9; Classen, *Gerhoch* 94–96.

64. "*Et omnis lingua confiteatur*: Hoc erit in die iudicii, quando uelint nolint Christum regem confitebuntur impii. Confiteantur, dico, quia idest quod Dominus Ihesus est in gloria Dei Patris, id est in equalitate secundum deitatem et post Patrem secundum humanitatem, secundum quam tamen constitutus est rex super omnem creaturam." Landgraf, "Kult" (n. 58 above) 134. The text ascribed to Bruno reads: "idest in equalitate Dei Patris secundum deitatem et post Patrem primus quantum ad humanitatem super omnem creaturam." PL 153.361. The same ambiguity reappears in Bruno's gloss on Hebr. 2: PL 153.498–500. On the author and transmission of this widely known gloss see Stoelen (n. 13 above).

65. "Quibusdam tamen uidetur homini donatum esse nomen quod est super omne nomen, quod nullo genere, nulla ratione conuenit." Landgraf, "Stellungnahme" (n. 58 above) 9. Cf. Rupert's "nullo modo" in n. 54 above.

ployed the concrete images and language of Scripture, warning skeptics to search the Gospel for increasingly evident signs of Christ's divinity, His possession, for instance, of perfect knowledge (one of the disputed questions).[66] In keeping with the received tradition, Rupert taught that Christ passed from a passible to an impassible, a mortal to an immortal state.[67] But reversing the criticism of those who objected that a suffering and an eternal Christ were incompatible, Rupert explained that the Son of Man was elevated to eternity "only by way of His suffering and death."[68] This was in fact the "necessary mode or order of His glorification": the passion or humiliation of the Son of Man had to precede the glory of the very same Son of God so that He received all glory and honor not despite but rather *because of* His passion.[69] Here Rupert quoted Hebr. 2:9 (*Eum autem, qui modico quam angeli minoratus est, uidemus Iesum propter passionem mortis gloria et honore coronatum*), and understood it to mean "Christ's human nature was crowned with a glory and honor it had not possessed."[70] Contrary to those who claimed that the Son of Man, made lower than the angels in His passion, had never attained equality with the Father, Rupert asserted that God exalted Him above the heavens precisely because of (*propter hoc*) His death on the cross, after which (*extunc*) He received the "name above every name" and was "*adored* at the right hand of God."[71] In sum, only after the Son of Man had suffered could the Son of God be recognized, preached, and adored (*adorari*) in His full divine dignity.[72] Or, to make the point still clearer, Rupert declared that before His passion the Son of Man was not

66. *John* 1, 2, 3: CM 9.12–13, 103, 133. Cf. Hugh, *De sapientia animae Christi, an aequalis cum diuina fuerit* (PL 176.845–56). See L. Ott, *Untersuchungen zur theologischen Briefliteratur der Frühscholastik* (BGPT 34, Münster 1937) 351–85.

67. *John* 12: CM 9.677.

68. "Verumtamen ad ipsam aeternitatem non nisi per uiam passonis et mortis ascendat." *John* 10: CM 9.591.

69. *John* 10, 2, 12: CM 9.581, 97, 689. Cf. CM 9.132, 388.

70. "Natura humana gloria et honore quem non habuerat coronata sit." *John* 4: CM 9.219.

71. *John* 4, 6: CM 9.181, 303; *Reg.* 5.14: CM 22.1429–30.

72. *John* 4: CM 9.178.

only not "adored" but also had not yet received "all power on heaven and on earth" (Matt. 28:18).[73] This was a strikingly original position built on a salvational-historical reading of the Gospel. Just fifteen years earlier St. Anselm had cited virtually all the same scriptural texts to argue the exact opposite position, namely that Christ always enjoyed the full adoration and power appropriate to His deity.[74]

To avoid the inevitable charge of adoptionism, Rupert explained that the "power" and the "honor and glory" conferred on the Son of Man came directly from His divine nature (though not until the resurrection, we must note). So there is still only one person of Christ, and there can be no proper talk of "merit." Yet the glorification of the Son of Man was also a glorification of God himself.[75] Indeed, had man not sinned and the Lord not assumed a human nature, He would not now be crowned with so much (*nec tantam quantam nunc habet*) glory and honor as He had gained through His passion.[76]

Comparison to the received tradition as Rupert knew it will further highlight his unusual position. In contrast to Rupert's emphasis upon Christ's passion as the source (*propter quod*) of his glorification, St. Augustine in his *Commentary on John* specifically argued that death as such meant nothing without the resurrection and that the resurrection could not be said to glorify God—another opinion Rupert directly and knowingly contradicted—simply because God is always fully and unchangeably God. Rupert knew this text not only from Augustine's commentary, but also as the Saint's gloss on Phil. 2:9, as compiled in the early ninth century by Florus of Lyon.[77] Haimo's Pauline

73. *Reg.* 1.5: CM 22.1205; *John* 9, 10, 14: CM 9.513, 590, 772.
74. *Cur Deus homo* 9: ed. Schmitt 2.62.
75. *John* 4, 11: CM 9.219, 619; *Reg.* 1.5: CM 22.1205.
76. *Spir.* 2.6: CM 24.1868. This passage was eliminated from earlier editions of Rupert's works: see PL 167.1610.
77. Augustine, *Tract. in Iohannem* 104.2–3: CC 36.602–03 (Florus, PL 119.385). Cf. *John* 11: CM 9.619. St. Lawrence had Florus' work in two volumes (Gessler, "Bibliothèque" 117), and the first, still extant, is from the eleventh century: Bibl. roy. MS 9369–70: van den Gheyn no. 283. For Hebr. 2:9, Florus adopted Augustine's remarks on Ps. 8:6.

commentary may possibly have offered scanty support for Rupert's distinction between the Son of Man and the Son of God and for his emphasis upon the cross.[78] The position Rupert developed at such length may also have been suggested by another isolated Augustinian text Florus copied out for Phil. 2:9.[79] But Rupert himself apparently changed positions on this issue. In *De diuinis officiis*, before he began to grapple with this problem and to write his *Commentary on John*, he stated clearly (like St. Anselm), citing both Phil. 2:9 and Hebr. 2:9, that even before He was glorified Christ (not referred to here as the Son of Man) had already received from the Father His kingdom and power.[80] The distinctions made in his *Commentary on John* were developed therefore in response to the errors propagated by the new teachers of Scripture.

In concentrating so upon the exaltation of Christ's humanity, Rupert always had uppermost in his mind the eventual exaltation of man's humanity. Though he knew and maintained the distinction between the Son by nature and sons by adoptive grace, he placed great emphasis upon the "solidarity" of the Son of Man with all human nature as the only hope for mankind; indeed, the title "Son of Man" brings out the "brotherhood" of man with Christ.[81] The "glory and honor of immortality" which the Son of Man once did not possess, man also can look forward to receiving, so that what the Father conferred upon the

78. On Phil. 2:9, Haimo said: "Quod nomen dedit illi? Ut Filius Dei uocaretur et esset, qui Filius hominis erat . . ." (PL 117.741). On Hebr. 2:9: "Hic aperte manifestat quia gloria et honor Christi crux eius fuit." This work too was found in the abbey: Gessler, "Bibliothèque" 123.

79. Augustine, *Contra Maximinum* 1.5 (Florus, PL 119.385): "Homini donauit ista, non Deo. Neque enim cum in forma Dei esset non excelsus erat aut non ei genua flectebant. [Rupert agreed, but did not emphasize this.] In qua ergo forma crucifixus est, ipsa exaltata est. Ipsi donatum est nomen super omne nomen ut cum ipsa forma Dei nominetur Unigenitus filius Dei" (Rupert developed this part). Notably, this text also appears in Abelard's *Sic et Non* for the question, "Quod creatura sit adoranda et non" (75: ed. Boyer and McKeon 311).

80. *Off.* 9.6: CM 7.313–14.

81. *John* 2, 3: CM 9.116, 155.

Son of Man, the Son of God will upon the sons of men.[82] On this basis Rupert quickly disposed of the question, posed first by Augustine and now again by the schoolmen, as to whether Christ assumed a "new man" or the same human nature as Adam's and ours.[83] Indeed, by the "vehicle of His divinity," Rupert contended, our humanity will be so elevated that adopted sons too may "participate in Him" in the eternal vision of God (*ad aeternitatem reducti consumamur in unum et participatio nostra fit in idipsum*).[84] Thus the christology designed to refute the new masters spoke just as effectively to the new religious sensibilities: imitation of Christ could extend potentially all the way from His suffering through His exaltation to ultimate union with God, and thus the suffering Son of Man be adored all the more for providing the way.

In sum, over against the dialecticians Rupert affirmed the unity (*unus idemque*) of the Son of Man and the Son of God, against the teachers of Scripture the necessity (*necessarius modus uel ordo*) of Christ's mortal passion for His exaltation, and against the background of a new devotion Christ's exemplary progression from suffering Son of Man to glorified Son of God. By combining all these potentially contradictory elements in a new christology based on a fresh explication of St. John's Gospel, Rupert had fulfilled the double mission of educated churchmen, to edify the faithful and confound heretics through the interpretation of Holy Scripture.

The biblical text (Phil. 2:6–10) key to the dispute and to Rupert's interpretation was familiar to every medieval cleric as the repeated verse (*capitulum*) of the divine office prescribed for Holy Week. Its interpretation therefore concerned more than just another random scriptural text; its right interpretation determined someone's view of the passion and the Person who suffered it. Likewise Hebr. 2:9 probably should be understood

---

82. *John* 12: CM 9.707. Cf. Hugh. *De sacramentis* 2.1.2: PL 176.371–73.
83. *John* 3: CM 9.155. See Augustine, *De Trin.* 13.18.23: CC 50.413–14. On this question, see G. R. Evans, *Anselm and a New Generation* (Oxford 1980) 152, and R. Grégoire, *Bruno de Segni* (Spoleto 1965) 264–65.
84. *John* 12: CM 9.708; *John* 3: CM 9.154.

in terms of the concrete visual image Rupert held of the Christ he worshipped and whose import he sought to communicate. That image came very close, in my judgement, to one midway in transition from the early medieval triumphant crucifix (Christ crowned with eyes open and body erect on the cross) to later medieval depictions of Christ in agony. It represents Christ suffering or dead upon the cross (eyes closed and body slightly curved) but with angels or even the hand of God bearing down the crown with which at the passion (*propter quod*) He was made King over creation and given the name above every name before which every knee should bow.[85]

About two decades later Gerhoch of Reichersberg discovered and exploited fully the resources of Rupert's christology.[86] Did anyone else take note of Rupert's contribution and react to it? Alger of Liège began his work on the eucharist, written just after Rupert's commentary (ca. 1117–19), with a chapter on the incarnation, not only as the basis of the eucharist but also and especially in order to treat "foolish" teachings about the Son of God and the Son of Man based on Phil. 2 and Hebr. 2. What "utter fool" (*insipientissimus*), Alger asked rhetorically, has suggested that the *Son of God* was not given the name above every name until after His passion and exaltation? To set the record straight Alger cited exactly the Augustinian glosses on Phil. 2:9 compiled by Florus, but like Augustine himself put no emphasis at all upon the sense of change in Christ's humanity potentially suggested therein. Rupert, it is true, had ascribed that change to the Son of Man, but he was sometimes wanting in caution, so that at least once he said plainly the "humiliation of the Son of Man preceded the glory of the Son of God" (see nn. 69 and 72 above). Alger's own preferred formula was more abstract, left

85. An example in ivory from Liège (now in Tongern) can be found in *Rhein und Maas: Kunst und Kultur 800–1400* (Cologne 1972–73) 2.220. It and several other examples in P. Thoby, *Le Crucifix des origines au Concile de Trent* (Nantes 1959) pl. XXIV–XXV.

86. Classen, *Gerhoch* 92–93 noted Rupert's influence but not his own polemical intent. Gerhoch's titles, *De glorificatione Filii hominis* and *De gloria et honore Filii hominis*, were very "Rupertian."

no room for a notion of growth, and apparently ascribed worship to Christ from the moment of His incarnation.[87] At least the leading master in his own city, in other words, perceived and criticized Rupert's attempt at new christological formulations. Hugh of St. Victor also criticized a position similar to Rupert's, but this one emphasized the *merit* of Christ's passion, which is not how Rupert normally expressed it.[88] In all likelihood Rupert's commentary never reached the scriptural masters at Laon, Reims, and Paris for whom it was partly intended.

3

Christ's Passion, the Holy Spirit, and Sacramental Grace

The eleventh-century reformers revolted against an established order in which Church and society, at least since Carolingian times, had become so interwoven that lay magnates appointed most of the priests and prelates and anointed kings assumed responsibility for upholding the sacred order. To destroy in a generation or two a world order built up over centuries, the reformers attacked with a combination of weapons, only the first of which has received adequate scholarly attention. To mount their offensive against kings and princes they formed ranks behind a revitalized Roman papacy championed as the unique source of authority in the Church, an office held in the place not just of St. Peter but of Christ Himself. The jurisdictional and even political thrust given thereby to the doctrine of Roman primacy rapidly gained general acceptance, and was never seriously challenged in principle or practice (outside a few heretical groups) until the Great Schism and the Protestant Revolt. But this alone could not have carried the day for the reformers. To their espousal of Roman primacy they brought an essentially sectarian mentality, convinced that outside the Ro-

87. *De sacramentis* 1.1: PL 180.743.
88. *De sacramentis* 2.1.6: PL 176.384–87.

man (that is, the newly reformed) Church there was no grace, no sacraments, no salvation; and this, as much as or more than the oft-studied political confrontation, lent the reform movement its real fighting spirit.[89] In 1059 simony, broadly defined as lay investiture, was pronounced heresy, and *ipso facto* countless priests and prelates in Latin Christendom found themselves at least in principle outside the Church with their sacramental powers declared suspect or, more often, null and void. Every major eleventh-century reform pope from Leo IX to Urban II ordered or performed reordinations. In 1075 Pope Gregory VII additionally enjoined the people to avoid and even physically to reject masses said by married or concubinate priests. Many instinctively agreed that hands which had touched a woman should not and *could not* consecrate the Body of Christ (after all, laymen had to abstain from intercourse simply in order to receive communion), and violent riots broke out in several places, compounding the troubled situations which already existed in Milan and Florence (to name just two well-studied instances).

This sectarian revolt against the established Church in the name of Rome quickly reproduced itself in particular localities. Numerous imperial bishoprics were rent in two: "purist" parties of reformers, often monks but also striking combinations of religious and townsmen (especially in Italy), separated themselves from the heretical (i.e. simoniac) pseudo-Church, while maintaining close communion with the Roman Church through papal legates and friendly bishops in nearby territories. By 1090— just as Peter Damian had predicted—the Church was in such chaos and doubts about sacramental efficacy were so rampant that Urban II, the reformers' pope, had to set down guidelines for determining which sacraments were valid and which invalid. These he based theologically on Augustine's argument against the Donatists (as historians have been quick to point out), but ecclesiastically on the one true *Roman Church* as the only valid source of sacramental grace (this emphasis usually

89. To substantiate and nuance this argument would require much more space than can be devoted to it in this book.

not appreciated in context). He ruled: priests ordained by ex-communicated bishops (meaning here, bishops of the imperial party) could remain in holy orders only if the bishop once belonged to the "Catholic" Church, if neither the priest's ordination nor the bishop's consecration involved any form of simony, and if there were signs of a godly life; but such persons could never be promoted beyond the priesthood.[90] This he considered a concession in "troubled times." For the rest, anyone who obtained office simoniacally or was ordained by an excommunicated bishop of the imperial party would not be granted this concession (*nullatenus hac uenia dignus habeatur*); the ordinations of such were null and void (*irritas, nullas umquam uires optinere*).[91] Pope Urban meant it, and commanded reordinations, one such order being preserved only in a St. Lawrence manuscript.[92] Rupert followed this general ruling when he refused to receive ordination from Otbert, excommunicated by Pope Urban at Piacenza. Following the death of Henry IV and the anti-popes, Paschal II moved quickly to end the schism and receive back the excommunicated bishops, requiring only that they swear loyalty to him, the one true Roman pope. This Bishop Otbert eventually did. Not to require as well a new "laying on of hands"—which Otbert might well have refused in any case—was a gesture of peace in extraordinary times, based perhaps on the theological arguments of Bernold's *De reordinatione uitanda*.[93]

90. JL 5393: PL 151.306–07. Repeated at the Council of Piacenza (1095) in canon 10: MGH Leges 4.1.562.

91. Piacenza, canons 2, 4, 8, 11: MGH Leges 4.1.561–63. L. Saltet, *Les réordinations* (Paris 1907); A. Schebler, *Die Reordinationen in der 'altkatholischen' Kirche* (Bonn 1936; repr. Amsterdam 1963). This issue is still badly confused by essentially confessional considerations, that is, the desire to ascribe to the reformers greater clarity on the objectivity of the sacramental order than they in fact possessed or for that matter were interested in. When they attacked ordinations performed by simoniac bishops as "*irrita*," they were not interested in making fine distinctions between "invalid" and "illicit"; they meant they were null and void, hence the reordinations.

92. JL 5442: see *Studia Gratiana* 15 (1972) 84–85.

93. U. R. Blumenthal, *The Early Councils of Pope Paschal II* (Studies and Texts 43, Toronto 1978) 32–73. Bernold's work in MGH LdL 2.150–56.

The canonists, the new spokesmen for the reform party now become the corporate Roman Church, never gave up in the twelfth century their strong conviction that only those in communion with Rome could confer or receive valid orders.

Once the initial schism had ended in 1106 (when Rupert too was finally ordained), the dispute moved largely to a theoretical level, that is, the reconstitution, on the hard-won base of the Roman Catholic Church, of an objective sacramental order. Those who clung to (Gerhoch of Reichersberg, for instance) or pursued further (Tanchelm, Henry of Lausanne) the sectarian, purist impulse which had inspired the early reformers suddenly found themselves at odds with the institutional Roman Church and in some instances condemned as heretics. Though much of the discussion became increasingly canonistic in orientation there lay behind the reformers' convictions and actions presuppositions about the Church and her sacraments which demanded consideration and better grounding. Rupert was one of the very few reformers who undertook this essentially theological task.

Utter loyalty to the Roman Church and sectarian rejection of the established Church describe almost exactly Rupert's stance in exile and in Liège over fifteen formative years of his early life (1092–ca. 1108). Even after Otbert was reconciled with Rome and Rupert ordained, the issues continued to simmer. Sometime between his ordination and his exile at Siegburg (late 1116), for instance, Rupert composed a separate treatise condemning the marriage of priests.[94] Unfortunately, this work has been lost, so neither its occasion nor contents are known.[95] Pope Gregory had charged that concubinage was a problem in Liège, and Sigebert

---

94. Reiner, MGH SS 20.596. Cf. Rupert, *John* 2: CM 9.97 (a reference to this heresy).

95. In a twelfth-century manuscript of St. Trond (now Liège, Bibl. univ. MS 230), D. de Bruyne discovered and published "Un traité inédit contre le mariage des prêtres," *RB* 35 (1923) 246–54, which C. Dereine, *Les chanoines réguliers au diocèse de Liège avant Saint Norbert* (Brussels 1952) 98 thought might be Rupert's lost work. Despite several striking similarities in language and thought, the weight of the evidence (differing citations of Scripture, for instance) leans against the ascription.

of Gembloux had prepared a defense, not of clerical marriage, but at least of those priests' sacramental powers. More striking still, St. Lawrence possessed a copy of Ps.-Ulrich's *Letter*, the most prominent apology for clerical marriage to come out of the reform era; and this may well have been the object of Rupert's critique.

His true inclination or calling, however, was that of a theologian rather than an activist. Twenty years after postponing his ordination Rupert explained and justified that action by citing a parable (John 15:1–4). So long as the vine is still connected to the branch, that is to say, a minister of the sacraments is still joined to the whole Church (*in concione uniuersitatis*), what he does is valid (*ratum*); but once the vine is cut off, that is, the minister publicly condemned and excommunicated (as Otbert was), his acts have only the appearance of piety and no efficacy (*uirtutem*) whatsoever.[96] So also in the *Commentary on John*: every word and every sacrament of those cut off from Christ and the unity of the faith is dead (*mortuum*), so that whatever they may appear to do or to sacrifice will only infect and pollute.[97] Nearly every strict reformer from Cardinal Humbert down to Rupert and beyond supported this view. But it is not quite accurate to say, as most historians have, that this merely represented a revival of "Donatism." Rupert clearly, and most other reformers too, taught that Christ actually administers the sacraments, so that prelates and priests are only "channels" (*canales*), not sources or fonts, of sacramental grace.[98]

What distinguished the reformers was their notion of an almost palpable grace which flowed only inside the reformed Roman Church. With virtually no notion as yet of sacramental "character"[99] (Rupert said simply that in the case of baptism

96. *Matt.* 12: CM 29.381.

97. *John* 11: CM 9.651; cf. ibid 68; *Levit.* 1.32: CM 22.843.

98. *John* 2: CM 9.67. This image appears to be Rupert's own; Augustine's commentary has another image Rupert also used (*serui*), but not the more material one closer to Rupert's own conception.

99. N. M. Häring, "Character, Signum und Signaculum," *Scholastik* 30 (1955) 481–512 and 31 (1956) 41–69.

God's name could not be invoked again), the whole power (*uir-tus*) of the sacrament consisted in the grace it conferred, and that grace was identified almost completely with the Holy Spirit (as we saw already in Rupert's "third age"). The Holy Spirit, in Rupert's words, is the arbiter and author of all the sacraments.[100] But, as every reformer insisted and Rupert declared in a chapter title, the Holy Spirit—here compared to a fountain whose water (grace) flows through channels—is not conferred (*non datur*) outside the Catholic Church; only bishops inside the Church and in the direct line of the apostles can "give the Holy Spirit."[101] Another image Rupert often used was that of the oil trickling down Aaron's beard (Ps. 132:2), that is, the grace of the Spirit flowing through the apostles and ministers of the Church.[102] Such teachings, Rupert claimed, were found "everywhere in the books of the Fathers" and he paraphrased a text from Leo the Great found in the *Collection in 74 Titles*.[103] But the Fathers, whose position on this was not quite so pointed as Humbert, Rupert, and others suggested, presupposed a broad, inclusive notion of the Catholic Church; Rupert and the strict reformers meant the Roman Catholic Church newly purged of simoniacs and immoral priests. What this did to sacramental efficacy is self-evident: for those sacraments which chiefly conferred the Spirit's grace (baptism, confirmation, ordination), the same ones later said to imprint a sacramental "character," returning heretics had to have "hands laid on" in order to receive the grace of the Spirit not conferred outside the Catholic Church. This was in effect to redo the sacrament, as many of the reformers' critics pointed out, and eventually it was stopped or reinterpreted as a "gesture of reconciliation." In the case of the eucharist there

100. *Off.* 10.18: CM 7.353; *John* 2: CM 9.68. So also Humbert, *Adversus simoniacos* 2.2: MGH LdL 1.140.

101. *Off.* 10.25: CM 7.361 (likewise the very first argument in Humbert's work: MGH LdL 1.100–01). *John* 7: CM 9.409.

102. *Off.* 1.22: CM 7.18–19; *Levit.* 2.4: CM 22.858–59. Cf. Augustine, *Enarr. in Ps.* 132.7–9: CC 40.1931–33.

103. Leo, *Epist.* 159.7, in *Diversarum Patrum sententiae* 221, ed. J. Gilchrist (Vatican City 1973) 139. Cf. *Off.* 10.25: CM 7.361.

could obviously be no consecration without the Holy Spirit, and so rather than a sacrifice theirs was only a blasphemous, polluting mockery.[104]

Rupert never altered his tough stand on sacramental validity. Indeed, the most progressive arguments for an objective sacramental order to come out of this era, those by Alger of Liège, were directed largely against him.[105] Instead Rupert explored at length, especially in his *Commentary on John*, two matters basic to the reformers' position: What is the nature of this grace of the Spirit which flows only through the sacraments of the Roman Catholic Church? And what is the ultimate source of it? In so doing Rupert acted chiefly out of his own experience and convictions, but he anticipated thereby both questions and answers later to become standard in the scholastic analysis of sacramental grace.[106]

To speak of those who "have" and those who "do not have" the Spirit's grace, as the reformers did, is to make of that grace and indeed potentially of the Spirit Himself a kind of object. So also historians of theology have frequently pointed to a shift during this era from grace understood essentially as "action" towards the scholastic notion of a "permanent habit."[107] Hugh of St. Victor, for instance, was the first to describe sacraments metaphorically as "medicine bottles" containing grace dispensed by priest-physicians.[108] When, as with Rupert and most early medieval theologians, sacramental grace was still identified so closely with the action of the Holy Spirit,[109] efforts to "objectify" or to "contain" that grace could become disastrous for the

104. *Levit.* 1.32: CM 22.843.

105. N. M. Häring, "A Study in the Sacramentology of Alger of Liège," *Mediaeval Studies* 20 (1958) 68–77, who overlooked the connection to Rupert.

106. Noted only, so far as I know, by Séjourné, in *DTC* 14.187–88.

107. Z. Alszeghy, *Nova creatura: La nozione della grazia nei commentari medievali di S. Paolo* (Analecta Gregoriana 81, Rome 1956), whose conclusion (pp. 259–65) cites other studies with similar views.

108. Hugh, *De sacramentis* 1.9.4: PL 176.323.

109. Just one typical example from Rupert: "Spiritus, quia gratis datur immo ipsa gratia est." *Off.* 9.3: CM 7.308.

doctrine of the Holy Spirit. That Rupert was later charged with heresy on this score will come as no surprise.

Rupert worked out his basic position already in *De diuinis officiis.* By way of introduction he declared that standard interpretations of the key texts (John 7:39, 16:7), meaning St. Augustine's in his *Sermons on John* and St. Gregory the Great's in his twenty-sixth homily on the Gospels, were weak (*infirma*) and failed to do justice to the majesty of the Spirit's gift.[110] Rupert refined his view in his *Commentary on John*, repeated it regularly thereafter, and defended it from attack at the end of his life. Both St. Augustine and St. Gregory had noted that the Spirit was given (*data*) twice, once by Christ after His resurrection (John 20:22–23: *insufflauit, et dixit eis: Accipite Spiritum sanctum; quorum remiseritis peccata, remittuntur eis, et quorum retinueritis, retenta sunt*), and then again at Pentecost; and this was done, they concluded, to teach and to inspire love of God and love of man.[111] Rupert's remarks occasionally reflected this teaching, but from early on he substantivized this into two different "givings" (*data*) understood as two distinct forms of the Spirit's grace—as Dom Séjourné noted, roughly comparable to the *gratia gratum faciens* and *gratiae gratis datae* of scholastic theology.[112] Rupert identified the second gift with the "diversity of graces" (*diuisio gratiarum*) of I Cor. 12:4ff conferred, salvation-historically, at Pentecost and sacramentally at confirmation. In practice this represented a largely traditional notion of the Spirit's independent gracious activity in both the Old and the New Dispensations.

Rupert's more distinctive contribution toward defining sacramental grace hinged upon his understanding of the Spirit's first gift (*datum*) in the form of "remission of sins." To distinguish this *new* role or task, the Spirit was given a new name, the Paraclete, which, Rupert held, following a suggestion of St. Augus-

110. *Off.* 9.2: CM 7.302.
111. Augustine, *Tract. in Iohannem* 32.6–8, 74.2: CC 36.302–05, 513–14; *De Trin.* 15.26.46: CC 50A.525; Gregory, *Hom. Evang.* 26.34: PL 76.1198–99.
112. Rupert's earliest exposition is *Off.* 9.3: CM 7.307; then *Gen.* 4:23: CM 21.308, 309; cf. *Num.* 1.13: CM 22.931. See Séjourné (n. 106 above).

tine and St. Gregory, meant *consolator*. But what greater consolation is there than the remission of sins, the regenerating grace
through which man ceases to be a child of wrath?[113] Rupert thus
identified justifying grace with the person of the Holy Spirit, a
concept requiring, as he saw, that this sanctifying Spirit "dwell
in" baptized believers, though never so fully and eternally as He
did in Christ upon whom the plenitude of the Spirit descended;
and this, he held, was necessarily so because only a divine Spirit
could penetrate and infuse Himself into the human spirit, a notion borrowed from John Cassian.[114] But clearly such sanctifying or redeeming grace was produced by Christ's sacrifice on
the cross. Hence Rupert's crucial reinterpretation of John 16:7
(*expedit uobis ut ego uadam: si enim non abiero, Paracletus non ueniret
ad uos; si autem abiero, mittam eum ad uos*). To St. Augustine and
St. Gregory this suggested that the apostles would not cultivate
a spiritual love unless Christ were bodily absent (thus referring
to the ascension). But how, Rupert objected, could they have
any love at all without redeeming grace? In other words, unless
Christ "departed" by way of His suffering and death, the Paraclete, the remission of sins, could not be given or sent.[115] This
interpretation Rupert saw confirmed in John 7:39 (*nondum enim
erat Spiritus datus quia Iesus nondum erat glorificatus*), which became the text he cited most often on this matter. St. Augustine,
in his commentary, had noted that after Christ's *resurrection*, and
again at Pentecost, the Spirit was given to the assembled apostles, but the only new, distinguishing mark was the gift of speaking in tongues.[116] Here Rupert disagreed, and to do so he drew

113. This definition is crucial to Rupert's argument. "Quo nomine [Para-
cletus = Consolator] nusquam antehac appellatus inuenitur, quia uidelicet
quamuis ueteribus sanctis et ipsis ante passionem Christi apostolis datus fuerit
[Holy Spirit], non sic ulli datus erat ut deberet appellari Paracletus, nec enim in
remissionem peccatorum fuerat datus antequam glorificaretur Iesus." *John* 11:
CM 9.635–36. Cf. *Spir.* 3.10: CM 24.1914–15.

114. First attempt to work this out in *Off.* 10.6, 10, 20–21: CM 7.335–38,
343–44, 354–57. For Cassian, see *Collationes* 7: CSEL 13.191.

115. First in *Off.* 9:3: CM 7.304; then *John* 12: CM 9.676–78; *Spir.* 2.19:
CM 24.1885. Very bluntly in *Exod.* 3:19: CM 22.710: "nisi Christus per passionem hinc abisset, ad nos . . . paracletus iste non uenisset."

116. *Tract. in Iohannem* 32.6: CC 36.302–03.

upon an essential aspect of his christology. Christ was glorified because He suffered sacrificial death on the cross, and the Spirit by which we are made sons of grace was given only after and because of His sacrificial atonement.[117] For Rupert the Holy Spirit as Paraclete or "remission of sins" represented sacramental grace, or, put in the reformers' terms, that effective sacramental grace conferred upon the faithful only within the Church.[118]

Rupert appears to be among the first to have worked out the main lines of the later scholastic doctrine *"de gratia capitis"*—as only Yves Congar, it seems, has noted.[119] Even Hugh of St. Victor, who shared many of Rupert's ecclesiological concerns and also attempted to define the work of restoration as much as possible in relation to Christ's sacraments, did not go so far in anticipating scholastic doctrine on the origins and nature of that grace. But to make sacramental grace and the Holy Spirit, at least in one aspect of His work, virtually interchangeable could pose dangers for the doctrine of His person. The "sending" (*missio*) of the Spirit at Pentecost, for instance, Rupert judged simply a visible extension of His "invisible procession."[120] Still more remarkably, Rupert argued only infidels would doubt that the "diversity of graces" might be considered the procession from the Father (that is, the Spirit's activity in the Old and the New Dispensations) and the "remission of sins" the procession from the Son (that is, the sacramental grace generated by Christ's sac-

117. "Porro hic Spiritus sanctus nulli in remissionem peccatorum nisi per Christi sanguinem datur." *Levit.* 1:14: CM 22.820. Cf. nn. 119, 121 below.

118. In the summary of his book on the sacraments: "Glorificato Domino Iesu et in ipsa eius glorificatione conditis salutis nostrae sacramentis . . . datus est continuo Spiritus." *Spir.* 4.1: CM 24.1938. A more concrete summary: "Duobus modis uobis appropinquabit [Spirit], quia paraclesim suam uidelicet remissionem peccatorum uisibilibus operando sacramentis apud uos manebit, idest numquam ecclesiastico conuentui deerit, et priuatam uel propriam cuique infundendo gratiam in uobis erit, etsi non semper manebit." *John* 11: CM 9.637.

119. "Ab hinc illa passione glorificata est de uentre eius [cf. John 7:38] . . . idest de profunda diuinitate eius coeperunt fluere duo uiuae acquae flumina, idest huius sancti Spiritus duo data. . . ." *John* 7: CM 9.410. See Y. Congar, *L'église de saint Augustin à l'époque moderne* (Paris 1970) 162 n. 29.

120. *John* 12: CM 9.671–72.

rificial death, which "first proceeded" (*illinc extunc processisse*) from His passion![121]

Once Rupert's interpretation of the Holy Spirit as the "remission of sins" is understood, its application to the sacraments follows straightforwardly. This grace which originated in Christ's passion was conferred upon the apostles and their successors when He breathed out the Holy Spirit upon them after His resurrection (John 20:22–23) and charged them with the power of remitting sins.[122] Rupert specifically rejected the widespread view that Christ "ordained" His apostles when He sent them to cast out devils, to preach, and so forth (Luke 9:1–6). For this was impossible: all ecclesiastical ordinations, especially the remitting of sins, wherein sacerdotal power ultimately consists, as gifts of the Spirit were necessarily founded in Christ's passion and conferred only after it through the apostles and their successors.[123] John the Baptist could not yet confer the Spirit, and his baptism consequently was only of "penance" with no power to grant the saving grace of the Spirit, since indeed before Christ there was no priest at all who could confer the Holy Spirit.[124]

Rupert applied this idea very concretely to baptism as well. Since the justifying grace of baptism could not be conferred until after the passion, the ancient faithful departed were held in limbo until the blood from Christ's side dripped down to cleanse them for transport into heaven.[125] Rupert's peculiar variation on the "Harrowing of Hell" emphasizes the grace produced by Christ's sacrifice and the need of the ancients physically to be "baptized" in it. His approach necessarily undermined the import of circumcision for anything other than promissory or figurative value, a position he defended at length in one of his

---

121. *Spir.* 1.28: CM 24.1855–56.

122. *John* 14: CM 9.771–73; *Reg.* 1.24: CM 22.1233.

123. *John* 2, 7: CM 9.60–70, 409–12.

124. *John* 1, 2: CM 9.47, 60, 61: ". . . non haberent [ancient Israelites] sacerdotem, qui Spiritum sanctum dare posset, cuius gratia uera et sola peccatorum remissio est" (9.61).

125. *John* 3: CM 9.140, 143–44; and *Gen.* 4.1: CM 21.281. Rupert's most synthetic treatment of the baptismal sacrament in *Spir.* 3.2–17: CM 24.1905–25. His first statement of it in *Off.* 6.15: CM 7.197, where he claims his teaching "Non est nouum hoc aut mirum."

"questiones."[126] There is in all this a concreteness which springs partly from Rupert's scriptural, salvation-historical approach to theological issues, and partly from his emphasis, as a reformer, upon the sacraments as the only and necessary means of receiving the Spirit's grace. At the end of his question on circumcision Rupert reasserted that heretics cannot and will not receive the grace of the sacrament until they return to the unity of the Church and the Holy Spirit is conferred upon them (without, however, repeating the baptismal rite).

In keeping with early medieval tradition, reflected also in Hugh's *De sacramentis*, Rupert spoke normally of two or three chief sacraments (baptism, [confirmation,] and the eucharist), whereby "ecclesiastical ordinations" were considered the divinely instituted administration of those sacraments, not themselves (either priestly ordination or episcopal consecration) "sacraments" in this narrowest sense of the term. Coming directly after the sacraments in his *De operibus Spiritus sancti*, and of virtually equal importance in his own religious life, was the reading, understanding, and preaching of the Word. Accordingly the same scheme was applied here: until Christ was glorified and the Spirit given, the apostles and their successors—not to speak of their "blind" predecessors—enjoyed no true spiritual understanding whatsoever of the mysteries of Scripture.[127] But Rupert linked the gift of "understanding" to Pentecost, making it one of the "diverse gifts" and thus not one conferred equally on all—something Rupert found eminently true in his own experience. Likewise, the gift of "fortitude" to face martyrdom or to preach boldly was given only after Christ's passion and only to a few.[128]

Even as in his new christological formulations, Rupert's treatment of sacramental grace was grounded in a fresh interpretation of Scripture, in concrete visual images (for instance, of

126. *John* 3: CM 9.140–46. Cf. A. M. Landgraf, "Die Wirkungen der Beschneidungen," in *Dogmengeschichte* (n. 58 above) 3.1.61–108.

127. "Libri namque aperti sunt, quando Spiritus sanctus per Christi passionem datus est hominibus, per quem aperta et intelligibilia facta sunt mysteria Scripturarum." *Reg.* 3.4: CM 22.1298. *Spir.* 4.1–2: CM 24.1938–39.

128. *Spir.* 6.7: CM 24.2016.

Christ's blood flowing down onto Adam's skull or into the chalice), and in a new piety. The cult later to be called devotion to the Sacred Heart apparently originated among Benedictine monks, and Rupert must be reckoned among its earliest representatives.[129] Characteristically, he gave this form of piety a salvation-historical and theological dimension quite beyond its more subjective and spiritual origins.

Generations of intellectual and religious leadership exercised by Black Monks had emboldened Rupert to take upon himself the task of teaching the faithful and refuting heretics. Whether or not he was himself a master in the abbey, he presumed to address secular masters as at least their equal. A religious dedicated to the followership of Christ, Rupert considered himself in a far better position to interpret Scripture and to set forth its christological teaching than any secular master. As a Benedictine theologian, he set out to provide scriptural grounds for the radical reforms undertaken by monk-popes. In all this, whether explicitly "going beyond" the seven-hundred-year-old interpretations of Augustine or implicitly responding to the teachings of the new masters, Rupert acted without hesitation or apology.

Rupert's firm stand on sacramental validity and his theological rationale for it gained at least one adherent. Gerhoch of Reichersberg borrowed heavily from Rupert in developing his views on this subject, which would have suffered condemnation in 1130 at Regensburg had not Bishop Cuno, Rupert's former patron, intervened.[130] Moreover, an unidentified letter found in a north German manuscript (Wolfenbüttler 782) echoed many of the same scriptural texts and positions Rupert had emphasized.[131] Back in Liège Alger reacted very negatively to Rupert's views on this subject, and the commentary itself caused a furor (chapter IV, parts 3 and 4).

---

129. J. Leclercq, "Le sacré-coeur dans la tradition Bénédictine au moyen âge," in *Cor Jesu* (Rome 1959) 2.3–28.

130. Classen, *Gerhoch* 47–57.

131. MGH LdL 3.12–20.

But outside Liège and Regensburg Rupert's *Commentary on John* remained almost unknown. It never entered the *Ordinary Gloss*, as did excerpts from his Genesis commentary, nor attracted the Victorines' attention, as did his *De diuinis officiis*. For this there are several possible reasons. Its near condemnation in Liège and Rupert's permanent departure soon thereafter may have closed off avenues of transmission to the south and west (except one mid-twelfth-century copy from an abbey in distant Cognac, now in Solesmes). The other three extant copies can be traced back either to Cologne–Deutz (Helmstedt, subject to Werden) or to Regensburg (Admont, Klosterneuburg).

More important, and in confirmation of the general argument of this chapter, Rupert's commentary evidently fell between two audiences. It was still far too contemplative in orientation to meet the needs of the schoolmen, and yet too "theological" to inspire his confreres, who were much more attracted by the meditational style of his commentaries on the Apocalypse, the Minor Prophets, and the Song of Songs. Nevertheless, in considering the origins of theology as a discipline—that is, the teaching of Holy Scripture and its divine truths—and in evaluating the contribution thereto of the Black Monks, Rupert's *Commentary on John* deserves attention, for it reveals much about the place between two worlds in which the Black Monks found themselves. In addition to christology and sacramental grace Rupert's commentary also took on the much debated question of eucharistic theology, and that very nearly brought his career as a scriptural theologian to a sudden and ignominious end.

APPENDIX

The Chronology of
De sancta Trinitate
and the
Commentary on John

In two chronologically ordered lists of his works Rupert placed the *Commentary on John* (hereafter: *John*) before *De sancta*

Trinitate (hereafter: *Trin.*),[1] and indeed in *Trin.* 36 (this work has 42 books in all) he referred back to his treatment of the eucharist in *John* 6–7 (14 books in all).[2] Moreover, *John* was completed before his trial in the fall of 1116 (chapter IV, part 3) and probably already by summer (chapter V, part 2). *Trin.*, Rupert tells us specifically, was "brought out" (*ad auditum publicum procedit*) at Siegburg in 1117.[3] Since his remarks on the eucharistic (note 2, which comes late in the work) and predestinarian issues all reflect the *pre-trial* state of the question, and since *Trin.* 39 concludes with a homily on St. Lawrence presumably written still in Liège, the work must have been finished in nearly all respects by mid-November 1116, when he went into exile.

It is much more difficult and important to determine when Rupert began these works. The point of the argument to follow is that Rupert began first to write *Trin.* even though he finished it after *John*. The prologue of *Trin.* is very close to a passage in the penultimate book of *Off.*,[4] and the eucharistic theology of *Trin.* 6 and *Trin.* 11 echoes or elaborates upon Rupert's original stand in *Off.*[5] Then suddenly in *Trin.* 12 and *Trin.* 14[6] he acknowledges problems regarding eucharistic theology which were to be argued out at length in *John* 6–7 and summarized, with reference back to *John*, in *Trin.* 33[7] and *Trin.* 36. So also with christology, the major theme of *John*. In *Trin.*, apart from vague references in books 9 and 12, there is no explicit treatment of the issue and especially of the relevant texts (Phil. 2:6–11) until *Trin.* 13, followed by expanded discussion of

---

1. *RegBen.* 1: PL 170.489; CM 7.3.
2. CM 24.1934.
3. CM 21.120, 122. Cf. Bischoff, *Controversy* 123–27.
4. *Off.* 11.17; CM 7.389–91 (see p. 78 above).
5. To *Trin.* 6.32: CM 21.410, cf. *Off.* 2.2 (the "quomodo est" and the Spirit's work), 2.4 (silence at consecration); to *Trin.* 11.7: CM 22.643–44, cf. *Off.* 1.28 (commemorative aspect); to *Trin.* 11.11, *Off.* 2.22 ("impanation" and the azymes question); to *Trin.* 11.22, *Off.* 2.9 (on communion of the "unworthy").
6. CM 22.698–99, 822.
7. CM 23.1809–11.

various aspects in *Trin.* 22, 25, and 28, including a direct echo of his attack upon the "*duos christos*" heresy in *Trin.* 24.[8] Then, apart from a brief reference in *Trin.* 37 simply explaining why St. John wrote his Gospel, silence returns on this issue.

Rupert's remarks about his progress through *Trin.* follow a strikingly similar pattern. Until *Trin.* 11 nearly every verse is treated, and he lingered over (*diutius immoramur*) "delightful" texts.[9] Then in *Trin.* 12 he spoke twice of "hurrying on" and in the next book of treating a topic "briefly."[10] At the beginning of *Trin.* 18 and even more clearly of *Trin.* 20, selection of relevant texts became the working principle.[11] *Trin.* 25 is a quick dash through the Psalms with a nod at the end to other Wisdom books. He admitted his treatment of Isaiah (*Trin.* 28) had been sparse; he hurried over the "obvious" in Ezechiel (*Trin.* 30); and he spoke repeatedly of haste and the need to finish in *Trin.* 32, which concludes with a token gesture towards the Minor Prophets.[12] He complained once more of weariness at the end of *Trin.* 33,[13] and then all such talk ceased in his powerful and original last nine books on the work of the Holy Spirit.

I suggest the following reconstruction. After completing *Off.*, probably in 1112, Rupert began work on *Trin.*, completing at least ten books before he encountered the eucharistic and christological issues. These he resolved to treat in *John*, where through eight hundred pages there is no talk of brevity, haste, or weariness. At just which point he ceased work on *Trin.* cannot be determined, though a long passage in *John* 13 appears to come verbatim from *Trin.* 18, and *Trin.* 19 has a somewhat formal closing[14]—confirming yet again the pattern whereby *Trin.* 20–32 show the complete breakdown of his original style and conception.

8. CM 22.779–80, 1205, 1301, 1307, 1361; CM 23.1569–71.
9. CM 22.635.
10. CM 22.730, 733, 766.
11. CM 22.1016, 1125, 1119.
12. CM 23.1569, 1667, 1738, 1758, 1765, 1772, 1780–81.
13. CM 23.1820.
14. Cf. *Deut.* 1.6: CM 22.1019–22, and *John* 13: CM 9.746, 748.

To this reconstruction there are two possible objections. In the dedicatory epistle of 1117 Rupert claimed to have finished the work as and when he could in three years (*utcumque et ubicumque coeptum opus triennio perficere*),[15] probably a hint at its interrupted progress but also suggesting that he began *Trin.* early in 1114. Quite apart from possible interpretations of the word *coeptum* in this passage and the notorious slipperiness of medieval time reckoning, it must be remembered that Rupert was actively seeking to impress his new-found patron. In a similar apologetic piece Rupert exaggerated by three or four years the date of an adversary's death,[16] whereas the mistake here would be only of a year or so. Secondly, as if in anticipation of my reconstruction, H. Silvestre has recently identified numerous verbal similarities between *John* and *Off.*, suggesting the close proximity of those two works.[17] But such repeated phrases, as Silvestre points out, can be found all through Rupert's work, and these works were in any case only a year and one-half or so apart. What Silvestre's list does not account for is the thematic development of *Trin.* with regard to its original intent, its progress, and the heresies it mentions or rebuts—all of which fit far better the pattern of my proposed reconstruction. To conclude: Rupert began *Trin.* by 1113 and *John* probably in 1114; he eventually concentrated on *John*, completing it by the summer of 1116, and then finished virtually all of *Trin.* by November 1116.

15. CM 21.123.
16. PL 170.483.
17. H. Silvestre, "La répartition des citations nominatives des Pères dans l'oeuvre de Rupert de Deutz," in *Sapientiae Doctrina: Mélanges Dom Hildebrand Bascour O.S.B.* (Louvain 1980) 296–98.

IV

The
Eucharistic
Controversy

IN 1049, the year Pope Leo IX mounted the papal throne, Berengar of Tours, a canon and teacher at the prestigious church of St. Martin's, began publicly and rather ostentatiously to defend views on the eucharist he had learned from a treatise ascribed to John Scotus Eriugena, written in fact by Ratramnus of Corbie. Thus this eleventh-century schoolman revived the Carolingian eucharistic controversy in what was to become for more than thirty-five years (1049–85) Latin Christendom's most celebrated theological dispute, the subject of repeated councils and papal interventions.[1] Berengar rested his case upon the authority of St. Augustine, as had Ratramnus before him, but he also employed arguments fashioned according to the newest techniques in speculative grammar. Flourishing schools and a mobile population of student-clerics carried those arguments and the ensuing debate to all parts of Europe. Nearly every aspiring theologian and many canonists as well gathered texts which reflected upon and reacted to Berengar's formulation of the issue. More-

1. Complete bibliography in J. Montclos, *Lanfranc et Berenger: le controverse eucharistique du XIe siècle* (Spicilegium Sacrum Lovaniense 37, Louvain 1971). See the review by O. Capitani in *Studi Medievali* 3rd ser. 16 (1975) 353–78, and the concise historical overview in M. Gibson, *Lanfranc of Bec* (Oxford 1978) 63–97.

over, in reversal of the ninth-century situation, Paschasius Radbertus' insistence upon the absolute identity between Christ's historically incarnate and His sacramental Body now held general sway, so that an outright denial of the Real Presence, whether or not Berengar and his followers so intended, never seriously threatened to prevail. But at the same time no particular formula defining the Real Presence had as yet gained general approbation, and none would until 1215 when Pope Innocent III canonized the term "transubstantiation." Long after Berengar's condemnation and death, therefore, eucharistic theology remained an open and much discussed topic.[2]

1

Rupert Takes a Stand

Exactly how much Rupert had learned about the Berengarian controversy is no longer ascertainable.[3] He had access to a rich variety of literature from both the Carolingian and the Berengarian disputes: the fundamental work by Paschasius,[4] a brief work by Heriger of Lobbes (d. 1007) and a related collection of authorities,[5] probably Adelman's letter to Beren-

2. For twelfth-century eucharistic theology in general, see J. de Ghellinck, "Eucharistie," in *DTC* 5.1233–1302. For Berengar's influence, see N. M. Häring, "Berengar's Definitions of *Sacramentum* and Their Influence on Medieval Theology," *Mediaeval Studies* 10 (1948) 109–46. For the range of eucharistic theology, see G. A. Macy, "The Theologies of the Eucharist in the Early Scholastic Period" (diss. Cambridge 1978). I wish to thank Dr. Macy for making his thesis available to me.

3. He noted once that Berengar claimed the authority of Augustine and that he made the Sacrament into a mere "figure." CM 9.2.

4. Darmstadt, Landes- und Hochschulbibliothek MS 700: see Bede Paulus, ed., Paschasius Radbertus, *De corpore et sanguine Domini*: CM 16.xvi.

5. See C. R. Schrader, "The False Attribution of an Eucharistic Tract to Gerbert of Aurillac," *Mediaeval Studies* 35 (1973) 178–204. There is an eleventh-century copy in the Séminaire at Liège, MS 6.F. 30bis. On the so-called *Exaggeratio*, a compilation of texts, see J. N. Bakhuizen van den Brink, *Ratramnus, De corpore et sanguine Domini* (2nd ed. Amsterdam 1974) 10–14, 29–32; H. Silvestre, *Scriptorium* 39 (1976) 324; J. P. Bouhot, *Ratramne de Corbie* (Paris 1976) 139–44.

gar,[6] and possibly Lanfranc's influential refutation of Berengar.[7] In the diocese of Liège, doubtless because of its excellent schools, the Berengarian affair was followed early and closely. Already in 1051 Bishop Dietwin intervened with the French king to quash a council he feared might exonerate Berengar; his letter cited the Fathers at length, drawing mostly upon Paschasius' *Epistola ad Fredugardum*.[8] Shortly thereafter, Adelman, formerly a master at Liège and then in Speyer, directed a lengthy critical letter to Berengar, whom he and several others from Liège had known personally during their student days together at Fulbert's Chartres. At least three copies of this letter-treatise once existed in the diocese of Liège; Berengar's response has come down only in a single manuscript, now fragmentary, from the abbey of Gembloux.[9] A decade later Gozechin, another master from Liège, cited Berengar's heresy as indicative of contemporary decline in religious learning.[10] And during the first decade of the twelfth century when Rupert took up the issue, interest was still keen enough for Alger to acquire Guitmund of Aversa's treatise, generally acclaimed the best to come out of the original debate.

Rupert's *De diuinis officiis*, I have argued, was intended mainly to serve as a devotional guide for monk-priests. For them and for Rupert himself the daily celebration of the Blessed Sacrament was the focal point of their religious lives, the moment in which they bore the person of Christ their head.[11] Monk-priests celebrated at least once and sometimes twice daily,[12] whereas

6. R. B. C. Huygens, "Textes latins du XI⁰ au XIII⁰ siècle," *Studi Medievali* 3rd ser. 8 (1967) 459–89. On Rupert's possible knowledge, see Bischoff, *Controversy* 217 and his nn. 246, 265, 495, 499.

7. Bibl. roy. MS 10807–11. Van den Gheyn 2.52 no. 980, dated this MS from St. Lawrence to the "twelfth century."

8. PL 146.1439–42. The *Epistola* in CM 16.145ff.

9. Huygens (n. 6 above) 461–62; Montclos (n. 1 above) 531–39.

10. J. Mabillon, *Vetera Analecta* 443. Gozechin was probably also the "ghost-writer" of Bishop Dietwin's letter (n. 8 above).

11. *Off.* 1.17, 19: CM 7.15, 17.

12. Gratian, *Decretum*, De cons. D.1 c.53 permits a daily and a requiem mass.

secular priests rarely celebrated daily and apparently required laws to encourage them to celebrate weekly. It was probably no accident that the ardent defenders of an uncompromised Real Presence, sometimes with crude and insufficiently qualified formulas, were nearly all monk-priests (Lanfranc, Humbert, Guitmund, Rupert), whereas those accused to one degree or another of "figurative" views (Berengar, Alger, Anselm of Laon) were mostly secular canons and sometimes only deacons.[13] Eucharistic theology was therefore utterly fundamental to Rupert's religious life: each day he meditated upon the mysteries of Christ hidden in Holy Scripture, but in the Blessed Sacrament he encountered Christ Himself. Any view which threatened to empty the sacrament of Christ's full and real presence required instant rebuttal.

In contrast to most other roughly contemporary monk-priests, however, such as John of Fécamp, Haimo of Hirsau, Wolfhelm of Brauweiler, Godfrey of Vendôme, and Franco of Afflighem,[14] Rupert was not content to reassert forcefully the incomprehensible mystery of Christ's bodily presence. In the second book of *De diuinis officiis*, he criticized those who were forever asking "how" (*quomodo*) of the sacramental mystery—a general reference to the Berengarian controversy and its aftermath—only, characteristically, to launch into his own explanation "lest we fail altogether to understand how."[15] To point up the seriousness of his attempted explanation Rupert employed special terminology—not, however, the language of "substance" and "accidents" which the new dialecticians preferred and William of St. Thierry would shortly use to correct him. He turned rather to the newer or "modern" *accessus ad auctores* for the terms

---

13. Macy's distinction (n. 2 above) between a "corporeal" (pp. 28–50) and a "spiritual" (pp. 51–74) approach to the eucharist may roughly distinguish the emphases of monks and secular clerics (as represented by schoolmen).

14. John of Fécamp, *Confessio fidei* 4: PL 101.1085–98; Haimo, *De corpore et sanguine Domini*: PL 118.815–18; Wolfhelm, *Epistola de sacramento*: PL 154.412–14; Godfrey, *Tractatus de corpore sanguine et Domini Jesu Christi*: PL 157.211–14; Franco, *De gratia Dei* 10: PL 166.771–72.

15. *Off.* 2.2, 8: CM 7.32–33, 40–41.

materia, intentio, and *utilitas,* used in a traditional rhetorical education, in his words, to introduce a distinguished author.[16] The *intentio* of the sacrament is daily to remind the believer both in mind and body of Christ's sacrifice without which devotion soon would wane. Its *utilitas* consists in uniting believers to Christ, making possible their eventual ascent into heaven with Him.[17] But to explain how Christ was truly present on the altar re-presenting His original sacrifice to and for the faithful, Rupert devised his own position on the *materia* of the sacrament— one which instantly got him into trouble.

For Rupert there could be no doubt that the Body of Christ on the altar was the incarnate Christ of the Gospels, but to show how this was (*quomodo est*) he chose to emphasize the unity rather than the identity of the two bodies and to develop a strong parallel between the eucharist and the incarnation.[18] Just as the incarnation effected the union of Christ's human and divine natures, so also the eucharist is constituted of a union between the bread and wine and the whole person of Christ. In each case the same Word is present and thus also the same sacrifice.[19] And just as neither of Christ's two natures was destroyed in the incarnation, so also the eucharistic union does not destroy the substance of the bread and wine evident to the five senses when it is conjoined to His crucified body and shed blood. Christ "assumed" to Himself a complete human nature, and so also the bread and wine on the altar are assumed or raised to a

16. *Off.* 2.8: CM 7.41. One likely source was the new *accessus* to Priscian: M. Gibson, "The Early Scholastic 'Glosule' to Priscian, 'Institutiones Grammaticae': The Text and Its Influence," *Studi Medievali* 3rd ser. 20 (1979) 235–54.

17. *Off.* 2.10, 11: CM 7.44–46.

18. The best interpretation of Rupert's eucharistic theology is now that of Bischoff, *Controversy* 57–68, but see also Séjourné, in *DTC* 14.196–203, and H. de Lubac, *Corpus Mysticum* (2nd ed. Paris 1949) 368–69. J. Geiselmann, *Die Eucharistielehre der Vorscholastik* (Forschungen zur christlichen Literatur und Dogmengeschichte 15, Paderborn 1926) 171ff, 222ff first named those who stressed unity rather than identity "mediating" theologians, and Bischoff (pp. 191ff) rightly linked Rupert to them.

19. *Off.* 2.9. For this important and controversial chapter, one must see the critical edition prepared by P. Classen in *DA* 26 (1970) 522–27, here 522.

higher unity with the "truth" of His divine and human substance.[20] This view, in Rupert's judgement, had two advantages.
For those doubters who objected that the elements remained unchanged on the altar,[21] it explained why the bread and wine, like
Christ's human nature, appeared unviolated, even though by a
kind of *communicatio idiomatum* the eucharist is rightly called the
Body of Christ, and He rightly said literally of Himself, "I am
the bread of life."[22] For the devout, on the other hand, the unity
established between the incarnate Christ and the assumed bread
and wine guarantees that it is the same sacrifice, making each
celebration of the sacrament, a daily event for monk-priests,
a real re-presentation of His incarnation and passion.[23] Alger
within months, William of St. Thierry soon after, and Bellarmine four hundred years later accused Rupert of the heresy of
"impanation" (a term also applied to Lutheran doctrine).[24]

20. "Totum attribuetis operationi Spiritus sancti, cuius effectus non est destruere uel corrumpere substantiam, quamcumque suos in usus assumit, sed
substantiae bono permanenti quod erat inuisibiliter adicere quod non erat.
Sicut humanam naturam non destruxit, cum illam operatione sua ex utero
Virginis Deus Verbo in unitatem personae coniunxit, sic substantiam panis et
uini secundum exteriorem speciem quinque sensibus subiectam non mutat aut
destruit, cum eidem Verbo, in unitatem corporis eiusdem quod in cruce pependit et sanguinis eiusdem quem de latere suo fudit, ista coniungit. Item
quomodo Verbum a summo demissum caro factum est, non mutatum in carnem sed assumendo carnem, sic panis et uinum, utrumque ab imo subleuatum,
fit corpus et sanguis Christi, non mutatum in carnis saporem siue in sanguinis
horrorem, sed assumendo inuisibiliter utriusque diuinae scilicet et humanae,
quae in Christo est, immortalis substantiae ueritatem." *Exod.* 2.10: CM 22.647.
21. Rupert regarded this as the primary stumbling block to belief in the
Real Presence: *Off.* 2.9: *DA* 26 (n. 19 above) 524–25; so too did his nearby
contemporary Franco of Afflighem, *De gratia Dei* 10: PL 166.777–78.
22. *Gen.* 4.5: CM 21.285–86. Cf. *John* 6: CM 9.357.
23. "Verbum quod humanam acceperat naturam, idem in carne manens et
sanguini quem de utero Virginis assumpserat et pani ac uino, quod de altari
assumit, medium interueniens unum sacrificium efficit." *Off.* 2.9: *DA* 26 (n.
19 above) 522 (cf. *Gen.* 6.32: CM 21.410–11). "Igitur cum Dei Verbum per
fidem ecclesiae descendens panem accepit de signo fidei, quod est altare, *re-
nouatur nobis illud* quod idem Verbum Dei per fidem Virginis descendens in
uterum eius carnem assumpsit." *Off.* 2.22: CM 7.54. (my italics).
24. Alger, *De sacramentis* 1.6: PL 180.754 (see n. 108 below); William,

Rupert worked out this view not long after his postponed ordination, and it served to bolster as well his severely restrictive stand on sacramental validity. Christ and the elements become one. Unworthy and doubting communicants cannot receive one part, the bread, while rejecting or flaunting Christ Himself, for by their unbelief they drive the Life out of the union, receiving only bread and wine, and thus, in parallel again with the incarnation, become literally "guilty of the body and blood of the Lord" (I. Cor. 11:27).[25] About ten years earlier Alger had struggled with this same problem in his *Liber de misericordia et iustitia*, and while he too at that point had little to say for the efficacy or validity of heretical sacraments, he nevertheless argued that in the case of the unworthy (*mali*) the Blessed Sacrament was true not only in its form, as he claimed for other sacraments, but also in its *res*, which is to say: it became the Body of Christ; only its gracious "effect" depended upon the faith of the communicant.[26] But for Rupert, the zealous adherent of the reform party, there was no *tertium quid*: believers were united bodily to Christ through the eucharist which "expanded" (*crescit*) on the altar to take in all believers and raise (*vehit*) them to heaven;[27] unbelievers were guilty literally of His body and blood.

The position Rupert took in *De diuinis officiis* and the first eleven books of *De sancta Trinitate* was essentially of his own devising, though several key points may have been suggested by Paschasius and Heriger of Lobbes. Paschasius had repeatedly cited a text from Ambrose's *De mysteriis* to the effect that the flesh on the altar is the same as that born of Mary and sacrificed

Epistola ad Rupertum: PL 180.342; *Roberti Bellarmini Opera omnia*, ed. J. Fevre (Paris 1874) 4.231ff, 244ff; see also Bischoff, *Controversy* 67–68, 278–81. Rupert never technically expressed an "impanationist" position in his printed works, but in his early works (nn. 19, 20, 23 above) he stressed the parallel between the species and Christ's human nature and said nothing about substantial change in the "assumed" bread and wine.

25. *Off.* 2.9: *DA* 26 (n. 19 above) 522–23.
26. *Liber* 1.62: PL 180.884. But cf. *Liber* 3.21: PL 180.941.
27. *Off.* 2.11: CM 7.46.

on the cross; Heriger later defended it as key.[28] This is the only
authority Rupert cited approvingly in his *Commentary on John*
(he criticized several others), and he apparently took it from
Heriger rather than directly from Ambrose or Paschasius.[29] From
Heriger Rupert also learned to draw analogies to Christ's assumed humanity and to emphasize unity rather than identity
with His incarnate body.[30] But where Heriger had presupposed
the Real Presence and sought to explain how the believer was
naturally (his keyword) unified to Christ's Body and thus brought
to heaven (that which Rupert considered the "utility" of the sacrament), Rupert meant rather to defend and explain the Real
Presence by showing how the elements became unified to the
crucified Christ. To do so he drew upon ideas normally reserved for the incarnate union. In a personal letter William of St.
Thierry, a native of Liège and a brother monk, warned Rupert
privately to clarify his use of language critics might consider
similar to Berengar's heretical "impanationism."[31] But local
clerics attacked Rupert directly and publicly, and thus fundamentally altered his thought and career.

2

Rupert under
Attack and in Debate

Almost four hundred years ago Bellarmine first suggested
that Rupert was the "impanationist" criticized by Alger of Liège;
but Gerberon and Mabillon, determined to defend their confrere

28. *De mysteriis* 53 is at the heart of Paschasius' exposition: *De corpore* 1, 4:
CM 16.14–15, 30; and becomes key to his later defense: *Epist. Fred.*: CM
16.145, 149, 170. So also Heriger, *De corpore* 1, 7: PL 139.179–80, 184–86.
On Rupert's sources, see Bischoff, *Controversy* 138–50, 191–219.

29. *John* 6: CM 9.336; see Bischoff, *Controversy* 210–11.

30. To Rupert's earliest pronouncements on the eucharist (nn. 20, 23
above), compare Heriger, *De corpore* 8: PL 139.186.

31. See my forthcoming note on "Rupert of Deutz and William of St.
Thierry," in *RB* 93 (1983).

from this Lutheran heresy, vigorously denied it,[32] and so the matter stood until fifteen years ago. In 1965 Guntram Bischoff's dissertation demonstrated the connection beyond any possible doubt and offered a thoughtful interpretation of their theological differences.[33] The eucharistic controversy between Rupert and Alger merits serious historical consideration for at least two reasons: it offers considerable insight into the state of eucharistic theology and piety in the second decade of the twelfth century, and it involves an early and neglected instance of trial for heresy.

Down to and including the eleventh book of *De sancta Trinitate*, Rupert echoed or expanded upon positions he had taken in *De diuinis officiis* 2.9. Then in Book XII, presumably written around 1113/14, he pointedly took up objections someone (*aliquis*) had raised.[34] The debate was on: "I had," Rupert wrote a good decade later (1125), "a most vexatious conflict (*permolestum certamen*) concerning the body and blood of the Lord with a master—or rather a monk—of great repute."[35] The most distin-

32. R. Bellarmine, *De scriptoribus ecclesiasticis*, in his *Opera omnia* (n. 24 above) 12.435–36. G. Gerberon, *Apologia pro Ruperto abbate:* PL 167.29–44, 99ff; J. Mabillon, *Annales Ordinis S. Benedicti* 76.83: ed. E. Martène (Lucca 1745) 240–43.

33. Bischoff, *Controversy* 14–31, 43–44. Bischoff held mistakenly that Rupert left Liège already in 1113 rather than 1116 (cf. chapter I, n. 5), that Rupert's and Alger's various works should be understood as a continuing series of responses to one another (for which I see no proof whatsoever), and that the *Commentary on John* responded to Alger's *De sacramentis* (the only evidence for this being a similarity in several quotations from Augustine which can be explained in other ways). Theologically, Bischoff saw their chief point of difference in Rupert's objections (as a "monastic theologian") to Alger's Augustinian terminology (*sacramentum* and *res sacramenti*). Rupert, though preferring scriptural language, objected much less to the terms than to the "figurative" view he thought they expressed and were meant to express. In this chapter I have acknowledged my debt to Bischoff where it is appropriate, but I have not argued points of difference since he has never formally published his dissertation.

34. *Exod.* 3.7–8: CM 22.698–99.

35. This is the basic narrative source: "Quorsum istud? Videlicet ut recogites qualem ob causam ego absens paene fuerim iudicatus, quatenus omnis

guished master in the diocese, Alger entered the abbey of Cluny in 1121, four years before this account.[36] But if Alger, Bishop Otbert's personal secretary since 1101, had initiated the debate, other clerics in Liège quickly joined in (*illi me ex hoc diffamare coeperunt*), and they more than Alger spearheaded the most crucial attack. There is circumstantial evidence that Alger made use of at least one manuscript found only in the library of St. Lawrence.[37] Occasions for Rupert and Alger to meet, in other words, and for the young monk to present his first work to this distinguished master could thus easily have arisen. But Alger objected to certain of his eucharistic views, and Rupert immediately leapt to his own defense.

Rupert's remarks suggest a protracted series of encounters. In Liège, long-standing interest in the Berengarian controversy and a large population of student-clerics eager to pursue a new

---

mihi licentia scribendi tolleretur, et quomodo tibi uelut de coelo a Deo missus pro me occurrerit beatus Hilarius, suumque librum manibus tuis et suam sententiam quam non quaerebas, sed nec usquam esse sciebas, tuis ingesserit oculis. Adhuc tibi eram fere incognitus, tantum autem semel uisus et tecum pauca locutus, quando istud actum est, aduersariis mihi nescienti et procul absenti magnam inuidiam conflantibus. Habueram quippe cum aliquo magni nominis magnaeque aestimationis scholastico licet monacho certamen permolestum de sacramento corporis et sanguinis Domini, qui inter caetera quibus deprimere conabatur maiestatem tanti sacramenti, illud mihi obiecerat, quia sacramentum illud Iudae quoque traditori suo Dominus dedit. . . . Quod autem illi, uidelicet Iudae proditori, dedisset simul cum caeteris in promptu erat illi astruere auctoritate beati Augustini. Eius rei necessitas me compulit ut dicerem non esse in canone scripta beati Augustini, non esse illi per omnia confidendum sicut libris canonicis. Putarem ego nouum uel incognitum hoc esse aduersariis praesertim nominatis et scientia non parum praesumentibus, maxime in comparatione mei rudis, ut putabant, atque iuuenculi? At illi me ex hoc diffamare coeperunt tanquam haereticum qui dixissem non esse in canone beatum Augustinum. Nosti ubi, quando uel quomodo tibi is . . . occurrerit beatus Hilarius taliterque me defenderit, ut sine illo non possem [non] iudicari haereticus. Illud mihi miraculum fuit. . . . *RegBen.* 1: PL 170.495–96. For Rupert's purpose in recounting this incident, see the Appendix to this chapter.

36. On Alger's life, see Nicholas' *Elogium* in PL 180.737–38.

37. See A. Michel, *Amalfi und Jerusalem im griechischen Kirchenstreit* (Orientalia Christiana Analecta 121, Rome 1939) 48–49.

turn in an old debate provided an alert and critical audience for Rupert's attempted solution. The second book of Alger's *De sacramentis*, for instance, treats ten problems, most of them old or new questions posed, it seems, by these student-clerics who looked to Alger as their master (in an informal sense). Rupert's later encounters with him took place almost certainly outside the cloister, most probably in the cathedral close. One must imagine Rupert walking down the Public-Mount less than a thousand yards into the city and directly east into the cathedral quarter, there to debate his eucharistic views with local secular canons, some of them possibly teachers. Alger apparently came armed with a battery of supporting authorities drawn chiefly from St. Augustine; this too suggests a lapse of time and prearranged debates.

Their dispute soon turned bitter. Age-old rivalry between monks and canons was further exacerbated by Rupert's confidence in his divine call to interpret Scripture and the clerics' pride in their modern education at the feet of renowned masters. The clerics found this contentious monk arrogant in defense of his own peculiar views, wholly out of touch with the fast-moving new world of schools and masters, and far too ignorant to comprehend basic philosophical techniques.[38] Rupert in turn accused these "false masters" and "would-be wise men" of preferring "Plato's Academy" to the Table of the Lord: in the name of seeking truth they dispute simply for the sake of disputing; and in pursuit of personal glory they devise their own ideas, scorning what the Spirit teaches about the sacrament in Holy Scripture.[39] This name-calling ought not to be taken too literally, however, for in fact the accusation of irreverent novelty was finally lodged most decisively against Rupert rather than the clerics. And just beneath the surface, indeed breaking through at crucial moments, lay deep antipathies arising out of irreconcilable party differences in the recent schism.

Rupert must have been bested in this "vexatious" debate, or

38. CM 9.1, 394.
39. *John* 6–7: CM 9.334, 335, 358, 393–96.

at least deeply embarrassed. But ever pugnacious and utterly convinced that Holy Scripture and honest piety were on his side, he resolved to set the matter straight in his *Commentary on John* (John 6:32–71), an act so much the more provocative in that the major source of authorities cited against him had been St. Augustine's *Sermons on John*. Many today, Rupert explained, find Christ's teaching about eating and drinking His body and blood (John 6:53–54) very hard. They murmur and dispute when we defend its truth. But the authority of the Gospel, rightly set forth, should now bind their resisting hearts and minds.[40] Which is to say, this section of his commentary (more than fifty pages in all) represents Rupert's response to the debate in Liège roughly during the years 1113–15. From it the major issues can be reconstructed.[41]

Old Testament figures frequently were made to yield doctrinally as much as New Testament teachings. The interpretation of manna had divided minds already in the Carolingian and Berengarian debates with respect to the sacramental grace which it could be said to have contained.[42] Three different times Rupert mentioned this issue first.[43] In *De diuinis officiis* 2.9, he had cited John 6:49 (*Patres uestri manducauerunt manna et mortui sunt*) chiefly to support his condemnation of reception of the sacrament by the unfaithful, and he had contrasted to it I Cor. 10:3–4 (*Patri nostri omnes eandem escam spiritualem manducauerunt et omnes eundem potum spiritualem biberunt*), interpreted as referring to efficacious reception. Certain "ignorant and little-known men," he reports, now contend (literally, "opine") that the ancient Israelites already ate and drank the body and blood of Christ in the

40. *John* 7: CM 9.368–69.
41. *John* 6–7: CM 9.329–83, summarized briefly in *Spir.* 3.18–25: CM 24.1925–34 (apparently written still before the trial).
42. Paschasius, *De corpore* 5: CM 16.31–34; Ratramnus, *De corpore* 20–26: ed. Bakhuizen van den Brink (n. 5 above) 48–50; Lanfranc, *De corpore* 9: PL 150.419–20.
43. *Exod.* 3.6–8: CM 22.697–99 (probably the first indication, chronologically, of the controversy); *John* 6: CM 9.329ff; and *Spir.* 3.19: CM 24.1926–27. Cf. Bischoff, *Controversy* 69–80.

form of manna and water from the struck rock, and they cite as proof I Cor. 10:3–4 and John 6:32 (the text he was then commenting upon).[44] These adversaries, presumably canons or students in Liège referred to in the context of another controversy as "ignorant rabble" (*indocto scholarum popello*),[45] had simply adopted St. Augustine's interpretation of John 6:32, doubtless out of respect for his authority[46] and also with a view to affirming the objective presence of sacramental grace.

This latter Rupert perceived to be the chief concern of these men who also preached that the sacrament was to be dispensed indifferently. After all, Rupert commented snidely, manna, unlike the priestly sacrifices or the Showbread, was available to all who would partake, including brute animals.[47] Rupert then expressly reiterated his original position: the spiritual sameness mentioned in the biblical text and in Augustine's commentary (*spiritalem utique eandem*) referred not to the grace of the sacrament (this was Augustine's position) and certainly not to Christ's actual broken body and shed blood, but rather to the spiritual truth that many avaricious, fornicating, and murmuring men partake of the sacrament who will nevertheless perish.[48] This description of those who would perish was hardly lost on the secular clerics in Liège, nor for that matter was his implication that the sacrament functioned only to the damnation of such "unfaithful" people. To establish his interpretation against the authority of St. Augustine, however, Rupert felt compelled to cite the manifold authority (*cum auctoritate multiplici*) of the prophet David (Ps. 77[78]:1ff), the apostle Paul who said all this happened to the ancients figuratively (I Cor. 10:11), Christ

44. *John 6:* CM 9.330.
45. *RegBen.* 1: PL 170.482.
46. Augustine, *Tract. in Iohannem* 26.11–12: CC 36.265–66. Rupert referred to their citation of Augustine: CM 9.334. Later, Alger likewise cited this text: *De sacramentis* 1.8: PL 180.762. Since, according to Rupert (CM 9.330), they defended this view in speech and writing (*scriptis et dictis*), they presumably had gathered texts from Augustine to rebut Rupert's position.
47. *John 6:* CM 9.335–36.
48. *John 6:* CM 9.330–31, 336, 354–55; *Exod.* 3.8: CM 22.699.

Himself who said only He was the bread (John 6:51), and not least the Lord's passion, the only and fundamental basis of the sacrament.[49]

So much for those who perished, but, the clerics fired back, what then about those faithful Israelites who partook of the "same spiritual food and drink" (I Cor. 10:3–4)? Rupert was forced in response to make explicit something implicit in his strict salvation-historical approach to theological issues: through His passion Christ became the "Food of Life," the antidote to the death-bearing food eaten in the Garden of Eden (a familiar image), and therefore this food (the eucharist), this salvation-bringing grace, could not have existed in any earlier form for the ancient Israelites. Otherwise stated, the Blessed Sacrament was instituted in Christ's passion, not earlier, for the passion itself is the effective power of the sacrament (*res et uirtus sacramenti*) whereby bread and wine are converted into His body and blood.[50] Even though this view, clearly related to his distinctive formulations on sacramental grace, directly contradicted the traditional teaching that Christ instituted the eucharistic sacrament at the Last Supper, Rupert never later abandoned it.[51] He insisted, moreover, that the faithful departed had also to receive both sacraments (baptism and the eucharist), and so at the moment of His sacrificial death Christ journeyed into the underworld—a traditional teaching[52]—and there personally extended to them His body (that is, the newly instituted sacrament) and the power of His divinity whereby they were transported into the state of bliss.[53] Unusual as the position was, Rupert's theo-

49. *Exod.* 3.6: CM 22.697–98.

50. *Exod.* 3.7–8: CM 22.698–99; *John* 6: CM 9.338–41; *Spir.* 3.22: CM 24.1930–31.

51. Reiterated, for instance, ten years later in *Cant.* 4: CM 26.101–02.

52. H. Quillet, "Descente de Jésus aux Enfers," in *DTC* 4.565–619; H. Grillmeier, "Der Gottessohn im Totenreich," *Zeitschrift für katholischen Theologie* 71 (1949) 1–53. The passage most familiar to Rupert, alluded to in the text of n. 53 below, was Gregory, *Homil. Evang.* 22.6: PL 76.1177.

53. Rupert spoke earlier, traditionally, of the saints held in limbo (*Gen.* 4.1: CM 21.281), but the notion of Christ liberating them by His bodily, i.e. sacramental, presence was a product of the debate: *John* 2, 6: CM 9.62, 340–

logical (as distinct from his ecclesiastical) intent was to be upheld by later medieval authors, for whom the relationship between manna and the eucharist became a standard school question. Hugh of St. Victor, like his master St. Augustine, tended still to blur the distinction, but Lombard's textbook declared that sacraments of the Old Dispensation only signified whereas those of the New actually conferred salvation.[54]

Rupert's emphasis upon the institution of the eucharist at Christ's passion and its higher status than the "figures" of the Old Dispensation provided the background for his attempt also to uphold a strict view on the efficacy and administration of the sacrament. In the course of the debate this came to turn on the question of whether Judas partook of communion at the Last Supper—Judas having become a general symbol of avaricious heretics during the reform era. In *De diuinis officiis* Rupert had spurned unworthy communicants as, effectively, slayers of Christ and His sacramental body, and seemed thereby to say that the Body of Christ existed for them in no sense whatsoever. This caught the attention of William of St. Thierry and even more forcefully of Alger and his fellow canons. In the oral debate— this is the incident Rupert later described most clearly—Alger objected that Judas too had received communion from Christ Himself; this argument, Rupert opined, was meant to disparage the sacrament, whereas in reality Alger surely wanted simply to assert the objective reality of the Lord's body. As proof Alger cited here St. Augustine's *Sermons on John*, a text and issue familiar to him from his earlier work.[55] Rupert in the meantime

---

41; *Spir.* 3.20: CM 24.1927–28; and more primitively *Exod.* 3.7: CM 22.698. Rupert's peculiar emphasis becomes especially clear when contrasted with another contemporary who dwelt on this idea, but in a traditional way: Manegold, *Contra Wolfelmum* 19: ed. Hartmann 85–87.

54. Hugh, *De sacramentis* 1.12.1–4, 24: PL 176.347–52, 362–64. Peter Lombard, *Sententiae* 4.1.6, citing Augustine, *Enar. Psalm.* 73.2.

55. Augustine, *Tract. in Iohannem* 26.11, 62.3: CC 36.265, 484; Cf. Alger, *Liber miser.* 1.52: PL 180.884–85; and the texts gathered and deployed later in *De sacramentis* 1.21: PL 180.798–803. See Bischoff, *Controversy* 81–88, who also noted the connection to ecclesiastical parties in Liège; and Pelikan, *Theology* 92, 196 for the position of others on Judas.

had come to greater clarity on the objective reality of the sacrament: once the bread is consecrated, he noted, it never ceases to be the body of Christ or loses its sanctifying power.[56] But this concession in no way diminished Rupert's zeal to exclude the unfaithful from the Church and her sacraments.

Many dispute, Rupert reports, about why the Lord elected Judas to the apostolic dignity, and some contend that he was originally good, otherwise the Lord would not have called him to such an office. This Rupert rejected. Is it not true, he asked these people (*quaerimus ab eis*), that even today many evil men manage to obtain and to exercise the episcopal dignity, modern Judases who seek Christ only out of cupidity and who use the revenues of the Church only to buy and sell sacred places?[57] A clearer reference to Bishop Otbert, as judged by both zealous and moderate reformers, could hardly be had. The Lord permitted the case of Judas, Rupert continued, in order to teach that evil prelates who cannot be corrected should be tolerated— a teaching suspiciously similar to Alger's main point in Book I of the *Liber de misericordia et iustitia*.[58] But still, should the holy sacraments be given to such as Judas? Here Rupert introduced a distinction not wholly without precedent. It is one thing to tolerate evil men who resist correction; it is quite another to suffer those publicly condemned in the Church: nothing (*nec ratio nec ueritatis regula*) permits us to become so indifferent (*indiscreta*) as to maintain communion with them or dispense the holy mysteries to them.[59] Two different popes had publicly condemned (*manifesto conuictos actu*) Otbert, in 1095 and again in 1106, and that was not forgotten in 1115. The secular clerics in Liège, who

56. *John 6*: CM 9.343. If Rupert understood this point before, he certainly never said it. I would be inclined to see this as a silent concession to Alger resulting from the debate.

57. *John 7*: CM 9.380–81. Cf. Alger, *Liber miser.* 3.85: PL 180.967–68.

58. *John 7*: CM 9.381; *Evang.* 23: CM 23.1809–10. Cf. Alger, *Liber miser.* 1.28, 83: PL 180.868, 892–94.

59. *John 11*: CM 9.616–17; *Evang.* 23: CM 23.1810–11. Rupert's view is related to that studied by S. Kuttner, "Ecclesia de occultis non iudicat," in *Acta Congressus internationalis Romae* (1936) 3.225–46.

had not broken off communion with their bishop as had Rupert's monastic reform party, knew exactly what his distinction was aimed at, and they were greatly angered by it—as, Rupert says, he "learned by bitter experience."[60] Rupert suggested, tongue in cheek, that they might be troubled by "guilty remorse" or simply "Christian humility," and he reminded them that judgements against one's self were not at issue here. Rather, the well-known and publicly unworthy were meant, those scandalous men judged unworthy by others; and such are "rightly repelled" (*iure repellimur*) from the sacrament![61]

Rupert clinched his argument by demonstrating that Judas in fact enjoyed no sacramental communion of any kind with the Lord. Since all sacraments were instituted (*condita*) in the passion, death, and resurrection of Christ, Judas self-evidently never received any priestly ordination, for the power to baptize, to consecrate the eucharist, and to remit sins was not finally conferred upon the apostles until Christ breathed out the Holy Spirit upon them after His resurrection (John 20:22–23). Judas shared with the other apostles, he conceded, the right and power to preach and to heal the sick, to which he likened evil but nonheretical bishops who continued to function in their offices—leaving the sacramental powers of and the appropriateness of communing with such bishops far from clear, exactly Rupert's sentiments still about Bishop Otbert.[62] Most important, Rupert also rejected outright Alger's and St. Augustine's notion that Judas had received communion. This required a bit of modern-sounding textual analysis. Rupert followed three of the Gospels, and especially St. John's, which reported that Judas went out immediately (*exiuit continuo*) after taking the "*buccella*," which

60. ". . . tantae dignitatis sacramentem *indignis* [n.b. not just hereticis!] et non probatis dandum non est. Cum autem haec dicimus, moventur plerique, sicut nos quoque *molesto experti sumus experimento*." *Spir.* 3.23: CM 24.1931 (my italics). Rupert later (n. 35 above) described this controversy as a "permolestum certamen."

61. Ibid. 1931–32.

62. *John* 7: CM 9.382–83; *Evang.* 23: CM 23.1810.

"no evangelist or doctor of the Church had ever identified with the Lord's Body." Christ then "representatively" ate the pasch, the prefiguration of His passion, with the remaining disciples. Only St. Luke told it differently. But, Rupert explained, he added the sacred words uttered later at the paschal meal to those said of the "*buccella*" by way of "anticipation."[63] Excluded from both ordination and communion, Judas had come to symbolize Rupert's indictment of simoniac prelates and immoral priests.

Quite apart from the problem of sacramental validity, Rupert and Alger differed markedly as well on basic questions of eucharistic theology.[64] Alger's critique in the debate, and possibly William's in his letter, forced Rupert now to say plainly that Christ's "assumption of" or "union with" the bread involved a "conversion" thereof. The charge of "impanation," which both Alger and William had leveled at him, he never deigned to answer directly.[65] But by the time he wrote his *Commentary on John*, it, like his ambiguity on the objective consecration of the eucharist, had been silently conceded and corrected. However, as with his severe stand on sacramental validity, he clung to his old view as much as possible, always preferring the language of Scripture and the canon of the Mass to any abstract terminology, and therefore insisting still that "Bread of God" (*panis Dei*: John 6:33) constituted an excellent and complete definition (*plena definitio*) of the Blessed Sacrament.[66] Alger, on the other hand, leaned heavily upon the authority of St. Augustine and introduced ever more of his language into the debate in an attempt to bring definitional clarity.[67] Rupert in turn perceived Alger/Augustine's distinction between the "sacrament" (*sacramentum*,

63. *John* 7: CM 9.382. Cf. *John* 11: CM 9.616.

64. Bischoff, *Controversy* 56–68 (an especially good analysis).

65. Here is his clearest reference to it: "Et sic Verbum, quod est panis angelorum, caro factum est, non mutatum in carnem sed assumendo carnem; sic idipsum Verbum iamdudum caro factum panis uisibilis fit, non mutatum in panem, sed assumendo et in unitatem personae suae transferendo panem." *John* 6: CM 9.357.

66. *John* 6: CM 9.343–45.

67. Alger, *De sacramentis* 1.4–5: PL 180.751–52. N. M. Häring, "A Study in the Sacramentology of Alger of Liège," *Mediaeval Studies* 20 (1958) 56ff.

meaning the external species) and the Body of Christ (*res sacra-menti*) as an attack upon the full reality of the Real Presence, and he ascribed it to his opponents' preoccupation with the unchanging species.[68]

In direct continuation, then, of the debate regarding manna, Rupert's adversary conceded that manna might well be only a figure, but so too, he said, was the bread on the altar a "figure" of the Living Bread and not itself that Bread. Outraged, Rupert asked what possible authority (*auctoritate canonica*) would support such a figural notion. The answer, as he knew very well, was St. Augustine.[69] But a figure, Rupert objected, is something which says one thing and means another. How could this possibly apply to the eucharist when Christ himself said "*hoc est corpus meum*" and "*Ego sum panis uitae*"? And when Christ stipulated that this is the body "which will be given for you," how can you say (*tu dicis*) that this sacrament is not the same body (*non est idem corpus*)? For if this is not the Living Bread from heaven, then it is also not the body given for us.[70] If anyone doubts, Rupert declared, that grain grown and wine pressed this year become Christ's body and blood, or that waters from the Rhine, the Tiber, or any other source signed with the cross become that which flowed from Christ's side, that person is utterly pagan and after the third warning should be shunned.[71] In a summary passage written somewhat later, Rupert rejected a certain argument (*contentiosa cuiusquam dissertatione*)—this could

68. *John* 6: CM 9.333–34.

69. *John* 6: CM 9.331. Alger probably cited as his "canonical authority" St. Augustine, *De doctrina christiana* 3.16.24: CC 32.92: "Locutio . . . figurata est. *Nisi manducaveritis*, etc." (John 6:54) (as he did later, *De sacramentis* 1.11: PL 180.772). For Rupert continued: "Etiam si quis [Augustine!] dicit figuratam esse locutionem, qua dicetur posterius, *Nisi manducaveritis*, etc. . . . non nobis adversatur, quia uidelicet ista figuratio locutionis ueritatem rei non perimit. . . ."

70. *John* 6: CM 9.333. Alger's meaning is manifest from his own work: "Quae ergo duo esse approbat ["Augustine"], uisibile scilicet sacramentum et inuisibilem rem sacramenti, non unum et idem sed aliud et aliud esse demonstrat." *De sacramentis* 1.5: PL 180.752.

71. *John* 6: CM 9.332.

only refer to Alger—and explained that Augustine's *res sacramenti* referred strictly to Christ's passion, with which believers commune by way of the "sacrament" which is always and only the body of Christ.[72] But identifying the "sacrament" with Christ's body—which to Rupert seemed obvious and necessary from the canon of the Mass—and the *res sacramenti* with His passion posed a new difficulty Rupert's adversaries immediately pounced upon.

If, they objected, the bread is not figuratively but truly Christ Himself, then He is made to suffer and die as often as the bread is broken.[73] Defending the Mass as sacrifice was utterly central to Rupert's piety and purpose, but given his salvation-historical approach, and indeed the state of theology generally on this point,[74] Rupert's proved a formidable task. The clerics cited texts from St. Augustine and St. Gregory to the effect that Christ died only once.[75] In a somewhat amusing and very condescending passage, Alger described how certain simple persons "blown around by every wind of doctrine" whom he "sought with God's help to straighten out," had become severely rattled upon hearing something they did not know, namely, that both the bread and the sacrifice are "figures."[76] Rupert reiterated in his Johannine commentary essentially what he had said earlier in his Genesis commentary about the "sacrifice of Isaac": the priest sacrifices the bread and wine while the Son of God, united to the bread, remains whole and impassible. A few pages later he stated it in still another way: the consecrated bread becomes one with Christ; but just like His divine nature during the passion, so also now His human nature is immolated on the altar without suffering death. These, Rupert concluded, are mysteries which must be left to the Holy Spirit.[77]

Thus the differences between Rupert and Alger mount up:

72. *Spir.* 3.22: CM 24.1930–31.
73. *John* 7: CM 9.369.
74. See M. Lepin, *L'idée du sacrifice de la Messe* (3rd ed. Paris 1926) 97–146.
75. See the texts gathered in Alger, *De sacramentis* 1.16: PL 180.786–90.
76. Ibid. 790.
77. *Gen.* 6.32: CM 21.410; *John* 7: CM 9.370, 374–75.

one a Benedictine monk, the other a secular canon; one a zealous reformer with "purist" impulses, the other more moderate;
one tending to ultrarealism in his view of the Host and the Sacrifice, the other struggling to define a real but "figurative" presence; one inclined to rely on Scripture, the other on Augustine.
All these differences came to summary expression in their sharply
diverging views on the relationship of Christ's sacramental to
His ecclesial body. St. Augustine regarded the body of believers
united in love as the chief end (*res sacramenti*) of the sacrament,
and Alger agreed.[78] Rupert attacked this directly. Let us not be
such incautious admirers of Father Augustine, he exhorted, that
through "hasty reading" we confuse his definition of Christ's
body (= Church) with the actual body broken for us on the
cross (that is, the eucharist). This Rupert repeated twice, the
second time in commenting upon the same verse (John 6:53)
which had first elicited Augustine's definition.[79] Against this
Augustinian view, in which much more emphasis falls upon
love binding the community of believers together into the body
of Christ, Rupert insisted that *partaking* of the eucharist is the
"chief and effective cause" of our salvation, that which binds us
to Christ and thence also to His body (= Church). Wherefore
communion, except in the case of infants, is absolutely necessary for salvation.[80] Christ enjoined those who would remain in
Him to eat His body and drink His blood (John 6:57), and
Rupert criticized any who would spiritualize this to mean "remain in Him by faith."[81] This latter position, again based on a
passage in Augustine's Johannine commentary, was taught at
Laon and thence entered the *Ordinary Gloss* for John 6:57, so it
may well have been touted by student-clerics in Liège.[82] Drawing upon elements of his christology, Rupert argued that this

78. *De sacramentis* 1.3–4: PL 180.749–51.
79. *John 6*: CM 9.341–42, 359. The Augustinian sentences Rupert quoted
and criticized are not exactly the same as those Alger cited later (n. 78 above).
80. *John 6*: CM 9.359–61.
81. *John 6*: CM 9.342, 360–61.
82. See Macy (n. 2 above) 46 n. 156, 53, 57–61. See Augustine, *Tract. in
Iohannem* 26.18: CC 36.268; and Alger, *De sacramentis* 1.21: PL 180.800–01.

"eating," joined of course to faith and love, should be understood more or less literally to produce eternal life, for by eating the divinized body of the Son of God believers too could become "as gods" (Ps. 81[82]:6).[83] By a "dissimilar similitude" it can be said that the Son of God lives because He was begotten of the Father and that "sons of God" will live eternally because they "eat" the Begotten of the Father.[84] This view of communing with Christ and of "divinization" by eating His flesh and drinking His blood may well have distinguished more generally the intense devotional approach of monk-priests like Rupert from the more communal emphasis of secular clerics like Alger.

Rupert's basic point was a simple one. When Christ said, *Hoc est corpus meum quod pro uobis traditum est*, He was to be understood literally. The eucharist is Christ's sacrificial, incarnate body and believers communicate directly with His saving passion; otherwise the whole would be of no value whatsoever. Rupert here gave voice to a piety very close to that of monk-priests and perhaps most Latin Christians. His insistence upon Christ's incarnate presence in the bread on the altar articulates theologically the pious convictions which went into the practice, first introduced in the early twelfth century, of burning candles before the reserved Host; it was also just a generation or so later that the elevation of the Host was first attested as accepted practice. His very literal notion of Christ's sacrifice upon the altar likewise has much in common with the numerous stories originating in this same era of "miraculous" and "bleeding" hosts.[85] In working this out, even against objections, Rupert always came back to the language of Scripture and the canon of the Mass. Alger and the student-clerics, on the other hand, came in the manner of schoolmen armed with authorities, drawn largely, it seems, from St. Augustine's *Commentary on John* and Book II of Ivo's recently published *Decretum*. On several occasions Rupert referred scornfully to their "scraps of paper" (*schedulis*, a favorite term of Jerome) and their writings (*dictis et scriptis*,

83. *John* 6: CM 9.363, 330.
84. Ibid. 364.
85. See Macy (n. 2 above) 5–13, with bibliography.

a common idiom).[86] The collision which inevitably occurred drove Rupert into ever stronger statements about the singular authority of Scripture.

In the course of this debate Alger cited Augustine on the question of Judas' communion, and so "necessity compelled me," Rupert says, to point out that Augustine was not in the sacred canon and therefore not to be fully relied upon in all things as Holy Scripture. Rupert's opponents immediately charged heresy. "I was amazed," Rupert goes on, "that this should be new or unknown to them, especially considering their great reputation and pride of learning in contrast to my youth and inexperience." Already in the earliest passage reflecting the debate (where the issue is manna) Rupert cited the "multiple authority" of Scripture and declared he would be bound only by Christ's Gospel even though "great Fathers" (in fact, Augustine) might hold another opinion. Again, in his *Commentary on John*: even if an angel from heaven (cf. Gal. 1:18) should hold something contrary to the plain sense of Scripture—Augustine was of course that angel—he was not to be received as an apostle of Christ on this matter (*in hac sententia*), lest he incur the curses invoked upon those who tamper with the text of Holy Scripture.[87]

"Necessity" forced him initially to adopt such a strong position, but it soon became a matter of principle, embedded, as so often, in religious practice. Devout religious were to "feed daily on the Word" (that is, on the eucharist and Holy Scripture), and Rupert's high regard for Scripture thus represented the exact counterpart to his insistence upon an uncompromised Real Presence. He was, moreover, technically correct to say that the Fathers had taught the singular authority of Scripture.[88] But as the clerics' reaction plainly showed, this cut directly against the grain of early medieval tradition which tended to consider the Fathers inspired as well. Yet even in its boldest expression,[89] Ru-

86. *John* 6: CM 9.337.
87. *Exod.* 3.8: CM 22.699; *John* 6: CM 9.336–38. Cf. nn. 35, 49 above.
88. De Lubac, *Exégèse Médiévale* 1.56–74, 2.227–29; Beinert, *Kirche* 142–144. Cf. Bruno of Segni, PL 165.977.
89. For instance, *Cant.* 4: CM 26.89: "sanctae omnes Scripturae, quae solae dicuntur et sunt canonicae."

pert's principle should not be construed in some proto-Protestant sense. He presupposed the teaching authority of the Church and was immersed in the Fathers' exposition of Scripture; but he also held, together with most others prior to the late middle ages, that Scripture was the unique source of divine truth, and tradition therefore the Church's authoritative exposition thereof.[90] Thus he described the Roman Church as authoritative in part because its teaching had always been consonant with Scripture.[91] To go back behind the Fathers to Scripture itself was a bold and risky step—reserved later for ordinary professors of theology following years of training and apprenticeship as "biblical bachelors"—but one consistent with prevailing views of ultimate authority on matters of divine truth. In the 1130's Peter Abelard was to prepare an original commentary on the Epistle to the Romans which created a furor in conservative circles, provoking William of St. Thierry to compile the Fathers' teachings on this book as a bulwark against Abelard's new interpretations. So also in the years 1114–16 Rupert turned to the Gospel of St. John in order to declare the plain scriptural truth on christology, sacramental grace, predestination, and the eucharist. Of course, Rupert knew full well that Augustine's exposition of St. John's Gospel had supplied many of the arms in his adversaries' arsenal.

3

Rupert on Trial

Rupert had completed his *Commentary on John* by the summer of 1116 at the latest, and soon after he challenged the venerable Anselm of Laon in a treatise entitled *De uoluntate Dei* (chapter V, part 2). Once these attacks had become known, his adversaries in Liège reacted swiftly, severely, and almost decisively. By the end of September Rupert was haled into court on charges of heresy and very nearly condemned to silence. On issues pertain-

90. See Pelikan, *Theology* 122ff, and F. Oakley, *The Western Church in the Later Middle Ages* (Ithaca 1979) 148–57, with further literature.
91. *Off.* 2.22: CM 7.52–53.

ing to the eucharistic debate—he was more successful on the other matter—only the unexpected intervention of Abbot Cuno of Siegburg saved him from certain condemnation (*paene fuerim iudicatus*). Nine years later Rupert still regarded Cuno's act as a "miracle" (*miraculum*) for which he would remain indebted to his dying day. But so great still was the hostility toward Rupert in Liège that Abbot Berengar, just before his death on 16 November 1116, arranged to have him sent for safekeeping to his new-found protector at Siegburg, where he remained in exile for several months (until about May 1117). Such, in brief, are the essential facts; since this account differs from previous ones,[92] the sources will be examined in an appendix and the actual reconstruction presented in the text that follows.

At the time he was charged with heresy, Rupert noted in his apologia of 1125, he was away (*procul absens*), uncertain even who his accusers were, and he as yet barely knew Abbot Cuno, whom he had met and spoken with only once before. Even allowing for some measure of distortion after nine years, both points are credible. As a leading member of his community and a likely candidate one day for an abbacy, Rupert doubtless undertook missions from time to time for his abbey. Most would have involved local ecclesiastical affairs or maintenance of the abbey's properties and incomes; at some time in the year 1116, for instance, Abbot Berengar witnessed a charter at Gembloux, and at least one of his monks presumably accompanied him there.[93] Some might also have taken him out of the diocese, as when he met and argued with Bishop John of Thérouanne (chapter VIII, part 2).[94] Particularly if Rupert were away with Abbot Berengar or Prior Heribrand, his adversaries might well have considered it advantageous to bring charges and set a trial in

92. A. Cauchie, *Biographie Nationale* 20 (Brussels 1910) 440–41 first distinguished the charges arising out of the eucharistic debate from Rupert's better-known controversy with Anselm of Laon; and Bischoff, *Controversy*, passim, first sought to reconstruct the actual events (with an incorrect dating).

93. C.-G. Roland, ed., *Recueil des chartes de l'abbaye de Gembloux* (Gembloux 1921) 51–53.

94. *RegBen.* 4.13: PL 170.536–37. Neither the time nor place is known.

motion before Rupert or his superiors could intervene with diocesan officials.

How Cuno became involved is much more difficult to say; it is worth repeating once more that Rupert too considered it "providential" and "miraculous." Abbot Cuno of Siegburg was easily the most powerful and influential abbot in the archdiocese and possibly the entire ecclesiastical province of Cologne. It is not surprising therefore that Rupert should have met him once. As an example of the ecclesiastical business which might have brought him to Liège, at a time unknown (Semmler estimated 1121–26) a canon (William of Millen) of the cathedral chapter donated properties and a parish church which became one of Siegburg's nine priories.[95] Cuno might also have taken a personal interest in Rupert's case. He had served for a time as master in the abbey school at Siegburg, and as bishop of Regensburg he promoted several ecclesiastical authors (Gerhoch of Reichersberg, Honorius Augustodunensis).[96]

In the prologue to *De omnipotentia Dei*, Rupert referred to a "trial" in which he had nearly (*paene*) been condemned.[97] Accompanied by Heribrand, he had appeared before Dean Henry, archdeacon for Condroz, the juridical district to which St. Lawrence (located just outside the city) belonged. Also present were two "*cognitores*," meaning something like "expert advisers,"[98] who apparently found in Rupert's favor, or at least (this is more likely) judged that he was not technically heretical (*iniuriam quam pro ueritate sustinui indoluistis*). Rupert himself described the debate aroused by *De uoluntate Dei* as the context of this hearing, and so scholars have, understandably, always taken it to re-

95. J. Semmler, *Die Klosterreform von Siegburg* (Bonn 1959) 68–69; E. Wisplinghoff, *Die Benediktinerabtei Siegburg* (Germania Sacra, n.F. 9.2, Berlin and New York 1975) 81–82.

96. Classen, *Gerhoch* 34–35, 50–52.

97. "Paene [cf. paene fuerim iudicatus, n. 35 above] istud mihi contigisse sentio, O doctores nostri et boni auditores Dei S. et A. qui cum abbate meo H. coram illustri uiro uestrae ecclesiae, archidiacono simul et decano H. cognitores causae Dei et nostrae adfuistis, et iniuriam quam pro ueritate sustinui indoluistis." *Omnip.* prologus: PL 170.455.

98. See Bischoff, *Controversy* 364 n. 30.

fer only to the predestinarian controversy. But at the end of this same prologue Rupert added: "And indeed the other things they say I do and once did as one depraved by arrogance and driven on by pride, I commit that all to God, who knows the secrets of the heart far better than they. . . ."[99] Now in the apologetic letter prefatory to his *Commentary on John*, Rupert also referred to charges of "pride" and "vanity" and also committed the matter lastly to God alone.[100] The best conclusion, then, particularly since there is no evidence whatsoever for a second trial, is that *both* the eucharistic and the predestinarian issues were handled at the *same trial*. Since on the predestinarian issue he had come through relatively unscathed, Rupert decided, determined as ever, to respond publicly and in writing so as to show that he had indeed been right all along; but since the eucharistic views argued in his *Commentary on John* had nearly cost him his theological life, he committed this matter to God alone.

Why have scholars not hit upon such a clear and elegant solution before? Because Rupert says he was accompanied to the trial by "my abbot Heribrand" (*cum abbato meo H.*). Yet this trial could not have taken place after Berengar's death and Heribrand's assumption of the abbacy (19 November 1116), because Rupert's flight to Siegburg, arranged still by Berengar, presupposed the trial and especially Cuno's intervention. There is, I think, a fairly simple solution. (There are, by the way, no surviving manuscripts to check the accuracy of that "H.") In his capacity as prior of St. Lawrence, as Rupert's former teacher, and possibly as heir apparent to the abbacy, it was Heribrand who took Rupert to the hearing. Abbot Berengar may simply have so ordered it, or he may have already been ill, for he would die in less than two months. But when Rupert wrote the prologue to *De omnipotentia Dei* in 1117, Heribrand was in fact his abbot and Rupert employed the present and greater title.

99. "Porro et quod praeterea dicunt id me agere olimque egisse arrogantia deprauatum et spiritu elationis excitatum Deo totum committo, qui melius nouit occulta cordium." PL 170.455.

100. ". . . illa praesumptionis uanitas, qua elatum me ad scribendum. . . . Ego autem testem habere me confido Deum in anima mea. . . ." CM 9.1.

By late in the summer of 1116, then, Rupert had completed the *Commentary on John* and *De uoluntate Dei*, and was temporarily away from St. Lawrence and Liège. Local student-clerics, in strong disagreement with his positions on eucharistic and predestinarian theology and outraged by his attacks upon Alger of Liège and Anselm of Laon, seized this opportunity to bring charges against him, particularly against these two newest works, and demanded he be totally silenced (*omnis mihi licentia scribendi tolleretur*, n. 35 above). The term "*licentia*" should be understood as referring to a general "right," not the specific *licentia docendi* first attested about two generations later;[101] but the legal situation was not significantly different. The power of the *magisterium* resided principally in the ordinary bishop, and in practice as regards teaching was conferred upon an official in the cathedral chapter, often a master or chancellor. In this instance the clerics at Liège simply went to the competent juridical official, the archdeacon for Rupert's district (Condroz), with the demand that this monk be proscribed from any further exercise of magisterial powers or rights, that is, any writing, teaching, or preaching. Archdeacon Henry, who presided at the subsequent trial, happened also to be dean of the cathedral chapter (1099–1123), the former patron of Sigebert of Gembloux, a man highly respected in the diocese (also by Berengar), and an adherent of the moderate reform party, roughly comparable in this to Alger.[102]

Two experts (*cognitores*) advised Archdeacon Henry on the technical theological matters at issue. Rupert identified them by

101. Gaines Post, "Alexander III, the *Licentia docendi*, and the Rise of the Universities," in *Anniversary Essays in Mediaeval History*, ed. C. H. Taylor (Boston 1929; repr. 1967) 255–77.

102. On Archdeacon Henry, see E. de Marneffe, "Tableau chronologique des dignitaires du chapitre Saint-Lambert à Liège," *Analectes pour servir à l'histoire ecclésiastique de la Belgique* 25 (1895) 441ff; G. Constable, "Monasticism, Lordship, and Society in the Twelfth-Century Hesbaye: Five Documents on the Foundation of the Cluniac Priory of Bertrée," *Traditio* 33 (1977) 171. Henry served as spokesman when the clergy brought charges of simony against Otbert, *ChronHub.* 96: ed. Hanquet 249; Berengar's good opinion, ibid. 77: 190–91.

initial ("S." and "A.") as members of Henry's (*uestrae*) church, that is, the cathedral chapter, and also as masters (*scholasticos, doctores*). "S." surely was "Stephanus," attested in the very year 1116 as the *scholasticus* of St. Lambert's.[103] And "A." was probably none other than Alger, the only other canon in the cathedral chapter known to have enjoyed such a scholarly reputation. But is it conceivable that Alger himself would be asked to sit as one of the "expert advisers"? In a system where judge and prosecutor often were in effect the same person that hardly seemed extraordinary at all. Precisely this happened just five years later (1121) when Abelard was tried for heresy at Soissons: the same two masters who had initiated charges against him were appointed by the papal legate and the archbishop of Reims also to sit in judgement (*cognitores*, as it were) on the theological contents of his book—much of course to Abelard's dismay.[104]

This identification, rather than complicating the matter, actually explains several things. Long after the debate and trial, Rupert continued to refer to Alger with great respect (*magni nominis magnaeque aestimationis scholastico*). Moreover, particularly with regard to the predestinarian issue, Rupert distinguished clearly between the "rabble of ignorant students" who brought charges and the "wise" and "prudent" masters who found in his favor. The same distinction is hinted for the eucharistic controversy: his adversaries, Rupert reports, charged him with accusing an "honest and learned cleric" of heresy.[105] This suggests Alger did not personally bring charges or defend himself against

103. *Cartulaire de l'église Saint-Lambert de Liège*, ed. S. Bormans and E. Schoolmeesters (Brussels 1893) 1.53. On the identification, compare A. Cauchie, *Biographie Nationale* 20.437 and Bischoff, *Controversy* 236, against H. Silvestre, *RTAM* 28 (1961) 11 n. 17 and *Saint-Laurent* 64, 75 n. 12.

104. ". . . ipsi inde iudicarent qui me super hoc accusabant, ut illud in me etiam compleretur: *Et inimici nostri sunt iudices*" (Deut 32:31). *Historia calamitatum*, ed. J. Monfrin (Paris 1959) 84. See Miethke (n. 106 below) 92–94.

105. "Aiunt me arrogantum et incredibiliter elatum, nullum pati uiuere probum clericum, quo nomine designare mos est cuiuscumque ordinis uel habitus ualenter litteratum, nullum eiusmodi sinere quin illum arguam esse hereticum." CM 9.2. Rupert means Alger was a "very learned man" but not a priest.

the attack in Rupert's commentary; rather, enthusiastic disciples sought to silence this arrogant monk in his behalf. If Alger served as adviser, it becomes even clearer why the eucharistic issue posed the greatest danger for Rupert, and also why he never dared speak to it again in Liège.

On the actual format of the trial next to nothing is known.[106] Presumably charges were brought, and under Heribrand's supervision Rupert responded to them. The experts then weighed the arguments and advised Archdeacon Henry, who rendered the final judgement. The issues considered at the trial, however, can be reconstructed: with regard to eucharistic theology, from Rupert's letter and Alger's De sacramentis; with regard to predestinarian matters, from the De omnipotentia Dei (chapter V, part 3).

The most fundamental charge held that Rupert's Commentary on John had impugned the authority and teachings of St. Augustine. The clerics accused him of overweening pride, of attempting like a "new man" to engraft himself into the "ancient nobility"—a striking social metaphor applied to the authority of the received tradition. Clearly, these student–clerics had singled out and understood very well those pages in the middle of Rupert's commentary which dealt so polemically with the preceding eucharistic debate. Rupert effectively countercharged that they, just like that heretic Berengar of Tours, sought to make St. Augustine sanction a "figurative" or "symbolic" view of the Lord's body, whereas he with the Holy Catholic Church (sicut ecclesia catholica tenet; uniuersa sciente ecclesia catholica) reaffirmed that the sacrament is necessarily Christ's body broken for us and His blood shed for us.[107] All of Rupert's brave language about Scripture as the ultimate and unique source of truth had disappeared. He claimed now to stand with the Holy Catholic Church,

106. There is no adequate study of heresy trials in the middle ages, but see J. Miethke, "Theologenprozesse in der ersten Phase ihrer institutionellen Ausbildung: Die Verfahren gegen Peter Abaelard und Gilbert von Poitiers," Viator 6 (1975) 87–116 (nothing on Rupert's case).

107. CM 9.1. Compare Alger's defense of this definition in De sacramentis 1.4: PL 180.751, where he cites Augustine, De civitate Dei 10.5 and De doctrina christiana 2.50.

charged his adversaries with misreading and violating St. Augustine's intent, and insisted in both letters written at Siegburg (see Appendix) that his commentary represented merely pious meditations, the reflections of a devout and harmless contemplative. So also the trial—in keeping with tradition—came down ultimately to a battle of authorities. Rupert had stated things in his commentary which clearly stood contrary to St. Augustine's authoritative commentary. Unless he could find other authorities to support his position, he would be proved manifestly in error and rightly made to keep silent thereafter.

The trial almost certainly reviewed Rupert's rejection of an Augustinian definition of Christ's body, his position on manna, and the question of sacrifice, for Alger devoted long chapters to these matters, replete with authorities, in the first book of *De sacramentis* (respectively cc. 3, 8, 16). But Rupert's letter does not refer to them. According to it, the primary question (*causarum supradictarum prima*) was Rupert's "incarnational" as opposed to his adversaries' "figurative" understanding of Christ's words, *Hoc est corpus meum quod pro uobis traditum est.* To support his strong analogy to the incarnation, Rupert produced a citation from none other than "St. Augustine" to the effect that the Church's sacrifice is confected of two things just as Christ's person consists of God and man. This authority effectively bedeviled the attack of Rupert's critics upon his "impanationist" views; later Alger worked hard at least three different times to interpret it "properly."[108] In fact, the ascription to St. Augustine, so important to Rupert in his dire circumstances, was false; the sentence came ultimately from Berengar of Tours (!), as quoted by Lanfranc, and was mistakenly attributed to Augustine by

108. "Dicunt ita personaliter in pane impanatum Christum, sicut in carne humana personaliter incarnatum Deum [cf. Rupert, as in nn. 20, 23 above]. Quae haeresis, quia noua et absurda est, rationibus et auctoritatibus, prout Deus aspirauit, radicitus est exstirpanda. Ex quadam enim similitudine beati Augustini in libro Sententiarum Prosperi, suam sumunt et defendunt haeresim, qua dicit: *Sacrificium ecclesiae duobus confici duobusque constare sicut persona Christi constat et conficitur ex Deo et homine.*" *De sacramentis* 1.6: PL 180.754. Cf. Alger's concern to interpret this text again in 1.5, 20: PL 180.752–53, 797–98.

way of Ivo's *Decretum*.[109] But Rupert found still other authorities, for Alger's account and refutation continues: when it is objected that the species are not united to Christ's person but rather are only a "mystery" or "figure" thereof, this "impanationist" goes on to cite additional texts from Ambrose, Maximus, and the Scriptures which seem to support his position.[110] Indeed, to substantiate his way of talking about the bread as assumed into union with Christ, Rupert cited still another text from Ambrose's *De sacramentis*, likewise found in Ivo's *Decretum*, and to the proper interpretation of which Alger also devoted considerable effort.[111] In short, Rupert had managed to muster a whole series of texts which appeared to support his particular view of the sacrament, one of which was even ascribed to St. Augustine and all of which served to defend the reality of Christ's body against "figurative" views his adversaries insisted upon finding in St. Augustine. The evidence indicates that he had gleaned several of his authorities from Book II of Ivo's recently published (ca. 1095) *Decretum*.

But, for his insistence that Judas had not received communion—this, he said, was what really made him "black" in their eyes[112]—Rupert could find no authoritative support. Judas, as a symbol of the unworthy, came up for treatment in virtually every eucharistic treatise as well as in Ivo's *Decretum*, but all followed St. Augustine in saying he had indeed received communion and was thus a symbol of the "mixed" church. Here finally they had caught Rupert; here was definitive proof of his heresy (*pro magno criminis argumento*). Then, wholly unexpectedly, Ab-

109. *Decretum* 2.9: PL 161.152–53. The true source noted and an explanation of the false ascription given by Häring (n. 67 above) 52–55. There is no reason to believe Rupert falsified the source, since Alger would have caught that.

110. *De sacramentis* 1.6: PL 180.754. The text from Ambrose is *De fide ad Grat.* 2.7.50, referred to but not cited in Lanfranc, *De corpore* 20: PL 150.437–38. See Häring (n. 67 above) 55–56. I have not located the passage from Maximus.

111. Alger, *De sacramentis* 1.7: PL 180.756–57. The text is Ambrose, *De sacramentis* 4.4, found in Ivo, *Decretum* 2.7: PL 161.144.

112. CM 9.2.

bot Cuno produced a passage from Hilary's *Commentary on Matthew* which took exactly Rupert's position.[113] Authority balanced authority; Rupert was saved by a breath from condemnation (*sine illo* [the Hilary text] *non possem [non] iudicari haereticus*). His relief and gratitude knew no bounds. According to Rupert, Cuno came upon this text "providentially," without knowing it or seeking it out. A likely hypothesis—but no more—is that the search for countervailing authorities had become frantic, and that Cuno, a former teacher, began to rummage through all Gospel commentaries, only to come unexpectedly upon this passage in Hilary's relatively unknown work. The twelfth-century library catalogue of St. Lawrence in fact lists Hilary's work[114] (though of course it could also have been acquired later as a result of the trial). In any case the text did its job and frustrated the clerics' attack. In his *De sacramentis* Alger devoted a lengthy chapter to interpreting this passage from Hilary, which, he said, was used to deny any reception of the Lord's Body by Judas and the unworthy.[115]

Thus Rupert escaped condemnation, but only by the thinnest of margins: an unknown text produced unexpectedly by a powerful abbot from outside the diocese. He was not ordered to keep silent (as was Roscellin, who soon ignored the order, but in another diocese) or to burn the offending book (as was Abelard, who recalled it bitterly).[116] But the clerics' hatred of this "arrogant" monk was now beyond telling. Several months later Rupert still compared himself to Ishmael: "His hand will be against

113. Hilary, *In Matt.* 30.2: PL 9.1065.

114. Gessler, "Bibliothèque" 108.

115. "Unde etiam aliqui errantes Christum a sacramento suo separari autumant, ita ut malos purum sacramentum [only bread] et non corpus Christi sumere astruant, et ipsum Iudam proditorem quibusdam sanctorum auctoritatibus contendant in coena Domini communioni corporis Christi non interfuisse, quasi corpus Christi non possit nisi qui incorporatur Christo uere sumere [an accurate reading of Rupert's intent]. . . . Sed iterum B. Hilarium . . . [*In Matt.* 30.2: PL 9.1065] quasi testem huius rei faciunt, qui manifeste uidetur asserere, a Domino Iudam a tanti sacramenti communione exclusum quasi indignum." *De sacramentis* 1.21: PL 180.798–99.

116. *Historia calamitatum*: ed. Monfrin 87–88.

every man, and every man's hand against him." In the days just after the trial Rupert was made to "suffer their undeserved hatred" (*me inimicitias sustinentem odientium me gratis*),[117] and grew increasingly frightened as his powerful abbot-protector lay dying. In the dedicatory epistle to Cuno, written just afterwards, Rupert recalled a dream he had then which, in his view, foretold Cuno's patronage, but which for our purposes accurately reflected his state of mind at that time. In the dream Rupert found himself in the middle of a church with people all round screaming charge and countercharge at him. He remained safe because Abbot Berengar held his hand. Then the abbot put Rupert's hand into that of another. This was the foretelling of Cuno's protection—which clearly then had not yet been arranged. As the volume and intensity of reproach reached its climax Rupert cried out: "Now, Lord, receive me with my brothers, your servants, through martyrdom!" This text came, as Rupert noted, from the *Passion* of Dionysius the Areopagite. If—as is often the case with dreams—Rupert had heard or chanted this shortly before, it was then just after October 3, Dionysius' feastday. This would put the trial itself in late September. Before he died (*migraturus*) a month later on November 16, Abbot Berengar arranged for Rupert to find refuge with Abbot Cuno at Siegburg, since Heribrand could no longer protect him from the hostility which had mounted against him.

4

Rupert under Judgement

As Rupert's chief adversary in the oral debate and probably also one of the "experts" required to sit in judgement upon his views, Alger resolved, in the aftermath of both the debate and the trial, to restore a measure of order by setting forth clearly and authoritatively the truth about the Blessed Sacrament. The "saints" (patristic authorities), he began, have spoken variously about the sacrament, and certain "simple people," seeking to

---

117. This and the remainder of the paragraph from CM 21.121–22.

know more than is necessary or than they themselves can understand, are producing heresies; unless they are corrected, by continuing to teach and to defend things they do not know about they will bring themselves and others to ruin. In particular, they fail to understand basic distinctions between Christ the Head and His members, between what is said about Him sacramentally and nonsacramentally, so that they tend in their confusion either to humiliate the Head (that is, to sacrifice Him again on the altar) or to glorify the members (the "assumed" bread which will "divinize" believers).[118] Such, in brief, was Alger's view of Rupert's contribution to eucharistic theology. Though various works have analyzed Alger's theology and sources,[119] the specific setting and purpose of his work still require comment, for beyond general analysis of problems raised since the Berengarian controversy its structure and argument must be understood in reference to the debate and trial in Liège.

Alger's *De sacramentis corporis et sanguinis Dominici* was finished sometime before he gave up his secretarial post to enter the abbey of Cluny around May 1121.[120] Repeated reference to authorities Rupert had used at the trial and his defense of Augustinian texts attacked in Rupert's commentary require that the final draft of Book I be dated sometime after the trial (September 1116). He never referred specifically and literally to Rupert's *Commentary on John*. Around 1117 there was presumably only one copy in existence, which Rupert may have taken with him to Siegburg, or simply refused to make available after the attack upon it. Alger's tone remained confident and sometimes condescending throughout. After all, he was still the bishop's secretary and the most highly regarded master in the city, whereas the monk of St. Lawrence had temporarily been driven out of town and effectively, if not legally, silenced.

Alger also began with the incarnation (c. 1), but in part, as

118. *De sacramentis* prologus: PL 180.739.
119. Haring (n. 67 above) passim; Bischoff, *Controversy*, passim (at least as good on Alger as on Rupert); L. Brigué, *Alger de Liège* (Paris 1936) passim; and Macy (n. 2 above) 31–38.
120. See Nicholas' *Elogium* (PL 180.738) for the *terminus ante quem*.

we saw earlier (chapter III, part 2), in order to criticize Rupert's unusual approach to christology. In the same spirit (cc. 2–3) he rejected Rupert's notion of personal union and "deification" by means of the sacrament as an assault upon Christ's uniqueness (*singularitas*) and an unwarranted (*superextendere*) exaltation of our poor humanity. Then he argued at length for Augustine's teaching that the end (*res* or *uirtus*) of the sacrament is to bind believers in love to Christ and one another by grace.[121] But Rupert's critique of his spiritualizing interpretation had manifestly put Alger on the defensive, for he cited many Augustinian texts and explained their meaning at length. The same is true for the next two chapters (4–5), where he laid down basic Augustinian definitions of "sacrament" and justified "figurative" (*figuratiua*, *similitudinaria*) language applied to the "sacrament," that is, the species or the form as distinct from the *res sacramenti*, the substance of Christ's body. On the strength of these definitions Alger then attacked fundamentally the "new and absurd heresy of impanation," first by rebutting improper analogies to the incarnation, including all talk of "assuming" the bread (c. 6: n. 108 above), and then by rejecting any notion that the substance of the bread and wine remained unchanged (c. 7).

Alger responded next (c. 8) to the debate about the sacramental significance of manna. Manna and the eucharist are alike in so far, he reaffirmed with Augustine, as they have a signifying function and confer the "same spiritual grace." So also in chapter 9 he refuted an extreme realist idea Rupert had taken over from Paschasius to the effect that the transformation of bread and wine is comparable to that of food into human tissue.[122] Chapters 10–12 constitute an extended commentary on John 6:54 designed, it appears, to teach Rupert by means of many different authorities that the eating and drinking Christ enjoined upon his followers was to be understood spiritually but nonetheless truly of the substance of His resurrected body. Where

121. *De sacramentis* 1.3: PL 180.749–51.
122. *De sacramentis* 1.9: PL 180.766–69. See *John* 6: CM 9.332–33. Bischoff, *Controversy* 63.

Rupert had openly differed with Augustine here, Alger cited the Fathers lest, he emphasized, he seem to interpret Scripture in his own way (*ne meo sensu interpretari uidear*). He "presumed" to add the testimony of the Fathers to that of Christ because Christ did not always speak so plainly; and this particular interpretation was not of "his own presumption" but rather of all "Catholic authority."[123] So much for Rupert's insistence upon the literal text of Holy Scripture against the received teachings of the Fathers!

Beginning with chapter 14, which Alger himself noted as a break, the connection to Rupert becomes less apparent, though two chapters still are crucial. Chapter 16 deals at length with the eucharistic celebration as sacrifice, identical with that on Calvary as regards the substance of Christ's body but "figurative" with respect to Christ's unique sacrifice. And then in his penultimate chapter (21: n. 115 above) Alger took up the question of Judas' communion. He defended Augustine's view and upheld the objective status of the sacrament so that the good can take communion with or even from the "evil." The Lord purposely included Judas, Alger added pointedly, in order to remove a major cause of schism, namely, that many, more out of pride than religion, drive from themselves with kicks (*calcibus etiam a se repellerent*) those who seem to them less good (*minoris aestimationis*).[124] So much for the self-righteousness of the zealous reformers!

Alger's Book I expounded the truth in large measure by way of indicting Rupert's "absurd" and "erroneous" views, and Book II, with its ten questions, seems to have reflected the general debate about eucharistic theology among students, clerics, and monks in Liège. This was the shape of his work when Alger composed the prologue, which mentions only two parts; and at least one manuscript (originally from the Benedictine house of St. James in Liège!)[125] has in fact only the first two books. But

123. *John 6*: CM 9.358–61; *De sacramentis* 1.12: PL 180.776, 777.
124. *De sacramentis* 1.21: PL 180.803. Cf. Rupert, as in text at n. 61 above!
125. Now Darmstadt, Landesbibliothek MS 766.

Alger decided to add a third book to deal explicitly with the validity of sacraments administered by heretics and schismatics, once again because the "saints" had spoken variously on this issue, probably the most openly contended in Rupert's dispute with the clerics in Liège. However much Alger himself had wavered twenty years earlier in the third book of his *Liber de misericordia et iustitia*, he now insisted uncompromisingly, as St. Augustine had for baptism (cc. 2–8), that *all* sacraments are of God and as such are fully and unchangeably true in and of themselves irrespective of the quality of their ministers. No other theologian or canonist in the reform era argued quite so clearly and cogently for the *ex opere operata* position[126]—and this, historically speaking, in opposition to Rupert and the strict reform party in the diocese of Liège.

Alger considered several possible objections, two of which relate directly to Rupert. Some seem to think, he noted, that Augustine's language applies only to the unworthy (as opposed to heretical or schismatic) and to those who are unknown or perforce tolerated (c. 8)—precisely Rupert's position (nn. 59, 60 above). They also object, he continues, that there is no place of sacrifice outside the Church, that neither Christ nor the Holy Spirit is to be found anywhere among the heretics—likewise Rupert's view almost literally.[127] They further object that the priesthood does not subsist among heretics.[128] Rupert never said this in writing, although Alger may have inferred it from his insistence that publicly condemned prelates be content with lay communion. Alger finally closed his case, the objective status of the Church and her sacraments established not as a result of but rather in opposition to the reformers. Still in his lifetime, a monk of Afflighem in Flanders strongly recommended *De sacramentis* to the monks of Maria Laach for its theology and spiritual teachings, with no reference at all to its controversial ori-

126. *De sacramentis* 3.1–2: PL 180.831–34. Häring (n. 67 above) 61–63, 67–71.

127. *De sacramentis* 3.9: PL 180.841–42. Cf. *John* 6: CM 9.314; *Levit.* 1.32: CM 22.843.

128. *De sacramentis* 3.10: PL 180.842.

gins in Liège.[129] And in the 1130's Peter the Venerable, Alger's abbot-father during his last years, praised it as the best defense of orthodoxy to come out of the Berengarian controversy.[130] And so it has been understood, with few exceptions, until now.

Rupert holds the dubious honor of having provoked the only two full-length treatises on eucharistic theology known from the early twelfth century, the one (Alger's) espousing more clearly than ever before the objective validity of the sacrament, and the other (William of St. Thierry's) one of the earliest to apply the distinction between substance and accidents. News of controversy in Liège traveled as well to the Benedictine abbey of St. Nicholas-aux-Bois near Laon. Sometime during or before the year 1119, Sigfried, prior of St. Nicholas, requested advice from Abbot Guibert of Nogent on two controversial questions, namely, whether the Lord dispensed the sacrament to Judas in the "*buccella*," a view held by St. Augustine and Leo the Great but opposed by Hilary and "Victor Campanus," and whether that "sacrament" was itself only a "sign," whence Christ's readiness to do so.[131] Prior Sigfried clearly had learned of the debate and more particularly of the trial in Liège where the opposing authorities were publicly deployed. Abbot Guibert professed not to know who would raise such questions and thus cast doubt on the harmonious authority of the Fathers. But according to his famous work *On Relics* written at about the same time, a friend had told him about someone who held Christ was crucified daily on the altar.[132] This too sounds like an echo of the debate in Liège. Yet, however news of Rupert's controversy

129. See C. Coppens, in *Ons Geestlijke Erf* 21 (1947) 92–98.
130. *Contra Petrobrusianos*: CM 10.87–88.
131. For the date of Guibert's *De buccella Iudae*, see M.-C. Garand, "Le scriptorium de Guibert de Nogent," *Scriptorium* 31 (1977) 24–26. The text of the letter is in PL 156.527–38. Compare Bischoff, *Controversy* 19–23, 175–78; J. Pelikan, "A First-Generation Anselmian, Guibert of Nogent," in *Continuity and Discontinuity in Church History*, ed. F. F. Church and T. George (Studies in the History of Christian Thought 19, Leiden 1979) 71–82, esp. 73–74; and J. Geiselmann, "Die Stellung des Guibert von Nogent in der Eucharistielehre der Frühscholastik," *Theologische Quartalschrift* 110 (1929) 60–84, 279–305.
132. *De pignoribus* 2.5, 6: PL 156.644, 646. Pelikan (n. 131 above) 74.

may have spread by word of mouth, especially in Benedictine circles at Laon and Reims, this affair remained essentially a local one. Texts ascribed to the "School of Laon," Hugh of St. Victor's *De sacramentis*, and Lombard's textbook take no note, even polemically, of Rupert's particular views.[133]

In November 1116 Rupert fled to Siegburg in the Rhineland. There he "brought out" and dedicated to Abbot Cuno his massive *De sancta Trinitate*, then addressed to the "expert advisers" his considered response to the predestinarian issues (*De omnipotentia Dei* cc. 1–18), and finally prepared the brief letter explaining why his *Commentary on John* had been attacked. This last letter suggests that his heart and mind were already intent upon returning to his homeland and mother abbey. Siegburg was a house at least four times larger than his own (one hundred twenty compared to about thirty monks), where he could not understand the native tongue[134] and knew no one except its powerful and busy abbot. He apparently longed to return as soon as his adversaries' hostility had subsided sufficiently and Abbot Heribrand judged it safe. But he was also, it seems, itching to return to the fray, and the predestinarian controversy would take a dramatic new twist immediately after his return (chapter V, part 3). The eucharistic controversy, however, was over, and Rupert now stood personally and psychologically, if not legally, under judgement. The mood betrayed in those two letters written at Siegburg (Appendix) is unlike anything since his confident announcement at the beginning of his first work six years earlier that he would go his own way in treating Holy Scripture and the divine office. The man divinely called to instruct the faithful and repel heretics had himself very nearly been condemned to silence and forced into exile. The man who bravely challenged inadequate interpretations by the Fathers now compared himself to the innocent woman persecuted for pouring out precious ointment on Jesus.

133. This certainly applies to Rupert's "impanationist" views. Hugh's discussion of Judas (2.8.4: PL 176.464) may contain a distant echo.
134. As he could not initially at Deutz: *Incendio* 14: ed. Grundmann 458.

Still in Siegburg, Rupert briefly reaffirmed his position with a scheme developed earlier: the eucharist is the body of Christ in "name" (*nomen*), because Christ himself, the chief high priest, said it (*Hoc est corpus meum*); in "*re*," because it is the "Holy of Holies crucified on the cross" (*traditus et lanceatus*); and in effect (*effecto*), because the species work the remission of sins just as his bodily appearance (*in illa specie, qua pependit in cruce*) worked remission for all the departed faithful gathered in limbo.[135] After his return, however, Rupert never again discussed eucharistic theology in Liège and despite its great importance to his religious life commented on it only rarely in works written later at Deutz. About eight years after the trial he restated his position on manna, and later still his position on Judas (citing Hilary explicitly).[136] Otherwise he avoided this topic, quite unlike the predestinarian issue to which he returned time and again.

In retrospect the eucharistic controversy appears to represent defeat in most regards, a series of strategic retreats from his original stand through near condemnation to virtual silence. Yet his views should not be dismissed as peculiar or aberrant. They grew out of a piety, ultrarealist and incarnational in character, which corresponded very closely to that of most monk-priests, as did his argument for the salvific, "divinizing" effect of eating Christ's body worthily; and his attempt to protect the purity of the sacrament expressed that high view of the sacrament which had inspired the reformers. But Rupert's thought represented much more than the reflection of a particular eucharistic piety: it was also a considered attempt to ground that piety theologically in a new exposition of Holy Scripture. For over fifty years historians have repeatedly insisted that Berengar's application of speculative grammar to the Blessed Sacrament marked a crucial turning-point in medieval thought, particularly since after a

135. CM 9.3; first developed in *Levit.* 1.16: CM 22.822; *Spir.* 3.21: CM 14.1929–30.

136. *Cant.* 4: CM 26.101–03; *Matt.* 10: CM 29.313–14; and *RegBen.* 1: PL 170.495–96.

century and a half of grappling with this problem Pope Innocent III sanctioned as orthodox a formula which presupposed
Aristotelian logic. This is undoubtedly true. But it also merits
attention that Rupert sought to find definitions of the sacrament
by freshly interpreting and applying texts from St. John's Gospel. Though not nearly so influential as Berengar's dialectical
approach, Rupert's scriptural approach to eucharistic theology
was equally innovative and contentious. And its initial results
were as crushing.

APPENDIX
Sources Pertaining to Rupert's Trial

There are four sources which bear in some way upon Rupert's trial on charges arising out of the eucharistic theology argued in his *Commentary on John*. Three were written from exile
in Siegburg just months after the trial, and the other, the only
narrative account, nine years later at Deutz.

In an apologia written in the spring of 1125 (see chapter IX,
part 2), Rupert described at length three successful theological
battles. He concluded with a hasty summary of the eucharistic
controversy (PL 170.495–96:n. 35 above), which had actually
taken place before the other three. This reversed order he explained at the outset of his apologia, addressed to Abbot Cuno:
he would tell first about his various critics and then (*posthac*)
about how Cuno had come so generously to embrace (*libenter
amplecteris*) his work.[1] Rupert referred to the eucharistic controversy, in other words, *only* in order to recall the origins of
Cuno's patronage and to repay his debt of gratitude publicly.
Rupert never otherwise described exactly what happened, and
the reason is fairly obvious. At the trial he had come within a
breath (*paene iudicatus*) of being judged a heretic (*iudicari haereticus*) and condemned to total silence (*omnis mihi licentia scribendi
tolleretur*)—a blow struck to the very heart of his religious and
intellectual vocation. This he would not talk about publicly, ex-

1. *RegBen.* 1: PL 170.480.

cept formally to thank Cuno for so "miraculously" saving him. Rupert's narrative account therefore glossed over or ran together many phases of the debate and trial, and it recounted in detail only the issue (Judas) which required Cuno's intervention to defend him.

The source nearest to the trial was written early in 1117 at Siegburg.[2] There, probably soon after his arrival, Rupert dedicated *De sancta Trinitate* to his new-found patron, and his dedicatory epistle (CM 21.119–23) reveals much about his situation. He emphasized that Cuno's authority and protection alone enabled him now to bring this work out. Twice he alluded in forceful language to the recent efforts to silence him and to Cuno's authoritative intervention.[3] It was, he believed, "only by the providence of God that he had come to Cuno's attention," so that when Abbot Berengar was about to die and Heribrand could no longer protect him from such great "envy" he could still find refuge at Siegburg. The opening one and one-half pages of the letter make clear that Rupert was thinking primarily of the near condemnation which resulted from his eucharistic views and his *Commentary on John.* Just like the woman who anointed Christ with precious ointment, Rupert began, so he has carried out his religious service (*impendit officium pietatis*) with meditations upon the incarnate Word become flesh, only to meet reproach from the apostles (clerics), to whom he now quoted Christ's words: Why do you trouble this woman? For she has wrought a good work upon me (Matt. 26:10). The contemplative, he reminded them, anoints Christ when he succeeds in extracting from the marrow of Holy Scripture meditations on the Word who was with God and became flesh to dwell among us (John 1:1–3, quoted verbatim here). Indeed how much sweeter

---

2. Rupert gave the year: CM 21.120. Cf. Bischoff, *Controversy* 123–25.

3. "Nosti, inquam, haec, nam nisi quia tu [Cuno], immo per te Christus praesidio adfuit, nimirum qui molesti fuere huic operi tantummodo dictis, fremuissent etiam in me factis." CM 21.120. "Tua namque maxime post Deum tutus ope et fretus testimonio, ecce respondeo exprobrantibus mihi uerbum. Et dum facis otium scribendi auctoritatemque concedis superno muneri. . . ." CM 21.122.

in fragrance the ointment (meditations) poured out by this woman than the stink of that thief Judas who wished to sell it![4] (Secular masters, of course, taught Scripture for money.) Her ultimate defense, however, lay in God Himself who knew more truly the secrets of her heart.[5] This letter, in sum, reveals nothing about the trial itself, but much about Rupert—stinging under the charges brought against his commentary, frightened by the attempt to silence him, and wholly dependent upon Cuno to protect his person and patronize his work.

In this letter Rupert remarked that he would now also respond (*ecce respondeo*) to his adversaries. This probably refers to the first eighteen chapters of *De omnipotentia Dei*.[6] The "advisers" at the trial had judged Rupert favorably on the predestinarian issue, and this little work, addressed to them, spelled out his position at length. The prologue to *De omnipotentia*, written either at Siegburg or upon his return to Liège when the whole work was finished, contains his only direct reference to a trial (n. 97 above), with language similar to that in the dedicatory epistle (cf. n. 99 to n. 5 here) and in the letter about to be described (cf. n. 100 to n. 5 here), but with no mention of the eucharistic issue.

Finally, in every extant manuscript and in its first printed edition Rupert's *Commentary on John* is prefaced by a letter (CM 9.1–4), which in three of four extant manuscripts bears the title "Letter of Rupert to Cuno explaining why this commentary on St. John's Gospel was attacked."[7] Whether that title came from Rupert's hand or from a later scribe, it accurately describes the letter's contents. Its dating, unfortunately, is not certain; but there is sufficient evidence, in my judgement, to place it still in the period of exile at Siegburg.[8] Rupert addressed Cuno exactly

4. CM 21.120.

5. "Defensa est illo defensore, qui cor eius melius nouerat." Ibid.

6. See chapter V, part 3; and Bischoff, *Controversy* 228–51, who also saw these chapters as the original core of the work.

7. CM 9.1.

8. Bischoff, *Controversy* 131–38, rightly saw that the "*tractauerim*" with which Rupert introduced his view of the eucharist refers back to his presenta-

as he had in the dedicatory epistle (*pater mi*). He also opened with the very same theme: "I meditate in the night," he says, "and the result is that I write; but behold now my work has brought lightning down upon me and turned every eye toward me." More clearly still, he applied to himself a scriptural text pertaining to Ishmael: "His hand will be against every man and every man's hand against him, and he shall pitch his tent over against (*e regione*) his brethren" (Gen. 16:12). By way of comment Rupert asked plaintively of Cuno: "What shall I do then, except pitch my tent away from (*e regione*) theirs and consider their gratuitous hatred stronger than the good will (*pace*) of those others who testified that I spoke truly?"[9] Thus, even though he had not formally been judged a heretic the hatred (*odia*) of his adversaries had forced him to live outside (*e regione*) his homeland, and, as he also said elsewhere, to repose true judgement now in God alone. However, he had already completed (*ante haec scripsi*) his apologetic defense addressed to the "advisers" (here called "masters," *scholasticos*), the core of his *De omnipotentia Dei*; and there was apparently nothing more he could do. This letter must date therefore to the last weeks of his exile at Siegburg (roughly April 1117). An *argumentum ex silentio* may be added in confirmation. Rupert listed here various other charges made against him, but not a new one raised soon after his return to Liège (chapter V, part 4).

What then was the original occasion or purpose of this letter? Rupert listed here the major charges made against his *Commentary on John* and concluded with an exposition of his revised stand on eucharistic theology. Bischoff labeled it an "open letter of defense" addressed especially to friends and supporters like Cuno.[10] Rupert himself said that his conscience and the matter

---

tions in *Levit.* 1.16: CM 22.822, and *Spir.* 3.21: CM 24.1929–30, meaning that the letter postdates *De sancta Trinitate*. But he misunderstood Rupert's use of Gen. 16:12 (n. 10 below) to mean he was *in* rather than *outside of* Liège, and therefore he dated the letter to sometime after Rupert's return.

9. CM 9.3. Cf. n. 97 above.

10. Bischoff, *Controversy* 137.

itself demanded he now cry out with Holy Church (Cant. 1:4), "I am black but beautiful."[11] But if this were so, a very brief and quite vague handling of the charges was all he dared muster in his defense as yet, quite in contrast to the twenty or so pages of rigorous scriptural argument in *De omnipotentia Dei*. Although it lacks the commonplaces of a dedicatory epistle, I suggest that Abbot Cuno had ordered a copy of the Johannine commentary prepared at the scriptorium in Siegburg and that Rupert then wrote this explanatory, apologetic preface regarding the recent attack on it. If he added it to his own copy, the letter would thus have entered the general transmission of the work.

11. "Tibi [Cuno] itaque tuique similibus nunc anima mea pro causa et conscientia sua illud recitat quod de pressuris suis sancta dicit ecclesia, *Nigra sum sed formosa*" (Cant. 1:4). . . . CM 9.1.

V

The
Predestinarian
Controversy

OF ALL Rupert's theological controversies his confrontation
with two leading French masters and their disciples during the
years 1116–17 is the best known by far. Such notoriety goes
back in good measure to Rupert himself, who referred to this
dispute more often and described it more thoroughly than any
of his others. The eucharistic controversy, despite its vehement
course, had remained essentially a local affair, and its dubious
outcome kept him from anything other than vague allusions.
The teachers of dialectic and Holy Writ criticized earlier for
their christological views either were not local men or never
rose to defend themselves in any recorded public encounter. But
the predestinarian controversy pitted Rupert eventually against
renowned masters of logic and Scripture in a dispute contemporary historians have come to regard as the first major collision in
twelfth-century Christendom between "monastic" and "scholastic" theology. This interpretation of the incident, widely influential by way of Chenu's essay on the origins of theology as a
science, now dominates nearly all presentations of it and, beyond that, most general depictions of Rupert's life and works.[1]

1. M.-D. Chenu, "Les *magistri*: la 'science' théologique," in *Théologie*
323–50; Magrassi, *Teologia* 179–218; H. Silvestre, "A propos de la lettre
d'Anselme de Laon à Heribrand de Saint-Laurent," *RTAM* 28 (1961) 5–25;

On the basis of what has already been learned about Rupert's career and aspirations, this chapter will attempt to place it in a somewhat different interpretative framework. The underlying issues and inciting moment of the controversy must first be examined before returning to take up the narrative just prior to Rupert's trial in the fall of 1116.

1

The Will of God:
Predestination
and the Incarnation

The ninth-century Carolingian reformers disputed long and divisively over christology, the eucharist, and predestination. Rupert addressed himself to each of these matters, still unresolved and taken up anew more than two centuries later, and he was soon charged with heresy for his position on the last two. The term "predestination" here encompassed several theological problems much broader in scope than the single question of sovereign grace and free will.[2] Just before the year 1100 St. Anselm of Canterbury's *Cur Deus homo* fundamentally recast the Western approach to redemptive theology, focusing attention almost exclusively upon the necessity of Christ's atoning sacrifice and thus eventually so transforming the received tradition as to make early medieval views seem quaint and obscure by comparison.[3] In the wake of St. Augustine and then of the Carolingian reformers, early medieval thinkers had approached this

---

idem, "Notes sur la controverse de Rupert de Saint-Laurent avec Anselme de Laon et Guillaume de Champeaux," in *Saint-Laurent* 63–80; Bischoff, *Controversy* 220–71.

2. See Pelikan, *Theology* 80–95; and compare B. Lavaud, "La controverse sur la prédestination au IXᵉ siècle," in *DTC* 12.2901–35.

3. R. W. Southern, *St. Anselm and His Biographer* (Cambridge 1963) 77–121; J. Rivière, *Le dogme de la rédemption au début du moyen âge* (Bibliothèque Thomiste 19, Paris 1934); G. R. Evans, *Anselm and a New Generation* (Oxford 1980) 139–73. On Abelard's redemptive theology, see R. E. Weingart, *The Logic of Divine Love* (Oxford 1970).

matter from the long view of God's plan ("will") for the salvation of His chosen angels and men. Presupposing for the most part Christ's actual power to redeem, and content usually to explain His victory over the Devil in terms of the "fish-hook" theory, they concentrated upon the question of how the Devil, the demons, and mankind, all under God's purview and power, came originally to fall and thus to set the entire process in motion. Rupert belonged to this older, traditional school of thought. But familiarity with discussions in the new schools by way of a confrere (thus not unlike Anselm's familiarity by way of the monk Boso) and an inner compulsion to set forth clearly and cogently God's plan for salvation drove Rupert too, in a movement best thought of as parallel to St. Anselm's, to reconsider several questions concerning predestination.

Treating the office prescribed for the Christmas vigil (thus among his earliest works, ca. 1110), Rupert devoted a lengthy chapter to the question, put precisely in its traditional form. Certain people, he noted, commonly thrust upon us a most inappropriate question: why did God permit the fall of man, which in His omnipotence He could have prevented, and thus make necessary His own incarnation? Three pages later, still in the same chapter, he took up another question (*Addit adhuc quaerere aliquis*): since there can be no evil disobedience without precepts, why did God command something He foreknew would not be heeded?[4] Rupert returned to these questions at the outset of his next major work, the *Commentary on Genesis*, and took up related matters in his *Commentary on John* (1114–16), referring twice specifically to people now raising difficult and scandalous questions about predestination.[5] Despite such protests, these "impious and useless" questions clearly intrigued Rupert from the beginning.

Among the new French masters who might raise such questions none enjoyed so great a reputation, also in Rupert's eyes,

4. *Off.* 3.14: CM 7.81–85.
5. *Gen.* 1.10–19: CM 21.136–49 (cf. *Gen.* 2.30–31: CM 21.221–24; Gen. 3.22–23: CM 21.259–61). *John* 5, 8, 9, 10: CM 9.263–74, 465–74, 593–94.

as Master Anselm of Laon (ca. 1050–1117).[6] Both John of Salisbury and Otto of Freising, an Englishman and a German come to France for higher study, considered Anselm the first luminary in the new schools of theology, and a chronicler ascribed to him the honor of having "reinvigorated" scriptural study.[7] Beyond compiling the *Ordinary Gloss*, the basic tool for the teaching of Scripture, Anselm and disciples from his "school" prepared handbooks of theological topics which basically followed a biblical order.[8] He intentionally avoided Trinitarian questions raised by the new dialecticians because he "feared to go beyond the Fathers,"[9] meaning especially, the Fathers as mediated by their teaching on Scripture. Such an approach manifestly reinforced the more traditional long view of predestination or re-

6. On Anselm of Laon, see the article by H. F. J. Reinhardt in *Lexikon des Mittelalters* 1.687–88; A. Landgraf, *Introduction à l'histoire de la littérature théologique de la scolastique naissante*, ed. A.-M. Landry, trans. L.-B. Geiger (Montreal and Paris 1973) 67–76 (with literature); H. Weisweiler, *Das Schrifttum der Schule Anselms von Laon und Wilhelms von Champeaux in deutschen Bibliotheken* (BGPT 33, Münster 1936); B. Merlette, in *Pierre Abélard—Pierre le Vénérable* (Paris 1975) 250–53. The extant fragments of Anselm's works are conveniently gathered in Lottin, *Psychologie* 5.9–183.

7. *Metalogicon* 1.5: ed. C. C. J. Webb (Oxford 1929) 17; *Gesta Friderici* 1.47: MGH SS 20.376–77; MGH SS 26.230.

8. V. I. J. Flint, "The 'School of Laon': A Reconsideration," *RTAM* 43 (1976) 89–110 rightly questioned the earlier ascription of nearly all twelfth-century theological sentence collections to a mythical "School of Laon," but that does not negate at once all the complex literary relationships worked out by Weisweiler and others. See H. Weisweiler, "Die ältesten scholastischen Gesamtdarstellung der Theologie," *Scholastik* 16 (1941) 231–54, 351–68; "Die Arbeitsweise der sogenannten *Sententiae Anselmi*" and "Wie entstanden die frühen Sententiae Berolinenses der Schule Anselms von Laon?" *Scholastik* 34 (1959) 190–232, 321–69; "Die frühe Summe *Deus de cuius principio et fine tacetur*, eine neue Quelle der *Sententiae Anselmi*," *Scholastik* 35 (1960) 209–43; and "Die Klagenfurter Sentenzen, *Deus est sine principio*, die erste Vorlesung aus der Schule Anselms von Laon," *Scholastik* 36 (1961) 512–49 and 37 (1962) 45–84. A useful summary of Weisweiler's results by H. F. J. Reinhardt, *AHDL* 36 (1969) 26–29.

9. John of Salisbury, *Historia pontificalis* 8: ed. M. Chibnall (London and New York 1956) 18–19.

demptive theology, and also raised the crucial questions concerning man's fall right at the beginning.

For Master Anselm and others who followed this scriptural arrangement and made few or no preliminary remarks on the doctrine of God, the question of God's will arose most often just at the point where St. Augustine had put a difficult question in his *Literal Commentary on Genesis*: the moment of man's temptation and fall.[10] While this specific question still appears in the *Summa sententiarum* (3.6) and Peter Lombard's textbook (2.23.1) in the context of the fall, Peter Abelard and other dialecticians began instead with a doctrine of God to which they then appended discussions of predestination and the divine will; and this general approach eventually came to predominate by way of Lombard's *Sentences*. Hugh of St. Victor, the leading second- or third-generation master of the Sacred Page, dealt first with creation (1.1), then the doctrine of God (1.2–3) and His will (1.4), before continuing with the creation and fall of angels (1.5) and the creation (1.6) and fall (1.7) of man. So also Hugh of Reading, a Black Monk preparing a kind of *summa* in the mid–1120's, devoted almost two full books in seven to the relationship of God's will to the origins of evil, taken up directly after a book on creation.[11] This salvation-historical placement of the issue and the influence of St. Augustine's commentary (especially Book XI) massively affected the nature of the questions asked about God's will, with that original exegetical base still evident in Peter Lombard's exposition.[12]

10. Augustine, *Gen.* 11.4–5: CSEL 28.337–38 devoted several chapters to the question "Cur Deus tentari permiserit hominem quem tentatori consensurum esse praesciebat." Bede (CC 118.59–60), Rhabanus Maurus (PL 107.487), and the *Ordinary Gloss* took this over for commentary on Gen. 3:1. The process by which this "question" expanded into a full treatment of God's will can be followed in the work of Weisweiler, in *Scholastik* (n. 8 above) 34 (1959) 207–15, 336–37, 350–56 (where he labeled it "eine der umstrittensten Fragen der Zeit und der Schule") and 36 (1961) 527–31.

11. Hugh, *Dialogi* 3–4: PL 192.1165–92.

12. *Sent.* 1.41.1, 1.45.1–2, 1.46.1 with the notes in the third edition (Grottaferrata 1971) 286, 306, 312.

All began with the conviction that God was utterly omnipotent, and this they expressed by way either of Ps. 113(115):3 (*Omnia quaecumque uoluit fecit*) or Ps. 134(135):6 (*Omnia quaecumque uoluit Dominus fecit*).[13] The Gloss to the former verse, not attributed to any Father and therefore quite possibly from Master Anselm himself, commented simply: *Per quod omnipotens apparet*. To define, secondly, God's saving or predestinating will the masters nearly always cited I Tim. 2:4 (*Qui omnes homines uult saluos fieri*). The gloss for this verse came from St. Augustine's *Enchiridion*, almost certainly by way of Florus' compilation (and therefore also known to Rupert).[14] The teaching of Augustine's *Enchiridion* 95–103 became crucial in Rupert's controversy and was still debated in Lombard's time.[15] To relate, finally, God's omnipotent, predestinating will to men and angels the masters asked with Rom. 9:19: *Voluntate enim eius quis resistit?*[16] These three texts, brought together in this combination, got theologians into a terrible tangle from which they could hardly extricate themselves. Already in Carolingian times Haimo had put the texts together and asked simply why then God in His almighty will had not saved all men.[17] Less than a generation before Anselm, Master Bruno of Reims sought to distinguish here a "twofold" will in God; and just after Rupert's controversy Peter Abelard lined up these three texts one after another in his *Sic et Non* for the question: *Quod quicquid uult Deus faciat et non.*[18] To these he added another scriptural text (Matt. 23:37) and Jerome's commentary on Dan. 4:32—the latter, quite re-

13. These texts and the question of how to interpret them echo all through Lombard's discussion of omnipotence: *Sent.* 1.42.1–3; cf. Abelard, *Theologia 'scholarium'* 3.4, and the *Summa sententiarum* 1.14.

14. *Enchiridion* 103.

15. *Sent.* 1.46.1–2.

16. Later discussions appear to have centered increasingly around Rom. 9:18–19 (see Lombard's *Magna glossatura*, PL 191.1462–66), whereas Carolingian and early twelfth-century scholars—probably owing to Augustine's *Enchiridion*—focused more on I Tim. 2:4.

17. Commenting on I Tim. 2:4 (PL 117.789).

18. PL 153.435–37; *Sic et Non* 36: ed. Boyer and McKeon 186–87.

markably, also cited by Rupert at the end of his *De omnipoten-tia Dei.*[19]

To resolve this difficulty Master Anselm of Laon proposed a threefold distinction in the will of God. His teaching on this point gained enormous influence during the first three or four decades of the twelfth century, providing, for instance, the gloss on "Thy will" of the Lord's prayer in the *Enarrationes in Mat-thaeum*, the earliest extant scholastic commentary on a Gospel.[20] Master Anselm applied his distinction in various ways (presum-ably in dealing with different texts), sometimes trimming it to two, other times expanding it to four; but, reduced to a for-mula, he distinguished an "efficient" (*efficiens*) will which ef-fected all things (Ps. 113[115]:3), an "approving" (*approbans*) will which desired the salvation of all men (I Tim. 2:4), and a "permitting" (*permittens*) will which "willed" even those things displeasing to God such as evil.[21] This last category, by which God could be said to have "willed evil," provoked heated and widespread debate down through Lombard's textbook. Once again, in a lengthy chapter containing the major scriptural and patristic authorities, Peter Abelard's *Sic et Non* (c. 31) raised the question directly: *Quod Deus malorum quoque causa uel auctor sit et non.* Master Anselm regularly cited Rom. 9:18 (see n. 21), on which the *Ordinary Gloss* quoted St. Augustine, *De praedestina-tione*, 4.4, describing God as "not willing" (*noluit*) to call or to

19. *Omnip.* 27: PL 170.477. Just how Rupert came upon the same author-ity as Abelard I have not yet determined.

20. PL 162.1307.

21. See Lottin, *Psychologie* 5.32–34 (nos. 31–32), 116–17 (nos. 152–53), 234–40 (nos. 290–95). The key part, to which Rupert would object in *De uoluntate Dei*, reads: "Permittens uoluntas est qua permittit aliquid fieri, etsi displiceat quandoque: hoc modo dicitur Deus uelle mala que permittit fieri; unde dicitur: *quoniam quem uult indurat et cui uult miseretur*" (Rom. 9:18). Lot-tin, no. 290, p. 236. This text is from Anselm's "school." It is important to the later discussion that all authentic texts from Master Anselm are more cautious: "Malos uult perire, non tamen sine eorum uoluntate, quia aliter iniuste; itaque Deus preuidet de hominibus futura, licet sint necessaria, non tamen implentur, nisi facientium uoluntate libera." Ibid. 34.

"soften" (*emollire*) certain sinners.[22] More telling still and equally important to Anselm's case was Rom. 1:24 (*Propter quod tradidit illos Deus in desideria cordis eorum*), for which his *Ordinary Gloss* had excerpted a text from Augustine's *De gratia* 21.42–43, where God is said to incline men's hearts either to good or to evil by His will.[23]

It was in the context of teaching man's fall, or more specifically of teaching Gen. 3:1ff, that Master Anselm and his disciples fully developed their views on the will of God. But the issue arose already in conjunction with the angels' fall, in no small measure because St. Augustine had dealt with both together in Book XI of his *Literal Commentary on Genesis*, and Master Anselm now excerpted from that book at truly extraordinary length for the *Ordinary Gloss* on Gen. 3:1ff. Rupert reported the question this way in his *Commentary on Genesis*: if God willed salvation for His creatures (I Tim. 2:4), why did He not create them all incapable of suffering any evil?[24] Honorius, perhaps ten years earlier, had included in his *Elucidarium* a very similar question, one which also went back ultimately to St. Augustine;[25] but in the schools, to judge from the extant texts, this was spun out into a more complicated form: Did the angels originally have free will? Was there an interval between their creation and fall permitting them to exercise it? And if not, must God be said to have "created them evil" (*creati malos*)?[26] From remarks made by Hugh of St. Victor and Peter Lombard, it is clear that one party

22. This Augustinian gloss was found also in Florus' compilation, whence it was known to Rupert and to Abelard (texts 29, 30 in c. 31).

23. One key sentence from Augustine as Master Anselm quoted it later: "Manifestum est Deum operari in animis hominum inclinando uoluntates eorum quocunque uoluerit, siue ad bonum pro sua misericordia, siue ad malum iudicio suo." Lottin, *Psychologie* 5.176, where the Augustinian passage (also known to Rupert and Abelard, text 18 in c. 31) is not identified.

24. *Gen.* 1.15: CM 21.142.

25. *Elucidarium* 1.45: ed. Lefèvre 368–69; cf. Aug., *Gen.* 11.7: CSEL 28.340.

26. *Sententiae Anselmi*: ed. F. Bliemetzrieder (BGPT 18) 50–55. See Weisweiler, in *Scholastik* (n. 8 above) 34 (1959) 194–202, 323–37; 35 (1960) 214–23; 36 (1961) 514–20. By Hugh of St. Victor's time these were much discussed

of masters and students argued precisely this position, but just as with extreme views on christology it cannot be attributed with certainty to any of the known, prestigious masters. Anselm of Laon seems to have fumbled uncertainly, constrained at once by Augustine's teaching that angels were created and fell instantaneously (*statim*) and by his own conviction that all things took place under the purview of God's omnipotent will.[27]

Much of the discussion came to focus increasingly upon Lucifer, the extraordinary angel become the Devil, to whom Augustine in his Genesis commentary had applied John 8:44 (*Ille homicida errat ab initio et in ueritate non stetit*). Augustine warned that this should not be construed so as to have God "create the Devil evil," and St. Anselm used this same text as a springboard for his discussion of *The Fall of the Devil*.[28] Although Master Anselm made no mention of this problem in the *Ordinary Gloss* for John 8:44, Rupert reported indignantly that this verse had become the occasion for all manner of puerile, complicated, and almost blasphemous (*nimii scrutatores*) questions about God's omnipotent will with respect to the origins of evil.[29] As ever, Rupert also felt compelled to interpret the verse truly. It taught, in his view, that evil is an "accident" of which the Devil, the "father of lies," is in his own pride and hatred the cause, an accident which then "infected" good things made by the Truth, Himself consubstantial to the Father.[30]

Already in his earliest commentary, Rupert held that neither angels nor men fell in any sense of the word "by the will of God." Yet this did not resolve the problem of how angels, and Lucifer in particular, created in goodness and truth, nonetheless

---

questions: *De sacramentis* 1.5.19: PL 176.254, whence the *Summa sententiarum* 2.1–4: PL 176.79–85, and Lombard, *Sent.* 2.3–4. For St. Anselm's attempt to sort out these questions and the various kinds of "will" in God, see Evans (n. 3 above) 126–34, 180–86.

27. See Lottin, *Psychologie* 5.126 (nos. 176–77), 244 (no. 307).

28. Augustine, *Gen.* 11.23: CSEL 28.355; Anselm, *De casu Diaboli*: ed. Schmitt 1.233–76. Cf. Evans (n. 3 above) 24ff.

29. *John* 9: CM 9.474.

30. *John* 8: CM 9.472. Cf. ibid. 269–72; *Gen.* 3.4: CM 21.239.

fell. Rupert noted that angels were "mutable" creatures, created like man from nothing, and therefore they like man had to progress (*sicut habuit initium, sic habere debuit et profectum*) in order to attain eternal beatitude. Many people too preoccupied with the greatness of angelic being had failed to recognize this. These "many people" owed their misunderstanding, as Rupert knew very well, to Gregory the Great, who had taught on the basis of Job 40:14 and Ezech. 28 that angels, particularly Lucifer, were created at a higher level than mankind (*Distat conditio angeli a conditione hominis*).[31] But, Rupert objected, God meant what was said in Ezech. 28 only ironically (*cum improprio et ironia*), as what might have been had Lucifer not rebelled. Indeed this must be so, because only God is immutable, and though He "begot" His own likeness in His Son He could not "make" such a likeness out of nothing. Men and angels must either progress toward God or regress toward nothingness. It may be hard to say that Lucifer was created not yet perfect, but it is harder to say that he already possessed the perfect love of God and fell from it.[32] To preserve God's omnipotence, it suffices to say that He made one creature capable of fully receiving His Creator and gaining by His work (*industriam*) divinity not possessed by nature![33] By removing angels thus from the realm of the divine and requiring "progress" of them too—presupposing therefore an interval of time, free will, and the eventual bestowal of God's love and grace—Rupert believed he had established sufficient distance between the good and immutable will of God and the failings of mutable creatures.[34] As for those other questions, mostly taken over from St. Augustine, such as why God created creatures He foreknew would fall, Rupert simply rejected them out of hand as "violent, importunate, and irrational."[35]

31. *Moralia* 32.23: PL 76.664–66. This teaching was excerpted by Paterius for Ezech. 28 (PL 79.991–92) and by Isidore for the discussion of angels in his *Sententiae* 1.10.6: PL 83.555. Thence it entered the mainstream of theological teaching, including Lombard, *Sent.* 2.6.1.

32. *Gen.* 1.16: CM 21.144.

33. Shades of that adoptionist christology: *Gen.* 1.15: CM 21.143.

34. *Gen.* 1.13–17: CM 21.140–46; cf. 1.37, 2.18: CM 21.165–66, 203–05.

35. *Gen.* 1.17: CM 21.145.

On theological matters as such—their ecclesiastical and sacramental views have received much less attention—the masters at Laon developed two doctrines so significantly that all twelfth-century theologians had thereafter to deal with them. One was their all-encompassing view of God's will. (The other, the question of original sin and how it was transmitted, Rupert seems also to have known about, but not to have found as interesting or "deviant.")[36] From his very earliest writings Rupert addressed the "predestination" issue. Though resident near Laon during the years 1092–95, he claimed never to have met or heard these masters in person. Contact between the dioceses of Liège and Laon was such, however, that several of the masters' disciples now resided in Liège either as masters themselves or still as students, and indeed one had become Rupert's confrere.

2

Rupert's Challenge
to the French Masters

Up until 1116 Rupert had worked out independent positions on at least four disputed doctrinal questions (the Trinity, christology, the sacraments, and the eucharist) entirely by way of commentary on Scripture and the divine office. What he had argued on predestination might have remained buried in his commentaries, hidden like his christological views from most contemporaries and historians alike, had he not resolved to write a separate treatise on *The Will of God*.[37] This unusual step he took roughly in the summer of 1116, probably just after completing his massive commentary on St. John's Gospel.[38] Not

36. *Gen.* 2.21: CM 21.209–10.

37. The only extant manuscript, Bibl. roy. 9607, fols. 171–77, which originated in St. Lawrence (though it is not Rupert's autograph) and was the basis of the extant editions, bears the full title: *Liber eiusdem apologeticorum de uoluntate Dei*.

38. *De uoluntate Dei* borrowed from and summarized materials worked out in the *Commentary on John* (nn. 54, 55, 58–60 below). Reaction to it, including the subsequent trial probably in late September (chapter IV, part 3), erupted "*statim*" (PL 170.472).

even the debate with Alger had produced a separate work, and neither *De sancta Trinitate* nor the *Commentary on John* constituted "treatises" on the Trinity or christology. Such doctrinal pamphlets arose almost exclusively from disputes, the Berengarian controversy, for instance, or the sacramental and canonistic debates of the reform era. The wholly extraordinary and brilliant works of St. Anselm have tended to mislead historians on this score. The early teachers of dialectic and Scripture— Lanfranc (except the treatise on the eucharist), Roscellin, Bruno of Reims, Anselm of Laon, William of Champeaux, and countless lesser known persons—left no treatises at all, only glosses on Scripture, the Fathers, or the prescribed texts of the arts curriculum. The occasion and intent of Rupert's treatise, therefore, require closer scrutiny.

One of his confreres at St. Lawrence (*quidam nostrorum*), Rupert reports, had studied with Master Anselm of Laon and now held, purportedly on the master's authority, a view of God's will with respect to evil which Rupert judged outrageous.[39] He had already argued with his brother monk for a long time (*longa contentione*), presumably at least since before writing the *Commentary on Genesis* (1112/13) and probably those contentious chapters in *De diuinis officiis* (ca. 1110).[40] Just how one of Rupert's confreres came to study with Master Anselm is unknown. It is possible Abbot Berengar had sent one of his monks to Laon for study, especially during the exile, as Abbot Anselm of Bec did one of his to Master Roscellin at Compiègne; but there is another more likely explanation. The reform of the abbey about 1100/05 brought a large influx of new recruits, including several

39. ". . . de uestris scolis hoc se quidam nostrorum [cf. nostri ordinis, in *Off.* 2.23: CM 7.59] accepisse fatetur, ut diceret, quia Deus malum fieri uult, et quia uoluntatis Dei fuit quod Adam praeuaricatus est. Non Scripturarum auctoritatibus sed uestri nominis innititur traditamque a uobis huiusmodi diuisionem longa contentione testatur: Voluntas, inquit, mali alia approbans, alia permittens." *Vol.* 1: PL 170.437. Cf. n. 21 above.

40. Rupert's language in *Off.* 3.14: CM 7.82–85 already suggests a personal encounter: "Quaerimus nunc ab eis, qui supradicta quaestione moueri solent. . . . Hic ergo respondeat qui altiora quaerit. . . . Dicet fortassis. . . . Addit adhuc quaerere aliquis. . . ."

former secular clerics,[41] one of whom may have studied at Laon before joining the abbey of St. Lawrence in Liège.

Rupert's confrere was not, however, the only student of French masters to be found in Liège. In the midst of his polemical commentary on John 8:44 Rupert alluded to a band of "ignorant folk" (the same words he would later apply to his adversaries) contending about these matters publicly. Later he referred to them as students of dialectic (*apud ipsos quorum dialectica professio est*).[42] This most fashionable of the arts doubtless had many enthusiasts among the student population in Liège—Rupert noted wryly its new-found "fame"[43]—and they may also have occasioned his remarks on dialectical aspects of Trinitarian and christological dogma, though he himself never made that identification. Rupert was irritated with them on at least two scores: first, that the plain scriptural truth proclaimed everywhere (*ubique*) and so reasonably (*rationabiliter*) should be contested by these "enemies of the truth"; and secondly, that such divine matters should be bandied about in the marketplace, in town squares and at crossroads (*in plateis uel compitis*).[44] That Rupert himself nonetheless had already argued bitterly with them, perhaps even in a public street, is evident from his remarks. He was specific too about how best to deal with them. The churchman should defend truth with moderating reason in such a way as not to fuel the flames of contention: when there is disagreement with a brother, he should explain his position again in patience and charity; but if someone teaches heresy publicly, he should be condemned in a public court as a "murderer" (*homicida*, i.e. of the soul)[45]—all this written confidently less than a year before his adversaries sought just such a judgement against him. Rupert failed in fact to follow his own advice. Perhaps he had be-

41. *Gesta abb. Trudon.* 8.16: MGH SS 10.278 (quoted in chapter II, n. 17).
42. *Omnip.* 24: PL 170.474.
43. *Omnip.* 23: PL 170.473.
44. ". . . ut nullam exinde habuerint occasionem indocti turbae popelli contendendi in plateis uel compitis. . . ." *John* 8: CM 9.466. Cf. "indocto scholarum popello," PL 170.482.
45. *John* 8: CM 9.467, 469; *Levit.* 1.9: CM 22.812–13.

come frustrated in arguing to no apparent effect with his confrere and these local dialecticians. He now determined to appeal over their heads to their esteemed teachers. Just as clearly, he aimed to discuss these matters himself with those acclaimed masters and as their equal.

Rupert addressed his treatise to "the most renowned masters of our time," Bishop William of Champeaux and Master Anselm of Laon; and in his opening chapter, as the first order of business (*hoc primum*), he asked to discuss the issues with them in person, that is to say, in effect challenged them to debate.[46] To underscore that purpose in his concluding paragraph (a "*peroratio*"), Rupert again called upon them to renounce any opinion which ascribed evil to the will of a righteous God.[47] This was a bold, even brash, act on Rupert's part and was perceived as such; but it was not unprecedented. For it was by challenging distinguished masters that learned careers were made, and in the years 1100–15 none ranked higher than Bishop William and Master Anselm. Peter Abelard developed his early career in challenges to those very same masters; by his own account he triumphed repeatedly over William, his former teacher, and just three years or so before Rupert's challenge had easily surpassed Anselm in teaching Scripture at Laon. Already two generations earlier, at the beginning of this new era (ca. 1050), the infamous Anselm Peripateticus had toured German and Italian bishoprics to show off his intellectual prowess in hopes of gaining a good clerical post, and in 1049 Master Berengar of Tours had challenged Lanfranc (the most renowned master of his time) to "discuss" eucharistic theology and thus set that controversy in motion.[48] A generation later Roscellin's claim regarding Lanfranc

46. "Haec idcirco nunc ad uos dicere incipimus, O magistri temporibus nostris inclyti, Wilhelme Cathalaunensis pontifex et Anselme Laudunensis lucifer. . . . Hoc primum a uobis optaremus, si copia uel opportunitas mutuis uocibus colloquendi praeberetur, utrum uerum esse possit quod uos artium magistri tam inertem fecisse diuisionem dicimini?" *Vol.* 1: PL 170.437.

47. *Vol.* peroratio: PL 170.454.

48. See Anselm's *Rhetorimachia*, ed. K. Manitius (MGH Geistesgeschichte 2, Weimar 1958), and H. E. J. Cowdrey, "Anselm of Besate and Some North-Italian Scholars of the Eleventh Century," *Journal of Ecclesiastical History* 23

and Anselm had provoked proceedings against his Trinitarian views.

Rupert recognized Anselm and William explicitly as the "luminaries" of all France, the masters to whom students flocked from every province.[49] A challenge to them, coming several years after he had first learned about and treated the disputed questions, was clearly a premeditated act, an attempt to make public solutions he had already worked out in his commentaries. For his own illumination he invoked at the outset the omnipotence and mercy of God which he wished here to confess and preach. He rebuked those who sought to make God responsible for their own sinfulness, and equated the unforgivable sin against the Holy Spirit with thus willfully contradicting the truth of Holy Scripture. The penultimate book of *De sancta Trinitate*, which, I have argued, deals with "current affairs," opens, notably, with exactly the same themes.[50]

On the basis of Master Anselm's distinction between an "approving" and a "permitting" will in God, his disciple, Rupert's confrere, had claimed God could be said to have willed Adam's fall. Rupert quoted the distinction as pertaining specifically to God's will with respect to evil, a qualification which indeed reflected the spirit, if not precisely the letter, of Anselm's teaching (cf. nn. 21, 39 above), for the "permitting will" always had reference to evil. As in his handling of christological heresy, so here Rupert first refuted his brother monk's false logic, substantially aided therein by the variant form "*uoluntas mali*." For, he reasoned, if the "*uoluntas mali*" is a species divided between an "approving" and a "permitting" will, is this "permitting" will good or evil? If it is evil, how is it distinguished from that other "approving evil"? But if it is good, how can it belong to the species of "*uoluntas mali*"? Surely, Rupert says, addressing the distinguished masters directly, you were not the authors of

---

(1972) 115–24; Berengar's letter, ed. R. B. C. Huygens in *Studi Medievali* 3rd ser. 8 (1967) 456.

49. *RegBen.* 1: PL 170.482.

50. *Vol.* prologus: PL 170.437; cf. *Spir.* 8.3–4: CM 24.2075–77.

such a senseless distinction, which both accuses God of evil and fails to preserve dialectical consistency.[51] In the third to last book of his *De sancta Trinitate*, while treating the liberal arts as the Spirit's gift of "*scientia*," Rupert made the point emphatically that evil, in dialectical terms, can only be called an "accident," never anything "substantial," and that truly wise philosophers would concentrate only upon how God through the incarnation worked to remove this accident.[52]

With this dialectical nonsense (c. 1) out of the way, Rupert put the question in scriptural terms (c. 2). The "authority" of Holy Scripture teaches that the "permission of God" means His "patience" (Rom. 9:22), whereby he bears with (*sustinuit*) evil in order to allow sinners time to repent. But (c. 3) Rupert's adversary retorts, since you agree that God "permitted" evil to be, did He do so willingly or unwillingly? For if He did so unwillingly, He was evidently compelled and therefore is not omnipotent. Rupert rejected the conclusion: God permitted evil unwillingly in order to allow time for repentance. But (c. 4) the man persisted (*Dicit homo adhuc*), coming now to a scriptural rather than a dialectical argument, what then did the apostle mean when he said that God has mercy on whom He will and—especially—hardens whom He will (Rom. 9:18)? This argument came straight from Master Anselm (nn. 21, 23 above). Rupert's response paraphrased Augustine's treatment of this text, as he knew it from Florus' compilation, whence it would also enter the *Ordinary Gloss*: God did not *cause* evil, but in some instances He did not soften (*emollire*) the hearts of those caught in Adam's sin. Unlike Master Anselm, Rupert never spoke of this "permission" or "patience" as in any sense an aspect of God's will.

So much then, in Rupert's own words, for such foolish and unprofitable arguments.[53] But, he adds immediately, for our own instruction we must proceed further (*pro nostra eruditione*

51. *Vol.* 1: PL 170.437–38. See Magrassi, *Teologia* 192–94.
52. *Spir.* 7.13: CM 24.2063–65.
53. "Haec pro illa tam inepta quam inutili argumentatione hactenus dicta sunt." *Vol.* 5: PL 170.440.

adhuc ultra progrediendum est) and examine those questions which have raised such scruples among the "curious." Rupert then named three questions, all of which he had dealt with or at least noted before (as cited in, respectively, nn. 4, 5, 24, and 29 above). Those questions, his quotation of Rom. 11:13 on God's unsearchable wisdom, and his attack upon "curious" masters and students all closely echoed a chapter from the *Commentary on Genesis*.[54] There, as here, Rupert presumed not to investigate God's incomprehensible judgements and unsearchable ways, but simply with the Spirit's help to say a few things (*pauca respondeamus*) in response to these sowers of suspicion. First of all, he insisted, such questions are not the product of honest and balanced minds. For how should an ignorant little man presume to counsel the Ancient of Days on how best to run the universe? And how should the clay tell the potter what to do (Rom. 9:20–21)? But as in his treatment of the eucharist, after declaring the unsearchableness of these divine mysteries and seeking the Spirit's guidance, Rupert nevertheless took up the questions himself.

If God did not "will evil," the first question asks, why did He not create man unchangeable, "incontrovertible," so that he could not fall into evil? The bulk of his answer (cc. 7–8) Rupert took over word for word from his first treatment of this problem in the *Commentary on Genesis*.[55] The only noteworthy difference between the text written in the summer of 1116 and that of 1112/13 is slightly greater emphasis in the later one upon the concept "incontrovertible," which, Rupert maintained, could be predicated only of God.[56] It might be "hard," Rupert conceded (c. 9), to say that God could only generate like (the Son) and "could not make" an incontrovertible creature, but it would be harder to assert that He did not "will" to create a good crea-

---

54. To *Vol.* 5–6: PL 170.440–41, cf. *Gen.* 2.30: CM 21.221–23, and also *John* 9: CM 9.474.

55. From the second sentence of c. 8 on ("Horum quae dicimus . . ."), Rupert copied the text of *Gen.* 1.15: CM 21.142–43. The argument of c. 7 is virtually the same as that of *John* 5: CM 9.269–70.

56. But he knew the question already in this form: *Gen.* 2.30: CM 21.222.

ture.[57] To uphold God's omnipotence (c. 10), one ought to look beyond this curious question to the incarnation, for only God, neither man nor angel, could fully join to Himself a complete human nature—again an argument first presented in the *Commentary on Genesis* but taken now word for word from the *Commentary on John*.[58] In short, the omnipotent Word of God alone "willed" (*uoluit*) and was able (*potuit*) to assume human nature. And this New Creature, the God-Man, not only did not "will" to sin but "could not" (*non posset*) sin (c. 11), an essential point taught by John 5:19, 30, from his commentary on which (the latter verse, here) Rupert appropriated verbatim his argument.[59] Even angels, by contrast, though now confirmed in their ranks by grace, were once subject to change (c. 12).[60]

In sum, what Rupert wrote "for our instruction," at least on the first question, was in fact meant to enlighten the French masters on solutions he had arrived at as much as four years earlier. He likewise dismissed the third question out of hand as violent and irrational, again quoting his own *Commentary on Genesis*.[61] This left only the second question (cc. 13–23), which Rupert himself designated the real heart of the matter: if God foreknew what would happen, why did He order Adam and Eve not to eat of the tree, unless He in fact "willed" their fall? The schoolmen sometimes raised this question, as Rupert knew earlier,[62] by way of interpreting Gen. 2:15–17. An original exposition of this text, therefore, one which refuted the scandalous questions and interpretations of the schoolmen, represented *De uoluntate Dei*'s most original contribution. Rupert knew also that God's com-

57. Cf. *Gen.* 1.16: CM 21.144 (in this instance, not a literal quotation).

58. *Gen.* 1.13, 16: CM 21.140, 144–45. *Vol.* 10 = *John* 3: CM 9.168.

59. From "Ergo non possum" to "facere non potest" in *Vol.* 11 = *John* 5: CM 9.282. But "omnipotence" and "incontrovertibility" are addressed at length in his commentary on both texts: CM 9.260–62, 280–83; cf. also *Spir.* 1.30: CM 24.1858–59 (roughly contemporary to *Vol.*)

60. *Vol.* 12, from "Et quidem" to "Patrem facientem" = *John* 5: CM 9.261.

61. *Vol.* 24: PL 170.452 = *Gen.* 1.17: CM 21.145.

62. See *Off.* 3.14: CM 7.85; and *Gen.* 2.30–31: CM 21.221–24. Cf. n. 10 above.

mand was sometimes discussed in relation to Rom. 5:20 (*Lex autem subintrauit ut abundaret delictum. Ubi autem abundauit delictum, superabundauit gratia*). The idea was that God in His omnipotence "disposed" man's fall by His "permitting will" so that greater glory and grace might abound through the incarnation of Christ.[63] Rupert rejected this, seeking a better intention and holier will in God's command.

Rupert understood God's command rather as a test of the proto-parents' faith, hope, and love; if they had demonstrated these in obedience, they would have gained eternal life, for the rational soul lives by the word of the Lord (cc. 14–16).[64] The fruit itself was of no consequence, only a means for the test; here Rupert cited Horace on the importance of a small item to prove a larger relationship.[65] Man himself sinned with swelling pride against God, provoking a forbidden desire for the fruit. God bore (*sustinente*) this; He in no sense caused it or willed it (c. 18). Indeed, how could God have willed something He had previously forbidden? To this they respond, Rupert reports with scorn in his voice, that God had once prohibited it but ceased to at the very moment of Eve's act (c. 19). God's second command concerning the tree of life was, moreover, an act of mercy to prevent man from living forever in his miserable state (c. 20).[66] But finally, Rupert continues (cc. 21–23), even if God is proved not to have willed evil, why did He not make man obedient since "*omnia quaecumque uoluit fecit*" (Ps. 134[135]:6)? Rupert related this key text directly to Christ's incarnation. God accomplished what He willed for man, but He had to do it Himself through Christ's incarnation and passion, since only a God-Man could do perfectly what God had willed.

63. See the *Sententiae Anselmi*, ed. Bliemetzrieder (BGPT 18) 62–64; and Master Anselm's fragmentary comment on Rom. 5:20 in Lottin, *Psychologie* 5.88 (no. 112).

64. A pointed summary of Rupert's argument earlier in *Gen.* 3.7–9: CM 21.241–44.

65. *Vol.* 17: PL 170.447–48. Horace, *Epist.* 1.16.

66. *Vol.* 20: PL 170.449–50; a summary (but not verbatim) of *Gen.* 3.29–30: CM 21.269–71, and *John* 8: CM 9.468–69. Cf. Augustine, *De ciuitate Dei* 9.10.

In his penultimate chapter (25) Rupert, from his own vast knowledge of Scripture, brought up three texts (Is. 45:27, Amos 3:6, Jonah 3:10) which speak of God "causing evil," and he interpreted them to mean "afflictions" designed to bring man to repentance. And, in his last chapter (26) he insisted again that man, not God, is responsible for evil: texts which speak of God "hardening hearts" (Rom. 9:18) or "blinding" people (John 12:39–40) mean simply that God has "permitted" them to continue in their sinful state.[67]

Thus Rupert had spoken, as one theologian to another. He had refuted the masters' erroneous dialectic, reviewed the contested scriptural texts, and offered a better interpretation, one which did not seek "to accuse God and excuse man." In closing he called upon Master Anselm and Bishop William once again to take back this "horrendous teaching" (namely, *Deus uult malum*) which rested now neither on Scripture nor on reason, but solely on the authority of their teaching.

3

Public Disputes
at Liège, Laon,
and Châlons-sur-Marne

The series of events following in rapid succession between Rupert's completion of *De uoluntate Dei* in the summer of 1116 and his return from France about August 1117 are known from two accounts, both by Rupert himself and both expressly apologetic in purpose. *De omnipotentia Dei* was written mostly after and in reaction to the trial; in preparation already during his exile at Siegburg, it was completed in Liège just before his journey to France and thus itself reflects various stages of the controversy.[68] The first book of his *Commentary on the Benedictine Rule*, written in 1125, reviewed the events and issues again from a rela-

67. Cf. *John* 10: CM 9.593.
68. This first pointed out by Bischoff, *Controversy* 228–39, who spoke of two "revisions" after the "original draft."

tively triumphalist perspective with no concern at all to distinguish various incidents chronologically or to include them all (no reference here to the trial, for instance). There is, unfortunately, no account or treatise from the other side, comparable to Alger's *De sacramentis*. Any reconstruction, therefore, including this one, must remain subject to caution on matters of exact chronology and the precise charges hurled back and forth.

Master Anselm and Bishop William's disciples in Liège read Rupert's dialectical critique of their esteemed teachers, including his charge that such a feeble and senseless distinction was unworthy of them. They immediately (*statim*) exploded in rage, stirring up against Rupert a large rabble of student-clerics (*turbas auditorum; indocto scholarum popello fauente aduersariis*) who, Rupert claims, knew virtually nothing about the issue and understood still less of it.[69] These clerics also reproached Rupert in a way Alger, it seems, never had. They charged him with irremediable ignorance because, as a monk since childhood, he had never traveled to study with their distant and famous masters. This stung Rupert to the quick. He returned to it time and again as in some sense the basic cause of his adversaries' scorn for him,[70] and it made him increasingly conscious of the sources, essentially mystical and vocational, of his own authority as a teacher of Scripture. But—ever quick on the uptake—Rupert paraphrased Horace (*Ars poetica* 72) to point out that monasteries too could be places of great learning, scoffed at the idea that certain masters alone possessed an indispensable key to learning (*clauim scientiae*), and cited from Augustine's *Confessions* the Saint's description of how he had taught himself the Aristotelian logic his teachers could not grasp.[71] Yet however much bravado Rupert could muster in repartee and also in retrospect, the violence of their reaction (*Nequeo satis edicere quanta quamque iniuriosa uiolentia*)[72] frightened him, as well it might. At

69. *Omnip.* 22: PL 170.472; *RegBen.* 1: PL 170.482 (cf. n. 42 above).
70. *RegBen.* 1: PL 170.480, 482. Cf. *Omnip.* 22: PL 170.472; and *John* 7: CM 9.396.
71. *Omnip.* 22: PL 170.472.
72. Ibid. 23: 473.

work in the relationship between these disciples and their masters was that same fierce loyalty which in the lay world bound a squire to his knight and vassals to their lords; particularly among high-spirited young men, with as yet no official responsibilities or posts, this could easily assume extravagant, or as Rupert put it, even violent expression.[73]

Still another factor distinguished this debate from the eucharistic controversy. Alger was committed to the received tradition, especially to St. Augustine, and he sought above all to make it speak plainly and harmoniously to contemporary ecclesiastical (canonistic) and theological problems. These teachers and students of dialectic, on the other hand, touted the power of the logical arts to resolve all theological problems, and disdained this monk for not being properly schooled in them. But Rupert's adversaries had also received a modicum of scriptural training, presumably from Anselm of Laon. They had traveled far and wide, Rupert reports, to study philosophy with famous masters, only at long last "to discover Holy Scripture," a pearl for which they paid a great price in anxious wakefulness (probably something more concrete too); if only now they would discover it to perfection and hold onto it into eternity! He had, by contrast, stayed home like Jacob with Rebecca and there, in his monastery, discovered Holy Scripture early and completely.[74] Rupert's defense of Holy Scripture against dialectic, rather than against the received tradition, lent this dispute a different character and dynamic.

Enraged by Rupert's arrogant challenge to their masters and claiming to act in defense of God's omnipotence, these clerics stirred up a "great tumult" against him and his treatise. This, Rupert seems to suggest, precipitated his trial before Archdeacon Henry, in which the eucharistic theology of his *Commentary on John* also came under judgement. Quite in contrast to the complex problems at issue there and the large battery of authori-

73. For this ethos among the lay, aristocratic youth, see G. Duby, "Les 'jeunes' dans la société aristocratique dans la France du Nord-Ouest au XIIᵉ siècle," in his *Hommes et structures du moyen âge* (Paris 1973) 213–25.

74. *RegBen.* 1: PL 170.480.

ties wielded by each side, the masters of dialectic simply charged that Rupert had denied the omnipotence of God, for if God did not "will" evil and it nevertheless happened, God clearly was not omnipotent.[75] But, Rupert noted smugly, they could produce no scriptural evidence to prove that "God willed evil" or that his position in *De uoluntate Dei* was at odds with the doctrine of God's omnipotence, nor apparently did they as yet employ a patristic authority (again from St. Augustine) which later became crucial. Rupert, on the other hand, probably even before the trial, had begun to gather and even to write up the scriptural and patristic arguments which went into the making of his own rejoinder, the *De omnipotentia Dei* 1–18.[76] In the event, these successfully blunted the force of the dialecticians' syllogism. The "expert advisers," Master Stephen of the cathedral chapter and possibly Alger, found Rupert not guilty of denying or impugning God's omnipotence, or as Rupert put it, they too grieved the "injury he had suffered in defending the truth." But the combined hostility of his enemies from both the eucharistic and predestinarian controversies nonetheless forced him into exile.

Rupert resolved to defend his position in a pamphlet on *The Omnipotence of God* addressed to the "wise and prudent" masters in Liège who had ruled in his favor.[77] The best evidence suggests Rupert wrote most of his basic argument (cc. 1–18) while in exile at Siegburg: none of its particular themes appears in the

75. *Omnip.* prologus: PL 170.455.

76. In *Omnip.* 2: PL 170.456, Rupert appears to refer only to heated debate and not yet to his subsequent trial and exile: "Immo quis nos istud quaerere compellit? Nimirum is qui noua nunc temeritate uel temeraria nouitate dogmatizat, quia uult Deus malum fieri et quia uoluntate eius primus homo lapsus est, illud pro argumento satis esse contendens, quia malum illud ne accideret non auertit, quod facere poteret cum omnipotens sit. Diximus pauca pro re superiore libello [were they in the same codex?], sed non est mitigata contentio. Itaque amplius atque amplius ad Scripturarum et omnimodae rationis patrocinium recurrere compellimur. . . ."

77. On *De omnipotentia Dei* (PL 170.453–78), see also Magrassi, *Teologia* 181, 195–97; Bischoff, *Controversy* 228–51 (the best extant analysis); Silvestre, "A propos" (n. 1 above) 21–22. No MSS have survived.

last books of *De sancta Trinitate*; he did not yet know an authority the masters deployed after his return; in an appended chapter (23) he referred specifically to his absence; and in the prologue he claimed to have held silence for a time, meaning especially the anxious weeks just after his trial. Charges of heresy compelled him to cite Scripture and the Fathers at length, as apparently he had also done in defending his eucharistic views at the trial.

Rupert took as the theme of his exposition Ps. 24(25):10: *Universae uiae Domini misericordia et iustitia.* For indeed the simplistic syllogism of the dialecticians, which would have God either will evil or lack omnipotence, wholly failed to grasp the twofold nature of God's almighty power by which He acted sometimes in mercy and at other times in truth and justice. Rupert insisted again (c. 2) that the will of God can never be considered the source of evil or of man's fall—this not so much an argument as a basic underlying conviction—and its true source must therefore (*consequenter*) be examined. Evil arose, Rupert argued by way of citing at length Augustine's *City of God*,[78] because man's will was created out of nothing and tended ever to return to nothing either in a diabolic way, by contending for that which neither is nor seems to be (the Father of lies), or in a human way, by seeking after things which seem to be but are not real, are not God Himself (cc. 3–5). The real question, Rupert argued, is the reverse of that asked by the schoolmen: in such dire (nihilistic) circumstances how do men and angels ever acquire a "good will"? And the answer, clearly, is that it is a gift of God's grace, as the apostle taught: *Nam Deus est, qui operatur in nobis uelle et perficere pro bona uoluntate* (Phil. 2:13). This text, so appropriate to Rupert's argument, was also a favorite of St. Augustine's for the positive side of predestination. But this led to the chief question (*summum quaestionis*): why did God not then extend this gift to all His creatures (c. 7)? To say that He would not is to contradict I Tim. 2:4. Scripture and reason teach, however, that sometimes in His justice He cannot (*non*

---

78. *Omnip.* 3 = *De ciuitate Dei* 12.6: CC 48: 359–60, 361.

posset) act in mercy. In particular (c. 8), God cannot have mercy upon unbelief, the worst form of which—Rupert aimed this one straight at his adversaries—is to defend one's own sinfulness by ascribing it to the will of God.

In the remaining chapters (cc. 9–18) Rupert confronted a series of objections (*Sed dicis*) to this interpretation. Two concern texts crucial to Master Anselm's position and may therefore go back to debates with his confrere in St. Lawrence. Rom. 9:19 (*Voluntate enim eius quis resistit?*), Rupert contended, could be understood only to mean "*et pacem habere*," as in Job 9:4 (*Quis restitit ei et pacem habuit*); in support he cited St. Gregory's gloss on Job and St. Augustine's on Rom. 9:19.[79] He also cited "Ambrose" on I Tim. 2:4, but this text, even or perhaps especially from his reversed approach to the question, caused difficulty, for all men manifestly were not saved. As he struggled to explain this (cc. 12–16), Rupert assumed an ever more homiletic tone, warning his readers to repent in humility and respect the omnipotence of God manifest in judgement. As final proof of His omnipotence Rupert argued, with the help of Gregory the Great,[80] that God in His irresistible will can and does bring good even out of evil and rebellion. In sum, however impressive Rupert's knowledge of the Fathers, however great his theological ambitions, and however weighty his call to defend the truth and rebut heresy, he remained a monastic preacher whose instincts, finally, often went beyond his actual theological equipment.

Armed with such a fine array of scriptural arguments written out in full, and persuaded that at least on this matter the two leading masters in Liège supported him, Rupert longed to return from exile and take up the battle anew. This he did in about May 1117,[81] but whether at his own insistence (more probably) or at Abbot Heribrand's request is simply not known. He quickly found opportunities to present his case, enriched now with the idea of God's twofold omnipotence and all these patristic au-

79. *Omnip.* 9 = Gregory, *Moralia* 9.9; *Omnip.* 10 = *De Spiritu et littera* 58.
80. *Omnip.* 17 = Augustine? and Gregory, *Moralia* 16.33.
81. Rupert traveled to France from Liège in the second week of July 1117, and one must allow a month for the events which led up to that journey.

thorities. The results proved bitterly disappointing. The masters of dialectic and their student-clerics scoffed at him as much now as they had before his exile (*me absente, me interdum praesente irridentes*).[82] After eighteen chapters of careful theological argument, Rupert suddenly intervenes with a very personal outcry. No matter what we say, he laments at the beginning of c. 19, they tell everyone (*diuulgamur*) that it simply misses the point, that we are a rustic simpleton unable to comprehend this subtle thought by which they "most truly claim" and "most firmly hold" that God willed evil. The last eight chapters of *De omnipotentia Dei* (cc. 19–27), in other words, are an immediate and personal record of the renewed debate after his return to Liège, just before his journey to France early in July. Two problems, one of authority and another of theological method, emerged from this second round.

At the trial and earlier in the debate Rupert's adversaries apparently produced no authorities to support their position, something they learned to rue upon Rupert's exoneration; and so by the time he returned they claimed to stand with their distinguished masters on the authority of St. Augustine's *Enchiridion*.[83] In a passage, parts of which entered the *Ordinary Gloss* for I Tim. 2:4 and other parts the fragmentary teachings preserved from the "School of Laon" on the will of God, Augustine had argued that nothing could happen contrary to God's will and therefore even evil He evidently permitted (*sinere*) willingly (*uolens*).[84] Rupert marveled that they should rest their whole case (*totum patrocinium*) on this single authority, and he still openly doubted that the masters at Laon really subscribed to such a

82. *Omnip.* 23: PL 170.473.

83. "Conueniebat quidem de his [Augustinian authority] tractare uel ad haec respondere in exordio sermonis [i.e. cc. 1–18], sed cognitum nobis nondum fuerat quod inde istud collegissent uel confirmari putassent, et mirabamur unde nanciscerentur aduersarii nostri causae suae defensionem cum nullam de Scripturis auctoritatem proferre possent." *Omnip.* 26: PL 170.475–76.

84. *Enchiridion* 95–96, 100: CC 46.99–100, 103, quoted in *Omnip.* 20: PL 170.469–70, and explicated in texts from Anselm's "school": Lottin, *Psychologie* 5.235 (no. 290), 238–39 (no. 292).

position.[85] As the next order of business, then, Rupert set out to interpret this passage properly (cc. 20–22). First of all, Rupert pointed out emphatically, St. Augustine nowhere said "*Deus uult malum.*" What he said rather was that God "wills" to bring good even out of evil, quite another matter. To demonstrate his reading of the text, Rupert proceeded (c. 21) exactly in the manner of a professional teacher to gloss the Augustinian passage, explaining its meaning word by word and citing other of the Saint's works to elucidate difficult passages.[86] In concluding (c. 22), he claimed they had "violently distorted" St. Augustine's text in order to derive from it this distinction by which they would have God will evil.

The masters in Liège were not impressed. Here it finally became manifest to Rupert too that their differences lay at a much deeper level. Part of it was just personal antipathy between these high-spirited secular masters and this local arrogant monk.[87] They spread it all around, Rupert reports (c. 23), that he had intervened not for the love of truth and God's honor but rather for sheer vain display—which strongly suggests Rupert had made quite a show of his challenge—only shamefully (*turpe*) to reveal thus his complete ignorance when he thought to glory in his learning. More precisely: Rupert failed utterly to grasp the dialectical skills needed to comprehend this distinction in the nature of God's will. His attempted dialectical refutation of the masters had in monkly ignorance merely "usurped" rather than truly applied this art.

As if this were the sum of the whole business, Rupert goes on, before my absence and now again they scoff at me and say I

85. *Omnip.* 20: PL 170.469–70.

86. Note that the method, though not the interpretation, differs not at all from the "school" fragment: Lottin, *Psychologie* 5.238–39 (no. 292).

87. For background on the opposition between monks and canons, see J. Ehlers, "Monastische Theologie, historischer Sinn und Dialektik," in *Antiqui und Moderni* (Miscellanea Mediaevalia 9, Berlin and New York 1974) 58–79; and R. Kohn, "Monastisches Bildungsideal und weltgeistliches Wissenschaftsdenken," in *Die Auseinandersetzungen an der Pariser Universität im XIII Jahrhundert* (Miscellanea Mediaevalia 10, Berlin and New York 1976) 1–37.

came too late to the study of dialectic, that I cannot, in particular, comprehend the difference between a '*mediata*' and an '*immediata*' position with respect to two contrary terms and had also confused '*uoluntas mali*' with '*uoluntas mala*'. In the general term '*uoluntas mali*', they now argued, one can distinguish two contrary positions, one approving and one reproaching, of which the middle term is the "permitting" form of God's '*uoluntas mali*'. But, Rupert objected, what new nonsense is this? How can God both will and reproach evil? Two contraries—teachers of dialectic ought to know this—cannot be said of the same thing! See, Rupert concludes, they demand we consider "middle terms" and only degenerate thereby into even more illogical positions. Probably with the help of a passage from Gregory's *Moralia*,[88] however, Rupert himself now (cc. 24–25) construed God's "permission" as His "suffering" evil (*sinere* [Augustine's term], *pati* [Gregory's term]), or His "not blocking" it (*non obsistendo*), but still never as a positive act of will.

The dialecticians' attack upon Rupert's ignorance hurt and he reacted sharply. He conceded the fame of dialectic these days, but professed publicly to God and to all who might hear or read his treatise that he had neither taught this art professionally nor attempted to show off his knowledge of it; and if he did know anything of it, he had drawn upon it only when a fight was necessary to support the simple and holy truth of God against heretical lies. In other words, Rupert was perceived to have challenged the masters on their own turf (dialectics), charged with simply making a fool of himself thereby, and now forced to beat a hasty retreat. For, Rupert went on (c. 23), he found (*censeo*) the simple words of shepherds and fishermen much more powerful (*ualentiora*) than the arguments of philosophers and "intellectuals" (*sapientium*)! Thus, just as Alger's insistence that divine truth be gained by way of the received tradition drove Rupert into defending the "unique" authority of Holy Scripture, so now the masters' claims for dialectic compelled him to take his stand on the "simple and holy words of shepherds and fishermen."

88. *Moralia* 6.18.33; see Silvestre, "Notes" (n. 1 above) 70–71.

To his original theological argument (cc. 1–18) Rupert had just finished adding his reinterpretation of the Augustinian passage and his remarks about dialectic (cc. 19–25) when confirmation came (c. 26) by way of "messengers" from France that certain masters (*quosdam facundiae Franciae magistros*) did indeed assert that "*Deus uult malum*" and presumed to base their argument chiefly on St. Augustine's text (*uim paene totam praesumerent*). But Master Anselm, Rupert learned happily, had not confirmed this view with his own authority. May the light of truth, Rupert exclaims, always preserve such a distinguished man from the blemish upon his honor sure to come from holding such a horrendous position! But whatever Master Anselm's stance was, several of his disciples or colleagues clearly did hold the contested position; notably, Rupert had not excluded Bishop William. Rupert now quickly concluded *De omnipotentia Dei* (c. 27): he reviewed again for his readers, especially the two "wise masters" to whom it was dedicated, his defense of God's omnipotence and righteous will, adding still another authority;[89] he reasserted that Scripture alone is the source of divine truth; and he rejected all foolish dialectical argumentation. Finally, in the last sentence he warned his adversaries not to go against the truth of Scripture lest they become guilty of the unforgivable sin against the Holy Spirit, from which "omnipotent God could do nothing contrary to the teaching of Scripture either to will or to effect their deliverance!"[90]—a position almost as extreme as that of those dialecticians who claimed God could not contradict Himself.

Those "messengers" apparently also brought word of a promise from Master Anselm to respond eventually to *De uoluntate Dei*.[91] The news raised Rupert's spirits; he seemed to have accomplished just what his challenge had intended. But soon An-

89. Jerome, *In Dan.* 4.32 (see above at n. 19).

90. ". . . unde nos [but clearly meaning *uos*] liberare non possit ipse, qui extra ueritatem Scripturarum facere aut uelle nihil potest omnipotens Deus." *Omnip.* 27: PL 170.478.

91. ". . . quando superiori libello respondere dignabitur, ut se facturum promisit. . . ." *Omnip.* 26: PL 170.476.

selm sent only a brief letter, in the event his last known written work.[92] The master of Laon, commonly acknowledged to be the greatest teacher of Scripture in his day, assumed a very lofty stance toward Rupert's challenge and the ensuing debate. He addressed his letter to Abbot Heribrand rather than to Rupert, and spent the first half of it warning that those who failed to adhere to the Fathers would quickly fall into petty quarrels over words in the fashion of young boys; that was about all (*in hoc genere pugnantium uerborum*) this flurry over whether "God willed evil" in fact amounted to. He turned next, and briefly, to the issue itself. He avoided, just as Rupert reported, the specific formula "*Deus uult malum*"; but he interpreted Ps. 24(25):10, the thematic verse of Rupert's *De omnipotentia Dei*, to mean that God "willed" acts both of mercy and of justice.[93] He essentially agreed with Rupert that the scriptural language about "hardening hearts" and "giving them over" meant "leaving" (*relinquit*) people in their sin, but on the basis of Rom. 9:18 and of Augustine's gloss on Rom. 1:24 he insisted nevertheless that it was part of God's omnipotent will to "harden hearts" or to "incline them toward evil." This Rupert did not and would not accept, as he had said already in *De uoluntate Dei* 2. In closing, Master Anselm dismissed the matter as deserving no more of his attention: I have stated my position, he says, and I leave all the rest to the "prudence" of you (Abbot Heribrand) who are more familiar with it.

Around late June 1117 Rupert found himself in the following position: Master Anselm had dismissed his challenge, his attempt to speak as an equal on this weighty theological question, as a mere quarrel over words; it was confirmed that certain other French masters did in fact teach that "God willed evil" and drew upon St. Augustine for support; his own *De omnipotentia Dei* was finished; and masters and students in Liège continued

92. The best edition in Lottin, *Psychologie* 5.175–77; for historical interpretation and manuscripts, see Silvestre, "A propos" (n. 1 above) 5–14.

93. Presumably the disciples in Liège had requested an interpretation of this verse from their famous scriptural master, since it had played such a key role in Rupert's defense. There is no evidence Anselm knew the just completed *Omnip.*

still to deride him as hopelessly ignorant and out of touch, in large measure because he had not studied dialectics abroad. In this situation Rupert resolved to go himself to these French masters, to debate them in public, and thus demonstrate that their understanding of Scripture and St. Augustine was manifestly in error. For a Black Monk to travel more than one hundred fifty miles, several days' journey, in order to debate publicly with acclaimed secular masters was truly extraordinary. In this era Black Monks occasionally studied at secular schools (as we have noted), and leading figures sometimes intervened publicly when called upon (Lanfranc, for instance, in the Berengarian controversy), but with the exception of Abelard, who continued to teach at the schools in Paris, few Black Monks entered the theological lists, so to speak, on their own initiative and in such a notable way.

When almost ten years later Rupert described what happened, he was himself, in retrospect, both proud and amazed at the "spectacle" (*spectaculum*): I went to France, he says, to do mighty battle (*potissimum . . . praelium disputationis committerem*) with those famous masters whose authority was always held over and against me. Seated on a paltry ass, with only a single servant-boy to accompany me, I set out (*profectus*) for those distant cities to join battle (*ad conflictum*) with masters whose genius and dignity of both office (Bishop William) and teaching (Master Anselm) I knew full well. Just as I expected, a large band of masters and students, like a not inconsiderable army (*quasi non paruus exercitus*) met me in order to hear my arguments and defeat them. But I was still more amazed to discover that just as I approached the city the elderly and more distinguished of the two (Anselm of Laon) drew his last breath, dying immediately after my entry (15 July 1117). One adversary thus removed from the scene, Rupert traveled another sixty miles to debate Bishop William in Châlons-sur-Marne. I do not know, Rupert went on, whether he outlived that harsh conflict (*acerbum conflictum*) by even a full year; in fact, Bishop William did not die until January 1122 (Rupert wrote this in 1125). Thus Rupert described his ultimate challenge to these renowned mas-

THE PREDESTINARIAN CONTROVERSY

ters, in the language and with the spirit of a knight errant fighting his way to fame and power.[94] Clearly the Black Monk, riding on a poor ass and with only a single servant-boy, was in this instance the "white knight."

In his apologia of 1125 Rupert went on to review and reinterpret the four scriptural texts and the passage from St. Augustine's *Enchiridion* which he had contested with his adversaries.[95] But he did not specify whether these adversaries referred to the "small army" in Laon (*non paruus conueniret exercitus ad me audiendum, ad me conuincendum*), or to Bishop William in Châlons-sur-Marne (*cum quo acerbum habui conflictum*). Yet however much he may have reworked this material to prove his own position, his language reflects still the public, open-ended disputes in which he took part.[96] The importance to the debate of scriptural texts may point towards Laon, where Anselm's brother Ralph immediately succeeded him as master of the Sacred Page; but William of Champeaux, even as bishop, continued also to teach, something to which Rupert alluded (*magister simul et episcopus*).

William of Champeaux (ca. 1070–1122) was active in nearly all the leading intellectual and religious movements of his time.[97] Abelard acknowledged him the leading teacher of dialectic around

94. *RegBen.* 1: PL 170.482–83. For a similar use of imagery drawn from feudal society in Abelard's *Historia calamitatum*, see the remarks of J. Le Goff, "Quelle conscience l'université médiévale a-t-elle eu d'elle-meme?" in *Beiträge zum Berufsbewusstsein des mittelalterlichen Menschen* (Miscellanea Mediaevalia 3, Berlin 1964) 16–19.

95. *RegBen.* 1: PL 170.483–89.

96. ". . . ostendere quod eadem capitula non perfecte intellexerint. . . . Ad secundum capitulum . . . dixi. . . . Ego fere nil praemeditatus, ita protinus respondi. . . ." Ibid. 483–84, 486.

97. On William, see C. Lohr, in *Lexikon für Theologie und Kirche*, 1130–31; P. Delhaye, "Guillaume de Champeaux," in *Catholicisme* 5 (Paris 1963) 391–93; Landgraf (n. 6 above) 76; G. Machaud, *Guillaume de Champeaux et les écoles de Paris au XII*ᵉ *siècle* (2nd ed. Paris 1867); J. Ehlers, *Hugo von St. Viktor* (Frankfurter Historische Abhandlungen 7, Wiesbaden 1973) 5–7, 9–11; and Karin M. Fredborg, "The Commentaries on Cicero's *De inventione* and *Rhetorica ad Herennium* by William of Champeaux," *Cahiers de l'Institut du Moyen Age Grec et Latin* [Copenhagen] 17 (1976) 1–39. Fragments of his works edited in Lottin, *Psychologie* 5.189–227.

the year 1100, even though he was eventually compelled to "destroy" William's view of universals.[98] William gained posts as chancellor and archdeacon at Notre Dame in Paris, but resigned them in 1108 to found the famous house of canons regular at St. Victor. In 1113 he was appointed bishop of Châlons-sur-Marne, a see closely tied to the royal house in France; there he reformed the cathedral chapter to regular status or the common life and also continued his teaching, mostly now for the benefit of his clergy. In 1115 (in the absence of the bishop of Langres) he ordained St. Bernard to the priesthood upon his consecration as abbot of Clairvaux. In short, for Rupert to debate such a man, and in his own episcopal see, manifestly required no small measure of courage. Unfortunately, apart from the debate over Augustine's *Enchiridion*, which seems very probably attributable to the dispute with Bishop William, nothing is known about their confrontation except that, in Rupert's words, it was harsh (*acerbum*).

All four scriptural texts used to argue that "God willed evil" Rupert knew previously to be used for this purpose, and he had dealt with the first (Rom. 1:24) already in *De uoluntate Dei* 2. As Anselm's letter had revealed, however, this text together with St. Augustine's gloss was crucial to the masters' argument (see n. 23 above). Rupert argued again that God did not incline men to evil but rather "left" unrepentant men in their wickedness. The second (Apoc. 22:11) and third (Exod. 7:3) the masters had apparently learned, as Abelard's *Sic et Non* shows, from one of Gregory's sermons on Ezechiel.[99] And the fourth text (Is. 6:10) was debated, as Rupert had noted earlier, in the context of John 9:40, where Christ quoted it. Quite apart from Rupert's specific arguments, which consistently placed the blame for sinfulness ("hardness" or "blindness") on man rather than God, two general observations deserve mention. First, the French masters, including presumably a former teacher of rhetoric and dialectic such as Bishop William, debated these issues by way of

98. *Historia calamitatum*: ed. J. Monfrin (Paris 1959) 65.
99. *In Hiezech.* 1.11.25: CC 142.181; *Sic et Non* 31.31: ed. Boyer and McKeon 179.

teaching and interpreting Scripture and not just, as Rupert's adversaries back in Liège would have it, in terms of dialectical coherence. There was, secondly, already an emerging structure to such teaching, so that Rupert, Anselm, and Abelard, largely or wholly independent of direct influence upon one another, brought the same scriptural and patristic texts to bear on specific doctrinal points.

Rupert's adversaries, in this case probably Bishop William, insisted further that St. Augustine's *Enchiridion* also taught their position. Rupert saw, rightly in fact, that St. Augustine had struggled mightily in this passage to resolve the tension between God's omnipotence and man's evil. I myself understood, Rupert says, what the holy Father intended to say, but when my adversaries would not concede it I boldly (*intrepidus*) exclaimed: the most holy Father Augustine retracted many things, and this passage too he should have retracted![100] I still dare (*Audeo autem adhuc*), Rupert went on, to counsel Father Augustine, like Jethro advising Moses, on a better way to state his meaning. That better way, Rupert preached, was essentially to say that men who did not repent, God would leave in their sin. For those few biblical instances where repentance was nevertheless followed by destruction (Ahab, for example), Rupert distinguished between true spiritual repentance with a view only toward heaven and penance done for present gain. Alger and others in Liège had been shocked to hear that Augustine was not in the canon and therefore not fully reliable on all things. One can only imagine the reaction of Bishop William and others who heard Rupert counsel St. Augustine on what to retract and how to put things better.

After Master Anselm's death and the disputes at Laon and Châlons-sur-Marne, Rupert reported in 1125, many religious and learned men who had not spoken openly while the masters were still alive now likewise criticized this view (*Deus uult malum*). Rupert doubtless exaggerated both his boldness and his own impact, though his remark accurately reflected the spirit of

100. *RegBen.* 1: PL 170.488.

steadfast loyalty which prevailed between masters and their students. Unfortunately, it is impossible to determine just which "religious and learned men" Rupert may have had in mind. Hugh of St. Victor, deeply indebted to St. Augustine and indirectly to Master Anselm, still upheld a qualified version of the view that God in some sense "willed evil"; Peter Lombard reported this view, but rejected it, as did most later scholastic authors.[101] The debate on this matter became so complicated and many-faceted as to make it impossible now to prove that certain objections stemmed originally from Rupert. His influence was probably very limited. There is only one extant copy, originally from St. Lawrence, of *De uoluntate Dei*, whereas there are at least seventeen copies of Master Anselm's brief letter to Abbot Heribrand. The fact remains, nevertheless, that Rupert was the first theologian known to have challenged this view so prominently developed in the most famous school of his day, and to have adopted, though not with the same language and method, essentially the position taken by later scholastic authors.

4

New Charges,
and Rupert's Silence

Rupert's original adversaries, the masters and students in Liège, persisted nonetheless in their hatred of him, and now sought revenge. Their attitude is easily grasped: this arrogant local monk had challenged the teachings of their famous masters, had escaped largely unscathed from attempts to prove him heretical and to silence him, had rebutted their scriptural and patristic authorities, and now—this was the last blow—had knocked their most important prop, the source of their pride, right out from under them by going to confront personally the masters on whose authority their position ultimately rested.

101. Ibid. 483. Hugh, *De sacramentis* 1.13–14: PL 176.233–46; Peter Lombard, *Sent.* 1.46. On the later development of this issue, see Magrassi, *Teologia* 211–16; Silvestre, "Notes" (n. 1 above) 67–68.

Rupert returned to Liège about August 1117, there presumably to announce the death of Master Anselm and to recount his bitter dispute with Bishop William—and from what we know of Rupert, probably not in the most tactful and retiring manner. His adversaries took their revenge soon after, perhaps still in the year 1117.

St. Augustine had taught in his *Literal Commentary on Genesis* and more briefly in his *City of God* that the "light" of Gen. 1:3 referred to the creation of angels.[102] Bede in his commentary had rejected this and argued simply for "primordial light." His view was very influential in the early middle ages, but Augustine's view, in good part through the *Ordinary Gloss*, came to prevail again among early scholastic authors. The earliest masters, however, still hesitated between Augustine's and Bede's views. Rupert, on the other hand, boldly devised an unprecedented variation on Augustine's view which evoked strong objections from the masters in Liège. St. Augustine had taught that angels were originally created out of the highest spiritual material, the "*caelum*" of Gen. 1:1; the good angels were then fixed in their adherence to God when they "became light," the "*fiat lux*" of Gen. 1:3. Rupert held instead that angels neither were created in nor fell from "heaven" (*caelum*), partly because that is the realm of God alone and still more because of his less ethereal view of angelic being. From St. Augustine Rupert had learned that devils have bodies made of dense, wet air, which explains how they can suffer physical punishment.[103] He identified this "air," against the tradition, with the "*tenebrae*" of Gen. 1:2, from which, he argued, all angelic bodies were originally made. Just as mortal man returned to the dust from which he was made, so the angels, Rupert reasoned, now become devils, reverted to that from which they had been made. But, again just like man, certain angels, not by nature but by grace, "became

102. *Gen.* 1.5.2; *De ciuitate Dei* 11.9. See G. Tavard, *Die Engel* (Handbuch der Dogmengeschichte II, 2b, Freiburg 1968) 60–65. Cf. Lombard, *Sent.* 2.13.2.

103. *Gen.* 1.11: CM 21.138; cf. Augustine, *De ciuitate Dei* 21.10.1.

light," to which "little proposition" Rupert related II Cor. 4:6 (*Deus qui dixerit de tenebris lucem splendescere, illuxit in cordibus nostris ad illuminationem scientiae claritatis in facie Iesu Christi*).[104] Throughout this argument Rupert sought very consciously to remove angels from their predetermined celestial status and to have them go through a salvation-historical process akin to man's. This is one of the very few instances where an argument closely identified with Rupert entered into scholastic texts: whether angels fell from the celestial realms into "darkness" and thus into "bodies of dense air" (the traditional view espoused, for instance, by Hugh of St. Victor) or rather were created with "airy"—as distinguished from "earthy"—bodies and then were raised to heaven by grace became a question debated by every medieval theologian on the basis of Lombard's textbook.[105]

In his apologia of 1125 Rupert told still another story to illustrate (*ab uno disce omnes*) the relentless persecution of his adversaries.[106] Seeking vengeance for the "shame Rupert had brought upon them" in the controversy over God's will, the masters and student-clerics in Liège "pored over his works in search of the slightest hint of heresy." Meanwhile Rupert had brought out *De sancta Trinitate*, first at Siegburg on Cuno's authority because he feared to make it public in Liège; but upon his return it evidently became more widely available. His adversaries read less than ten (printed) pages before they came upon Rupert's novel teaching that angels were created out of "darkness" (*de tenebris creatos esse angelos*). This, they said, is manifestly heresy (*Hoc, inquiunt, manifeste haeresis est*). The passage probably caught their attention so much the more because the next several pages of his *Commentary on Genesis* contain arguments Rupert had later used verbatim in the first third of his *De uoluntate Dei*. This time the masters' charge took the form, it seems, of a personal attack rather than any new judicial hearing; but the incident created enough public commotion in Liège that Meingoz of St.

104. *Gen.* 1.11: CM 21.138–39.
105. *Sent.* 2.8.1
106. What follows is taken wholly from *RegBen.* 1: PL 170.492–94.

Martin's, a friend of Rupert's from a collegiate church near St. Lawrence, referred to it nearly ten years later.[107]

Rupert responded bluntly: heresy is to contradict the holy and canonical Scriptures, to affirm something denied by them (such as, God willed evil), or to deny something affirmed by them. What Scripture, then, have I contradicted? When his enemies, as before, could produce no such contradiction, Rupert charged them flatly with straightforward calumny, particularly since this was a question which concerned creatures rather than the Creator. Rupert then went on, somewhat less belligerently, to explain from Scripture that "darkness" need not necessarily have a negative sense. He quoted Augustine explicitly against Bede (unnamed) to prove that "*fiat lux*" referred to the creation of angels, and quoted from Augustine again on the "dense, humid air" of which devils' bodies consisted.[108] So, he concluded, drawing together his argument, either they can agree with St. Augustine that "*fiat lux*" refers to the angels, and then they must also listen to the apostle Paul teaching that God made the light to shine out of darkness (II Cor. 4:6); or else let them tell when and from what substance angels were created. For my part, Rupert declared, I do not fear their charges (*uoces*) so long as they cannot prove my position (*ego in sermone aliquo*) contrary to the teachings of Holy Scripture.

But Rupert feared their attack much more than he would admit even in 1125, six years after he had left Liège and four years after he had become abbot of Deutz. The masters almost certainly had brought still another charge, this too a very personal one, which Rupert dared not answer until he was safely established in Cologne. Rupert had attempted something original in his *De sancta Trinitate*: a commentary on the whole of Sacred Scripture. This, the masters charged, was a flagrant affront

107. In a letter to Rupert, ed. H. Grundmann, *DA* 21 (1965) 274. Half the letter is devoted to the question of Rupert's orthodoxy, indicating what a cloud still hung over his name in Liège about 1125/26.

108. Here (PL 170.493–94) Rupert quoted explicitly that which he had referred to implicitly in his *Commentary on Genesis* (nn. 102, 103 above).

to the authority of the Fathers. For it was not permitted to add anything to that already said by the holy Catholic Fathers. What's more, when holier and more learned men had already spoken, it was not only brash but burdensome to increase still further the number of commentaries.[109] Such a charge struck directly at Rupert's perception of his own calling, and this time his response was total silence.

From about August 1117, when he returned to St. Lawrence in Liège, until his permanent removal to Deutz in April 1119 Rupert produced, so far as is known, not one single scrap of writing—this in contrast to around thirty-five hundred pages written in the preceding seven years. Rupert either feared the hostility of his adversaries in Liège or was so depressed by their attacks that he could not bring himself to write; in all likelihood both were true. It was, moreover, during those years that Alger completed and brought out his work on the eucharist, which in Liège at least was surely read as a powerful indictment of Rupert's teachings. And in addition the predestinarian controversy continued still to rumble in the background. At some point during the year 1118, Wibald of Stavelot accompanied his teacher Reinhard, the *scholasticus* at the abbey of Stavelot, to Liège in order to see Rupert and read his treatises (*nam illuc propter uos et opera uestra de Stabulaus ueneramus*). Reinhard, Wibald reports, agreed wholeheartedly with them against Rupert's adversaries.[110] Rupert's challenge to the famous masters in France[111] and his raucous dispute with the masters in Liège had evidently become renowned throughout the diocese and probably beyond. Abbot Heribrand, however, possessed nothing of Berengar's power and prestige, and he could not act effectively as Rupert's protec-

109. *Apoc.* prologus: PL 169.825.

110. For the date and Wibald's letter in general, see Silvestre, "Notes" (n. 1 above) 72–73, and Bischoff, *Controversy* 360–62. PL 170.543–46; P. Jaffé, *Bibliotheca rerum germanicarum* 1.76–77. On Wibald, see G. Despy, in *Biographie nationale* 30.814–28.

111. Wibald refers to "apologeticos uestros quos illustribus scripsistis uiris" and claims to have read a Matthew commentary in which for the verse "*Fiat uoluntas tua*" (Matt. 6:10) "inuenimus calumniatoris uestri sententiam." By the

tor and patron. How long Rupert would have continued to suffer the clerics' hostility and to maintain silence, despite his conviction of a theological calling, cannot be known. In April 1119 the rapidly deteriorating ecclesiastical situation in Liège finally forced him, still unwillingly, to leave his homeland forever and to begin a new career in the archdiocese of Cologne.

---

early 1120's, in other words, Anselm's teaching on God's will had entered a scholastic commentary on Matthew; around 1140, it is also found in the *Enarrationes in Matthaeum*, PL 162.1307.

VI

Abbot
of Deutz

RUPERT SPENT the last ten years of his life (April 1119–
March 1129) in the archdiocese of Cologne, the latter eight and
one-half of them as abbot of Deutz. Freed finally from the op-
pressive hostility of his adversaries, Rupert immediately took
up his writing and produced even more at Deutz than he had
during the foregoing ten years (1109–19) at Liège. His work
came to fruition now; and although his basic themes remained
largely the same, individual works responded to new controversies on matters ecclesiastical, religious, and theological (chapters VII, VIII, and IX). At St. Lawrence Rupert's responsibilities beyond those of an ordinary monk-priest, probably as a
teacher, could be reconstructed only by way of circumstantial
evidence. His reign at Deutz and his activities in the large and
important archdiocese of Cologne are far better attested, though
still not with plentiful documentation. As an administrator and
churchman Rupert almost certainly maintained a collection of
his correspondence, but this invaluable source, possibly still extant around 1500, has since disappeared together with most
other manuscripts from Deutz.[1] Enough additional evidence

1. Johannes Trithemius, *Catalogus illustrium virorum*, in *Opera historica*
(Frankfurt 1601; repr. 1966) 136–37 refers to works of Rupert he had himself
discovered, and among them: *epistolarum ad diversos libr. 1*. Though a notori-
ously unreliable author, he was at Deutz around 1492 (probably other times

survives, however, to reconstruct the historical setting for his works and controversies at Deutz.

1

Refuge at
Cologne and Siegburg

Bishop Otbert's formal reconciliation with Rome brought no end to the deep ecclesiastical divisions inside his diocese. Down at least to 1116 Rupert had argued bitterly with secular clerics about sacramental validity, and as late as 1118 Otbert faithfully supported another imperial anti-pope, Gregory [VIII], otherwise known as the "Spanish ass."[2] Following Otbert's death on 31 January 1119, strife between the two parties broke into the open.[3] Neither the emperor (any longer) nor the papacy (yet) was strong enough to command assent from all; power devolved effectively upon local noble parties which formed up around each of the contending candidates. Frederick,[4] the cathe-

---

too) to give a speech in praise of Rupert, and made use of the manuscript collection there: see K. Arnold, *Johannes Trithemius (1462–1516)* (Quellen und Forschungen zur Geschichte des Bistums und Hochstifts Würzburg 23, Würzburg 1971) 33, 60, 63–64, 136. Moreover, one of Rupert's letters has recently been discovered in a manuscript containing mostly "school materials": see Lajos Csoka, "Ein unbekannter Brief des Abtes Rupert von Deutz," *SMBO* 84 (1973) 383–93. This may point to a collection of letters from which one was excerpted as a model.

2. Reimbald, *Chronicon*: CM 4.133.

3. Accounts of the schism in Liège in G. Meyer von Knonau, *Jahrbücher des deutschen Reiches unter Heinrich IV. and Heinrich V.* (Leipzig 1909) 7.97ff, 141ff; E. de Moreau, "Les derniers temps de la querelle des investitures à Liège," *Bulletin de la Commission Royale d'Histoire* 100 (1936) 301–48; P. Bonenfant, "La Lotharingie avant et après le Concordat de Worms: Observations tirées de la crise liégeoise de 1119–1123," *Annales de la XXXII° session (1947) de la Fédération Archéologique et historique de Belgique*, 95–104. That the divisions went back ultimately to a papal-imperial split is clear from Rudolph's *Gesta abb. Trudon.* 11.4: MGH SS 10.299.

4. F. Magnette, "Saint Frédéric, évêque de Liège," *Bulletin de la société d'art et d'histoire du diocèse de Liège* 9 (1895) 225–62; and M. de Somer, in *Dictionnaire d'histoire et de géographie ecclésiastique* 18 (1977) 1167.

dral provost and brother to Count Godfrey of Namur, expected
to succeed Otbert, but a pre-election assembly broke up in disarray, whereupon Alexander,[5] treasurer of the cathedral, provost
of two local collegiate churches, and son of Count Otto of
Jülich, seized the ring and staff, brought them to King Henry V,
and was immediately invested with the bishopric. Archbishop
Frederick of Cologne, a recent convert to the papal cause, forbade the clergy and people of Liège to receive Alexander, and
Frederick, as provost, attempted to enforce the order. The confrontation grew violent. In March, Count Godfrey of Louvain,
duke of Lower Lotharingia, forcibly quashed a "free election" in
Liège called by Archbishop Frederick. Provost Frederick and his
supporters withdrew to Cologne, where he was canonically
elected bishop of Liège on 23 April 1119. Pitched battle ensued.
Eventually Frederick won, and in October he was consecrated
by Pope Calixtus II at Reims. When he died only two years later
(1121), his supporters claimed he had been poisoned and in time
they had him canonized. Alexander then battled anew for the
episcopal see, but lost out this time to Albero I, brother of the
count of Louvain, his former supporter. Alexander finally succeeded Albero in 1128, only to be removed for simony in 1135.

Rupert accompanied Provost Frederick to Cologne and there
served as a witness to his "free election."[6] Abbot Berengar had
already established a close working relationship with the provost, so that when, for instance, Frederick had gone on pilgrimage to the Holy Land he had first confessed to the abbot of
St. Lawrence.[7] And after Frederick's death it was Nizo of St.
Lawrence, one of Rupert's confreres, who prepared the *Life*
which argued successfully for his canonization. Rupert may
have been present at the two earlier election assemblies which

5. J. Closon, "Alexander Ier de Juliers, évêque de Liège (1128–35)," *Bulletin de la société d'art et d'histoire du diocèse de Liège* 13 (1902) 403–73.

6. ". . . sanctae memoriae Fridericus in episcopum electus, cuius causam
conscius et testis Deus tantis tamque crebris miraculis defendit atque illustra-
uit, secum huc ad Agrippinensem metropolim cum electionis suae testibus adduxit me." *RegBen.* 1: PL 170.496.

7. Nizo, *Vita Friderici* 5: MGH SS 12.504.

broke up in disarray and violence. In any case, he expressed grateful relief to have escaped the violence, this "time of great tribulation" which beset his *patria*, even though initially he had refused to leave[8]—whether out of loyalty to his abbey, to his favored candidate, or to his *patria* is not altogether clear. As with the apostles' release from prison (Acts 5:19), it was as if an angel had finally seized him by the hand and led him out. In another reference to these events, Rupert made it clear he had not considered himself called to martyrdom, however firmly he supported the papal candidate for bishop in Liège.[9]

For approximately a year and one-half Rupert's status and future remained uncertain. Even after Bishop Frederick had gained secure control of Liège Rupert stayed in Cologne and Siegburg; evidently, beyond the immediate political situation the hostility of his theological critics provided yet more compelling grounds for his departure from Liège. But he still considered himself a monk of St. Lawrence: when Abbot Markward of Deutz pressed him to rewrite the *Vita Heriberti* Rupert pointed out that he was "going the extra mile," since as a monk professed elsewhere he was not bound to obey the abbot of Deutz.[10] During this period of enforced leisure Rupert probably lived mainly at Siegburg, though he also developed close contact with Archbishop Frederick and Abbot Markward.[11] His major project was a new *Commentary on the Apocalypse* (chap-

8. "Cum enim tribulatio patriae immineret—quis denique tribulationem illam non audiuit—cum, inquam, patriae tribulatio uehemens prope iam adesset [the violently quashed election of 23 March?], me dissimulante exire et reuerti ad te [Cuno] quo me magnopere inuitabas. . . . Extunc [election of 23 April] obedienter hic [archdiocese of Cologne] ego passus sum detineri. . . ." *RegBen.* 1: PL 170.496.

9. *Matt.* 8: CM 29.254.

10. *Herib.* prologus: ed. Dinter 31.

11. The latter implied by the prologue to Rupert's *Vita Heriberti*: ed. Dinter 30, 31. However, Rupert's "Ibam alias" and "diuerti huc" refer here to his forced diversion from his proposed project (the Apocalypse commentary), not to relocation from Siegburg to Deutz as H. Grundmann, *DA* 22 (1966) 399 n. 27 and Dinter, *Heribert* 103 suggested.

ter VII, part 3), but Abbot Markward managed to divert his attention at least briefly elsewhere.

Archbishop Heribert of Cologne (999–1021) founded the abbey of Deutz around 1003 and dedicated its church in May 1020. A generation or so later, Lambert, a monk and later abbot (1061–70) of St. Lawrence in Liège, then serving as *scholasticus* at Deutz (1045–56), wrote the *Life of St. Heribert.*[12] Abbot Markward (1110/13–20), with the support of Archbishop Frederick and Abbot Cuno, had reformed the abbey and now asked Rupert also to rewrite its founder's *Life* "in a better style." Rupert reluctantly agreed. With the charges of novelty leveled against his *Commentary on John* and *De sancta Trinitate* still ringing in his ears, he carefully pointed out in his prologue that he rewrote only at Markward's request and that others would have to judge whether he had indeed improved upon the original.[13] Peter Dinter's recent edition and commentary have thoroughly handled most philological and hagiographical matters. But a review of those themes and remarks Rupert added to Lambert's original will indicate something of Rupert's mood and concerns just after he went into exile again.

Twice in the course of his narrative Rupert referred directly to recent events in Liège. Prelates were to be called by election, he insisted; they were not to intrude by human presumption.[14] The clergy and people in Heribert's time had been split too, but they quickly united around him—unlike other times and places Rupert had heard about and seen (*audita uel uisa*) where unity was not restored until after the loss of many souls and even

12. Ed. H. Pertz, MGH SS 4.740–53; *Miracula* (also by Lambert), ed. O. Holder-Egger, MGH SS 15.1245–60.

13. Rupert's cautious prologue, contrasted with his much bolder preface to the Apocalypse commentary, and his reference to other writing as just begun (*Ibam alias . . .* , *proposito curso* [n. 11 above]) suggest to me that Markward's request and Rupert's rewriting came early on, probably still in 1119. On the *Vita Heriberti*, see Dinter, *Heribert* passim, and M. L. Arduini, "Il problema della *paupertas* nella *Vita sancti Heriberti Archiepiscopi Coloniensis* di Ruperto di Deutz," *Studi Medievali* 3rd ser. 20 (1979) 87–138.

14. *Herib.* 15: ed. Dinter 57–58.

lives.[15] Heribert's adversary had also attempted to bribe the emperor (like Alexander in Liège, it might be added, for this report is not found in Lambert's original or any other known source).[16] Again and again throughout the *Life* Rupert stressed that the episcopal dignity was a "gracious gift" of Christ not to be sought by human ambition. Bishops are called to a spiritual ministry, not to rule over secular principalities (*non ad regna gentium*).[17] To illustrate his point Rupert added an account of the awful death of an ambitious bishop of Strassburg, again based on no known source.[18] Rupert also explicitly condemned priests who made the sacraments venal and served only the wealthy.[19] Good prelates, on the other hand, must preach, and Rupert placed in the archbishop's mouth a sermon on one of his own favorite themes, Christ's victory over the Devil, the prince of this world.[20] In sum, the contested election and subsequent warfare in his homeland, attributable largely to the worldly ambitions of prelates like Alexander, was still very much on Rupert's mind during his first months in the archdiocese of Cologne.

Following Frederick's election on 23 April 1119, Rupert "obediently suffered himself to be detained" in the archdiocese of Cologne, and in all likelihood he never saw his homeland again. Cuno's offer of refuge and Rupert's permanent removal presupposed the connection established between them in 1116–17. But from April 1119 until May 1126 when Cuno was elected bishop of Regensburg that bond deepened steadily, becoming of immeasurable importance to the further development of Rupert's theological and ecclesiastical careers. Abbot Cuno's patronage enabled Rupert to begin writing again and doubtless also to receive an abbatial appointment outside his home diocese. Since Deutz and Siegburg are less than twenty miles apart, Rupert and Cuno were frequently together. At least four and

15. *Herib.* 6: ed. Dinter 39.
16. *Herib.* 7: ed. Dinter 40 and 110 (commentary).
17. *Herib.* 9: ed. Dinter 44.
18. *Herib.* 8: ed. Dinter 42–43.
19. *Herib.* 23–24: ed. Dinter 64–68. Cf. Arduini (n. 13 above) 112ff.
20. *Herib.* 17: Dinter 59–60.

probably five of Rupert's nine major works from this period were written expressly at Cuno's request, and in the last of them Rupert honored his patron with an almost hagiographic tribute upon his elevation to the episcopal dignity.[21]

Rupert's chief patron was born into a ministerial family (von Raitenbuch) near Regensburg.[22] As a young man he joined the monastic life in the recently (1070) founded abbey of Siegburg, soon rose to director of the abbey's school (which may explain his support for Rupert, who alone reports this detail),[23] and then was elected abbot (1105–26). During his reign the abbey nearly doubled in size (one hundred twenty monks in all), reaching the pinnacle of its power and extending its Observance and reforms beyond the archdiocese to houses in Utrecht and Minden. Abbot Cuno also established a system of priories, founded a house for women on an island in the Rhine (Nonnenswerth), and significantly enlarged the abbey's income, possibly with the help of forged charters—all this in close cooperation with Archbishop Frederick. Cuno's reputation as a monastic leader was unexcelled. Rupert called him a "pillar of the religious life" who was "most zealous in letters" and a "model of monastic discipline."[24] Norbert of Xanten went to Siegburg after his conversion for several months of ascetic training, and when in 1121 new warfare over the episcopal succession in Liège drove out the learned and devout Abbot Rudolph of St.

21. *Matt.* 12: CM 29.386–96; separately edited with an introduction by P. Jaffé, MGH SS 12.637–38.

22. On Cuno, see J. Semmler, *Die Klosterreform von Siegburg* (Bonn 1959) 46–48; E. Wisplinghoff, *Die Benediktinerabtei Siegburg* (Germania Sacra, n.F. 9.2, Berlin and New York 1975) 157–58; and R. Bauerreiss, "Honorius von Canterbury (Augustodunensis) und Kuno I., der Raitenbucher, Bischof von Regensburg (1126–32)," *SMBO* 67 (1956) 306–14. Apart from the cartulary edited by E. Wisplinghoff, *Urkunden und Quellen zur Geschichte von Stadt und Abtei Siegburg* (Siegburg 1964), Rupert's "*Vita*" (n. 21 above) is the major source.

23. *Matt.* 12: CM 29.388. For the possibility that Cuno patronized vernacular poets (the *Annoslied*) as well as theologians such as Rupert, Gerhoch, and Honorius, see Bauerreiss (n. 22 above) 311.

24. CM 21.120; *Matt.* 12: CM 29.388.

Trond, he too intended to take refuge at Siegburg, though in the end he stayed for a time with Rupert at Deutz.[25] In short, Rupert had gained as his protector and bosom friend the most powerful and probably also the most influential and able Benedictine abbot in the province of Cologne (which is to say, the entire northwestern corner of the Empire).

Through Abbot Cuno, possibly as early as 1117, Rupert was made known to Archbishop Frederick of Cologne.[26] Cuno had Rupert deliver a "meditation" before the archbishop on the Book of Apocalypse in order to demonstrate that Rupert could "go beyond the Fathers" in interpreting this marvelous and difficult book.[27] Archbishop Frederick was suitably impressed, and he too became Rupert's patron, a far more powerful figure both politically and ecclesiastically though never so close personally as Cuno. Frederick was the son of a noble Bavarian family (von Schwarzenbach).[28] He showed throughout his life a fascinating combination of the old and new. Quick to perceive and patronize new intellectual and religious movements, he was also an unreconstructed prince-bishop determined to solidify and expand his territorial holdings. After studying in France (Angoulême) as a young man, he returned to serve in two cathedral chapters much favored by the Salian dynasty (Bamberg and Speyer); from Speyer King Henry IV appointed him to the archbishopric of Cologne (1100–31). Frederick remained loyal to the old king longer than most but finally switched to Henry V's party only to be suspended by Pope Paschal II. In 1111 he accompanied the king to Rome where he witnessed the fiasco which culminated in the pope's imprisonment. In 1114, owing

25. MGH SS 12.671; PL 170.1261; *Gesta abb. Trudon.* 11.15: MGH SS 10.303.

26. CM 7.2; *Matt.* 8: CM 29.229. The archbishop was at Siegburg on 29 March 1117: Wisplinghoff, *Urkunden* (n. 22 above) 57–58.

27. *Apoc.*: PL 169.825.

28. On Frederick, see F. W. Oediger, *Das Bistum Köln von den Anfängen bis zum Ende des 12. Jahrhunderts* (2nd ed. Cologne 1972) 131–40; E. Wisplinghoff, in *Neue Deutsche Biographie* 5.511; J.-P. Sosson, in *Dictionnaire d'histoire et de géographie ecclésiastique* 18 (1977) 1157–59; R. Knipping, ed., *Die Regesten der Erzbischöfe von Köln in Mittelalter* 2. nn. 1–286.

partly to territorial ambition and partly to genuine conviction, he joined the papal party, organized a massive and violent rebellion against the emperor in the lower Rhineland, and assumed leadership of the Church party in the northwest down to 1122. It was at Cologne in April 1115 that Henry V was pronounced excommunicated for the first time on imperial soil, and Frederick's intervention at Liège in 1119 in behalf of the papal party was therefore to be expected.

After nearly thirty years of grave tension with Bishop Otbert, in other words, Rupert suddenly found himself under the protection of an archbishop who was both at the forefront of the papal party and enthusiastic in support of his own work. This too, at least initially, was liberating. Rupert dedicated the first two of his commentaries written at Cologne, that on the Apocalypse and the first half of that on the Minor Prophets, to Archbishop Frederick.

2

The Abbot of Deutz

On 11 September 1120 Abbot Markward died, and shortly thereafter (before 6 January 1121) Rupert succeeded him as abbot of Deutz.[29] According to a contemporary chronicler, Rupert owed his promotion to the "great fame of his learning in Holy Scripture."[30] That was doubtless correct, at least so far as it went, for without his reputation for divine learning and his "numerous, large, and magnificent books," as merely a foreign exile and probably a commoner, he could never have gained such a post. Nor would he have received the appointment if he had not already enjoyed the good favor of Archbishop Frederick to whose see the abbey of Deutz belonged, and especially the patronage of Abbot Cuno who had just effected Deutz's reform according to the Siegburger Observance.

29. On the date of Markward's death, see Semmler (n. 22 above) 76 n. 18, 331 n. 44, 332 n. 54. Rupert witnessed a charter as abbot on 6 January 1121: Wisplinghoff, *Urkunden* (n. 22 above) 75 no. 34.

30. *Gesta abb. Trudon.* 11.13: MGH SS 10.303.

In the early fourth century, the Romans built a castle (*tuitio* = Deutz) directly opposite the city of Cologne to guard the east entrance of their bridge over the river Rhine. When barbarians overran the city a century later, the castle fell first to Frankish kings and then in the ninth century to the archbishops of Cologne. The bridge eventually collapsed, but the castle with its massive Roman walls and some fifteen towers stood firm. As such it posed a grave threat to river traffic passing before the city and indeed to the city of Cologne itself.[31] Archbishop Bruno (953–65) may therefore have begun to dismantle it. But Archbishop Heribert (999–1021), in cooperation with Otto III, resolved instead—like Bishop Wolbodo (1018–21) with the Public-Mount in Liège—to render the site safe by founding a monastery inside the castle. Initial plans dated back to just before Otto III's death (1003); on 3 May 1020 the abbey church was dedicated to the Blessed Virgin and still later (1030's) to the newly canonized Heribert himself. The abbey of Deutz, like that of St. Lawrence, belonged to the bishop, who made or supervised the appointment of all its abbots.

Many of Deutz's early charters, including the founding charter dated 3 May 1020, are forgeries (at least in certain particulars), prepared during the generation after Rupert's death (1130–60).[32] But from the extant charters and Milz's study (here summarized), it is safe to conclude the monastery was sufficiently endowed initially to support forty monks (when thirty was closer to the average), continued to receive support from Archbishop Pilgrim (1021–36) and down to about the 1060's, and then suffered definite decline, both material and religious. Archbishop

31. Basic on all matters pertaining to the medieval history of Deutz: Joseph Milz, *Studien zur mittelalterlichen Wirtschafts- und Verfassungsgeschichte der Abtei Deutz* (Veröffentlichungen des kölnischen Geschichtsvereins 30, Cologne 1970); see pp. 3–22 on the castle.
32. The charters are newly edited by E. Wisplinghoff, *Rheinisches Urkundenbuch: Ältere Urkunden bis 1100* (Bonn 1972) 173–212, nn. 120–45. On the forged charters, compare O. Oppermann, *Rheinische Urkundenstudien* (Bonn 1922) 1.265ff; E. Wisplinghoff, "Beiträge zur älteren Geschichte der Benediktinerabtei Deutz," *Jahrbuch des kölnischen Geschichtsvereins* 29/30 (1957) 139–60; Milz (n. 31 above) passim.

Frederick and Abbot Cuno cooperatively reformed the abbey in the 1110's; under abbots Markward (1110/13–20) and Rupert (1120–29), Deutz enjoyed again its full material endowment. This was squandered by Rupert's disreputable successor, Abbot Rudolph (1130–46), and then rebuilt or recouped so far as possible under abbots Gerlach (1146–59) and Hartbern (1161–69), who were presumably responsible for some of the forged claims.

The purported founding charter, an authentic papal confirmation in 1147, and records gathered by the *custos* Thiodericus Aedituus around 1160 reveal the approximate extent of lands, churches, and rights over which Abbot Rupert presided.[33] His abbey possessed about twenty-five manors, located mostly in the archdiocese of Cologne along the Rhine or to the northeast, together with three onetime royal forests, a small castle on the Rhine north of Cologne (Bürgel), and vineyards on the Mosel.[34] Deutz also possessed around forty parochial churches—an extraordinary number, surpassed in the archdiocese only by the archbishopric itself and the church in Bonn. The abbey received the full tithe from twenty-five of those and normally appointed their parish priests (usually not monks).[35] Inside the castle and just in front of the abbey gate there stood an older parish church, St. Urban's, which served nearby townspeople as well as those from five surrounding villages. This church too, served in Rupert's time by a secular priest named Stephen, was made over to the abbey. Whether or not the archbishops also granted to the monks the entire castle of Deutz with its houses, walls, and towers was and is, as we shall see, a matter of dispute.

Little is known from Rupert's time about the lay lords who lived on and helped to administer these properties. They first

33. Wisplinghoff, *Urkundenbuch* (n. 32 above) 191–93; T. J. Lacomblet, *Urkundenbuch für die Geschichte des Niederrheins* (Düsseldorf 1840; repr. 1966) 1.244–45 = JL 9081. On Thiodericus, partially edited in MGH SS 14.560–66, see Milz (n. 31 above) 2; and Wattenbach-Schmale, *Deutschlands Geschichtsquellen im Mittelalter* (Darmstadt 1976) 1.370–71.

34. Milz (n. 31 above) 23–35 (systematic overview), 245–89 (list of all properties, rights, and incomes), and Map 3 for locations.

35. Ibid. 99–117, 150–61, 167–68.

appear (*cum testimonio laycorum fidelium ac ministerialium nostrorum*) in the only charter extant from Rupert's reign,[36] and several probably lived in the castle right next to the monks. The abbots of Deutz made extended visitations to hold court on their manors, to oversee incomes, and to inspect subject churches. *En route*, an abbot from just after Rupert's reign traveled with two or three chaplains, five or six knights, and various servants (chamberlains, cooks, bakers, etc.), in all as many as thirty people.[37] Even if this was an exceptional case (hence the documentation) and Rupert traveled with a far smaller retinue, it still represented a dramatic change from the single servant-boy who accompanied him to Laon and Châlons in 1117.

The church at Deutz was quite unusual and possibly even singular, for, though designed from the outset for monks, it had an octagonal interior with a rounded exterior, modeled perhaps on Charlemagne's famous chapel at Aachen.[38] To accommodate the forty or so monks who worshipped there, the easternmost bay was extended into a kind of apse, and a rectangular elevated platform with its own vaulted ceiling was built out from that choir into the center of the octagon. According to Thiodericus (ca. 1160) it was Abbot Rupert who had this vault completed with "marvelous decoration."[39] Given the importance of biblical images in his thought and the speculation among art historians about his influence, it is most regrettable that this "marvelously decorated" vault has long since disappeared. Rupert's church was renovated in gothic style around 1390, totally rebuilt in baroque style around 1775, and toward the end of the Second World War almost completely destroyed. The cloister and other monastic buildings have also disappeared, but Thiodericus ascribed to Rupert the building of another (the "new") dormitory.

The internal religious life at Deutz is known hardly at all.

36. Ibid. 173–78; the charter is that in n. 48 below.

37. T. J. Lacomblet, "Die Benediktinerabtei zu Deutz," *Archiv für die Geschichte des Niederrheins* 5 (1865) 278ff; Milz (n. 31 above) 68.

38. See H E. Kubach and A. Verbeek, *Romanische Baukunst an Rhein und Maas* (Berlin 1976) 184–86, with a ground plan and bibliography.

39. MGH SS 14.565.

The monks there resisted the Siegburger Reform longer than any other Benedictines in the archdiocese. Rupert referred once to his "negligent predecessors," and Thiodericus said of Abbot Lutfridus (dates unknown, but attested in 1110) that he lost his abbatial post in an even worse way than he had gained it.[40] Around 1110 Archbishop Frederick, as part of his growing support for monastic reform and for Abbot Cuno of Siegburg in particular, installed first an Abbot Bavo (1110) and then Abbot Markward (attested 1117), the latter definitely a monk from Siegburg.[41] In 1119/20 Rupert described Markward's reign as a green tree transplanted, a restoration of religion where it had almost died out, and in the *Vita* he omitted any reference to Heribert's original training at Gorze.[42] Unfortunately, the Siegburger Customary has been lost, and so the exact structure of its office and discipline is no longer known. As abbot, Rupert certainly upheld these reforms, but there is no evidence which would make of him a great spokesman for the Siegburger Reform.[43]

At Deutz Rupert was not at first well received. He compared himself later to Joseph who had also to rule over subjects whose tongue he could not understand and to suffer envy because he, a "foreign hired servant," was "promoted over local men" and "placed in charge of their material holdings."[44] By 1127, however, Rupert could manage a play on words in German,[45] and thirty years later Thiodericus regarded him as Deutz's

40. *Incendio* 9: ed. Grundmann 450; MGH SS 14.565; Milz (n. 31 above) 235.

41. Semmler (n. 22 above) 74–76 noted several bits of evidence which pointed to Bavo's connection with Siegburg as well, but rejected them largely because of Rupert's remarks about Markward's role in the reform (n. 42 below). But those remarks may only reflect the shortness of Bavo's reign, Rupert's ignorance thereof, or his own desire to flatter Markward. The fact that both Lutfrid and Bavo are attested for 1110, and that Lutfrid somehow lost his post (above at n. 40), suggests the reform began forcibly in that year.

42. *Herib.* prologus: ed. Dinter 31–32.

43. Semmler (n. 22 above) 77 n. 23 named Rupert "der eifrigste Verfechter des Siegburger Reformprogramms"—something for which there is no evidence whatsoever.

44. *Incendio* 14: ed. Grundmann 458.

45. *Matt.* 12: CM 29.388.

most distinguished abbot. The abbey's confraternity book, recorded in its present form around 1160 but reflective of Rupert's reign, began with Siegburg, mother house of the reform, followed by four related houses (Great St. Martin's and St. Pantaleon's in Cologne, Brauweiler and Gladbach in the archdiocese), but then listed St. Lawrence, which received the largest notice, and St. James in Liège.[46] Rupert also instituted special celebrations at Deutz for the feastday of St. Lawrence, dedicated a new chapel at Deutz to St. Lawrence, and called upon him for help (rather than the Blessed Virgin or St. Heribert) after a fire and other troubles.[47] As abbot of Deutz, in sum, Rupert had gained powerful and supportive patrons, a well-endowed house with a scriptorium at his own command (about which, unfortunately, almost nothing is known), and a reformed religious life. All that was very good. But the sense that he was a foreigner, a man dislocated from his homeland and his mother abbey, seems never quite to have left him.

Rupert assumed the abbacy of Deutz in the fall of 1120 and ruled until his death on 4 March 1129. Bitter and extended controversies with his temporal lord and his advocate, beginning in 1126, and a disastrous fire in the castle on 28 August 1128 marred the last years of his reign. Only one administrative document has survived, a charter he issued in 1128 extending pastoral care to the chapel at nearby Westhoven for those who could not make the journey to the parish church at Deutz.[48] Scattered documents testify to his involvement in archdiocesan affairs.[49] In September 1121 he was present, quite possibly in an advisory capacity, at the council in Cornelimünster which repelled and condemned Alexander of Jülich's second try for the bishopric of

46. B. Albers, *SMBO* 16 (1895) 97–98.

47. MGS SS 14.565; *Incendio* 18–23: ed. Grundmann 463–70.

48. F. Mering, *Geschichte der Burgen, Rittergüter, Abteien und Klöster in den Rheinlanden* (Cologne 1855) 10.143–44. Milz (n. 31 above) 117–19.

49. A witness at Siegburg on 6 January 1121: Wisplinghoff, *Urkunden* (n. 22 above) 75; witness in Cologne in 1123/26 and again in 1126: Knipping (n. 28 above) nn. 233, 234, 257; also in Cologne in 1124: H. Foerster, "Eine unbekannte Urkunde Erzbischofs Friedrichs I. von Köln (1100–31)," *Annalen des historischen Vereins für den Niederrhein* 121 (1932) 131–34.

Liège; and in 1128 he witnessed the settlement arranged by Wibald which definitively joined Malmedy to the abbey of Stavelot.[50] For reasons unknown, Rupert visited Rome and Monte Cassino during Advent 1124 (see n. 55 below), there possibly witnessing the enthronement of Pope Honorius II, and between January and March 1128 he traveled to the bishopric of Münster (see below at n. 77). How representative of his administrative acts and his travels these may be is simply unknown.

Just as Abbot Markward had persuaded him to rewrite the *Life* of Deutz's founder, so others from the archdiocese and beyond soon called upon his talents as a writer. Abbot Albanus (1110–38) of Great St. Martin's in Cologne asked him to rewrite the *passio* of Eliphius whose relics were preserved there. Since the older, unsatisfactory account proved the only source of information, Rupert complained that like an architect he could not build a great edifice upon such a small foundation; but he finally agreed and improved upon the original chiefly by adding more narrative of the persecutions under Julian the Apostate (the time of Eliphius' martyrdom).[51] Abbot Gerard (1123–47) of St. Pantaleon requested that he prepare a homily to be read annually on the feastday (July 28) of their patron.[52] Freed of the models he was forced to follow in his *Vita Heriberti* and *Passio Eliphii*, Rupert included many of his own favorite themes in this *Sermo de St. Pantaleone*: his notion of the Spirit's two missions (*data*) (cc. 2–4), the struggle between Michael and the dragon together with the struggle against the seven kingdoms (cc. 5, 7), the aid of the seven-form Spirit (c. 6), and even a comparison of St. Pantaleon to his own beloved St. Lawrence (c. 8). At the end Rupert mentioned several recent miracles, one in Constantinople (noting the destruction of the Pecheneg invaders), another in Russia (naming the ruling czar, and thus dating the sermon to 1125–28), and still another in England. These

---

50. *Gesta abb. Trudon.* 11.15: MGH SS 10.303; J. Halkin and G. C. Roland, *Recueil des chartes de l'abbaye de Stavelot-Malmedy* (Brussels 1909) 1.297–99.

51. *Eliph.* prologus: PL 170.427. *Bibliotheca hagiographica latina* 2482.

52. M. Coens, "Un sermon inconnu de Rupert, abbé de Deutz, sur S. Pantaléon," *Analecta Bollandiana* 55 (1937) 244–67.

miracle-stories reveal something of the news which circulated through the largest city in the Empire and indeed through its Benedictine abbeys as well.

Rupert's reputation for solving scriptural—which is to say, theological—problems brought another request his way, the delicacy of which at first embarrassed him; but once he began to write, the words, as usual, came quickly, and he produced a small treatise *On the Loss of Virginity*.[53] Wibald of Stavelot, who had met Rupert briefly in Liège, flattered him on his understanding of Scripture, requested copies of his two treatises associated with the predestinarian controversy, and then posed two questions which, he suggested, were much discussed at Stavelot.[54] The first was: did masturbation constitute a loss of virginity? In response Rupert condemned homosexuality (implied in Wibald's question) and sodomy as losses both of virginity and of human dignity. Lesser abuses, he argued, could be pardoned on the basis of a distinction: according to God's truth or justice evil thoughts already entailed the loss of virginity, whereas according to His mercy only physical intercourse caused an actual loss. Beyond insisting upon penance, humility, and daily contemplation upon the Word to gain and retain the palm of virginity, there was also a salvation-historical point to be made: until Christ's incarnation only virginity of the mind, that is, abstinence from idol worship, was required, particularly of those inspired to write Holy Scripture—Solomon, Rupert adds, being problematic in more than one regard (c. 9). Pious ears probably also would not tolerate any argument that St. John's bodily virginity procured for him a higher crown than that bestowed on the once-married prince of the apostles.

Wibald's second question was of an equally practical sort: could and should a non-virgin still be consecrated a nun? Rupert affirmed, somewhat hesitantly, that she could but, as was cus-

---

53. *De laesione uirginitatis*: PL 170.545–60.

54. PL 170.543–46; also P. Jaffé, *Bibliotheca rerum germanicarum* 1.76–79. The references to Liège (*dum adhuc essetis Leodii*) and to the predestinarian controversy suggest a date not long after Rupert became abbot, thus the early 1120's; so also H. Grundmann, *DA* 22 (1966) 426 n. 81.

tomary, with a covered head and without reception of a ring (c. 15). But if hers was a secret sin known only to her confessor, Rupert added, he favored the regular ceremony, on grounds that canon law permitted lapsed priests, whose sin was confessed in secret, to continue to function in their offices, and it would seem unfair not to permit the "inferior sex" the same. He hesitated only lest he appear to contradict Jerome's famous remark that God could not repair lost virginity, which Rupert took here not—like many of his contemporaries—as a logical conundrum but rather as a possibly authoritative moral or canonical teaching. On both matters, then, Rupert proved himself familiar with the Church's traditional teaching and laws, and he upheld them in a reasonable and thoughtful way.

Apart from three treatises to receive separate treatment below, the remainder of Rupert's numerous works written at Deutz were contemplative and theological in orientation. A review of their relative chronology here will make it unnecessary to handle chronological matters repeatedly in later chapters. Besides evidence taken from prologues, the chief guides will be three lists Rupert himself prepared: the first in the year 1125, probably earlier (about spring) rather than later;[55] the second in the summer of 1126;[56] and the third in the fall of 1128.[57]

Rupert's first project after leaving Liège was his *Commentary on the Apocalypse*, completed sometime after assuming the abbacy of Deutz (thus about 1121) and followed by a *Commentary on the Minor Prophets*, the first six of which he treated in seventeen books during 1122–23. He grew weary of this and turned at Abbot Cuno's insistence to his remarkable *De uictoria Verbi*

55. *RegBen.* 1: PL 170.489. In the third book of this work (PL 170.523) Rupert noted: "praesenti anno die Natalis Domini [Christmas reckoning of the new year in Cologne] cum essem Romae." Since this work was written before Cuno went to Regensburg (May 1126) and after *De uictoria Verbi Dei*, the only two possibilities are Christmas 1124 or 1125. But by about May 1126 he had completed so many more works that 1124 is the only reasonable possibility. Cf. Bischoff, *Controversy* 359–60.

56. CM 7.1–4. This letter dedicated *De diuinis officiis* to Cuno in honor of his episcopal elevation (elected 11 May 1126).

57. PL 169.9–12, to Pope Honorius II after 28 August 1128.

Dei in thirteen books (about 1123/24), and then hurriedly finished the six remaining Minor Prophets in fourteen books, almost certainly before going to Rome at Christmas 1124.[58]

After his return the tempo actually quickened, and the chronology also becomes more complicated. In all likelihood he began first, at Cuno's request, a commentary on St. Matthew's Gospel entitled *De gloria et honore Filii hominis*, and had completed three books when he yielded to Cuno's more insistent demand that he take up certain polemical issues in a *Commentary on the Benedictine Rule* (which contains the first list).[59] At the end of four books on that subject Rupert said he would hurry back (*festino redire*) to the Sermon on the Mount, but almost certainly, again at Cuno's demand, took up instead his famous—and relatively brief—commentary on the Canticle of Canticles called *De incarnatione Domini*. This work does not appear in the first list, nor is it hinted at in preceding works; and the fourth book of the commentary on Matthew, to which he would have returned next, begins with a verse from the Canticle.[60] He had barely returned to St. Matthew's Gospel when Archbishop Frederick demanded, and with vehemence, that Rupert prepare a commentary on the Books of Kings. Eventually completed in fifteen books, this work is—most unfortunately for historians—the only one of Rupert's major works to be lost.[61] Then just before (*nuperrime*) compiling the second list (summer 1126) Rupert acceded to another request, this time from Abbot Rudolph of St. Trond, to construct a dialogue between Jews and Christians.[62]

58. PL 168.525–28. Legate William of Palestrina had still only the first part in August–September 1124: PL 169.14.

59. *RegBen.* 1: PL 170.479, 489.

60. CM 29.84. So also at the very beginning of his second half on the Minor Prophets Rupert referred back to the central theme of the recently completed *De uictoria Verbi Dei* (PL 168.529–30). The reference to *Cant.* at the end of the second list (summer 1126) also strongly suggests it was a very recent work (CM 7.3). See H. Silvestre, *Bulletin de théologie ancienne et médiévale* 12 (1976) 64.

61. See H. Grundmann, *DA* 22 (1966) 436–39. Rupert noted it in his third list (for Pope Honorius): *In Samuelem et David libri XV* (PL 169.11–12).

62. CM 7.3.

By the summer of 1126, Rupert tells us in his second list, he had proceeded into the eighth book of his commentary on Matthew and the eleventh on Kings. In a passage probably written just before that dedicatory epistle containing the second list—Cuno was still abbot—Rupert began the eighth book of his commentary on Matthew with a remarkable prayer to the Wisdom of God, whose help he needed now more than ever before. For he could not, as before, concentrate on a single work and fulfill a single debt. He was now torn between two patrons, the archbishop of Cologne who had rescued him in time of persecution and was now both demanding and commanding a work on Kings, and Abbot Cuno to whom he owed more than he could ever say. He could not deny the archbishop (*maiori et digniori*), but he feared to slight his friend and patron who simply said, "I grieve for you" (*Doleo super te*). So Rupert prayed for assistance and gathered his resolve henceforth to have two scribes dip their pens at the same time into the ink of his mind.[63] In 1127 Rupert finally completed both works. He then took up his *De glorificatione Trinitatis* to meet another request from Abbot Rudolph and one also from the papal legate William of Palestrina. It was completed just before the fire at Deutz on 28 August 1128, for there was then still only one copy. Shortly after the fire Rupert wrote *De incendio* (fall 1128), and he died on 4 March 1129 while at work on a treatise entitled *De meditatione mortis*.

Safely removed from his enemies in Liège and protected by the two most powerful figures in the archdiocese of Cologne, Rupert of Deutz took the opportunity in the prologue of his first major work written there to answer those who charged that "better and holier Fathers had already written more than enough on Holy Scripture": the spacious field of Holy Scripture is common to all who confess Christ, and the right (*licentia*) to treat (*tractare*) Scripture can in no way (*nulli iure*) be denied to someone who, within the bounds of the faith, says or writes what he thinks. Even after the Fathers have dug their wells (Gen. 26), "he can and," Rupert declares, "he will so long as he lives dig new and additional wells with the ploughshare of his

---

63. CM 29.229–30.

own genius (*uomere* [spade?] *proprii ingenii*) in search of living water which will cause no harm to those who drink it, that is, cause neither error nor scandal for those who read his works!"[64]

Of all Rupert's commentaries, the most purely contemplative in orientation, the one freest of theological or ecclesiastical polemic, is probably that on the first six Minor Prophets. Here he could concentrate wholly on that which he always declared to be his chief purpose: uncovering the mysteries of Christ hidden in the text of Holy Scripture. In the prologue this theme alone (*ad quaerendum Christum*) came to expression—no asides against adversaries and no apologies for his own theological calling. Rupert's was nonetheless no easy undertaking. Like Augustine's commentary on St. John's Gospel, Jerome's on the Minor Prophets had reigned throughout the early middle ages. A decade or so before Rupert, Guibert of Nogent attempted a new commentary, defending himself specifically against charges of slighting Jerome's authority. He concentrated wholly, however, upon the moral or spiritual sense because, as he put it, he felt more secure dealing with something from his own experience and feared to go astray (*exorbitare*) if he treated the difficult allegorical mysteries of Christ and His Church.[65] This latter task Rupert set for himself.

Rupert believed that Christ's advent was foretold, not just generally but specifically and in the correct chronological sequence, in each of the Minor Prophets. He began his commentary on each therefore with a separate preface, as Jerome had, setting out the recapitulations of Christ's advent and passion found therein. With his strong sense for concrete historical event, Rupert noted that a prophecy might often refer immediately (*de propinquo*) to the Israelites (the exile, for instance) and ultimately (*de longinquo*) to the advent of Christ,[66] and he tried often, though not consistently, to do justice to both facets. He also referred the prophecies to aspects of the Church's history, one text, for instance, in his view pointing ahead to the monastic life identified

64. PL 169.827–28.
65. PL 156.339.
66. PL 168.14–15.

here with the "Black" (*niger tam professione quam habitu*) Monks.[67] The novelty of this commentary lies almost wholly in Rupert's exegetical boldness, his attempt once again to reconsider the received tradition of interpretation. Though extant still in several manuscript copies (nine for Part I and six for Part II),[68] it and the *Commentary on Kings* alone never reached St. Lawrence in Liège, and Rupert's own copy at Deutz he lost when Abbot Cuno presented it to the papal legate William of Palestrina (see n. 58 above). Cuno must have taken copies of both parts to Regensburg, for all fifteen extant manuscripts originated in Bavaria.

3
Disputes with Rhineland Jews

Rupert devoted much of his time and effort, as evidenced by his large *Commentary on the Minor Prophets*, to the discovery of christological meanings in the Old Testament. The small but active Jewish communities scattered throughout northern France and the Rhineland constituted a standing challenge to any such interpretation. The theological problems were built into Scripture and required consideration in any case: law and grace, circumcision and baptism, the Chosen People and the elect, the Messiah and the Son of God. But increased contacts in burgeoning towns, the growing role of Jews as moneylenders to bishops and abbeys, the renaissance of Jewish exegesis associated with Rashi and his disciples, and finally the awful pogroms and forced conversions of the late 1090's gave to those theological problems a definite social and personal dimension.[69] Benedictine monks were again the first to rise to the occasion, and they remained in the forefront of the debate at least until the 1120's when the Victorines attempted a more positive and constructive approach to Jewish exegesis. In Rupert's part of the world, Herman of Tournai, Odo of Cambrai, and Guibert of

67. PL. 168.740; cf. PL 168.809–10.
68. R. Haacke, *DA* 26 (1970) 535–36.
69. A summary, with literature, in L. K. Little, *Religious Poverty and the Profit Economy in Medieval Europe* (Ithaca 1978) 42–57.

Nogent all addressed this issue, largely in terms of "proving" the incarnation.[70]

Rupert's preoccupation with this matter, on both a theological and a personal level, stands out in all his work.[71] He repeatedly put emphasis upon the rejection of the Jews as a crucial stage in salvation-history, and he dealt with the Jewish question in the penultimate book of *De sancta Trinitate*, that treating "current affairs."[72] Liège had, so far as I can determine, no permanent Jewish settlement during the eleventh and twelfth centuries, but Jewish traders and moneylenders certainly would have passed through such an important city, riverport, and bishopric. In at least one passage of his *Commentary on John*, an argument about circumcision, Rupert seems clearly to reflect the objections of a real, not just hypothetical, Jewish adversary.[73] So also in *De sancta Trinitate* he referred to Jews who heard the prophets read on the Sabbath and yet stubbornly interpreted them in another way. Indeed, they know the Gospel message, for in the cities they look on (*aspicientibus*) when Christians celebrate feast-days; they hear and see the chorus of praise sung to Christ.[74] Once Rupert had moved to the Rhineland such contact and conversation became unavoidable and probably frequent. Several passages in his *Commentary on the Minor Prophets* definitely reflect such discussions.[75] The only record of an oral dispute to

70. Odo, *Disputatio contra Iudaeum Leonem nomine de Aduentu Christi Filii Dei* (PL 160.1103–12); Herman, *De incarnatione Iesu Christi Domini nostri* (PL 180.9–38); Guibert, *Tractatus de Incarnatione contra Iudaeos* (PL 156.489–528).

71. See M. L. Arduini, *Ruperto di Deutz e la controversia tra Cristiani ed Ebrei nel secolo XII* (Studi Storici 119–121, Rome 1979); Beinert, *Kirche* 356–66; Rauh, *Antichrist* 226–30; G. R. Evans, *Anselm and a New Generation* (Oxford 1980) 34–41. David Timmer, a theology student at the University of Notre Dame, is preparing a dissertation on this subject.

72. *Spir.* 5.1–12: CM 24.1977–91 (a miniature dialogue); *Spir.* 8.14–15, 21: CM 24.2091–94, 2098–2100.

73. "Solent irridentes obicere Iudaei cum dicimus eis. . . . Sed dicit ad haec Iudaeus. . . . Iudaeis argumentantibus. . . . Adhuc nihilominus aduersarius Iudaeus obicit. . . ." CM 9.142–44.

74. *Spir.* 8.14: CM 24.2091–92.

75. "Quoties cum illis sermonem conferimus. . . ." PL 168.366. Cf. PL 168.121, 369, 686.

survive, however, is late and comes from his Jewish adversary, a man named Herman who converted to Christianity and later as the Premonstratensian abbot of Scheda wrote a short work *On His Conversion.*[76]

The debate took place in Münster sometime during January or February of the year 1128.[77] Bishop Egbert of Münster (1126–32) had served earlier as master (1106–18) and dean (1118–26) of the cathedral chapter at Cologne. A supporter of the reform party, he had helped repulse Alexander's second try for the bishopric of Liège. The death of Bishop Albero of Liège on 1 January 1128 marked the beginning of Alexander's third campaign for the episcopal office, and Rupert evidently followed these events too.[78] He may have gone to consult with Bishop Egbert on this or perhaps other matters. In any event Rupert stayed for a time (*morabatur*) and there met Herman, who spent twenty weeks in Münster, partly to collect money loaned to the bishop and partly to escape family difficulties at home in Cologne.

Herman remembered Rupert as the most brilliant of all the Christians he had debated prior to his conversion.[79] Herman challenged Rupert to debate, and Rupert promptly accepted, promising to meet the Jew's arguments on any topic he chose. Herman reported only a small, exemplary portion of the debate, since the whole of it, he says, was much too long. The speech he put in Rupert's mouth defended the use in church of sculptured images, paintings, and so forth—a custom frequently attacked by Jews and of interest to Herman, who was much struck with the interior of the cathedral at Münster. Arguing

76. G. Niemeyer, *Hermannus quondam Iudaeus opusculum de conversione sua* (MGH Geistesgeschichte 4, Weimar 1963). See Wattenbach-Schmale (n. 33 above) 379–81, and Arduini (n. 71 above) 50–57.

77. Niemeyer (n. 76 above) 32–40 narrowed the date to either January/February or the late fall of 1128. But after the fire at Deutz (28 August 1128) Rupert is unlikely to have left his monks immediately, and in any case he wrote his *De incendio* then and died a few months later. Cf. Arduini (n. 71 above) 57 n. 197, whose objections to Rupert's presence at Münster are groundless.

78. *Gesta abb. Trudon.* 11.15: MGH 10.304; and Meingoz of St. Martin's letter, ed. H. Grundmann, *DA* 21 (1965) 276.

79. *Opusculum* 3: ed. Niemeyer 76.

first from "reason," Rupert pointed out that a cross, for instance, helped to kindle an inner love of Christ, and—this is Gregory the Great's famous line—that these images served as "books for the illiterate." Turning to the Old Testament, Rupert insisted that its altars and sacrifices were also, among other things, visual means of knowing and worshipping God. Thus, Herman concluded, Rupert met each of his objections with "beautiful arguments" and "powerful scriptural authorities." But Rupert's arguments were not in fact enough for Herman. The Jew's conversion took place only later, at Mainz and in different circumstances.

It is important to recognize that in personal encounters Rupert could adopt a friendly attitude and debate on common ground, whereas in his commentaries, written for Christian readers, he assumed toward Jews and Judaism that same combative stance he took toward all "enemies of Christ and His Church." Distinguishing between Jews as an ethnic and a confessional group, he ascribed to all the latter, those who still "cursed Christ in their synagogues," full hereditary responsibility for the blood of Christ. No matter how much they may read Scripture or observe the Sabbath, he declared, all they consider holy and indeed their very hands are covered with blood.[80] This charge was to loom ever larger as Christian devotion shifted increasingly from Christ's resurrection to His passion, a shift evident also in Rupert's spirituality. Rupert insisted more and more that the Jews' failure to receive Christ as the Son of God sprang from active rejection, from proud and stubborn resistance to God's ways and teachings.[81] This doubtless reflected his own experience at Cologne: Herman too, in 1128, would not yield to Rupert's arguments. His own dedication to interpreting Scripture likewise evoked much emphasis upon the "blindness" of Jewish understanding. In graphic language he described Jews as mired in the mud of their literal understanding and clinging to

80. *John* 7: CM 9.391; *Gen.* 8.26: CM 21.513.
81. PL 168.170 (may reflect actual debate), 459–61.

the dung of carnal observances.[82] Rupert's tone throughout all of his writings is noticeably sharper than that of many, perhaps even most, of his predecessors, owing partly to his own pugnaciousness and still more to the changing situation in the early twelfth century. But what set Rupert apart most clearly was his effort to fit the Jews too into the "present" stage of salvation-history.

The destruction of Jerusalem in 70 A.D. and the consequent dispersion of the Jews confirmed in Rupert's view the truth of Christ's Advent, the conversion of the Gentiles and rejection of the Jews. Here was undeniable historical proof of the Jews' error and guilt; Rupert often quoted from Josephus' description of the destruction to bring the reality of it home to his readers.[83] But more important, its enduring, visible reality persisted "today" in the exiled, wandering status of the Jewish people, something they shared with the marked and rejected Cain. They lost their land, Rupert declared, because of Christ's blood, an unquestionable historical fact even if they persist in denying it. Cast out both spiritually and temporally, they have become princes among exiles, ever desirous of land and other material things, ever plotting, but now made to settle in restricted quarters among scattered cities.[84] This is an unambiguous reference to the Jewish quarter found in most northern French and Rhineland cities and a very early example of Christians' conferring upon those quarters, soon to become ghettoes, a theological significance. To the treatment of Jews Rupert devoted one lengthy discussion less than fifteen years after the terror in the Rhineland. Christian princes ought not to kill these "brothers of Christ," Rupert announced, with Crusaders almost certainly in mind. But Jews should nevertheless be made subject to Christian kings and thus indirectly to Christ, and they should also be taxed severely so that by a kind of "pious torture" they might

82. *Deut.* 2.10: CM 22.1096–97, and very frequently; *Hier.* 83: CM 23.1635.

83. For instance, PL 168.339–45.

84. *Gen.* 4.6: CM 21.288; *Ps.* 5: CM 22.1356; *Hier.* 81: CM 23.1634.

be brought to do penance and acknowledge Christ. And even if they converted for base motives (to escape onerous taxation), at least their children would be baptized and raised Christian.[85]

Christian-Jewish relations worsened disastrously in Rupert's lifetime; but if, as so often, their relationship is conceived only in terms of the oppressor and the oppressed, the numerous friendly contacts that persisted and indeed the relative strength of the Jewish communities—and the threat they seemed therefore to pose—would be wholly overlooked. At Cologne, for instance, Rupert's friend and fellow exile Rudolph of St. Trond was made abbot of St. Pantaleon (1121–23), and while there had frequent amicable discussions with local Jews, becoming so trusted (*amabatur*) by them that even their women were permitted to go and converse with this Christian abbot.[86] Jews, moreover, could defend themselves ably and forthrightly. It was after all Herman who challenged Rupert to debate. They could also raise questions about Scripture certain to give Christians pause. One with which Rupert repeatedly struggled in the end affected a central point in his theology (chapter IX, part 3): how could God be trusted as constant in his salvific purposes if he had overthrown his Chosen People and started "anew" with Jesus Christ? There were many such questions; asked of an inexperienced or poorly trained Christian, they could create confusion and even doubt, something which surely happened much more often than the dominant Christians cared to record.[87]

Abbot Rudolph, doubtless while still at St. Pantaleon and in conversation with local Jews, asked and later demanded that Rupert prepare a dialogue in which a "Christian" invited a "Jew" to join the Church and the Jew then resisted with all the evidence he could muster from the letter of the Law and his interpretation of it. This, Rudolph judged and Rupert agreed,

85. *Gen.* 9.4: CM 21.536.

86. *Gesta abb. Trudon.* 11.16: MGH SS 10.304.

87. N. Golb, "Notes on the Conversion of European Christians to Judaism in the Eleventh Century," *Journal of Jewish Studies* 16 (1965) 69–74; W. Giese, "*In Iudaismum lapsum est.* Jüdische Proselytenmacherei im frühen und hohen Mittelalter (600–1300)," *Historisches Jahrbuch* 88 (1968) 407–18.

might not be necessary for experienced Christians; but younger monks would find it most helpful to have gathered in one place all the arms needed so they would not hesitate to battle Jewish interpretations contrary to the teachings of God. In his prologue Rupert expressed hope that the tournament (*conflictum, duellum*) he had arranged would give pleasure to his young readers (*Festiuum sit pueris fidelibus hoc spectaculum*); but he admitted it was the best he could manage just then, considering his many other preoccupations.[88] Though requested earlier, the work was written in the spring of 1126, probably the single busiest and most productive time in Rupert's life. And Rudolph was not in fact altogether satisfied; his request for something more must be considered later. But Rupert's work is noteworthy nevertheless, for it is the only such dialogue to come out of the critically affected Rhineland soon after the massacres and forced conversions of the later 1090's.[89]

The dialogue has many digressions, but in the main Rupert set out to treat baptism and circumcision in Book I, faith in Christ as opposed to the Law, the sacrifices, the Sabbath, and the terrestrial promised land in Book II, and Christ's sacrificial priesthood, the eucharist as the "new covenant," and the veneration of the cross in Book III. Rupert's Jew protested throughout against "figural" interpretations of Scripture, while Rupert's Christian insisted that the same God who had spoken through Moses also spoke through Christ and the New Testament, both grounded in the Old Testament. Rupert repeated many ideas found all through his commentaries, but clearly he also attempted to take account of particular Jewish interpretations, for instance their insistence that Jerusalem and Zion must now be exalted if the Messiah had truly come, or—as later with Herman—their enforcement of the Old Testament ban on graven images. Friendly but sometimes hard-hitting in tone, the dialogue ended with a long speech by the Christian inviting the

88. *Anulus* prologus: ed. Haacke (in Arduini, n. 71 above) 184, with an extensive analysis of the treatise, 19–49.

89. See the list in P. Browe, *Die Judenmission im Mittelalter und die Päpste* (Miscellanea historiae pontificiae 6, Rome 1942) 100ff.

Jew to convert, that is, to receive the ring (*anulus*) which the Father extended to his prodigal but now penitent son.

4

Strife over the Castle
at Deutz (1126–28)

On 28 August 1128 the castle at Deutz caught fire. The monastic church and its cloister were spared, but many adjacent buildings, including the parish church of St. Urban's, suffered severe damage. Rupert looked upon this as a judgement of God, a direct divine intervention in behalf of his struggle for almost two years past to claim jurisdiction over the entire castle at Deutz. To document that struggle and to provide an interpretation of the fire's providential meaning, Rupert prepared for his monks, and presumably also for his adversaries, a remarkable little work called simply *De incendio*. This, his last completed work, was probably much like one of his earliest works, the lost "little book" detailing what trials the house of St. Lawrence had had to undergo at the hands of its episcopal lords. Herbert Grundmann edited *De incendio*, and in an interpretative essay long to remain fundamental he first uncovered its historical setting and major themes.[90] What follows here is based upon Grundmann's essay, but differs from it on several historical details and also in its general presentation and interpretation of Rupert's argument.

The disputed point, to come to it directly, was whether the archbishops of Cologne had made over to the monks the entire castle inside which their abbey stood. The founding charter, a forgery, conferred this castle upon the monks—but in language borrowed from Rupert's *De incendio*.[91] Oppermann first noted

90. H. Grundmann, "Der Brand von Deutz in der Darstellung Abt Ruperts von Deutz," *DA* 22 (1966) 385–440 (commentary), 441–71 (edition). See the review by H. Silvestre, "Du nouveau sur Rupert de Deutz," *RHE* 63 (1968) 54–58.

91. Compare the charter in Wisplinghoff, *Urkundenbuch* (n. 32 above) 192 to *Incendio* 9: ed. Grundmann 450–51 (the towers and the keys); or ibid. 23:

the similarities and argued, curiously, that both the charter and *De incendio* were falsified. Wisplinghoff, the modern editor of Deutz's early charters, agreed the founding charter was falsified, but argued for the authenticity of a papal confirmation in 1147 which included claims to the "*castrum.*" Grundmann established the authenticity of Rupert's text and contended for a genuine claim to the castle already in the founding charter which Rupert would simply have paraphrased.[92] Both Milz and Lewald in turn rejected Grundmann's argument,[93] and rightly so. Rupert was desperate to find authoritative written support. In *De incendio* he actually cited (without naming its author) his own *Vita Heriberti*. If he could have produced a charter, or indeed if, as Lewald suggested, he himself had forged the falsified charter, he would surely have cited it explicitly and repeatedly.

It is still possible, though far less likely, that the monks in fact had a claim to the castle which was never properly documented or for which the documentation had been lost. Milz chose this position, citing Rupert's report that until recently the prior or provost of the abbey had held the keys to the castle and locked it up at night. Lewald dismissed this on grounds that the prior's task, a temporary one in the event, hardly constituted proof of possession. Hers doubtless is the correct view and can be substantiated by still another scrap of evidence taken from Rupert's own account. When Abbot Rupert sought to remove certain lay folk from the castle, they and their supporters resisted successfully, perhaps with litigation.[94] Even if they did so only by "quarreling," the abbot evidently could wield neither a documentary nor an historically established claim against them. The

471 (secular intrusion). Additional parallels noted in Grundmann (n. 90 above) 405 n. 40; Milz (n. 31 above) 6.

92. Oppermann (n. 32 above) 265ff; Wisplinghoff, "Beiträge" (n. 32 above) passim; Grundmann (n. 90 above) 404–05.

93. Milz (n. 31 above) 6–8; U. Lewald, "Zum Verhältnis von Köln und Deutz im Mittelalter," in *Festschrift Edith Ennan* (Bonn 1972) 387–88.

94. ". . . meque reclamantem aut litigio depresserunt aut silentio destituerunt." *Incendio* 9: ed. Grundmann 451; "*litigium*" could mean either a "quarrel" or a "lawsuit."

fact that the monks had no legitimate claim to the castle fundamentally affects the interpretation of *De incendio*. It is one thing, with Grundmann, to see Rupert insisting upon an established right temporarily lost through negligence. It is quite another to watch Rupert seek to make good a claim for which he had neither historical nor legal precedent.

The situation at Deutz was unusual. When monasteries were founded at Siegburg and later at Altenberg (both in the archdiocese of Cologne), the entire site, including the former castle, was made over to the monks. But that clearly did not happen at Deutz. Both Lambert's *Vita Heriberti* of about 1050 and Rupert's of 1119 (though Rupert's in somewhat stronger language) state that either a barn (Lambert) or a farmsite (*curtim*, Rupert) belonging to the archbishop was removed and a place cleared on which the monastic church and its buildings were built *inside* (*in eodem*) the castle.[95] An older parish church remained standing directly in front of the abbey's gate (*ante ualuas monasterii*). This "gate" was part of a stone wall which separated the immune territory of the monks, reserved for them, their servants, and their guests alone, from the parish church and other secular dwellings built inside the castle.[96] It would appear, from a reconstruction, based partly upon archaeological digs, that the abbey and parish church took up one-half to two-thirds of the space inside Deutz.

In 1128, but notably not in 1119, Rupert claimed that Archbishop Heribert had originally removed all lay folk (*nullam secularium habitationem*) and settled them on lands and in houses, also subject to the abbey, just outside the castle to the south. As proof Rupert cited the testimony of descendants who recalled their ancestors' move.[97] Many people doubtless were removed to make way for the abbey, but almost certainly all, as Rupert claimed in 1128, were not. For, as Rupert also reported, many good folk (*honesti*) had repaired and now inhabited the towers

95. *Vita Heriberti* 8: MGH 4.746; cf. *Herib.* 13: ed. Dinter 54–55.
96. *Incendio* 4: ed. Grundmann 445. On the "engere Klosterimmunität," see Milz (n. 31 above) 16 n. 42, and his reconstruction of it in Map 1.
97. *Incendio* 8: ed. Grundmann 450.

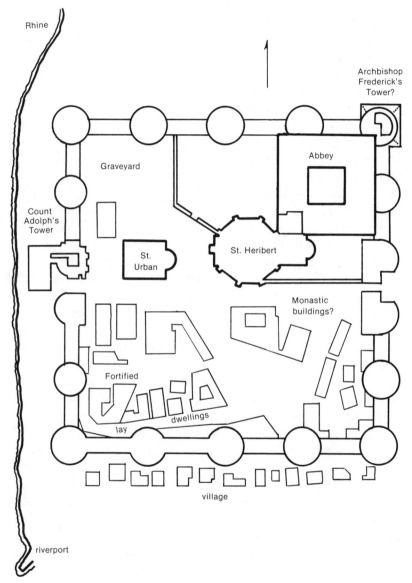

Rhine

Archbishop
Frederick's
Tower?

Graveyard

Abbey

Count
Adolph's
Tower

St.
Urban

St. Heribert

Monastic
buildings?

Fortified

lay dwellings

village

riverport

Figure 2. Castle and abbey of Deutz.

251

and walls (*interturria*) of the castle, and they in turn had allowed other, disreputable folk—especially scandalous so near a monastery—to inhabit the rooms, passageways, and cellars clustered beneath the walls.[98] This Rupert ascribed to the "*longa negligentia*" of his predecessors. That word "*longa*" is telltale, however, for despite his own claims he apparently could not, as with the removed villagers, produce testimony of a time when there were no lay folk living in the castle. More striking still, the removed villagers supported those inside the castle who resisted Rupert's demand that they leave (see n. 94 above). Many of those "good folk" in the towers and walls were probably *ministeriales* who served either the abbey or the archbishopric, and had probably been there as long as the abbey itself, if not longer. But the disreputable folk beneath the walls may well have been a relatively newer phenomenon, a reflection of the urban expansion found everywhere in the early twelfth century. It is noteworthy in this regard that the towers, walls, and "inhabited" area to which Rupert referred were apparently on the south and west of the castle, that is, contiguous to the village and the Rhine.

The archbishops of Cologne knew exactly why the entire site had not been ceded to the monks: the castle of Deutz was utterly crucial to the defense of their city. No enemy approaching from the east could mount a direct attack across the Rhine or indeed prevent resupply of the city via the river so long as forces friendly to the prince-bishop held the castle of Deutz.[99] Frederick (1100–31) in particular had many occasions to reflect upon this reality. In 1105 he belatedly joined Henry V's rebellion against his father, but the citizens of Cologne remained loyal to Henry IV, and they controlled the city. When Archbishop Frederick and King Henry attempted to besiege it, they failed because the citizens controlled all Rhine traffic, meaning they also controlled the castle at Deutz. In 1114 the archbishop and the citizens of Cologne together rebelled against King Henry V who, probably remembering the events of 1105, immediately

98. Ibid. 9: 451.
99. Lewald (n. 93 above) passim.

moved to take Deutz; but it was so valiantly defended he had to withdraw.[100] Evidently the towers and walls were already then in good repair.

In 1125 the political situation became critical again. (Earlier scholars have overlooked this immediate setting for Rupert's troubles.) Frederick's stance in the disputed royal succession is not fully known, but he was no supporter of the Staufer Lothar III: he crowned the new king, as was his right, but immediately broke with him; and when Lothar came to celebrate Easter at Cologne in 1126, the archbishop retreated to Siegburg and celebrated the feastday there.[101] It was about then, Rupert reports, almost two years before the fire (28 August 1128), that his "vexation" began.[102] Meanwhile Abbot Cuno had departed for Regensburg (May 1126), and Rupert was left to fight this battle without the aid of his powerful patron.

Archbishop Frederick, to whom Rupert referred throughout *De incendio* as his "right eye,"[103] began late in 1126 to rebuild a tower and erect a "fortified house" (*domum firmam*) at Deutz. The tower was scandalously offensive to Rupert for it stood in a corner where two sides of the cloister joined.[104] If this corner was also a corner of the castle, as Rupert seems to mean, it must have been the northeast corner, though it might also have been the southeast corner of the cloister, placing the tower on one side of the former *praesidium* or main guarded entrance to the castle. In either case, the defensive purposes of a tower looking out to the east and of a fortified house for the archbishop somewhere in the castle require no explanation. Abbot Rupert was utterly outraged. He marveled that the archbishop who in the past had revered and promoted religious life refused now to see how this act would destroy it. For months (until about mid-

100. *Chronica regia Coloniensis*: ed. G. Waitz (MGH in usum scholarum 19) 53.

101. Oediger (n. 28 above) 139; *Anselmi continuatio Sigeberti*: MGH SS 6.380.

102. *Incendio* 11: ed. Grundmann 452.

103. Grundmann (n. 90 above) 413–18 first made the identification.

104. *Incendio* 13: ed. Grundmann 456.

1127) Rupert pleaded, protested, and finally threatened to resign, until Frederick reluctantly gave in at last and ceased work
on the tower—but, Rupert noted, not without considerable anger and invective.[105]

No sooner had Rupert won over the archbishop than another
"friend," fully aware of Rupert's troubles and also of his required subjection to the archbishop, his lord both spiritual and
temporal, took advantage of Rupert's distraction and Frederick's
permission to begin work on still other towers, also with dwellings, built either as an extension of or just in front of the old
west gate facing the Rhine and the city of Cologne. This "friend"
was none other than Count Adolph III of Berg, advocate of the
abbey and of the archbishopric, whose powerfully ascendant
family was to supply five of Cologne's archbishops during the
twelfth century, beginning with Frederick's successor Bruno
(Adolph's son).[106] Count Adolph's desire for a fortified residence
and tower at Deutz, directly across from the cathedral and episcopal palace in Cologne, needs no more explanation than the
archbishop's. Abbot Rupert and Count Adolph remained at
odds for a whole year (*totum annum*); thus their fight must have
begun about the summer of 1127, just after the archbishop had
yielded. Rupert says he can hardly tell what anguish those towers cost him. Count Adolph, unlike Archbishop Frederick, ada-
mantly refused to reconsider, and the building proceeded at the
front of the castle just a few dozen yards from the abbey. In
great anger Rupert hurled at his advocate the curses Joshua had
called down on anyone who rebuilt Jericho: "Cursed before the
Lord is the man who undertakes to rebuild this city: at the cost
of his firstborn son will he lay its foundations; at the cost of his
youngest will he set up its gates" (Joshua 6:26). Count Adolph's
wife then died. In deep embarrassment and with no little guilt

---

105. *Incendio* 14: ed. Grundmann 457.
106. Ibid. 17–18: 461–63. See Milz (n. 31 above) 169–73 for the approximate location, and Grundmann (n. 90 above) 423–28 for the identification.
Cf. J. Milz, "Die Vögte des kölner Domstiftes und der Abteien Deutz und
Werden im 11. und 12. Jahrhundert," *Rheinische Vierteljahrsblätter* 41 (1977)
196–217.

Rupert sought to explain and excuse his curse as justified by the grave harm those towers would have wrought upon the religious life at Deutz. Following his wife's death, the count finally relented and entered into an agreement with Rupert, whereby the partially constructed dwelling was made over to the monks, as Rupert put it, "*partim pro anima sua, partim accepta pecunia.*" [107] Since it stood just before the front gate of the castle, Rupert resolved to make of it a hospice and almonry, and constructed a chapel there dedicated to St. Lawrence. This structure, nearly finished, was gravely damaged in the fire.

The towers of Archbishop Frederick and Count Adolph provoked Rupert's claim to the entire castle. But he then extended his campaign against secular intrusion to all lay inhabitants of the castle. In Liège Rupert had grown up near a large city with a major thoroughfare passing just in front of his abbey, but St. Lawrence stood outside the city gates and high upon a hill. At Deutz lay folk inhabited the towers, walls, and open areas all around the abbey. If from the beginning Rupert had judged this wholly unsuitable for the contemplative life, he nonetheless held his peace, so far as we know, until the confrontation with his archbishop and advocate. These resident lay folk, however, simply refused to give in. By the summer of 1128, therefore, Rupert had gained two significant victories, but not the removal from the castle of all military fortifications and other forms of town life for which he still pressed.

Prolonged confrontation, first with the archbishop of Cologne, then with the most powerful nobleman in the archdiocese, and still with neighboring laymen, completely exhausted Rupert. He was serious about resigning his abbatial post. Only another mystical experience, as he reports it, of the kind that first called him to his writing and had kept him going through the years, prevented him from abandoning his birthright like Esau, that is, his abbatial post and with it the conditions which made possible his "ministry" (*ministerium*), his commenting

107. *Incendio* 17–18: ed. Grundmann 461–63. The "*sua*" meant presumably Adolph's departed wife for whom the monks would now be obliged to pray.

upon Holy Scripture. In retrospect Rupert directed against himself what he had once insisted upon in Liège, that lost pastoral charges could never be regained.[108] During the heat of the dispute Rupert in fact wrote only one work, and that a short one by his standards (two hundred columns)—quite in contrast to his stupendous output during the years 1124–26. In the prologue to *De gloria et honore Filii hominis*, finally finished in 1127, Rupert complained to Cuno, now bishop of Regensburg, that the burden of his abbatial office made it difficult for him to write.[109] But despite weariness Rupert stuck fast to his claim, and he understood that in the end he, a foreigner and commoner, had won a considerable victory against the archbishop and the count. To record the outcome of this controversy, to put into writing his claims, and to press them further against the resisting lay folk, Rupert prepared *De incendio* right after the fire. Though certainly a polished literary work in its final form, it was apparently delivered first to the assembled brothers (*Scitis hec, fratres dilectissimi*).

De incendio, Rupert declared in his opening chapter, gave expression to the monks' gratitude for God's special mercy by which He had saved their abbey from the flames. Indeed, had the abbey not been so miraculously spared, the monks' "friends," like Job's, might have mistakenly misinterpreted the "test" Satan had just put them through. As it happened, providentially, the "conquering flames" quickly enveloped those "hateful towers" (*Turres circumstantes odiosas nobis*) and other dwellings so that the entire castle became as a single furnace, and yet the flames stopped just short of the abbey and its cloister (verbal echoes here of Daniel's friends in the furnace, Dan. 3). Rupert next recounted three miracles of preservation: of a Host cast into the fire (c. 3), of the abbey even though the parish church directly in front of it was severely burned (c. 4), and of a Host negligently left in the parish church (c. 5). To conclude this opening section he warned his monks against ingratitude and

108. Ibid. 14–16: 459–61.
109. CM 29.3.

especially against the error which ascribed such things to "accident" rather than to God's providence (c. 7).

Rupert then (c. 8) went directly to the heart of the matter (*Causam nunc dicere libet*). Not the towers themselves, Rupert explained, but the injustice they represented, he hated with a "perfect hatred," because the entire castle ought to be a legal sanctuary (*Debuerat enim totum castelli huius spatium esse legale sanctum*), meaning, it ought all to be included in the abbey's narrow immunity (now bounded by the stone wall) so that no lay folk at all could "contaminate" the monks' religious life.[110] Argued through several chapters (cc. 8–12), his case rested on religious convictions set out most clearly in the chapter (c. 13) summarizing his battle with Archbishop Frederick. *Silence* is the key, all-inclusive concept. For religious men and women silence is the "privilege or assurance, even the fortified guardian of, contemplative solitude," whereas the noisy hustle and bustle, the mode of life, and especially the (military) obligations associated with towers and armaments mean only further enslavement to the world. The Lord Christ wanted His priests in no way to become caught up in cities and castles, especially not us monk-priests. But what's the use finally of devising still more subtle arguments? The archbishop knows full well that monks need a quiet house as fish do water.

Most monks and abbots would have agreed. But the fact is, Black Monks over the last several generations had frequently been located near population centers where they performed numerous social, charitable, educational, and religious functions, and it should not be taken for granted that all of Rupert's monks, who after all had steadfastly resisted the Siegburger Reform until about fifteen years earlier, were as displeased as their abbot with the "world's" impingement upon Deutz. Rupert closed this chapter with a blunt warning to them: if any of you (*uestrum*) should perhaps think otherwise (about the need for solitude), that person clearly has not yet washed away all the dust of the world from the eye of his mind.

110. *Incendio* 9: ed. Grundmann 450.

Rupert's problem, however, was to translate his religious conviction into a legal claim when lay folk inhabited at least one-third of the castle and Archbishop Frederick, his spiritual and temporal lord, and Count Adolph, his advocate, were each busily rebuilding fortified towers on the east and west sides respectively of the castle—the archbishop's indeed in a corner of the cloister. Rupert began (c. 8), not surprisingly, with a divine law culled from Holy Scripture, a conflation of texts from Levit. 27:28, 21: "Anything once consecrated is thereafter most holy to the Lord, and a consecrated possession becomes the property (*ius*) of priests." Now, he asked rhetorically, who does not know that this castle was dedicated to the Lord Christ and to the Blessed Virgin? To show that it was, he quoted anonymously from his own *Vita Heriberti* a passage now taken to mean that the whole castle, not just a place (*locum*) for the abbey, was cleared and consecrated (see above at n. 95).

Rupert turned next to a history of Deutz seen from the perspective of his battle for control of the entire castle. Founded by Constantine rather than Julius Caesar as was popularly believed,[111] the castle, he held, had been dismantled by Archbishop Bruno to the great displeasure of his brother the emperor, and the ruined site was then consecrated wholly to the Blessed Virgin by Archbishop Heribert. As proof that Heribert removed all secular inhabitants, Rupert cited the memory of those who had moved and the prior's onetime possession of the keys (cc. 8–9). Only later did lay folk come to "occupy" the towers and walls which they "repaired." Rupert's narrative, so plausible on the surface, is in fact wholly misconstrued: there is no evidence Bruno destroyed the castle to any substantial degree, if at all, no evidence Heribert cleared the entire castle, and no evidence lay folk had to reoccupy and repair the castle. These lay inhabitants and especially their continued resistance were in fact, as Rupert now saw it, the major cause of the fire, a judgement of God (*causa ista maxima fuerit et iudicio Domini actum sit*). It was no accident that the fire started in their dwellings and

111. Rupert, sounding like a historian, quoted a recently uncovered inscription: *Incendio* 8: ed. Grundmann 449.

most severely damaged them! Rupert only hopes (*O ergo utinam*) that they will have learned now to fear the flames of the Last Judgement, cease their invasion of a site dedicated to the Lord, and give up their sacrilegious effort to undo the above-named archbishops' holy destruction and dedication (c. 9).

With the righteous zeal of a preacher Rupert castigated the wickedness of these builders of cities and fortifications (cc. 10–12).[112] No biblical saints ever built cities; they were all patriarchs and pilgrims. Cain reportedly built the first city (Gen. 4:16); the Canaanites lived in cities; and since this world generally is the atrium of the well-armed Devil (*atrium fortis armati*, Luke 11:21), earthly cities are rightly judged *atria* or forecourts of the Devil's real abode in Hell. The patriarchs, by contrast, set up altars, not cities; the import of this scriptural teaching, Rupert commented, had become much clearer to him in the course of his present vexation. Christ, according to Luke 11:21–22, as the stronger man eventually threw out the well-armed Devil. But how then should His followers continue to cast him out? Rupert named two ways: either by steady preaching against all forms of error, that which Rupert evidently considered his own chief calling, or by overthrowing so far as possible the titled claims of this world's proud. By way of example Rupert pointed to the reign of Peter and Paul in the place where Romulus and Remus once lay buried in honor. So also in an earlier work Rupert had used this text to justify the Church's reign (*principatum*) in the present age.[113] And, to come to the point, the archbishops of Cologne were engaged in the same task as Christ, Peter and Paul, and all the saints when they destroyed a pagan castle (as the Israelites did the heathen cities) and dedicated this entire site to the Lord. Those lay folk who continued to resist in behalf of their fortified dwellings had clearly aligned themselves with the Devil (the *fortis armatus*) and stood in grave danger of hellfire, of which this fire was but a premonition.

This, in sum, is the whole of Rupert's argument: a religious

112. See Grundmann, *DA* 22 (1966) 409–13.
113. *Vict.* 8.25: ed. Haacke 269; and for the importance of this text generally in Rupert's thought, see Van Engen, *DA* 35 (1979) 61–62.

conviction regarding the monks' need for and right to solitude; a theological argument that things dedicated to God become forever sacrosanct and that the dedication of whole religious sites in particular constitutes one of two essential weapons in the continuing fight against the Devil; a mustering of such historical facts as would bolster his case (all of them, intentionally or not, distorted to some degree); and finally an interpretation of the fire as a judgement of God. These arguments had sufficed to turn back the archbishop of Cologne and Count Adolph of Berg but not, interestingly, the lay folk who lived right next to the abbey.

Once Rupert had set out his claim and placed the struggle for its maintenance in an overarching framework of battle between Christ and the Devil (cc. 8–12), he went on to describe his confrontation with Archbishop Frederick (c. 13), his near resignation and the divine intervention which prodded him to continue (cc. 14–16), and finally the unexpected and much more difficult contention with Count Adolph (cc. 17–18). The last five chapters take the form of a summary prayer to St. Lawrence. Rupert prayed that the lessons of the fire, again compared to the Last Judgement, be impressed upon the lay folk, especially the fact that while one of their women was burned to death, the monks were wholly spared. He prayed also for patience and fortitude in this time of testing and suffering (cc. 20–21), and related a dream (c. 22) that revealed his own great terror. He concluded with two specific requests: that the chapel dedicated to St. Lawrence be completed, or in lieu thereof—he was in fact to die within a few months—that his good intentions be accepted; and, turning now to the Blessed Virgin, the patron of the abbey, that the half-burnt fortifications not be rebuilt, so that the intrusion of lay folk and their much too close cohabitation with the religious life would not be allowed to continue.

The effect of Rupert's treatise upon his monks at Deutz is not known. Its impact upon Archbishop Frederick was negligible, for he appointed as Rupert's successor a worldly abbot who squandered the abbey's resources in pursuit of the high life at

the prince-bishop's court. Count Adolph, five years later and
at the behest of his zealous brother, converted the family castle at
Berg entirely into a Cistercian monastery (henceforth: Altenberg) and himself made profession as a Cistercian in 1138. The
monks at Deutz were never able to make Rupert's claim stick:
both the archbishops and Count Adolph's heirs eventually built
and maintained fortified houses and towers at Deutz until rebellious citizens of Cologne totally destroyed the castle and its
fortifications in 1243.

In 1119 Rupert left his homeland under a cloud of suspicion
and in the midst of ecclesiastical strife. Within months his situation was reversed. He enjoyed the patronage of Archbishop
Frederick and Abbot Cuno, the most powerful and respected
religious figures in Cologne. The abbots of Great St. Martin's
and St. Pantaleon called upon his talents as a writer; Wibald of
Stavelot and Abbot Eberhard of Brauweiler consulted him on
religious and monastic questions; Abbot Rudolph got him to
prepare the only Jewish-Christian dialogue to come out of the
Lower Rhineland in this era; Norbert of Xanten challenged him
on theological and canonistic questions; and Archbishop Frederick and Count Adolph III of Berg were forced to yield, at least
temporarily, to his insistence upon Deutz's religious immunity.
There were still other testimonies to his reputation. Bishop
Thietmar of Verden requested copies of his work; Abbot Erkenbert of Corvey praised Rupert for the high quality of his commentaries, as did Prior Reginhard of Helmarshausen; and Anselm of Havelberg claimed to have met Rupert and read several
of his works "out of curiosity."[114] In short, resident in an abbey
facing directly the greatest city in the German Empire, Rupert
had become the leading Benedictine theologian in the archdiocese and probably the foremost theologian during the 1120's
anywhere in the northern and western part of the Empire.

114. *Cant.* epistola: CM 26.3–4; *Proph.* prologus: PL 168.526–28; Anselm,
Epistola: PL 188.1120.

VII

The Church
and
the Reformer

T HE HOLY CATHOLIC CHURCH encompassed all of Rupert's life and writings. Reform of both the secular Church and the religious life forced him and his contemporaries to reflect often and deeply upon the nature of the Church, that is, upon her origins and membership, her historical course, and the relative ranking of her constituent parts. Nothing could be taken for granted anymore: the pope had cast "God's anointed ruler" out of Holy Church, dioceses and the papacy itself had been rent in two, White Monks and canons regular had challenged Benedictine leadership. To formulate their ecclesiologies Rupert and his contemporaries drew upon and reaffirmed much that was traditional, but nearly always with the present situation in mind.[1] Two of Rupert's three works treated below, for instance, introduced significant variations into well-formed exegetical traditions; the third proved wholly original.

1. Thus B. Smalley, "Peter Comestor on the Gospels and His Sources," *RTAM* 46 (1979) 93 n. 40 rightly criticized R. Grégoire, *Bruno de Segni* (Spoleto 1965) 329–82 for concentrating upon traditional aspects of Bruno's ecclesiology with little regard for their new meaning in this age of reform. On Rupert's ecclesiology, see Beinert, *Kirche* passim; Magrassi, *Teologia* 87–124; and M. Bernards, "Die Welt der Laien in der kölnischen Theologie des 12. Jahrhunderts: Beobachtungen zur Ekklesiologie Ruperts von Deutz," in *Festgabe für Josef Kardinal Frings* (Cologne 1960) 391–416.

1

The Church

Rupert's *Commentary on Leviticus*, written still in Liège, offers a good introduction to his general view of the Church. Like Rhabanus Maurus in the ninth century, Bruno of Segni in his own lifetime, and Ralph of Flaix in the 1140's, Rupert understood this book to teach about the Church's priestly ministry. But where Ralph aimed a distinctly polemical thrust at Jewish law and sacrifices, Rupert set forth the whole well-ordered makeup (*status*) of the Church and her priesthood, with emphasis more upon spiritual than institutional matters.[2] The sacrifices prescribed in the Book of Leviticus were founded upon a celestial exemplar, which Rupert here expounded for the benefit of those now in its service. Christ is the head (c. 4), but his chosen people, his "royal priesthood," is divided into three distinct orders, represented by Job, Noah, and Daniel. The laity (c. 5) must be faithful in marriage and good deeds, and serve the altar as "priests" in so far as they bring gifts of faith and rectitude (presupposing more material ones). Prelates (c. 6) must show mercy and charity in ruling the Lord's flock. Contemplatives (cc. 7–8) must cast aside the cares of the flesh in order to meditate upon Holy Scripture. But, Rupert continued (c. 9), those who treat Scripture in the Holy Spirit with no heretical blemish and no show of vainglory will immediately encounter persecution, derided from within by false brothers and openly attacked from without by the impious! A good monk must, then, act with discretion and patience, seeking still to extract from Scripture that which will encourage sanctity and root out concupiscence (cc. 10–12).

Christ's sacrifice (cc. 13–14) instituted the two chief sacraments, baptism (c. 15) and the eucharist (c. 16); but even as His passion was a unique event (c. 17), so the sacrament of baptism

---

2. Cf. *Levit*. 2.30: CM 22.892–93. B. Smalley, "Ralph of Flaix on Leviticus," *RTAM* 35 (1968) 35–82.

remits all sin only once. Concretely applied, this meant that priests and prelates caught in public crimes must be relegated to lay communion (cc. 18, 26), and laymen (c. 19) who defend or continue in their sin receive no remission at all. The only certain way to gain forgiveness is to join the religious life (c. 20), the life of continual penance (and also a second baptism). What then about those who merely "observe" corruption? All heretics must be reproached and shunned, the reformer insists, for their sacraments are "dead" and "polluting" (c. 21).

The second half of this first book interprets the sacrificial law prescribed for various sins. Oaths are to be sworn with great care, if at all (c. 22); monk-priests deserve material support only if they pray faithfully and sincerely for their benefactors (cc. 23–24); sins committed in ignorance weigh less heavily than those done in concupiscence (c. 25). The pure religious life, defined in terms of the three cardinal virtues and the seven gifts of the Spirit (c. 27), requires complete chastity (c. 28) and daily nourishment from Scripture and the Fathers (c. 29). For priests, Rupert argued forcefully (c. 31), this is not a matter of counsel but precept; they have no right at all to become involved with women or worldly affairs. Valid sacrifices are performed only within the Church and only by those with pure and believing hearts (cc. 32–33). But Rupert distinguished between an essentially private mass said by those striving toward the vision of God (for whom his *De diuinis officiis* was intended as a guide) and public masses said, for instance, for kings. When priests bring sinners to repentance, they deserve to reap material rewards (c. 34), but greedy priests and bishops who accept gifts from unrepentant sinners should, in Rupert's judgement, be removed.

Book II places the Church in a salvation-historical framework, beginning with the foundation of the priesthood in Christ's sacrifice and the pouring out of the Holy Spirit (cc. 1–9) which enabled priests to understand and to preach the Word and required of them continence to perform the sacrifice. Then (cc. 10–23) Rupert dealt with those to be included in and especially those to be excluded from the community, adopting a very hard line (*statim eicienda et separanda*) toward those guilty of false teaching, immorality, and simony. Next (cc. 24–29) he treated reconciliation, admitting that a second laying on of hands virtually constituted reordination (c. 25). False teachers (cc. 26–27) must be properly examined, warned, put under silence, and finally removed completely if they persist in their errors. The conversion of the Jews (c. 30) and the persecutions of Antichrist (c. 31) will bring the earthly pilgrimage of the Church to a close. The remaining chapters comment on the three major feastdays of the Christian Church (cc. 32–37) and on the religious life (cc. 38–46), with emphasis upon confession, penance, and mutual forgiveness.

The view which emerges from Rupert's *Commentary on Leviticus* is striking both for its monastic perspective and for its preoccupation with matters of reform. The two were potentially at odds: the new Church definitively brought the secular hierarchy to the fore, and popes looked increasingly to canons regular and later to mendicants rather than to monks for religious support; the new monks, on the other hand, shunned involvement in the secular hierarchy—at least initially, though it would be hard to prove this from the life of St. Bernard. Rupert, a Black Monk like most of the reform popes down to 1119, sought still to uphold both the superiority of the religious life and the role of monks in reforming the Church.[3]

To express the superiority of "contemplatives" in the Church, Rupert used a variety of biblical images, most of them (such as the distinction among Job, Noah, and Daniel) either originating with or known to him from the first monk-pope, Gregory the Great.[4] The stricter a form of life, the more intent already upon the vision of God, the higher it stood in the Church.[5] The re-

3. See Y. Congar, "Modèle monastique et modèle sacerdotal en Occident de Grégoire VII (1073–85) à Innocent III (1198)," in *Mélanges E. R. Labande* (Poitiers 1975) 153–60, who, however, did not comment on the precarious overlap between these two models just in Rupert's lifetime. On these different models, see also G. Tellenbach, *Church, State and Christian Society at the Time of the Investiture Contest*, trans. R. F. Bennett (New York 1970) 38–60.

4. *Reg.* 3.10: CM 22.1304–05. Originating in Origen, the distinction among Job, Noah, and Daniel was known to Rupert from Gregory, *Hom. Ezech.* 2.4.5: CC 142.261–62. See Beinert, *Kirche* 249–61, 272–312.

5. *Gen.* 4.18: CM 21.303; cf. *John* 14: CM 9.781–82.

form movement had, moreover, effectively sharpened the division between those who administered the sacraments, especially the eucharist, and those who did not. But as Rupert pointed out so frequently, monks alone among clergymen were to feed daily on the Body and the Word of the Lord. Thus Benedictine monk-priests who lived the strictest form of life and celebrated mass daily became, for Rupert, the ideal for the whole Church. Still another image deserves attention: while bishops presided as ordinary judges in the secular Church, devout monks, Rupert observed, would one day serve with Christ as judges in the Last Judgement.[6]

Rupert's monastic approach to ecclesiology, together with the scriptural nature of his writings, fostered the use of biblical images expressing an essentially spiritual conception of the Church: Noah's ark, the tabernacle, the temple, the Bride of Christ, the body of Christ, the New Jerusalem, and so forth.[7] The Church considered as "Kingdom of God," however, enabled Rupert not only to insist upon its fundamentally spiritual nature but also to trace its development in the history of salvation over against the "kingdoms" of this world. The Church as Kingdom of God was founded in the incarnation, passion, and resurrection of Christ, whereby the Devil was cast out as the prince of this world and God's "seat" established in the "present Church."[8] The baptized have already been joined to God's Kingdom but continue to live in tension with the flesh and the kingdom of this world until the final resurrection of their bodies.[9] Those few who deny themselves even what is licit and are thus liberated from the Devil and the passions of the flesh anticipate the coming "third condition" (*tertius mundi status*), the Kingdom in all its fullness.[10] The primary aim of this Kingdom, as set out in Rupert's *Commentary on the Gospels*, is to liberate sinners. It is

6. *Spir.* 9.12: CM 24.2113.

7. Fully treated in Beinert, *Kirche* 151–89.

8. *Apoc.* 2: PL 169.906, 909–10; *Matt.* 9: CM 29.277–79.

9. *Off.* 7.11: CM 7.37–38; *John* 14: CM 9.761–62; *Iosue* 16: CM 22.1137–38; *Apoc.* 11: PL 169.1183–85.

10. *Spir.* 4.24: CM 24.1973.

not a kingdom of this world: Christ never sought great tracts of land, large cities, or many brave knights, and he never posed a threat to any earthly empire including Rome.[11] While kings and knights of this world cruelly subjugate lands and peoples, the soldiers of Christ, the apostles, preach mercy; but they also preach the hard and narrow way, and do not, like courtiers, seek only to flatter the vainglorious. Thus the Beatitudes constitute the law of God's Kingdom, whereas kings and princes of this earth—here addressed directly (O reges terrae et principes)—are "proud, cruel, scoffers, impatient of doing justice, lacking in mercy, immoral, and restless." Citizens of God's Kingdom would rather be pilgrims than reign, would rather be killed than kill. But since Christ taught all this originally to His apostles, Rupert's real point here was to impress upon prelates (such as Otbert) the great difference (distantiam) between the Kingdom over which they preside and that governed by dukes and princes of this world.[12]

Because Christ's Kingdom is not of this world, His ministers manifestly may not become entangled in worldly affairs. Indeed, the law has decreed that such worldly bishops and priests must be removed (deicitur).[13] Christ's ministers, like the Levites before them, must be distinguished from the people; otherwise they will become unfruitful in both spiritual and worldly affairs.[14] The apostles were already warned against secular involvement, and their successors too must remember that they receive powers in the Church and rewards from wealthy kings and emperors on condition that they function as "teachers and pastors," not as "commanders and tyrants."[15]

Despite such vigorous criticism of imperial bishops and of priests and monks inordinately concerned about their properties and incomes, Rupert never for an instant questioned the Church's

11. Evang. 9–12: CM 23.1789–93; John 13: CM 9.729.
12. Evang. 18–19: CM 23.1799–1805; John 1: CM 9.41; and esp. Matt. 8: CM 29.246, 250.
13. Num. 1.4: CM 22.918–19. Rupert cited Canones Apostolorum 7.
14. Deut. 1.17: CM 22.1036–37; Exod. 3.22: CM 22.714.
15. Iosue 8: CM 22.1126; Deut. 2.17: CM 22.1108–09.

right to control extensive lands and resources. As the Book of Daniel teaches, every kingdom of this world is threatened by the rock which will destroy all others. Even as the martyrs and confessors triumphed over pagan Rome, so since Constantine the Christian religion is rightly defended by both the "swords of kings and the authority of bishops."[16] Their triumph so enriched this world, moreover, that large parts of its kingdoms were seized as the "richest spoils" for the use of the victors, Christ's ministers. Rupert specified here the wealth of kings and emperors together with control over castles and cities. This text of about 1113/14 laid claim, in other words, to precisely those material possessions Pope Paschal II had just (1111) vainly agreed should be returned to kings and emperors.[17] But Rupert always insisted these were meant only to support the service of the altar, the upkeep of churches, and the care of the poor.[18] The strict reformers steadily resisted any compromise which would return to secular control properties and incomes once dedicated to the Lord. About 1123 Rupert quoted the Donation of Constantine in the midst of his *Commentary on the Minor Prophets.*[19] His "little reminder" of the "Roman privilege" may just possibly represent his reaction to the Concordat of Worms' recent compromise settlement, which his archbishop had witnessed as archchancellor of the realm.

Rupert was no less clear on the Church's leadership generally. The preaching of the apostles, martyrs, and confessors had conquered the Roman world.[20] The sacerdotal power of saints Peter and Paul now extended far beyond the military sway of the pagan Roman emperors—this borrowed from a well-known sermon by Leo the Great.[21] Though aimed at the spiritual end of

16. *Dan.* 6–11: CM 23.1744–53; *Gen.* 7.9: CM 21.439–40. Cf. *Off.* 5.5: CM 7.152; *Gen.* 6.24: CM 21.401–02.
17. *Num.* 2.15: CM 22.984. Cf. *Priuilegium Paschalis* II: MGH Leges 4.1.140–42.
18. *Gen.* 7.37: CM 21.473–74.
19. *Ionah* 2: PL 168.432.
20. *Num.* 2.10: CM 22.978. Cf. *Off.* 11.2: CM 7.372; *Dan.* 8–10: CM 23.1747–51.
21. *Gen.* 7.10: CM 21.441; *Ionah* 2: PL 168.432. Cf. Leo, *Sermones* 82.1.

instilling Christian faith and practice, the Church's leadership (*principatum*) was nonetheless very real.[22] The Church need never seek counsel now from drunken princes and foolish worldly philosophers, but rather under Christian kings and Catholic princes she is permitted to reign over public assemblies and to govern a divine empire with heavenly laws.[23] Holy Church needs the protection, the "sword-power," of princes and kings: when the two work together, nothing is better, but when they are at odds, nothing could be worse for the state of Christendom in this world.[24] Thus material power played a necessary, but manifestly subservient, role; it was to foster and to enforce the preaching and teaching of the Church. Any time it ceased to do that it reverted essentially to an opposition role more or less comparable to that of the pagan Roman emperors. Christ's victory over the Devil meant that "in the present age He and His Church reigned supreme in a public religion marked by mutual cooperation between imperial power and the ecclesiastical priesthood."[25] The crucial practical problem of just how the Church should govern its own affairs and administer its extensive lands and incomes without becoming entangled in worldly affairs interested Rupert hardly at all, quite in contrast to several other contemporary monastic reformers and his intellectual protégé, the canon Gerhoch of Reichersberg, who devoted his first book to this subject.

2

Preaching Reform
to Prelates and Priests

Once the tensions over sacramental validity (chapter III, part 3) and political authority began to subside, and the reformers had, so far as possible, removed, penalized, or threatened into submission those prelates and priests deemed unfit for their

22. *Proph.*: PL 168.640, 771–72.
23. *Reg.* 2.13: CM 22.1259; *Levit.* 2.26: CM 22.887.
24. *Num.* 1.5: CM 22.920.
25. *Vict.* 8.25: ed. Haacke 269.

offices, the new Church faced a fresh challenge: to produce worthy churchmen. Pope Gregory VII charged bishops with the support and maintenance of schools in their dioceses, but in general the reformers had hardly foreseen this development, and the relationship between the new Church and the new schools remained at first haphazard and indirect. Individual reformers, writers, and prelates had therefore to take up the slack, seeking as best they could to train and instruct worthy priests and prelates. Much of the mysterious Honorius Augustodunensis' work, for instance, should be understood in this context.[26] In Rupert's part of the world Norbert of Xanten, following his conversion and brief stay at Siegburg (ca. 1115), toured various bishoprics, preaching reform and castigating the vices of their resident bishops. Neither the bishops nor more established monks found Norbert's conduct in the least amusing, and at the Council of Fritzlar in 1118 they successfully challenged his right to preach; but Gelasius II, a reform pope, soon licensed him to continue his reform preaching.[27] In 1127/28, at the request of Henry of Boisrogues, the archbishop of Sens and primate of Gaul, St. Bernard prepared an influential letter-treatise on the office and virtues of the good prelate.[28] And probably in the 1130's another monk, the father of the science of canon law, devoted the entire first part of his *Concord of Discordant Canons*, save an introduction on the law itself, to an exposition of this same theme under the leitmotif of I Tim. 3:2ff.[29]

26. B. Smalley, *The Becket Conflict and the Schools* (Totowa, N.J. 1973) 18–58. Cf. L. K. Little, "Intellectual Training and Attitudes toward Reform, 1075–1150," in *Pierre Abélard—Pierre le Vénérable* (Paris 1975) 235–49, whose argument, however, would not account for Rupert; and V. I. J. Flint, "The Place and Purpose of the Works of Honorius Augustodunensis," *RB* 87 (1977) 97–127.

27. *RegBen.* 1: PL 170.492; *Vita Norberti A* 4–5: MGH SS 12.673–75. L. K. Little, *Religious Poverty and the Profit Economy in Medieval Europe* (Ithaca 1978) 87–89. On other reform preachers, such as Henry of Lausanne and Peter of Bruys, who ended up outside the Church, see R. I. Moore, *The Origins of European Dissent* (New York 1977) 82–114.

28. *Epist.* 42: ed. Leclercq 7.100–31.

29. *Decretum* D. 21–101. See G. Le Bras, "Les Ecritures dans le Décret de Gratien," *Zeitschrift der Savigny-Stiftung*, Kan. Abt. 27 (1938) 47–80.

The most readily available instrument for the instruction and improvement of the clergy was preaching (understood here in a fairly broad sense). The reformers encouraged preaching, and so too did the new schools. Masters of the Sacred Page were expected not only to lecture on Scripture but also to preach from it, and several of the new masters—Smalley pointed particularly to Robert Pullen and Geoffrey Babion—"used their lecture courses as material for sermons."[30] In fact the same was true for at least one Black Monk. The homilies of Bruno of Segni are taken directly from his commentaries, and two other works distinctly ecclesiological in orientation, his *Libri sententiarum* and his *De sacramentis ecclesiae*, are also in effect sermons with manifold correspondences to his biblical commentaries.[31] Only from the mid-twelfth century can scholars trace in detail the homiletic work of the masters, an important source for understanding their ecclesiastical setting and purposes.[32] But for the wandering preachers of the early twelfth century, the message, though often delivered in a popular style to an enthusiastic laity, was aimed at least as much at the "corrupt" clergy as at the people. Many other reformers accomplished the same end within the structures of the Church and in a far less rabble-rousing form. Bishop William in Châlons-sur-Marne, we noted earlier, reformed his clergy to the common life and then instructed them in the faith. Rupert too, beginning with his guide to the divine office, had this same concern and purpose.

Addressed to monk-priests and interested prelates, Rupert's works interpreted Scripture so as to instruct and edify those in clerical office. In descriptions of their calling, he quite consistently placed preaching first among their responsibilities, time and again making it the central requirement for true ministers of Christ (thus including both bishops and priests).[33] In his

30. Smalley (n. 26 above) 24.
31. Grégoire (n. 1 above) 83–101, 104–08.
32. J. W. Baldwin, *Masters, Princes and Merchants: The Social Views of Peter the Chanter and His Circle* (Princeton 1970); J. Longère, *Oeuvres oratoires de maîtres parisiens au XIIᵉ siècle* (Paris 1975).
33. *John* 5, 8: CM 9.246, 455; *Matt.* 2: CM 29.58; *Gen.* 5.15, 6.13: CM 21.348, 390.

clearest reference to the reformers' demand for "free election" of bishops, for instance, Rupert declared that only such properly chosen men could rightly and effectively teach the mysteries of Christ and His kingdom.[34] When a conviction assumed this much importance for him, Rupert would also find a place for it in his exposition of salvation-history—in this instance, in fact, two places. The coming of the Holy Spirit at Pentecost and the illumination of the apostles enabled them to preach and thus to spread the Church throughout the world.[35] And now in the "peaceful state" of the Church, as successors to the martyrs, all prelates and priests, here equated with Mother Church, must renounce this world and preach in order to bring forth spiritual sons, for by preaching they now carry on the fight against the Devil (*Praedicando pugnauerunt*). Preaching (*constantissima praedicatione ueritatis*), remember, was also the first of the two ways to wage battle mentioned in Rupert's *De incendio*.[36]

The problem, Rupert once remarked, is that so many prelates now live as though they were not reading Holy Scripture and did not know its mandates.[37] Otloh of St. Emmeran believed that a serious reading of Scripture would chasten and correct the simoniacs of his day.[38] In this context the task of a scriptural commentator was manifestly to make plain the teachings of Scripture and to instill in the hearts of priests and prelates renewed zeal to carry out their tasks. Heretics and the unfaithful must be admonished diligently, Rupert declared, and finally cast out if they fail to respond, for the House of God should have in it nothing unclean or heretical; other faithful servants should then be brought in to replace them and thus "by constant preaching (*sedula praedicatione*) and improved learning the whole condition (*status*) of the Catholic Church (*pacis catholicae*) reformed."[39]

34. *Num.* 1.7: CM 22.922–23.

35. *Spir.* 4.1–10: CM 24.1938–51. For the apostles as preachers, see *John* 12: CM 9.703; *Exod.* 3.4: CM 22.694–95; *Num.* 1.18: CM 22.936–37.

36. *Spir.* 6.14–15: CM 24.2027–29. *Incendio* 12: ed. Grundmann 454.

37. *Hier.* 18: CM 23.1595.

38. PL 146.77–78.

39. *Levit.* 2.27: CM 22.889.

Accordingly, Rupert himself constantly preached moral and spiritual reform. Taking the reformers' key text as his own guide (Phil. 2:21: *quae sua sunt quaerunt, non quae sunt Jesu Christi*), he relentlessly condemned the avarice and ambition which "now" reigned everywhere, threatening the whole Church. He singled out particularly those priests who committed themselves to the service of the altar only in order to obtain their daily bread, thus under the guise of "religious piety" pursuing only the "service of idols" (Eph. 5:5).[40] What's more, Rupert observed, once avarice enters the Church it soon devours all else besides—chastity, respect for the religious life, and devotion to sacred learning.[41] Rupert struck here at the heart of a problem endemic to the religious life in the middle ages, particularly in prosperous times. The monastic life, conceived of still in essentially functional terms, represented the pinnacle of the spiritual order and also guaranteed material security and often ease, thus attracting many whose motives were not of the most spiritual sort. Unlike the White Monks and others who called for a return to the desert, however, Rupert insisted only that the publicly condemned be removed and called upon all others to examine their own motives in seeking the priestly office. Reform began, in Rupert's view, with individual renewal and extended to others by way of preaching and teaching.[42]

Beyond innumerable remarks on the virtues of priests and

40. *Apoc.* 6: PL 169.1025; *Off.* 4.16: CM 7.131; *John* 6: CM 9.303,313; *Gen.* 8:45: CM 21.482: *Levit.* 1.36: CM 22.849; *Hier.* 31: CM 23.1603; *Iosue* 21: CM 22.1134.

41. ". . . continuo tamquam de mala radice uitiorum omnium pullulant fructus mali primumque ecclesiae castitas et omne decus religionis perit, scientiae nulla cura, nullus honor, nullus fere sacri feruor studii, sed auaritiae, quae idolorum seruitus uorago bona cuncta submergit." *Apoc* 2: PL 169.879.

42. ". . . ad cor suum quisque nostrum redeat et interroget semetipsum, qua mente ad thronum uel mensam eius adeat, idest quid quaerens, quid desiderans ad sanctum altare eius accedat." *John* 6: CM 9.323. "In isto gradu uincere est doctrinam Balaam, idest fornicationes, primum in semetipso per uirtutem continentiae, deinde in aliis per uirtutem scientiae destruere. Porro qui hoc modo uincit, ille sacramentum corporis et sanguinis Domini digne percipit. . . ." *Apoc.* 2: PL 169.880.

prelates scattered all through his commentaries,[43] Rupert twice set forth specific examples of model prelates, first (about 1119) in reworking the *Vita Heriberti*,[44] and then (1126) in a tribute to Cuno upon his elevation to the bishopric of Regensburg.[45] He consciously modeled the latter account on the *Life of St. Martin*, the paradigm of a monk-bishop. Cuno left wealth, a well-placed family, and his homeland to follow Christ and His Gospel, only to reap a manifold harvest of souls as abbot of Siegburg. He was humble almost to a fault, an effective counselor, teacher, and preacher, and a reluctant prelate, a peacemaker freely elected to reconcile divisions in his native city. Rupert implies he retained his monastic habit, as had St. Martin; and to conclude he reminds even Cuno that prelates are called to serve Christ and His people, not to rule over subjects. Earlier Rupert had described Heribert in similar ways: a gentle, honest, and humble prelate who preached to his people, cared for the poor, generously supported the religious life, and curbed abuses among his clergy—with virtually no mention at all of Heribert's relatively important role in the affairs of the German Empire. This was the ideal Rupert taught and aimed to instill: men committed above all to the Kingdom of Christ who served that Kingdom through their intercession at the altar, their preaching (whether written or spoken), their pastorate, and the prudent administration of properties and incomes. Rupert's work functioned in practice as criticism of adversaries such as bishops Otbert and Alexander, as encouragement and praise for friends and patrons such as Frederick of Liège and Cuno, and finally as earnest and rather courageous admonition to the compromised and wavering such as his second patron, Archbishop Frederick of Cologne.

43. See Beinert, *Kirche* 262–93; and José M. Arancibia, "Las virtudes de los prelados según Ruperto de Deutz," *Scriptorium Victoriense* 17 (1970) 241–82.

44. Useful discussion from this point of view in M. L. Arduini, "Il problema della *paupertas* nella *Vita sancti Heriberti archiepiscopi Coloniensis* di Ruperto di Deutz," *Studi Medievali* 3rd ser. 20 (1979) 87–138.

45. *Matt.* 12: CM 29.386–93.

3

The Labors of
the Church: *Commentary*
on the Apocalypse

Monks normally read the Book of Apocalypse (together with the Acts of the Apostles and the Pastoral Epistles) between Easter and Pentecost. The Latin Fathers had interpreted it as a general allegory on the continuing struggle of the Church and individual Christians, despite Christ's victory, during the time between His first and second comings. Thus early medieval monks, who saw themselves on the front line of this moral and spiritual battle against the wiles of the Devil, became greatly attracted to the book, whence the important commentaries by Bede, Beatus, Ambrosius Autpertus, Haimo, and others, and also the many important illuminated manuscripts of it.[46] Bruno of Segni commented on this book very early, probably when Rupert was still in his youth; he evidently attempted to rework certain exegetical problems, but all still within the framework of the received interpretative tradition,[47] which soon received its definitive form in the *Ordinary Gloss* prepared at Laon. It was Rupert who first interpreted the Book of Apocalypse in a distinctively new way, to have it bear concretely on the course of salvation-history.[48] Near the end of *De sancta Trinitate* Rupert

46. The basic work is still W. Kamlah, *Apokalypse und Geschichtstheologie* (Berlin 1935); but see Y. Christe, "Ap. IV–VIII, 1: de Bède à Bruno de Segni," in *Mélanges E. R. Labande* (Poitiers 1975) 145–51, and *L'Apocalypse de Jean: traditions exégètiques et iconographiques IIIe–XIIIe siècles*, ed. R. Petraglio et al. (Geneva 1979).

47. Grégoire (n. 1 above) 81–83; Kamlah (n. 46 above) 15–25; Christe (n. 46 above) 147–49.

48. See Kamlah (n. 46 above) 75–104, who concluded: "In der Reihe der Ap-Kommentare des 12. Jahrhunderts ist Ruperts Werk das eigentümlichste" (p. 103). Kamlah emphasized the commentary as a product of monastic meditation; without in any way denying that, I have developed a different theme.

dealt with several texts crucial to his later commentary,[49] and his first presentation before Archbishop Frederick also expounded verses from this book. But it was only in the protected leisure (*otium*) afforded him at Cologne–Siegburg–Deutz and at the insistence of both Abbot Cuno and the archbishop that Rupert finally wrote the entire work. Dedicated to Archbishop Frederick, who had probably just appointed him to the abbacy of Deutz, his *Commentary on the Apocalypse* was well received, becoming with twelve extant manuscripts and another eleven attested in catalogues his second most popular commentary (or, counting *Off.* and *Vict.*, his fourth most popular work).[50]

Rupert stated more clearly in this prologue than anywhere else that meditation on Scripture offered the beginnings of the eternal vision of God, and his commentary was intended first of all to guide souls toward that vision. But Cuno was also persuaded, Rupert notes, that he could "add something useful" (*utiliter supererogare*) to what the Fathers had already said on this book, and with the powerful support of his new patrons behind him he no longer feared charges of "novelty." This prologue closes in fact with the single most vigorous defense of his "right (*licentia*) within the faith to turn over the field of Scripture with the ploughshare of his own genius."[51] The Book of Apocalypse fascinated, too, simply because of its difficulty, containing— Rupert quoted Jerome in the prologue—almost as many mysteries as words. Unresolved exegetical problems had apparently provided a major stimulus to Bruno of Segni. With a proven genius for recasting exegetical traditions, Rupert now undertook this task with unusual brilliance and boldness. Though he knew and often followed the work of his predecessors, especially Haimo, he sought consciously "to go beyond them in search of something more befitting the majesty of Holy Scripture."[52] More basically, he rethought the entire structure of this complex book and came thus to stand apart from both the re-

49. *Spir.* 6.3, 14: CM 24.2010–11, 2027–29.
50. R. Haacke, *DA* 26 (1970) 534–35.
51. PL 169.825–28.
52. *Apoc.* 3: PL 169.907–08. Kamlah (n. 46 above) 88: "Rupert hat die Frage des Aufbaus der Apokalypse ganz neu durchdacht."

ceived monastic tradition, followed still by Bruno of Segni, and the school tradition, a streamlined version of the former, upon which later commentators such as Richard of St. Victor were to build.

The "greater usefulness" of Rupert's spiritual teachings and his innovative exegesis of St. John's visions—the two points stressed by Kamlah—stemmed ultimately, in my judgement, from a new perception of this work's essential theme or purpose. Rupert treated introductory matters in Book I: an *accessus* to the Book of Apocalypse, a confession of faith, a theory of visions,[53] and the first vision of the Son of Man (with much emphasis upon Christ's divinity). Book II then went to the heart of the matter. The seven churches of Asia Minor must be understood as the one Church filled and directed by the seven-form Spirit so that what was said to each applies to all. For the instruction of the Church as a whole, then, the Spirit's seven gifts, in ascending order from fear to wisdom, spoke to each of the seven churches, and those messages, briefly summarized, Rupert read as follows. To Ephesus (fear) came a strong warning that penance is required of those who have fallen away, something Rupert directed particularly at the "many fallen priests today", especially those guilty of false teaching and immorality. To Smyrna (piety) the Spirit teaches that persecutions and tribulations must necessarily be borne by those who seek to live in piety and truth. The message to Pergamus Rupert turned into his single most vivid and angry condemnation of the "simony and immorality which now threaten the whole Church." In particular, his attack upon "violent secular powers" who set up "simoniac bishops" and "adulterous anti-popes" referred almost certainly to Henry V, who had supported an anti-pope in 1118 and the scurrilous Alexander at Liège in 1119.[54] The Spirit's word to Thyatira (fortitude) Rupert understood as an admonition to priests and prelates to pluck up their courage and preach against these evils. The entire message to Sardes (counsel) concerns the handling of secret sins by priests and prelates (especially sins of the flesh) and how to counsel them privately to do

53. Ibid. 106–08.
54. *Apoc.* 2: PL 169.877–78.

penance while maintaining their offices. To Philadelphia (understanding) the Spirit spoke of the true understanding of Scripture which only He could provide, and admonished those who had this gift to use it for the benefit of others despite the "envy" directed against them. Finally Laodicea (wisdom) speaks of the eternal sabbath of charity, humility, and wisdom, toward which true believers must be striving. In short, Book II offers nothing less than Rupert's view of the Church's current state, or better, of the pressing needs which the Spirit's messages clearly addressed.

More so than in his *Commentary on Leviticus*, Rupert now saw the Church as under siege, threatened on every hand by violent kings and lords, avaricious prelates, venal, immoral priests and, not least, false teachers—much of this owing doubtless to his own recent exile and the violent schism in Liège. When evil looms so large in Christendom, Rupert declared, the Scriptures must be examined to determine why such persecutions have been allowed to rise up against the Church.[55] Just such an investigation lay at the very heart of Rupert's theme and purpose. What intrigued him was the Book of Apocalypse understood as a vision of the Church laboring in time toward its eternal destiny in the Heavenly Jerusalem. Near the end of Book I he provided an "outline" (*schema uel habitus*) of his entire work: it would deal first (Book II) with "what was to be corrected or praised in the seven churches," and then (Books III–XII) with "the various labors of the Church which were to come."[56] At the outset, however, Rupert presented a definition of prophecy or "what was to come" as comprehending the past, present, and future: Christ revealed to St. John what the status of the Church had been, then was, and would be.[57] By this definition a commentator had

55. "Cum autem multa sint peccata in populo Christianitatis, non abs re est scire uel quaerere Scripturarum exemplis, quo maxime uel quali pro peccato illa talis tribulatio contra ecclesiam consurgere permittenda sit." *Apoc.* 6: PL 169.1024.

56. *Apoc.* 1: PL 169.862. The phrase "uarios ecclesiae labores" Rupert took over from Bede's commentary on Apoc. 1:19 (PL 93.137).

57. *Apoc.* 1: PL 169.831. Though apparently original in Rupert's formulation, it may have been suggested by Gregory's first homily on Ezechiel: CC 142.5–16.

actually to deal with the entire course of the Church's history, all of its "labors" from the beginning to the end.

One resultant and unusual feature of Rupert's commentary is his claim to find various Old Testament events in the Church's course "prophesied" in this New Testament book. This reversal of normal allegorical procedure yielded several of his more extraordinary interpretations: the twenty-four elders around Christ's throne (Apoc. 4:4) understood as the judges who preceded and succeeded David, the dragon's kings and kingdoms as enemies of the Israelites (Egypt, Babylon, etc.), the vision of the Lamb as referring first back to the paschal lamb and then forward to Christ's passion. By contrast the Tyconian tradition Rupert inherited had referred all of St. John's revelation generally to the New Testament Church or the New Testament age. Kamlah suggested that Rupert had confronted that tradition with the entire story of salvation familiar to him from St. Augustine's *City of God*.[58] But the schemes Rupert employed and his own purposes went far beyond that. To search the Scriptures for insight into the Church's tribulations meant necessarily that the entire Church extending back to Abel (the *ecclesia ab Abel*) was to be included so that present readers could be instructed and encouraged also by the example of Old Testament saints.

Even as Rupert sought to provide readers of the Apocalypse with a clear vision of the Church's past, so he offered them also a new understanding of her "present" and "future" labors. The Tyconian tradition, in fear of millennialists, had opted for vagueness rather than specificity, for general types (martyrs, preachers, etc.) rather than concrete events. Rupert insisted instead upon exact chronology: St. John's revelation prophesied events in the history of salvation accurately, one after another, from Old Testament times down to the "Catholic Peace" following Constantine's conversion and the Nicene Council's rejection of heresy. In support thereof Rupert was the first commentator to draw on historical sources from outside Scripture, chiefly Eu-

58. *Apoc.* 3, 7, 9: PL 169.907–08, 1043ff, 1088–89. See Kamlah (n. 46 above) 98–102, who found, however, only two persuasive examples of such influence: 99 n. 77, 100 n. 79.

sebius/Rufinus' *Ecclesiastical History* and Josephus.[59] Rupert's view of Antichrist was also much more specific than the vague "*corpus diaboli*" of the Tyconian tradition, for it included specific past (and present: Rome) kingdoms as well as real sinners (the avaricious, the immoral, and so forth).[60] Yet he stopped short of any Joachite-like prophecy, and he did not now, as earlier in his poem, apply apocalyptic images specifically to contemporary events or personages, though several passages came close to it (especially that at n. 54 above). It was startling enough that Rupert insisted the Apocalypse be read as a concretely historical picture of the Church's labors.

The scheme Rupert discovered in the Book of Apocalypse, his own ingenious interpretation of this wealth of visionary imagery, entailed seven recapitulations of the Spirit's work in the Church past, present, and future. By dividing the Book of Apocalypse into seven sets of visions—not counting the opening one, the letters to the churches, and the final one—Rupert came closest to Autpertus' scheme. But this organization was of his own devising, and he felt compelled to note in the prologue to Book III that his discovery of seven visions, each one linked to a different gift of the Spirit, was true to St. John's revelation and not forced upon the text.[61] Rupert outlined there the entire remaining commentary, a scheme he restated at several later points.[62] The Apocalypse reveals that the work of the Spirit's seven gifts, treated and "recapitulated" in descending order—the same order, incidentally, Rupert had employed in the third part (the New Testament age) of *De sancta Trinitate*[63]—

59. Kamlah (n. 46 above) 81, 101.

60. See Rauh, *Antichrist* 206–26.

61. *Apoc.* 3: PL 169.903–04.

62. Perhaps the clearest and briefest is at the beginning of Book XII where he summarized what he had done: "Septem spirituum Dei opera spectauimus, quae uel qualia cum genere humano operati sunt ab initio usque ad finem saeculi, singuli ordine suo a primo qui est Spiritus sapientiae usque ad ultimum eiusdem ordinis Spiritum timoris Dei." *Apoc.* 12: PL 169.1193. Cf. ibid. 11: 1163.

63. The rationale is also the same: Christ's fullness of grace (= Spirit) "descends" to us. Cf. *Apoc.* 12: PL 169.1193 and *Spir.* 1.31: CM 24.1860–61.

encompasses the whole of salvation-history. Most of the recapitulations, though not all (Rupert was never that consistent),
begin in the Old Testament and work forward through Christ's
incarnation to the coming of Antichrist. By way of example,
the seven trumpets (under the aegis of "counsel") and the seven
angels bearing plagues (under "*scientia*") figure a series of judgements stretching from the Old Testament into and beyond the
New, each with a noteworthy moral, spiritual or ecclesiastical
thrust.

That Rupert saw the Book of Apocalypse in much more ecclesiological than eschatological terms can be confirmed from
beginning to end. Thus Book III (under the aegis of "wisdom")
has the vision of Christ enthroned figure the Church, the throne
He established through those four acts (incarnation, passion,
resurrection, ascension) figured in turn in the four celestial
beings. And in Book VII (under the aegis of "fortitude") the battle between the dragon and the woman (Apoc. 12) figures the
battle of God's people against wicked kingdoms, from Egypt
through Rome to Antichrist. All these works of the Spirit, these
seven recapitulations of salvation-history, lead finally to the establishment of the Church as the Heavenly Jerusalem, described
in his final book by way of the last vision, though with much
time spent still on the Church as the Kingdom of God even in
its pilgrim state.[64]

The battle of the righteous against the agents of the Devil
had become particularly intense in his own day, and Rupert attempted to show the persecuted faithful where in the larger
course of salvation-history they stood relative to the prophets,
the martyrs, and the Lord Himself, all of whom had fought
this battle before them. It was this relatively concrete vision of
the Church in the long-term development of salvation-history

---

64. "Nunc tandem in calce uisionis siue reuelationis huius uniuersitas huic
Ioanni demonstratur totius operis, quod Jesus Christus tot impensis, tot spirituum suorum gratiis uel donis aedificauit, scilicet ciuitas sancta Jerusalem quae
est ecclesia Dei, non qualis in ista peregrinatione est . . . sed qualis post
iudicium in gloria aeterna erit, sola et tota, alienis omnibus foras missis, per-
fruens visione Dei." *Apoc.* 12: PL 169.1193.

which Abbot Cuno, Archbishop Frederick, and others could not find in the works of Rupert's predecessors and which seemed to speak so well to the needs and concerns of priests and prelates "today."

4

De uictoria Verbi Dei

About the year 1123 Abbot Cuno of Siegburg visited Rupert at Deutz, and as was their wont the two abbots withdrew from the other monks to pursue in solitude spiritual conversation on the majesty of Holy Scripture. That particular day they reflected upon Daniel's vision of the four beasts rising from the sea (Dan. 7), usually understood to represent four world-empires. They agreed that such fierce and bloodthirsty beasts rightly figured the cruel and bloody kingdoms of this world which had so bestially ground to pieces the saints of God. By contrast, the Son of Man who appeared on the clouds of heaven and came before the Ancient of Days figured the Kingdom of God, the empire of peace, justice, truth, and mercy. But why then, Abbot Cuno suddenly intervened, does the Church read, in addition to the *Lives* of saints and martyrs, the Books of Maccabees with their detailed accounts of fierce wars waged against the third of the beasts (leopard = the Greeks)? (Maccabees was read at table and at the night office throughout the month of October.) Spontaneously, it seems, Rupert responded: their battles and military prowess were of great benefit to us and to all ages, for they preserved, against the devious and destructive wiles of the Devil, the chosen race, the "branch" from which the saving Word had to be born in order to gain the ultimate victory. The same, Rupert added, could be said for Esther and Mordecai who battled against the second of the beasts (the bear = the Medes and Persians). (The book of Esther was read in the month of September). Excited and also spiritually enlightened by Rupert's interpretation of these books, a not inconsiderable part of the monastic office each fall, Abbot Cuno exclaimed: Write me a book on the victory of the Word of God![65] He then kept after Rupert until he had in fact done so, at the latest by the end of the year 1124. This work proved to be Rupert's third greatest success, with twenty-four extant manuscripts and more than ten others known from catalogues. The copy Rupert presented to Cuno was probably one still extant, complete with illuminated initials and a dedication picture.[66] Unlike his commentaries on the Apocalypse and the Song of Songs this work also became known outside the German Empire, at Clairvaux, for instance, and at St. Vaast outside Arras.

Rupert's work held great appeal at three different levels: the cosmic or salvation-historical, the ecclesiological, and the personal. *De uictoria Verbi Dei* contains the briefest, most compelling account since St. Augustine's *City of God* of salvation-history, that is, of the cosmic-historical battle between the Kingdom of God led by the Word and the kingdom of evil led by the Devil.[67] Freed from the genre of commentary with its inevitable maze of digressions, Rupert focused upon this single theme, which he also considered the greatest of all Christ's works. And since God is known primarily through His works, an exposition of Christ's battle and victory must greatly enhance our knowledge of God Himself.[68] But the core of Rupert's thought on salvation-history also provided the general framework for his approach to ecclesiology, that is, the Kingdom of God advancing, despite battles and persecutions, toward its ce-

65. *Vict.* prologus: ed. Haacke 1–3.

66. On this manuscript (Clm 14055), see Haacke's introduction, xxix–xxxiii, and on its text, E. Meuthen, "Ruperts von Deutz 'De victoria verbi Dei' nach clm 14055," *DA* 28 (1972) 542–57, which, unfortunately, must be used in conjunction with Haacke's new edition.

67. Magrassi, *Teologia* 142–71 and Rauh, *Antichrist* 196–226 depicted Rupert's views of ecclesiology and salvation-history largely in terms of the *De uictoria Verbi Dei*; but cf. now Peter Classen, "*Res gestae*, Universal History, Apocalypse: Visions of Past and Future," in *Renaissance and Renewal in the Twelfth Century*, ed. R. L. Benson, G. Constable, and C. D. Lanham (Cambridge, Mass. 1982) 404–05.

68. *Vict.* 1.5: ed. Haacke 10.

lestial destiny. This framework afforded Rupert the opportunity to speak, sometimes directly but more often by implication, to the place of kings and secular power, the role of prelates and preachers, and the power of the sword. This same battle, finally, was also fought over each individual soul, something monks especially as the "soldiers of Christ" should know and appreciate. Rupert expected each reader to apply this account of battle and victory to his own life, as he did later to his patron's life in describing Cuno's spiritual wrestling with his religious vocation.[69]

Rupert's story began in heaven with the rebellion of Lucifer and the other angels. But this was only the prelude. Rupert structured the remainder of his epic around an interpretation of Apoc. 12, the vision of the seven-headed dragon attacking the woman in labor, which he had employed twice before to present either a crucial stage or the whole of salvation-history from the perspective of "fortitude."[70] The received exegetical tradition, in addition, referred the vision of four beasts in Dan. 7:3–7 to four successive world-empires and that of the seven-headed dragon in Apoc. 12:3 to all evil kings active as agents of the Devil.[71] Rupert combined these two traditional strands in a unique way, so that following the initiation of conflict in heaven (Book I) the Word of God, first through His chosen people and then in His own flesh, had to fight off the attack of seven successive historical empires or kings: Egypt (Book II), the kings of

69. The passage shows how Rupert expected his fellow monks to read this book: ". . . ita rudis fuisti, ut putares de te solo inter partes tam contrarias eiusmodi certamen haberi? Immo et de toto genere humano certamen hoc fuit ab initio. . . . De hoc certamine ego tibi efflagitanti nuper scripsi opusculum libellorum duodecim intitulatum De uictoria Verbi Dei. . . . Certamen istud uetus est et pro omnibus certatum est et adhuc pro singulis certatur et in omnibus uel pro omnibus electis suis uincit Deus." *Matt.* 12: CM 29.388.

70. *Spir.* 6.14: CM 24.2027–29; *Apoc.* 7: PL 169.1039–64 (this, written two or three years earlier, was the real foundation for the exposition in *Vict.*). There is a very useful overview of Rupert's scheme in Haacke's introduction, xxvi–xxviii. Cf. Rupert's own summaries in *Vict.* 1.6, 3.10, 4.1, 8.23: ed. Haacke 12, 95, 118–19, 266–67.

71. Jerome, *In Dan.* 2: CC 75A.838–43; Haimo, PL 117.1082. Cf. Bede (PL 93.166) and Autpertus (CM 27.447).

(northern) Israel (Books IV–V), the Babylonians (Book VI), the Persians (Books VII–VIII), the Greeks (Books IX–X), the Romans (Books XI–XII), and the Antichrist (Book XIII). In each case particular saints (kings, judges, prophets, martyrs, etc.) rose up to defend God's cause, some of them figures otherwise rather neglected such as Esther (Book VIII) and the Maccabees (Books IX–X), since they especially, as he noted again, were the original occasion for this work.[72]

In the battle, as Rupert recounts it, the dynamic lies to some degree with the aggressor, the seven-headed dragon; but Rupert's driving theme throughout is the repeated and ultimate victory of God's predestined plan of salvation, for which the unifying image (*summa praesentis opusculi*) is the woman in labor and under attack,[73] figuring either Mary or the Church giving birth to her victorious Son.[74] Evocative as this image was, it did not in and of itself answer Cuno's original question completely. To defend the divine necessity of these bloody battles, and thus their usefulness even for monastic *lectio diuina*, Rupert applied his notion of predestination very concretely to sacred history. From the very beginning God had a plan (*propositum*) whereby those whom He had called He would also save and exalt (Rom. 8:29–30) by way of the Son's incarnation and victory.[75] The Devil sought to frustrate God's plan in general and Christ's incarnation in particular by destroying the chosen line from which He was to be born—hence the Egyptian slavery, the Babylonian exile, the wars of the Maccabees, Slaughter of the Innocents,

72. *Vict.* 9.2: ed. Haacke 278.

73. *Vict.* 9.28: ed. Haacke 305. Cf. *Vict.* 3.11: 96–97.

74. "Hic iam nomen mulieris duplicem sensum habet. Antequam esset beata uirgo Maria, ante (inquam) et longe prius erat mulier quam in sacramento sentimus, idest ecclesia, et utique praegnans mulier mente grauida gerens uerbum promissionis." *Vict.* 12.1: ed. Haacke 373. Cf. *Vict.* 2.16: 64. Rupert referred to this image already in *Off.* 2.2: CM 7.34–35, but first offered the present exposition in *Spir.* 6.14: CM 24.2027–29.

75. *Vict.* 1.1: ed. Haacke 5–6, and applied as assurance to all elect readers: *Vict.* 13.15: 420–21. Cf. also *Vict.* 2.32, 3.21, 8.32, 11.3: 83, 107–08, 275, 343.

and so forth.[76] Rupert managed thus to give all Old Testament history a clear and concrete christocentric focus, while also making all those bloody battles (always a potential embarrassment to Christians and especially to monks) an essential part of God's plan for redemption. For instance, he found new grounds for interpreting the twenty-four elders as figures of the Old Testament judges, since their reigns and battles manifestly served to preserve the chosen line from which the victorious Word was to be born.[77]

To describe this running confrontation and the Word's ultimate victory over the Devil, Rupert resolved not to investigate in this work the mysteries or allegories of Christ hidden in the text of Holy Scripture but rather to concentrate upon His deeds understood and reconstructed as a story or narrative (*hystoriam texere*).[78] Here is that same lively sense of history we have noted so often before, which stemmed in good part from Rupert's concern to locate the traumatic "present" in the grand scheme of salvation-history. The same basic image of dragon and woman was first employed in Rupert's early poem, where the dragon clearly was Henry IV. Still in 1123 he and Cuno were discussing the appropriateness of "beasts" to figure all worldly kingdoms. Yet Rupert also declared that Christ's victory over Satan's sixth head, bloody Rome, constituted no direct threat to the Roman Empire as such, and he was content to repeat his familiar scheme: the apostles broke with the Jews, the martyrs suffered under the emperors, the confessors repelled false brothers, and finally—somewhat anachronistically—the Nicene Council established the rule of Christian faith.[79] Rupert knew the argument, based on II Thess. 2:17, that the Roman Empire (the sixth head) would survive until the coming of Antichrist (the

76. One clear example to stand for all others: "Et idcirco quidquid in eundem populum agebat per Pharaonem et seruos eius, in illum Filium recte refertur, cuius originem carnis praecidere festinabat, ne nasceretur." *Vict.* 3.17: ed. Haacke 104.

77. *Vict.* 4.7: ed. Haacke 126. Cf. *Apoc.* 3: PL 169.907–09.

78. *Vict.* 3.1, 15: ed. Haacke 85, 101.

79. *Vict.* 12.1–9, 13.3–8: ed. Haacke 373–81, 406–13.

seventh head), and basically he accepted it; but identifying Rome with the sixth head of the dragon, something borne out more than once in his own experience, effectively robbed that notion of any apologetic value. In fact he warned against idle speculation on this subject.[80]

Rupert's *De uictoria Verbi Dei* was an early and remarkable product of the new twelfth-century fascination with salvation-history. Both in concept and in execution it went dramatically beyond St. Augustine's *City of God* as well as contemporary works of a more traditional orientation such as Franco of Afflighem's *De gratia Dei*. Yet it manifested nothing of that self-consciousness about methodology evident in Hugh of St. Victor's salvation-historical approach to theology.[81] It was the work of a Black Monk and a reformer, whence its biblical and ecclesiological orientations, and to that extent it must be distinguished from the work of imperial apologists such as the Cistercian imperial bishop Otto of Freising. As the inhabitant himself of two important imperial bishoprics, Rupert recalled royal coronations favorably, prayed for the kings under whom he lived, and may even have considered, like Sigebert, that royal anointing conferred an "irremovable" sign.[82] But kings and emperors had virtually no positive role to play in Rupert's vision of the Church and of salvation-history. The Roman Empire receives mention almost exclusively in connection with past persecutions; other worldly kingdoms are specified as agents of the Devil, whose persecutions God has used for his own purposes.[83] Royal power meant the cruel subjugation of peoples, a drunken quest for ever more land, incessant warmongering, and a lust for power sparing not even of the royal family[84]—a reference probably to Henry V's rebellion in 1105–06 which Rupert

80. *Vict.* 13.12–13: ed. Haacke 416–18.
81. See J. Ehlers, *Hugo von St. Viktor* (Frankfurter Historische Abhandlungen 7, Wiesbaden 1973) passim; and Classen (n. 67 above) 406–07.
82. *Off.* 4.13: CM 7.122; *Levit.* 1.35: CM 22.847; *Gen.* 4.9: CM 21.293.
83. *Spir.* 6.14: CM 24.2028; *Exod.* 2.37: CM 22.686.
84. *Apoc.* 10: PL 169.1131, 1133, 1139, 1141; *John* 11: CM 9.621, 662; *Reg.* 1.27: CM 22.1235–36.

would have followed very closely in Liège. Kings converted to Christianity cannot kill and consider such shedding of blood a form of Christian service.[85] Earthly kingdoms arc in fact ever-failing and uncertain; Christ's victory has already begun to be realized.[86] The victory over these various heads of the dragon is therefore assured, but secure only within the religious life.

There is still another genre to which Rupert's work deserves comparison, however, and that is the epic literature or *chansons de geste* which flourished among the secular aristocracy. Monks, especially Black Monks, were not isolated from the manners and mores of the warriors who supported and protected them and for whom they were expected to pray. Particularly as an abbot administering his monastery's incomes and attending the archbishop's court, Rupert would regularly have encountered the entertainments of those courts, including presumably the minstrels. Not only prince-bishops but abbots too sometimes patronized vernacular poets.[87] In any case, Rupert's *De uictoria Verbi Dei* read wonderfully well as a biblical epic written for the entertainment and edification of monks engaged in their own religious strife who identified with the preservation and victories of a particular "chosen lineage." Rupert even used the language appropriate to such an epic. In his account of the Maccabees, he referred twice to their "*res gestas*," which may be taken over from reading Roman history as a schoolboy but also recalls the "gestes" of famous knights.[88] Before setting out to "narrate the victory," he introduced the two antagonists (*primum ipsas demonstrare nitimur personas uictoris atque uicti*).[89] Book I then described the beginning of their combat in heaven (*initium duelli, principium certamimis, exordium inimicitiarum*),[90] and Book II the battle site (the earth) and its chief object (man).[91] With the decla-

85. *Apoc.* 8: PL 169.1083.

86. *Vict.* 6.16, 8.28: ed. Haacke 200, 272; see Rauh, *Antichrist* 206–26.

87. E. Faral, *Les jongleurs en France au moyen âge* (Paris 1910) 25–60.

88. *Vict.* 9.29, 10.8: ed. Haacke 306, 320.

89. *Vict.* 1.3: ed. Haacke 8.

90. *Vict.* 1.7, 9: ed. Haacke 13, 16.

91. "Quid longius morer? Positus est locus certaminis, et factus est homo, legitima possessio Dei et causa totius certaminis." *Vict.* 2.5: ed. Haacke 51.

ration of enmity between the woman and the snake in Gen. 3:15, the gauntlet was flung down: "here began the books of the wars of the Lord!" Indeed, Rupert declares the whole of Scripture to be the "books of the wars of the Lord."[92] Precedent for this phrase can be found in Origen's *Homilies on Judges*,[93] but no other medieval author transformed it into the central theme of Holy Scripture, and none dared reverse Origen's allegory so as to make the wars literally and materially necessary to the history of salvation. So also the words "duel," "conflict," and "victory" resound throughout Rupert's work. It was a stroke of literary and spiritual genius to recount the religious warfare of Christ, His Church, and His devoted monks in terms familiar from the prevailing social and literary milieu, particularly in view of the decidedly aristocratic makeup of most medieval monasteries.

Secular knights were trained and privileged to bear the material sword. Likewise, reversing the allegorization of Israelite warfare which had prevailed since Origen, Rupert held that Old Testament saints had legitimately wielded bloody swords in order to protect and preserve the chosen line from which Christ the Victor was to come.[94] But what could this possibly have to do with the religious warfare of monks? During the reform era a major discussion began on those enigmatic biblical verses regarding the "two swords" (Luke 22:38, 49–51), a discussion which culminated a generation or two later in the application of this figure to Church and state.[95] Rupert had in fact treated this

92. *Vict.* 2.18: ed. Haacke 66.

93. *Homiliae in libro Judicum* 6.2: ed. W. A. Baehrens (Griechische christliche Schriftsteller 30, 1921) 500. See G. Caspary, *Politics and Exegesis: Origen and the Two Swords* (Berkeley 1979) 18–39, esp. 19 n. 28.

94. *Vict.* 12.19: ed. Haacke 392; cf. *Vict.* 4.8: 127. This first suggested in *Spir.* 6.13: CM 24.2026, and *Apoc.* 7: PL 169.1051. But Rupert did not justify all battles: *Vict.* 4.13: ed. Haacke 132–33.

95. On the "two swords," see W. Levisohn, "Die mittelalterliche Lehre von den beiden Schwerten," *DA* 9 (1952) 14–42; H. Hoffmann, "Die beiden Schwerter im hohem Mittelalter," *DA* 20 (1964) 78–114; A. Stickler, "Il 'gladius' negli atti dei concili e dei RR. pontefici sino a Graziano e Bernardo di Clairvaux," *Salesianum* 13 (1951) 414–45, and numerous other articles by

text in earlier works,[96] but he devoted a whole chapter to it in his biblical epic where its relevance was manifest.

Interweaving once again the old and the new, Rupert maintained traditional views of the spiritual sword, views going all the way back to Origen,[97] but he enriched and sharpened them, first with his unprecedented defense of Israelite warfare at a particular time in the history of salvation. The incarnation then ushered in a new dispensation in which the Word Himself, which is to say, the preaching of the Word (see Eph. 6:17, Hebr. 4:12), became the Church's chief weapon[98] (together, it might be said, with the other spiritual powers of coercion, above all excommunication, but Rupert assumed rather than dwelt on those). Rupert presupposed and enjoined again the strict ban on clerical use of the material sword.[99] His identification of the spiritual sword with the Word was also traditional, but it received here a new emphasis. Rupert saw the vigorous wielding of this sword—that is, preaching, teaching, and meditating upon the Word—as the chief means to reform unworthy and indifferent priests and prelates.[100]

Rupert was not a proto-mendicant, but he was a Black Monk and not a White one. Those who wielded this sword best and most courageously were, in his view, the religious who cast off all secular cares and duties in order to devote themselves wholly to learning and teaching the Word.[101] Thus Rupert's un-

Stickler conveniently summarized by Y. Congar, *L'église de saint Augustin à l'époque moderne* (Paris 1970) 142–45.

96. *John* 13: CM 9.717; *Levit.* 1.36: CM 22.849–50; *Apoc.* 2: PL 169.884.

97. Essential now is Caspary (n. 93 above), who noted Rupert's interpretation specifically on pp. 99 n. 149 and 188.

98. ". . . [the apostles] contenti meliori gladio qui iam uenerat, qui iam datus est, quod est ipsum Verbum Dei." *Vict.* 4.8: ed. Haacke 127. The good angels had used this weapon already in heaven: *Vict.* 1.16: 24.

99. *Proph.* 2: PL 168.477–78; *Matt.* 3: CM 29.94.

100. "Praedicando pugnauerunt. . . . Tota itaque pugna caelestis, tota uictoria spiritualis est." *Spir.* 6.15: CM 24.2029. Cf. *Vict.* 13.5: ed. Haacke 409.

101. *Vict.* 12.19: ed. Haacke 392. Cf. *Spir.* 6.13: CM 24.2026–27; *Apoc.* 7: PL 169.1051; *John* 13: CM 9.718.

derstanding of the sword as the Church's right and duty to preach, teach, and inculcate the Word aptly captured the thrust of his reforming ecclesiology, one that was monastic in origin but with a vigorous sense of mission toward the whole Church. In this way the victory of the Word of God would also be made real in the present Church and in the lives of those who read this epic story.

5

The Church and the
Blessed Virgin: *Commentary*
on the Song of Songs

Rupert set out to plant the Church firmly in the course of salvation-history and thus to provide a broader religious perspective on her continuous battles and present troubles. The figure of the persecuted woman in labor (Apoc. 12) served as the unifying ecclesiological image in *De uictoria Verbi Dei*. Early medieval commentators had already identified her with the Church and sometimes with the Blessed Virgin Mary.[102] From early on Rupert had perceived the Virgin as bearing the person of the Church, and in successive works had identified Mary ever more completely with this woman in labor, the figure of the whole Church.[103] In his *Commentary on the Song of Songs*, composed just a year or so after *De uictoria Verbi Dei* (1125), he finally made it explicit in the *first consistently Marian* interpretation of that love song ever to appear in Latin Christendom.

This work, the briefest of his commentaries, attracted considerable attention in his own day, and has again in ours. With more than forty extant manuscripts it was by far his most read, but all those manuscripts originated in the German Empire.[104]

---

102. Bede identified the woman only with the Church: PL 93.165–66. To this Autpertus (CM 27.443ff) and Haimo (mostly an abbreviation of Autpertus) cautiously added an important reference to the Virgin: PL 117.1081.

103. *Spir.* 1.8: CM 24.1829; *Vict.* 12.1: ed. Haacke 373. Cf. n. 74 above.

104. On manuscripts, see R. Haacke's edition: CM 26.xv–lx.

Over the past generation scholarly investigation into medieval commentary on the Song of Songs has made Rupert's contribution clear; indeed, more has been written on this work than on any of his others.[105] Rupert's commentary brought nothing new, however, by way of doctrine. He took a negative stand on the Immaculate Conception, just then coming under discussion, and he avoided the title "mediatrix of graces," employed by several other twelfth-century authors.[106] The novelty which stirred up conservative readers then (chapter IX, part 1) and has captured scholarly interest now sprang rather from his exegetical approach and the ecclesiological accent of his Marian interpretation.

Rupert interpreted the Song of Songs to contain four "recapitulations" of a central theme to which he gave expression in his title, De incarnatione Domini. Already as a young man he had undertaken a work in heroic verse bearing the same title and theme, but the versifying became too burdensome and he abandoned the project.[107] Then early in the 1120's Abbot Cuno asked him to prepare a meditation on this love-song—a great favorite of monks—and apparently was not disappointed with the results (tu tanto libentius legisti). But to break so radically with the received tradition was not an easy matter. Rupert described himself as wrestling with the Word of God to wring out of this song a work which would both celebrate the incarnate Lord and honor the Blessed Virgin. Still christocentric in orientation, as in all his work, Rupert approached the Lord's incarnation here

105. E. Ohly, Hohelied-Studien: Grundzüge einer Geschichte der Hoheliedauslegung des Abendlandes bis um 1200 (Wiesbaden 1958) 121–35, under the title "Der Bruch mit der Tradition"; H. Riedlinger, Die Makellösigkeit der Kirche in den lateinischen Hoheliedkommentaren des Mittelalters (BGPT 38.3, Münster 1958) 208–12; M. Peinador, "El commentario de Rupert de Deutz al Cantar de los Cantares," Marianum 31 (1969) 1–58.

106. M. Peinador, "La actitud negativa de Ruperto ante la Immaculada Concepción," Marianum 30 (1968) 192–217; idem, "La Mariologia de Rupert de Deutz," Ephemerides Mariologicae 17 (1967) 121–48; and H. Graef, Maria: Eine Geschichte der Lehre und Verehrung (Freiburg 1964) 208–09.

107. Cant. prologus: CM 26.6–7.

by way of the Mother of God, the blessed vehicle of the incarnation. In a letter to Bishop Thietmar of Verden (1116–48) and in the commentary itself, Rupert declared he had written this work wholly in meditation upon the Blessed Virgin.[108]

Liturgical usages had prepared the way for a Marian interpretation of the Song of Songs. Readings from the Song were assigned to the feasts for Mary's Assumption (August 15) and Nativity (September 8); monks also read this book in the night office during the month of August.[109] Yet, though various foreshadowings of this interpretation were to be found in Carolingian authors, it was Honorius Augustodunensis in the first decade of the twelfth century who first drew all the elements together in his *Sigillum*.[110] But it was one thing to write a treatise honoring the Blessed Virgin which drew upon selected verses of the Song hallowed by liturgical usage; it was quite another to interpret the entire Song with reference to Mary. Even Honorius, when he wrote a commentary many years later, stopped short of doing that, and the Venerable Bede, largely under the influence of St. Augustine, at one point had specifically rejected such a Marian interpretation.[111] So also St. Bernard ten years later, despite his veneration of the Virgin, avoided any such Marian interpretation in his influential *Sermons on the Song of Songs*. To be sure, ever since the time of the Fathers particular verses were referred to her; but in general the spouse was understood either as an individual Christian soul or as the Church, the collective body of the faithful, in dialogue and spiritual communion with Christ—and these two, obviously, were not mutually exclusive. Rupert knew very well that his interpretation was novel; he claimed later that he had not sought to contradict the

108. CM 26.4. Since the abbey church at Deutz was dedicated to the Virgin, the likelihood is very great that Rupert studied a painted or sculptured image (*in contemplatione faciei*) while preparing his meditation.

109. See J. Beumer, "Die marianische Deutung des Hohen Liedes in der Frühscholastik," *Zeitschrift für katholische Theologie* 76 (1954) 411–39.

110. PL 172. 495–518. See V. I. J. Flint, "The Commentaries of Honorius Augustodunensis on the Song of Songs," *RB* 84 (1974) 196–204.

111. PL 91.1206. See Ohly (n. 105 above) 69–70.

tradition but rather to "add a little something" to what the Fathers had already said.[112]

Rupert spoke directly to his exegetical difficulties at the end of the prologue. To set forth the Marian meaning of each verse he had first to lay a firm foundation in the historical sense. But the "historical" sense of this book meant for Rupert the events in the Gospel which pertained to Mary's role as the Mother of God.[113] This he justified on grounds that just as all Scripture tends toward Christ the Word, so also all prophecy converges upon Mary, the bearer of that Word.[114] For roughly each verse of the Song, therefore, Rupert found a corresponding verse in the New Testament (chiefly from St. Luke's Gospel). Thus the "kiss" of Cant. 1:1 prophesies or corresponds to the Annunciation (Luke 1:28) and the "breasts better than wine" to the Holy Spirit in His twofold "*data*" which "overshadowed" the Blessed Virgin at the conception of Christ (Luke 1:35). Each of the "*uoces*" of the Song had in this way specific reference to Mary, a difficult exegetical undertaking indeed (*Labor magnus et difficilis*), but one Rupert carried off with an ingenuity which clearly delighted Cuno, and many of his contemporaries as well, to judge from the number of extant manuscripts.[115] Rupert understood the Song's dialogue to take place between Mary and her Son and, as a Black Monk devoted to the performance of the divine office, conceived of it as a kind of play. As Mary, bearing for her pregnancy the scorn of her adversaries, pondering the ways of her Son, suffering through His rejection and death, yearning for His presence after His ascension, and humbly turning away

112. ". . . sicut aliquid supererogatum ultra lectionem ipsorum, adundando et congregando uoces tam magni tamque diffusi corporis ecclesiae in unam animam singularis et unicae dilectae Christi Mariae." *Glor.* 7.13: PL 169.155.

113. On the question of how monks read this love song and what they understood to be its literal and historical meanings, see J. Leclercq, *Monks and Love in the Twelfth Century* (Oxford 1979) 29–40.

114. *Cant.* 1, 4: CM 26.12–13, 147.

115. Rupert's scheme is laid out clearly in R. Haacke's introduction (CM 26.xii–xiii) and Peinador (n. 105 above) 19–39. Cuno's reaction in CM 7.3.

from the honors bestowed upon her, the "*sponsa*" of the Song comes alive in his commentary.

Rupert's devotional understanding of the Blessed Virgin's role in the history of salvation was essentially traditional, and strikingly similar in intent to a nearly contemporary (ca. 1140) mosaic in S. Maria Trastevere in Rome, where the lower panels depict various scenes from Mary's life and the apse's upper zone presents the Blessed Virgin crowned and enthroned on Christ's right, holding a book with verses from the Song of Songs.[116] But he also understood the Virgin to embody and give voice to the Church (see n. 112 above). This too had earlier precedents, most clearly in the Carolingian author Paschasius Radbertus, but Rupert was apparently the first to work out the implications fully.[117]

Whatever this world receives in the way of virtues, graces, or celestial operations are sent from the Blessed Virgin, through whose gifts the Church, diffused throughout the world, is made one.[118] Therefore Mary's "*ecclesia nostra*" is also the "*universa terra*."[119] Though rejected by her own people she now has churches throughout the gentile world—including Deutz—

116. On this mosaic, see G. B. Ladner, *Die Papstbildnisse des Altertums und des Mittelalters* 2 (Vatican City 1970) 9–16, Pl. 1–2.

117. "De hac [Mary] specialiter dictum sit in Canticis, quamuis generaliter de ecclesia significatum intelligamus. Nimirum quia quidquid in speciali narratur affamine, totum expressius monstratum signatur in genere." *Matt.* 2.1: PL 120.106. Rupert almost certainly knew both this and the sermon in Paul the Deacon's *Homiliary* for the feast of the Assumption where it says: "Quod licet et de uniuersali ecclesia possit accipi, conuenientius tamen specialiter huic potest Virgini coaptari" (PL 95.1568). An excellent survey of the sources by H. Barré, "Marie et l'Eglise du Vénérable Bède à Saint Albert le Grand," in *Marie et l'Eglise* (Etudes Mariales 9, Paris 1951) 1.59–125; and H. Coathalem, *Le parallelisme entre la sainte vierge et l'église dans la tradition latine jusqu' à la fin du XIIᵉ siècle* (Analecta Gregoriana 74, Rome 1954); cf. H. de Lubac, *Méditation sur l'Eglise* (3rd ed. Paris 1954) 273–329. Specifically on Rupert, see M. Peinador, "Maria y la iglesia en la historia de la salvación según Ruperto de Deutz," *Ephemerides Mariologicae* 18 (1968) 337–81.

118. *Cant.* 4: CM 26.88–89.

119. *Cant.* 2: CM 26.49.

which rely upon her protection and intercession. Indeed, preachers, priests, martyrs, and all true servants of Christ are brought forth out of her womb, so that apostles and prelates are her "domestics."[120] The Church will endure, like her womb, inviolate and will continue to serve as the gate of heaven until the end of time, when, like the Church, Mary's motherhood and royal status will be brought to perfection in the heavenly Jerusalem[121] (think of the last book of the *Commentary on Apocalypse*). Already in this life, however, she is crowned, for the evil kingdoms (again compared to beasts)[122] once converted will bow down before her as the queen over her Son's Kingdom.[123] Rupert also depicts Mary as the leader of the apostles: the Gospel truth they preached was first taught and confirmed to them by her; it was she who rendered the decisions in the apostolic councils and through her preaching brought divergent opinions into unity.[124] Rupert drew out still further the implicit parallel between the incarnated and the written Word and concluded that the Gospel had its origins in Mary. She is, in brief, the "*secretarium omnium Scripturarum sanctarum.*"[125] Though she yearned to be with her Spouse, she was left behind specifically in order to testify to His deeds, teaching His doctrine and serving as a bulwark of truth against heresy in His absence.[126]

Rupert completed his depiction of Mary as the spiritual embodiment of the Church with one last great parallel to his ecclesiological views: it is she who wields the spiritual sword persistently and unwaveringly, her Beloved having taken the material sword away from her.[127] She stands thus in the midst

120. *Cant.* 1, 7: CM 26.22, 35, 158–59.

121. *Cant.* 1, 6: CM 26.35, 139.

122. *Cant.* 4: CM 26.93 (image of the seven-headed dragon).

123. *Cant.* 3: CM 26.79. This is in comment upon Cant. 4:8, one of the texts written on the scroll Mary carries in the mosaic of S. Maria Trastevere! Cf. Rupert's comment on Cant. 8:3, the other text in the mosaic (CM 26.160).

124. *Cant.* 1, 3: CM 26.24, 74.

125. *Cant.* 4: CM 26.89. Cf. CM 26.115–16, 156.

126. *Cant.* 1, 4, 5, 7: CM 26.24, 28, 95, 104, 112, 117, 163. This partly echoes the antiphon "Gaude Maria."

127. *Cant.* 3, 7: CM 26.63–65, 164.

of all preachers as the effecter of virtue and the mistress of holy religion. In her chastity and freedom from avarice—the two vices against which Rupert and the reformers fought and preached so hard—she is a perfect mirror to all churches.[128] But Mary also gave preeminent expression to the contemplative life. She turned away from the cares of the world in order to reflect only upon the ways of her Son, that is, to meditate upon the Word, and she expects those friends and servants who are powerful in the world to support her contemplative vocation so that they too may benefit therefrom.[129] So also her humility is a constant inspiration, and her longing for her absent Spouse and Son captures the innermost desire of all true contemplatives for communion with their Lord.[130] To ascribe to the Blessed Virgin all the virtues of the contemplative life as Rupert envisioned it was not unusual. But this Black Monk and reformer perceived Mary also to embody all the virtues necessary for the active life, at least those deemed important for the reform of the Church: the bearing of the spiritual sword, the preaching and teaching of the Word, chastity, honesty in all tasks, and decisive intervention in behalf of the truth.

The reform movement focused Christian thought upon the nature and the task of the Church to a degree unprecedented in the early middle ages. The reformers insisted that salvation and grace were to be found only in and through the true Roman (reformed) Church. But institutions generally are too amorphous, too impersonal, and much too evidently human to become wholly satisfying objects of devotion as such. In this setting there arose a rapid and very significant expansion of Marian devotion during the early twelfth century. She becomes the embodiment and personal presence of the true Church, the mediatrix or channel of grace, as St. Bernard would say. None of Rupert's phrases were to be as influential, but they were all equally significant from this perspective: she is the source of the Gospel and of doctrinal truth, the font of all virtue and grace, a

128. *Cant.* 1, 4, 5, 6: CM 26.11–12, 17, 87, 103, 106, 147.
129. *Cant.* 3, 4, 5, 6: CM 26.73, 88–89, 106–07, 134–35.
130. *Cant.* 1, 5: CM 26.30–31, 113.

steady bulwark to preachers and saints. In the Blessed Virgin the reformers saw all they sought to realize in the new Church, and in his *Commentary on the Song of Songs* Rupert set forth all the virtues to be ascribed to the Blessed Virgin.

Rupert's ecclesiology contains much that is old and also much that is new, a notable combination of the Black Monk and the reformer. There was indeed nothing new about using the books of Leviticus, the Song of Songs, and the Apocalypse to speak of the Church; but to each Rupert brought a distinctive interpretation meaningful ultimately only in the context of the reform movement. Then too Augustine and especially Gregory the Great had already labeled preaching an important virtue of the good prelate; but Rupert seized upon it as the chief instrument for reform. Likewise, Origen had identified the preaching and understanding of the Word as the wielding of the spiritual sword; but Rupert so emphasized this perception of the sword in the context of reform as to make it very close to the chief purpose and goal of his own works. Or yet again, the pattern of sacred history from Adam and Abraham down to the martyrs and confessors had become thoroughly familiar during the early middle ages; but Rupert lent it a concreteness and sense of direction which led by implication right down to the religious and ecclesiastical struggles of the present. And, finally, to conceive of the battle for reform in essentially spiritual rather than institutional terms, and thus effectively to place monks in the vanguard of the movement, was in fact to retain the religious world-order of the early middle ages. But this vision of Black Monks removed from the cares and corruption of the world while also involved in teaching and guiding the whole Church met ever stiffening opposition from new monks and canons alike, forcing Rupert to defend the form of religious life to which he had been committed since childhood.

VIII

Defender
of the Black
Monks

℟UPERT ENTERED the abbey of St. Lawrence at a time (ca. 1082) when Black Monks still enjoyed essentially unquestioned respect from clergy and laity alike. In his lifetime, however, new monks and regular canons rose up on every hand to challenge the Benedictines' once exclusive representation of the communal religious life.[1] Right outside Rupert's monastery, in the forests atop the Public-Mount, a certain Goderranus established a hermitage (1080–90) which attracted several followers; around 1115 he transformed it into a house of canons regular (St. Gilles), probably the second such house in the diocese.[2]

1. G. Morin, "Rainaud l'Ermite et Ives de Chartres: un épisode de la crise du cénobitisme au XIᵉ–XIIᵉ siècle," *RB* 40 (1928) 99–115; C. Dereine, "Odon de Tournai et la crise du cénobitisme au XIᵉ siècle," *Revue du Moyen Age Latin* 4 (1948) 134–54; J. Leclercq, "La crise du monachisme aux XIᵉ et XIIᵉ siècles," *Bullettino dell'Istituto Storico Italiano per il Medio Evo* 70 (1958) 19–41; N. Cantor, "The Crisis of Western Monasticism," *American Historical Review* 66 (1960) 47–67; M.-D. Chenu, "Moines, clercs, laics au carrefour de la vie évangélique (XIIᵉ siècle)," in his *Théologie* 225–51. Good overviews by B. Lackner, *The Eleventh-Century Background of Cîteaux* (Cistercian Studies 8, Washington, D.C. 1972), and L. K. Little, *Religious Poverty and the Profit Economy in Medieval Europe* (Ithaca 1978) 59–112.
2. See H. Silvestre, "Goderan, le fondateur de l'abbaye liégeoise de St. Gilles, était-il un jongleur provençal?" *RHE* 55 (1960) 122–29; C. Dereine,

While still in Liège (1109–19), Rupert argued both in person and on parchment against various critics, and when the confrontation with White Monks and canons regular heated up all across Christendom in the 1120's, Abbot Rupert wrote several letters and treatises in defense of traditional Benedictine life—all of which deserve more attention than they have thus far received.[3] Scholars have cited Rupert on these matters, to be sure, but most often as author of the *Dialogus quae sit uita uere apostolica*,[4] a treatise he did not in fact write.[5] After describing his general views, this chapter will examine the circumstances of his various pamphlets and then analyze his differences with the new monks and the canons regular.

1

The Religious Life

Reared from childhood in a monastery, Rupert knew no other life than that of a Black Monk. Benedictine monasticism came to him as something given, its basic constitution established centuries earlier by Benedict and its superiority as the only sure way of salvation grounded in Holy Scripture. Reform certainly was possible and sometimes necessary—that he had experienced in Liège and heard about at Deutz—but a funda-

---

Les chanoines réguliers au diocèse de Liège avant St. Norbert (Brussels 1952) 121–37; *Monasticon Belge* 2.3 (Liège 1955) 301–06.

3. The only exceptions are J. Semmler, *Die Klosterreform von Siegburg* (Bonn 1959) 270–73, 314–15, 356–63; Beinert, *Kirche* 294–301; and C. W. Bynum, *Docere verbo et exemplo: An Aspect of Twelfth-Century Spirituality* (Harvard Theological Studies 31, 1979) 123–24.

4. Thus A. Mouraux, "La 'vie apostolique' à-propos de Rupert de Deutz," *Revue liturgique et monastique* 21 (1935–36) 71–78, 125–41, 264–76; Chenu (n. 1 above) 227–28; and, for instance, D. Lapsanski, *Perfectio evangelica* (Munich 1974) 5–7.

5. Ever since Gerberon (1669), no historian with a good knowledge of Rupert's work has maintained the attribution to him, which goes back entirely to a suggestion by E. Martène, reprinted by J. P. Migne. The best recent review of the issue is by M. O. Garriques, "A qui faut-il attribuer le *De uita uere apostolica*?" *Le Moyen Age* 79 (1973) 421–47, who ascribed it, quite persuasively, to Honorius, and in *RHE* 70 (1975) 421 dated it to the late 1120's.

mental reconsideration of monasticism's very structure and purpose seemed unthinkable. Practiced for centuries, the way of penitential piety nourished by constant prayer in choir and daily intercession at the altar was plain. Consequently Rupert took up questions of structure and practice only in self-defense. It was not the form of religious life as such but rather the fervor and commitment of individual religious which required constant renewal, and it was to this end that he devoted his biblical commentaries, his own reforming use of the spiritual sword. In one sense, therefore, all his works spoke to the nature and quality of religious life. But he rarely attempted to summarize or to systematize that which had shaped the whole of his conscious life.[6]

Even if they obey all the commandments, those who marry, who possess and use the things of this world, can hope only to avoid punishment; they cannot merit grace, since they do only what is required, whereas to receive grace creatures must do something more (*supra adicere*): they must commit themselves wholly in love to seeking the vision of God.[7] To open the way toward that vision, the counsels of perfection demand, initially, a series of negative steps. First, monks are to forsake all fleshly bonds, of both marriage and kindred. Rupert had aimed considerable invective at concubinage among the clergy but said little about chastity among monks. For them familial bonds proved a greater obstacle. Because monks were pledged to poverty and had normally little expectation of high office, parents sometimes resisted the "loss" of their children to the cloister—a problem Rupert addressed more than once.[8] Enthusiasm for the religious life nevertheless remained high in Rupert's day, even in traditional Benedictine houses. The harvest is plenty, he noted, but the workers, those who can "safely" be charged with the care of lesser brothers, are "very few."[9]

Religious were also to forsake all worldly goods. Not that

6. There is no work as such on Rupert's spirituality, but see J. Huijben, "L'école bénédictine," *La Vie Spirituelle*, supplement 59 (1939) 116–26; and J. Leclercq, *La spiritualité du moyen âge* (Paris 1961) 213–15.

7. *Spir.* 5.16: CM 24.1996.

8. *Spir.* 5.21: CM 24.2001–03; *Matt.* 7: CM 29.220–21.

9. *Matt.* 8: CM 29.239.

such goods were evil in and of themselves: it is "permitted" to provide necessities for home and family, but this is dangerous (*Haec uia periculosa est*), for what begins as necessity easily can become the service of mammon.[10] Rupert fully embraced the ideal of voluntary religious poverty, and preached at length to those religious who were "too anxious about the source of their food and clothing."[11] But the enthusiasm for total poverty which swept across Christendom in Rupert's lifetime touched him hardly at all. He fully expected that the wealth of kings and princes, including the "incomes of cities and villages," would be made over to monks in return for their spiritual intercession.[12] This he considered a biblical principle; most often, especially in the 1120's, he cited Ps. 103(104):16–17: the birds can safely make their nests in the cedars of Lebanon, which is to say, those who soar aloft in contemplation can expect to have their material necessities provided.[13] Rupert never questioned this; he only insisted—at nearly every available opportunity—that in return for such material gifts monks faithfully carry out their spiritual service.[14]

For Rupert and most Black Monks, "poverty" referred much more to obedience, their voluntary assumption of a humbled status in this world.[15] Religious men and women were by definition the "poor" (*pauperes*) because they had voluntarily renounced personal use of and command over the goods of this world. Thus the "poor" merged almost indistinguishably with the "poor in spirit," the humbled and the mild-mannered (*humilis, mitis*), for with their property most had also given up that

10. *Matt.* 6: CM 29.180.

11. Ibid. 177–91.

12. *RegBen.* 3.11: PL 170.519–20; *Matt.* 2: CM 29.40; *Spir.* 9.17: CM 24.2118–19.

13. *Herib.* 12: ed. Dinter 52–53; *RegBen.* 3.7: PL 170.515; *Cant.* 4: CM 26.88; *Matt.* 6: CM 29.181. Rupert adopted this interpretation from St. Augustine, *Enar. Ps.* 103, *Sermo* 3.16–17: CC 40.1513–15, and especially Cassiodorus, *In Ps. 103* 16–17: CC 98.932–33.

14. *Herib.* 12: ed. Dinter 53–54.

15. See M. L. Arduini, "Il problema della *paupertas* nella *Vita sancti Heriberti archiepiscopi Coloniensis* di Ruperto di Deutz," *Studi Medievali* 3rd ser. 20 (1979) 106–07, 109.

arrogance of power which often took haughty and cruel expression. Like St. Benedict, Rupert frequently listed humility and gentleness or mercy as the chief virtues of the religious life, in contrast to the pride and cruelty especially evident among aristocrats who were also the monasteries' major benefactors and therefore the chief objects of the monks' prayers.[16] In sum, without wholly losing sight of religious poverty, Rupert together with most other Black Monks placed far greater emphasis upon being "poor in spirit" than upon being absolutely "poor" in material goods.

The ascetic rigor characteristic of those pledged to strict material poverty was also foreign to his spirit. Cuno commented that he saw Rupert practice none of those fasts and vigils the holy fathers had needed to reach his level of scriptural illumination, and once even called him an "Epicurean."[17] A man who admitted to corpulence, something confirmed by Anselm of Havelberg,[18] Rupert regarded the religious life as penitential in its essence (whence, he noted, the appropriateness of the Benedictines' black garb).[19] He certainly practiced fasts and other prescribed devotional exercises, but spiritual forms of penance remained uppermost in his mind. This meant, for instance, frequent confession as well as the exercise of mutual censure among the brothers.[20] Above all it meant constancy in performance of the divine office and in meditation upon Holy Scripture. Rupert spoke movingly of the way in which chant opened one's heart to receive the grace of the Holy Spirit, much more indeed through the singing even than the simple reading of Scripture.[21] Yet in making explicit what was always more or less

16. *Off.* 8.6–7: CM 7.275–78; *John* 2: CM 9.72–73; *Spir.* 8.3: CM 24.2075–77; *Matt.* 4: CM 29.106. See L. K. Little, "Pride Goes before Avarice: Social Change and the Vices in Latin Christendom," *American Historical Review* 76 (1971) 16–49. But avarice among the clergy was of great concern to Rupert too.

17. *Matt.* 12: CM 29.366.

18. *RegBen.* 1: PL 170.479; PL 188.1120.

19. *Spir.* 8.1–3: CM 24.2074–77; *RegBen.* 3.13: PL 170.520–22.

20. *Levit.* 2.40–45: CM 22.905–13; *Spir.* 8.20–21: CM 24.2097–2100.

21. "Non dubito plerosque esse, qui huius rei experimentum quantulumcumque assecuti sint et secundum illud exemplum nonnumquam persenserint

implicit in Benedictine life, Rupert added something new. As he put it in the prologue to his first work, monks should go beyond the mere doing of the office—though that was meritorious in itself—and come to a "prophetic" understanding, an *inward experience*, of the mysteries, the images and works of God known from Scripture and the office. This required not only a better understanding of the office and of Scripture, something Rupert believed himself called to provide in his innovative, "more useful" commentaries, but also greater intensity and personal commitment on the part of Black Monks, something he pleaded for throughout his works. The point of comparison once again is the secular aristocracy: he exhorted his monastic readers, who, he said, now showed less prudence, vigilance, and desire in their vocation than did secular folk in pursuit of temporal goods and earthly well-being, to rouse themselves (*excitemur*) to imitate (*exemplo illorum*) their zeal—redirected, however, toward seeking God and eternal well-being.[22]

What then were the personal qualities of this more intense Benedictine life? Rupert provided a systematic exposition in his interpretation of the Sermon on the Mount, which is in fact a brief treatise on the religious life. Recognizing that this sermon had been treated before—he probably meant St. Augustine's commentary—Rupert claimed to add (*superaddere*) only a little of his own.[23] To the Beatitudes he added Old Testament precedents, which, he said, established their divine authority. He next reviewed the high calling of those gifted with a spiritual understanding of Scripture, who must serve their fellow Chris-

---

in auditu siue decantatione laudis, siue orationis bene et morose cum musico modulamine sonantis, quod ipsorum uiscera concuteret impetus Spiritus sancti, inundans affectus diuinae inspirationis, uis magna sanctae compunctionis. Fit denique nescio qua naturae ui, ut multo amplius afficiar audiendo sublimiter canentem ecclesiae chorum cum multitudine sonorum . . . quam si simplicem eiusdem orationis litteraturam . . . legam uel audiam." *Matt.* 5: CM 29.156. Rupert's entire discussion (pp. 154–59) is rooted in his experience as a choirmonk.

22. *Spir.* 8.21: CM 24.2100.
23. *Matt.* 4–7: CM 29.104–207, esp. 106, 123.

tians as "salt of the earth" and the "light of the world." Then he divided Christ's sermon into four parts corresponding to the four principal virtues (justice, temperance, fortitude, and prudence), which the pagans had already known but not in their full heavenly dimensions.

The first division (Matt. 5:20–48) treats justice or righteousness under the guideline of Christ's declarations: "I came not to destroy the law but to fulfill it," and "Be ye perfect even as your Father in heaven." Rupert understood Christ to have transformed six different parts of the law into "counsels necessary for the religious seeking perfection."[24] Rather than kill, for instance, they are to dwell together in faith and brotherly love; as an example of difficulty or disunity Rupert discussed at length the simoniac brother who turns a house of prayer into a den of thieves and hates implacably those brothers who reproach his avarice.[25] The religious must also "work to maintain chastity" and must preach it, but not in such a way as to cause adultery, that is, division and hardship among the legitimately married. Religious are likewise forbidden to swear oaths: this, Rupert explains, requires that they free themselves from all secular affairs since oaths are necessary in worldly business.[26] Religious, in the fifth place, may not seek vengeance in order to do justice, but rather should suffer evil if necessary and should seek only to live the contemplative life in peace. Finally, they must all seek to dwell together in perfect charity.

Next Rupert turned to temperance (Matt. 6:1–34), and this he subdivided into three parts: religious must refrain from vainglory or self-righteousness, from excessive eating and drinking, and from avarice or undue concern about the morrow—all of these, it might be said, familiar monastic vices which Rupert here confronted squarely. In the spirit of the text "Do not your justice before men to be seen of them" (Matt. 6:1), Rupert attacked hypocrisy in alms-giving, which most Benedictines had institutionalized in the form of hospices or almonries at the gate (Rupert was soon to found one himself), and hypocrisy or

24. See his own summary in *Matt.* 5: CM 29.136–37.
25. *Matt.* 4: CM 29.133–34.
26. *Matt.* 5: CM 29.140–42.

vainglory in the magnificent prayers which had become the distinctive mark of Benedictine houses. Rupert ardently defended the Benedictine choir, but he emphasized the need for sincerity and spiritual attentiveness in prayer. Then he took up fasting, and with Christ Himself he attacked those who made a great public show of their asceticism. Rupert saw it much more as a religious exercise prescribed by the Church and as a call for moderation in food and drink, especially on the part of religious. Finally, Rupert attacked those hypocritical religious who, despite entering the cloister, continued to be concerned about their incomes, their clothing, and numerous other worldly affairs.

Rupert treated the virtues of fortitude (Matt. 7:6–14) and prudence (Matt. 7:15–27) much more briefly. Fortitude means largely perseverance, especially perseverance in seeking the spiritual sense of Scripture, that which true contemplatives were always to be doing and from which they were not to be deterred either by the difficulty of the letter or the "envy" of others. Prudence, lastly, involves the ability to discern and the strength to resist all those false leaders who will eventually be found out by their evil fruits. Rupert intimates here (and elsewhere) that enemies lurk all around seeking to betray the true religious. Just as Rupert's commentary on certain chapters of the Benedictine *Rule* was to be the first in almost three centuries, so also his exposition of the religious life by way of the Sermon on the Mount had few if any precedents in the tenth and eleventh centuries. Personal rather than structural renewal was his aim, from his first commentary to his last. But many of Rupert's contemporaries were calling for a much more profound reform of Benedictine monasticism.

2

Disputes over the Religious Life

In concluding his commentary on the Mass, about 1110, Rupert vigorously defended the luxurious appointments of altars and churches. The critics he had in mind presumably were advocates of the new poverty.[27] Rupert's defense at several points in *De diuinis officiis* of monastic usages against those of canons may reflect not only the numerous collegiate churches in Liège but also the foundation of new houses of canons regular at Flône (ca. 1090) and Rolduc (1104).[28] However Rupert had learned of their critique, he now mustered a variety of arguments in behalf of the splendid Benedictine celebration of the office. The sacrosanct ministry of the altar is called *missa*, "mass," he began, because it is the "only effective and pleasing envoy sent to resolve the enmity between God and man," and even though its spiritual rationale is "splendid" enough, whatever may be done to adorn its external cult is all the more laudable. For the gold, silver, and precious stones which are signs of ambition among lay folk—again the parallel to the aristocracy—constitute in ecclesiastical and divine matters the dutiful service of piety. Rupert conceded that the poor ought also to be fed and that in cases of necessity crude and barren altars would suffice. But on the strength of the Lord's anointing with precious oil just before His passion and His rebuke to the apostles who disapproved of this "waste," Rupert concluded that where the opportunity and the riches were present the Lord had "commanded" works of gold and silver be prepared by the "finest craftsmen," lest—here revealing much about what was expected of the Benedictine office—the Lord's table be despised for its lack of splendor. He further argued that Old Testament descriptions of the tabernacle and temple still had a literal import, and to sustain this point he took on (*nec statim illud nobis obicitur*) by name Jerome, Gregory, and Leo, who had offered only moralizing or spiritualizing interpretations.

27. *Off.* 2.23: CM 7.56–60. For this new poverty and its critique of Benedictine luxury, see Lackner (n. 1 above) passim, and M. Mollat, ed., *Etudes sur l'histoire de la pauvreté* (Paris 1974).

28. See esp. *Off.* 1.10: CM 7.10–12. Flône shared with St. Lawrence the partial possession of at least two parochial churches (Incourt, Haneffe). See Dereine (n. 2 above) 106–20, 169–217. The customary followed at Rolduc has been edited by S. Weinfurter, *Consuetudines Canonicorum Regularium: Springirsbacenses-Rodenses* (CM 48, 1978).

Still at Liège, sometime therefore between his ordination (ca. 1108) and his departure (1119), Rupert also wrote a separate treatise, now unfortunately lost, on one of the more controverted problems of his day, transition from one order to another.[29] According to Reiner, Rupert refuted the arguments of someone who defended his right to leave a monastery and join the secular clergy.[30] Around the year 1108 a canon of the cathedral chapter in Utrecht named Ellenhard secretly joined a strict house ("monastery") of canons regular in the archdiocese of Trier, doubtless Springiersbach which had attracted converts from all around, including five canons from Utrecht and four from Liège. Ellenhard took vows under the stricter Augustinian *Rule* (*ordo nouus*), but then grew weary of this monastic asceticism and sought to return to the cathedral chapter at Utrecht, on grounds he had never received permission from his ordinary bishop to leave. The chapter was divided and sought advice from several nearby cathedral chapters.[31] The response from Liège, the most detailed and interesting, was probably written by Alger, who argued from canon law that one could not justifiably renounce vows or move from a higher to a lower form of religious life. This issue aroused so much discussion that Reimbald, another canon in the cathedral chapter, composed a separate

29. On this problem in general, see K. Fina, "*Ovem suam requirere:* Eine Studie zur Geschichte des Ordenswechsels im 12. Jahrhundert," *Augustiniana* 7 (1957) 33–56; and for its canonistic aspects, P. Hofmeister, "Der Übertritt in eine andere religiöse Genossenschaft," *Archiv für katholisches Kirchenrecht* 108 (1928) 419–81. See n. 39 below.

30. Reiner, *De ineptiis* 1: MGH SS 20.595.

31. Dereine (n. 2 above) 94–97. The documentation is edited in P. Jaffé, *Bibliotheca rerum germanicarum* 5.366–82, and more completely in S. Muller and A. C. Bouman, *Oorkondenboek van het Sticht Utrecht tot 1301* (Utrecht 1920) 1.237ff. Springiersbach was not founded until 1107 (Weinfurter [n. 28 above] vi), Ellenhard sought to return sometime after two full years (*transactis duobus annis*) at the abbey, and the canons at Utrecht sought and received advice while Rodulphus (1101–12) was still provost. Given, too, that Ellenhard seems not to have understood fully what he was getting into, a date nearer the house's foundation makes good sense; this then places the exchange of letters and subsequent discussion at about 1111.

treatise, which included an exchange of letters with Wazelinus of St. Lawrence, Rupert's former student.[32]

In his *Commentary on John* Rupert seems also to refer to Ellenhard's case, or at least to one very much like it. People have been criticizing zealous leaders (Richard of Springiersbach?) who go about recruiting (four from Liège), bind their converts with vows, rule them with undue severity (the *ordo nouus?*) so as eventually to drive them away, and thus render them even more damnable than before. Rupert cited the authority of Christ Himself for casting the net widely in order to take in both good and bad, the latter of which cannot be blamed upon prelates. Indeed, Christ Himself chose at least one evil follower; should human prelates be expected to do better?[33] Whatever incident had elicited this passage and his lost pamphlet, Rupert's stand diverged hardly at all from that of the cathedral chapter in Liège (Alger's): men and women may always choose to follow a higher and stricter (*arctior*) form of life but never the reverse. To judge from Reiner's notice, Rupert probably argued this point with an interpretation of Noah's ark.[34] It is possible, moreover, that the "*Epistola ad L.*," once ascribed to Rupert but now to Wazelinus, either excerpts from or paraphrases Rupert's lost work.[35]

While still in Liège Rupert argued a similar point with Bishop John of Thérouanne, who was the most vigorous promoter of the canons regular in all of Flanders, first at Arras as a canon of St.

32. G. Demeester, "Note sur le canoniste Alger de Liège," in *Fédération archéologique et historique de Belgique, Congrès de Bruges* (1903) 451–58. Dereine (n. 2 above) 96–97 mistakenly confused this official letter (Jaffé [n. 31 above] 373–79) with that composed later by Reimbald: *Stromata seu de uoto reddendo*: CM 4.39–116.

33. *John* 7: CM 9.376–77.

34. Cf. *Gen.* 4.18: CM 21.303 (written about 1112/13, but without polemic). See also Beinert, *Kirche* 256–58.

35. R. Vander Plaetse, "Notities betreffende Wazelinus, abt van Saint-Laurent," *Sacris Erudiri* 24 (1980) 245–64, has a critical edition of the *Epistola*, pp. 254–64. Many of its arguments and some of its language (as noted by Vander Plaetse) are very "Rupertian," and elsewhere Wazelinus drew upon Rupert's argument on lapsed clergy and penance in his letters to Reimbald: CM 4.92–94, 97–101.

Eligius and then at Thérouanne as bishop (1099–1130).[36] Just where and under what circumstances Rupert met and debated Bishop John is unknown; but as with Bishop William, Rupert, though still a little-known monk, showed no fear of debating a renowned religious leader and a bishop closely tied to the reformed papacy. As Rupert recounts it, a canon regular had left to join a monastery. On the authority of canon law, the *Rule* of St. Benedict, the structure of Noah's ark, and all manner of arguments Rupert held that this was and always would be permissible. John, who even as bishop maintained the habit and discipline of a canon regular, was manifestly displeased to have his new form of the religious life referred to as lower (*inferior*) and less strict (*latior, laxior*). Moreover, the *Constitutions* he followed explicitly forbade transit to another (monastic) order without extraordinary permission.[37] And so, Rupert says, Bishop John found it very hard to concede the point, meaning, doubtless, he never conceded it at all.

The first treatise Rupert wrote at Cologne was to become his best known by far, the *Altercatio monachi et clerici quod liceat monacho praedicare.* With fifteen extant manuscripts, this little dialogue ranks in fact among the most widely read of all these religious disputes,[38] for outside St. Bernard's *Apologia* and perhaps Peter the Venerable's *Letter 28* most never gained wide distribution. But Rupert's *Altercatio* instructed and entertained, among others, monks and canons throughout Bavaria (doubtless by way of Cuno), the monks of St. Denis at Paris, and the Premonstratensian canons of Belval and Bonne Espérance. The dispute moves briskly, in language still close to colloquial Latin and often sharp in tone. The chief issue was the right of monks to preach and teach publicly in the Church; the argument turned on

---

36. *RegBen.* 4.13: PL 170.536–37. The identification was first made by Dereine (n. 2 above) 99. See the contemporary *Vita* of Bishop John in MGH SS 15, 2.1140–45, and on the foundation at Arras, L. Milis, *L'ordre des chanoines réguliers d'Arrouaise* (Bruges 1969), with his edition of the *Constitutiones canonicorum regularium ordinis Arroasiensis* (CM 20, 1970).

37. *Constitutiones* (n. 36 above) 200: CM 20.183.

38. PL 170.537–42; R. Haacke, *DA* 26 (1970) 539–40.

a widely quoted text from Jerome to the effect that monks had the task of penitential weeping, not teaching.

Such evidence as there is suggests the *Altercatio* was based on an actual debate, but the identity of Rupert's clerical adversary and the circumstances of their dispute cannot be determined with complete certainty. In the 1150's Philip of Harvengt, the Premonstratensian abbot of Bonne Espérance, refuted Rupert's *Altercatio* at length in his own *De institutione clericorum*. Philip referred distinctly to such a debate, and reported that the monk had transcribed this dispute and manipulated its outcome so as to make himself the victor.[39] This cleric whom Philip "knew so well" was probably Norbert of Xanten. A twelfth-century manuscript from Ottobeuron (now Clm 27129) bears the title *Conflictus Ruodperti Coloniensis abbatis . . . cum Noperto clerico, si liceat monacho praedicare an non.*[40] For reasons given presently, the *Altercatio* should be dated to Rupert's early years in Cologne (1119 to about 1122), and Norbert in fact visited Cologne in 1121 and again in 1122.[41] Moreover, Rupert once criticized Norbert's too rapid promotion to the priesthood and his vigorous exercise of the preacher's office.[42] Might this have provoked

39. *De continentia* [*De institutione clericorum*] 103: PL 203.807. See Douglas Roby, "Philip of Harvengt's Contribution to the Question of Passage from One Religious Order to Another," *Analecta Praemonstratensia* 49 (1973) 69–100; and N. J. Weyns, "A propos des Instructions pour les clercs (*De institutione Clericorum*) de Philippe de Harvengt," *Analecta Praemonstratensia* 53 (1977) 71–79. On Philip, see N. J. Weyns, in *Nationaal Biografische Woordenboek* 4 (Brussels 1970) 329–40; and the earlier work of G. P. Sijon, in *Analecta Praemonstratensia* 14 (1938) 37–52 and 15 (1939) 129–66. It is quite possible that the copy of Rupert's work Philip consulted still exists: Mons, Bibl. Munic. 46/220, Catalogue no. 286 (12th c., from Bonne Espérance).

40. *Catalogus codicum manuscriptorum bibliothecae regiae monacensis* (Munich 1881; repr. 1969) 4.4.246–47. See G. Constable, *Monastic Tithes from Their Origins to the Twelfth Century* (Cambridge 1964) 173–74, and idem (n. 94 below) 567.

41. *Epistola Roduphi*: MGH SS 10.330–31; *Vita Norberti A* 12: MGH SS 12.681–82. See C. Dereine, "Les origines de Prémontré," *RHE* 42 (1947) 352–78; G. Niemeyer, "Die Vitae Godefridi Cappenbergensis," *DA* 23 (1967) 423–25.

42. *RegBen.* 1: PL 170.492.

Norbert into an attack on Abbot Rupert's right to teach and preach?[43] However that may be, there is a complication. An early manuscript from Huysburg bears the title *Disputatio Rodberti abbatis contra Willehelmum diaconum*, and a sixteenth-century copy the title *Altercatio Ruperti monachi contra Timundum clericum*.[44] I could discover no clue to the possible identity of a Deacon William or a Timundus, but these manuscripts cannot be dismissed lightly, and so the identification with Norbert must remain tentative.

Next, Abbot Eberhard of Brauweiler (1110–26) consulted with Abbot Rupert as to whether he could assign monks to parish churches belonging to his monastery.[45] In his response Rupert referred to the *Altercatio* as finished and gone, but he did not mention his commentary on the *Rule*, written in 1125; this dates his letter to about 1123–24 and the *Altercatio* to 1119–22. Rupert's letter notes the clerics' age-old attack upon the monks' right to exercise the cure of souls, and offers a pithy summary of all the themes taken up below in his dispute with the canons regular. The same issue was hotly contested in Bavaria as well, where Endres discovered a *Quaestio* on the subject ascribed to Rupert and elaborated upon by Honorius.[46] As bishop of Regensburg (1126–32) Cuno could well have brought Rupert's opinion with him or requested it at a later time. In any case, the position taken is exactly Rupert's, that is, a strong affirmation of

43. See the remarks on the "self-defensive" character of Rupert's position in Bynum (n. 3 above) 139 n. 35.

44. London, British Library MS Add. 10957, fol. 158; see the description in R. Haacke's edition of *Vict.*, xli–xlii. Wolfenbüttel, MS Extravagantes 264.37, fol. 55ᵛ; see H. Butzmann, *Kataloge der Herzog August Bibliothek Wolfenbüttel: Die mittelalterlichen Handschriften der Gruppen Extravagantes, novi, und novissimi* (Frankfurt 1972) 123.

45. Rupert's letter is preserved in the *Chronicon Brunwylrense*, ed. G. Eckertz, in *Annalen des historischen Vereins für den Niederrhein* 17 (1866) 138–39, and reprinted in PL 170.541–44.

46. The manuscript originated in Windberg (now Clm 22225); see J. Endres, *Honorius Augustodunensis* (Munich 1906) 145–47 (*Ruodbertus, Questio utrum monachis liceat predicare*), 147–50 (*Honorius, Quod liceat monachis predicare*). See Bynum (n. 3 above) 109 n. 10.

the monks' right to exercise pastoral care, and therefore this *Quaestio*, however it originated, is probably authentic.

Rupert's last and most extensive work in defense of Benedictine monasticism is his *Commentary on the Benedictine Rule*, which should be dated to the year 1125 (chapter VI, n. 55). Consultation of the only complete twelfth-century manuscript (British Library, Add. 10957) is helpful in determining its original appearance and composition.[47] In both the twelfth- and sixteenth-century manuscripts, the commentary is preceded by an *Epistola Roberti* [or: *Ruperti*] *abbatis ad Cunonem*, that is, a prefatory letter such as Rupert used to introduce nearly all his works.[48] There Rupert explains he had consented to write this "little but useful work on certain chapters of the *Rule* disputed by other monks" only because Cuno demanded it of him (*petis atque instanter exegis*). About a year earlier he had addressed his monks in conference on the office of matins, and Cuno, greatly taken with his spiritual explanation, had insisted he write it down. Although this seems not to have involved one of the disputed questions, Rupert nevertheless had resisted for a long time, and in his very next sentence he broadly hinted at the reason. Let that person in whose sight we stand and in whose ears we speak know, Rupert says, that we "assent to do this with no little trepidation" for there is an "invisible auditor who is to be feared lest what we say not totally please him." That "invisible auditor" was none other than Archbishop Frederick, who about 1121 had brought the first Cistercian foundation into the Empire and then the first house of Augustinian canons into his archdiocese. Abbot Cuno plainly was annoyed and no little concerned. Hence he began to pressure Rupert, from around 1124 at least, to write something against the self-righteous claims of these two new orders. Rupert finally agreed in 1125, but first he made sure that the archbishop, who had appointed him and re-

47. This manuscript, which belonged to Huysburg, may be the one used by Abbot Egbert of Huysburg (see below, n. 119). A sixteenth-century copy now at Wolfenbüttel (n. 44 above), fols. 1^r–55^r, has the same form.

48. PL 170.477–80 includes the letter, which runs through "*Quid est illud*," but does not set it off as such with a separate rubric.

mained both his temporal and spiritual lord, knew full well who it was that had put him up to this.[49] And since Cuno had successfully forced these controversial matters upon him, Rupert first made his patron and friend listen to several matters that were troubling him, namely, his various theological controversies.

Rupert's work is divided in manuscript as follows: Book I, containing the account of his theological battles, bears the appropriate title *Liber primus Rodberti abbatis de apollogeticis suis*; Book II, containing chiefly the conference Rupert once gave on matins, has the title *Incipit secundus de ordine uigilarium nocturnarum dominice noctis*; and the present Books III and IV, the polemic Cuno actually wanted from Rupert, are separated from the foregoing with an "*Explicit liber Rodberti abbatis de apologeticis suis*" and described as, *Incipit eiusdem de eo quod altaris officium precellat opus manuum* [=Book III], *et quod abbatibus non prepositis liceat baculos portare sicut episcopis, et quod monachi ordinati sint etiam clerici* [=Book IV].[50] The manuscript, in other words, makes clear that this work comprises three different elements: Rupert's apologia, his spiritual conference, and his dispute with the new religious. The lumping together of Books III and IV need not be considered decisive, for a manuscript now in Vienna (Nationalbibliothek 2235) contains just the fourth book, the dispute with the Augustinian canons, which must have been perceived and possibly even separated out as a distinct unit.

3

Ministry at the Altar:
Rupert against the New Monks

In January 1122 Archbishop Frederick of Cologne issued a charter founding the first Cistercian abbey in the German Empire at a site named Camp (near present-day Kamp–Lintfort). Both Frederick's charter and a later chronicle state plainly that

49. "Proinde si quem scribendo haec offendero, tibi [Cuno] totum imputet quiscumque fuerit, siue iuste siue non iuste offensus ille sit." PL 170.479.
50. On microfilm I cannot read the folio numbers.

the initiative lay with the archbishop, who made his request of a native cleric named Arnulf who had become the first abbot of Morimond. In response, Arnulf sent his brother Henry, who served as abbot (1122–37), together with the required twelve monks. They reportedly stayed in the archepiscopal palace until a suitable site could be found for their "new monastery." Frederick's founding charter speaks of "grafting branches of this new plant" into his diocese so that he might find rest in their spiritual shade, and refers to these monks as "preserving rightly the Benedictine *Rule*."[51] He understood and appreciated their reforming claims. It is little wonder that Abbot Cuno felt distinctly threatened. In the event, Camp was to prove an amazingly successful foundation, responsible for the spread of Cistercian houses all across northern and eastern Germany (fourteen male houses, twenty-four female houses, and fifty "granddaughter" houses). But Cuno and Rupert were successful too: Archbishop Frederick still chose to be buried, a few years later (1131), at Siegburg.

Just what connections developed between the new monks at Camp and the powerful abbot of Siegburg is not known in detail, but Rupert referred indignantly to their efforts, apparently successful (*multis didicimus experimentis*), to recruit certain "simple brothers" from among established houses for their new and stricter way of life. Particularly at Siegburg (*tu melius nosti*), this occurred more than once when White Monks visited there, something both Cuno and Rupert considered a serious and subversive breach of monastic hospitality.[52] These White Monks for

51. See the *Chronicon monasterii Campensis*, ed. H. Keussen, in *Annalen des historischen Vereins für den Niederrhein* 20 (1867) 263–64, and T. J. Lacomblet, *Urkundenbuch für die Geschichte des Neiderrheins* (Düsseldorf 1840; repr. 1966) 1.194. Cf. M. Dicks, *Die Abtei Camp am Niederrhein* (Kempen 1913) 31. On Camp, see also J. M. Canivez, in *Dictionnaire d'histoire et de géographie ecclésiastique* 11 (Paris 1949) 618–23; K. Spahr, in *Lexikon für Theologie und Kirche* 2 (Freiburg 1958) 906; and Semmler (n. 3 above) 355–56. Historians have sought to make Arnulf a relative of the archbishop, but "our mother" clearly is the church at Cologne and "*lactatus*" refers to the training Arnulf received there.

52. *RegBen.* 3.1: PL 170.511.

their part charged the Benedictines with scandalizing young and zealous monks, who, as Rupert put it, soon came to discover that monks were still men, that vessels thought to be of gold and silver could crumble and melt into the mere lead of jealousy, anger, and worse. Rupert agreed that those who so scandalize the young are worthy of condemnation, but he judged it an even greater and more dangerous scandal when young monks are encouraged to break their original vows of stability in order to pursue an elusive vision of a stricter life—something he had evidently witnessed (*quod experimento didicimus*). For, Rupert pointed out, however religious these new monks might be, they too were still mere men, and he cited biblical texts warning against false prophets who led men ultimately to destruction.[53] Rupert respected their zeal and holiness, but he resented their assertive self-righteousness. The adversary he had in mind at several points in Book III (*tu dicis, inquis*) was probably Abbot Henry, brother to the first abbot of Morimond.

The new monks prided themselves on their strict adherence to the *Rule* of St. Benedict: Rupert called them "scrupulous investigators (*studiosos scrutatores*) of the *Rule*."[54] They radically cut back all accretions to the divine office, the heart of Benedictine monastic life, and insisted that that office be performed exactly as the Blessed Benedict had prescribed. Noting that differences of this kind had occasioned his work, Rupert took up one such question near the end of Book II: that of when to cease singing the "alleluia" in psalms and responses (at Lent or Septuagesima). It struck Benedictines, including Peter Abelard, as presumptuous to break with established "Roman" usage. Rupert observed, correctly, that Benedict might not yet have known later "Gregorian" usage, admonished the new monks not to be such enthusiastic admirers (*incauti adulatores*) of one saint as to dissent from the entire tradition on his authority alone, and

53. *RegBen.* 3.14–15: PL 170.522–23.
54. *RegBen.* 2.13: PL 170.509. See in general Lackner (n. 1 above) 239–53; idem, "Friends and Critics of Early Cîteaux," *Analecta Cisterciensia* 34 (1978) 17–26; and Little (n. 1 above) 91–92.

reinterpreted Benedict to make him conform to the received usage.[55] For the rest, Rupert concluded, their liturgical usages differed inconsequentially from his own, a conclusion that suggests he knew less about them in 1125 than did several slightly later Benedictine polemicists. This may explain why these remarks were appended to Book II, his spiritual conference on matins, over which there was also as yet little hint of controversy.

The new monks were just as zealously committed to religious poverty as to the pure observance of the *Rule*.[56] Rupert had no quarrel with that but warned against taking false pride in their coarse habits. In perhaps the earliest extant record of the white Cistercian habit, he suggested that they had chosen to wear this odd, off-white color (undyed wool) simply to set themselves apart from generations of monks and nuns who had worn penitential black, and that, had the others worn white, they would probably now wear black.[57] Likewise, their literal insistence on two tunics and two cowls for each monk went contrary to Benedict's own prescription that abbots should decide these matters for particular regions. After all, Adam and Eve (*tunicas pelliceas*: Gen. 3:21) and even Benedict himself (*uestitum pellibus*) had worn woolen garments, as had some of the desert fathers.[58] The same applied to breeches worn under the habit. Benedict did not mention them because they were not then worn in Italy (and still were not in Rupert's own day, as he had discovered to his embarrassment during a recent trip to Rome). Monks had adopted them to cover their shamefulness

---

55. *RegBen.* 2.13–15: PL 170.508–12. See B. Lackner, "The Liturgy of Early Cîteaux," in *Studies in Medieval Cistercian History* (Spencer, Mass. 1971) 18–19; and C. Waddell, "Peter Abelard's *Letter 10* and Cistercian Liturgical Reform," in *Studies in Medieval Cistercian History II*, ed. J. R. Sommerfeldt (Cistercian Studies Series 24, Kalamazoo 1976) 82.

56. *RegBen.* 3.13: PL 170.520. Lackner (n. 1 above) 268–75; Little (n. 1 above) 92–96.

57. The next notice would be Peter the Venerable's (ca. 1128) in his *Epist.* 28: ed. Constable 57; see Constable's commentary, 2.116, and see also the sermon probably by Abelard (n. 82 below, 227–28).

58. *RegBen.* 3.16: PL 170.523–24. Gregory, *Dialogi* 2.6.8.

while walking and riding outside the monastery or while eating and sleeping inside; monk-priests in particular should always wear them while serving at the altar.[59]

The new monks' zeal for the letter of the *Rule* and for religious poverty came together in their emphasis upon manual labor as an integral part of the monastic life. This was the heart of the difference between them, as Rupert saw it, and it was to this issue that he devoted most of Book III (*de eo quod altaris officium precellat opus manuum*). Rupert's argument was not tightly constructed, probably reflecting still the give and take of oral disputes. For purposes of clarity the points at issue may be distinguished as three: the right interpretation of St. Benedict's prescription regarding manual labor; the relative role of the priesthood in monastic life and Benedict's failure to say more about it; and the right of monks, especially monk-priests, to live off the tithes and oblations owing to the service of the altar. Rupert concluded with his own summary: his purpose was not to impugn their religious poverty nor to excuse idleness, but rather to defend the service of the altar and the Work of God as higher occupations.[60]

There are those now, he began, who go about recruiting from traditional houses with the claim that monks "can be saved only if they do manual labor as St. Benedict prescribed," and that "only those who live from the labor of their own hands have attained apostolic perfection."[61] Rupert had met zealots of the new "apostolic" poverty already in Liège. He thought highly of Bishop John of Thérouanne (*religioso et uenerabili uiro*), and noted favorably those canons who chose today to live the common life.[62] He even conceded, somewhat grudgingly, that religious could, like St. Paul who worked at Corinth and the apostles who continued to fish, choose without culpability (*culpa non est*) to practice legitimate crafts and to live from the

59. *RegBen.* 3.17: PL 170.524–26.
60. *RegBen.* 3.13: PL 170.520.
61. *RegBen.* 3.2, 4: PL 170.511, 513.
62. *RegBen.* 4.13: PL 170.536.

labor of their own hands.[63] He probably had in mind the canons regular at Rolduc and Springiersbach, who placed great emphasis on manual labor as *necessary* for all true religious.[64] But now, because Benedict said so little about the celebration of mass, these new monks too "placed almost all their hope in the labor of their hands." They actually neglected the priestly office in order to spend time cutting down trees and gathering the harvest![65]

This interpretation of Benedict's *Rule* Rupert considered wholly wrongheaded. One must distinguish those commands truly necessary for salvation from others "permitted" because of local and finite necessity—a distinction Rupert had first developed to separate the "permitted" Jewish law (especially cultic law) from the immutable will of God.[66] St. Benedict had foreseen labor in the fields (c. 41) only in cases of particular necessity (c. 48) and desired that such labor be restricted to the monastery so that monks would have no cause to wander abroad; nonliterate monks could still, for instance, do small crafts inside the walls.[67] As for the notion that manual labor was "apostolic," taken by the White Monks directly from the *Rule* (c. 48), the abbot of Deutz argued to the contrary from Scripture and monastic history. The prince of the apostles declared that it was not fitting for them to abandon the Word in order to serve tables (Acts 6:3); St. Paul firmly upheld his right to live off his ministry (I Cor. 9:4ff), working only once in a case of necessity (the avarice of the Corinthians); and the Blessed Maurus, Benedict's very own disciple, accepted the largesse of kings and princes (this precedent cited again three years later by Peter the Venerable).[68] The new monks also claimed that work was necessary to

63. *John* 14: CM 9.777.

64. See the *Consuetudines* 98: CM 48.53–57, where St. Paul is cited to prove the "necessity" of manual labor for religious.

65. *RegBen*. 3.10: PL 170.517.

66. *RegBen*. 3.4–5: PL 170.513–14. Cf. *Spir*. 5.11: CM 24.1989.

67. *RegBen*. 3.5, 8: PL 170.513, 516.

68. *RegBen*. 3.5, 7: PL 170.514–15, citing Gregory, *Dialogi* 2; cf. Peter's *Epist*. 28: ed. Constable 71, with commentary, 2.118.

avoid idleness (*Rule*, c. 48). Rupert agreed it was useful, but best was, as Christ Himself taught Mary and Martha, to be wholly free to meditate on the Word.[69]

The new monks stressed manual labor at the expense of the divine office. This raised the question Rupert perceived to be at the heart of the matter: whether it was more "apostolic" to be engaged in manual labor and live therefrom or to minister at the altar and receive incomes owing to it.[70] These new monks, Rupert reported with shock, had nearly forgotten they were also priests, principally because Benedict had said so little about celebrating mass.[71] Rupert cited Benedict's lone chapter on the subject (c. 62), but mostly he argued, on the strength of Benedict's famous last chapter (c. 73), that his *Rule* was meant merely for beginners, freshly interpreted by Rupert to mean those training themselves in monastic discipline prior to receiving ordination. To their monastic status they were then to add the priestly, and these two together constituted true apostolic perfection.[72] Indeed, secular priests were more nearly "apostolic" than lay monks! But, Rupert's adversary countered, what then have so many priests to do in a monastery? And he apparently cited the example of the first desert fathers, Paul and Anthony, who were not ordained. Theirs, Rupert answered, were different times, times of persecution and mere survival. But now (*at nunc alius ecclesiae status est*), so many kings and princes have founded monasteries and churches and so many faithful Christian people have brought their oblations and commended themselves to the prayers of monk-priests that the harvest truly is plentiful and the workers few. If monk-priests were to shorten their office and spend several hours a day working in fields, it would wholly disrupt their intercessory duties.[73]

69. *RegBen.* 3.8: PL 170.515–16. Cf. Peter's *Epist.* 28: ed. Constable 70.
70. *RegBen.* 3.4: PL 170.513.
71. *RegBen.* 3.1: PL 170.511.
72. ". . . in his autem qui monachi simul et clerici sunt apostolica perfectio est." *RegBen.* 3.9: PL 170.517.
73. *RegBen.* 3.11–12: PL 170.518–20.

Such a view left little place for lay or illiterate (the terms were synonymous for Rupert) monks. The first task he assigned them, in fact, was to minister to priests at the altar, with gardening and small crafts inside the monastery reserved for any time that might be left over.[74] For almost two centuries, priestly intercession, a function (de officio altaris) requiring both discipline and literacy, had come increasingly to define the role and purpose of monastic life. Nothing, to Rupert's mind, could be more important than the monk-priest's constant service of praise and intercession at the altar.[75] The new monks cut directly against that tradition, putting emphasis instead upon personal ascesis and private meditation leading to personal salvation, and opening up the monastic life to lay brothers who could apply their only skill, usually field work, to the religious life. It is no accident that St. Bernard, for all his manifold influence upon Christian doctrine and devotion, said very little about the eucharist, the chief sacrament of the Church.[76] More than forty years after he had entered the monastery as a child and almost twenty years after he had been ordained, Rupert found wholly incomprehensible the notion that daily prayer in choir and intercession at the altar should be curtailed in order to spend time doing field-work like an illiterate peasant, and he wrote to make sure his own and other monks were not misled by these false notions of the "apostolic life."

Something very concrete was also at issue: the source of the monks' income. Many of the reforming groups, the new monks in particular, rejected all lands and incomes which entailed worldly obligations, including all tithes and oblations requiring

74. *RegBen.* 3.8: PL 170.515–16.

75. Rupert put it thus in his Matthew commentary: ". . . tota quidem illi [Christ] offert ecclesia credens et confitens, quia uere Deus est, et *omnis in eo plenitudo diuinitatis corporaliter inhabitat* (Col. 2:9), maxime autem sanctorum ordo sacerdotum qui propter eum caelibem ducentes uitam semper altari praesto sunt, offerre illi incensum dignum et omne sanctum iugiter exsequi sacri altaris eius ministerium." *Matt.* 2: CM 29.39.

76. This point, which deserves more attention, was noted by Y. Congar, "L'ecclésiologie de S. Bernard," *Analecta Cisterciensia* 9 (1953) 148ff.

intercessory service.[77] Rupert vigorously upheld the monks'
right to receive gifts from wealthy laymen (see above, at nn.
12–14) so long as the monks faithfully carried out their intercession at the altar and remained true to their contemplative vocation. The whole world could be starving, he once argued, and
yet the teachers of the Word would have a right to see their
needs provided for;[78] but his argument presupposed that monk-
priests taught and interceded for others, not just themselves.
Even the most zealous of the new monks, moreover, depended
to some degree upon the gifts and protection of the powerful, so
Rupert managed to dismiss this issue rather easily. But the right
to tithes, which Benedictines often lumped with their other incomes, met a much more formidable challenge in the protests
of the regular and secular canons (below, part 4).

Rupert's arguments against the new monks had no demonstrable influence outside the archdiocese of Cologne. But his
is nevertheless the earliest full-fledged polemic against White
Monks anywhere. At virtually the same time (1125/26), and at
the behest of Rupert's friend and critic William of St. Thierry,
St. Bernard prepared his *Apologia*, a stinging indictment of
Cluniac monasticism.[79] Hugh of Reading soon issued a response,
defending Benedictine monasticism;[80] and Abbot Peter the Venerable independently drew up his own apology for Cluniac monasticism.[81] Soon there was a large polemical literature, includ-

77. *Exordium paruum* 17; and, for instance, Odo at Tournai in Flanders:
Dereine (n. 1 above). The *Libellus de diuersis ordinibus* 3: ed. Constable and
Smith 45–55 describes these new monks accurately, and Peter Abelard rather
nastily (n. 82 below, 225–28).

78. *Matt.* 8: CM 29.239–40, 247–48.

79. *Apologia*, ed. J. Leclercq and H. Rochais 3.63–108. For background
see A. H. Bredero, "Cluny et Cîteaux au XIIᶜ siècle: les origines de la controverse," *Studi Medievali* 3rd ser. 12 (1971) 135–75.

80. A. Wilmart, "Une riposte de l'ancien monachisme au manifeste de
saint Bernard," *RB* 46 (1934) 296–344. On its author, see C. H. Talbot, "The
Date and Author of the 'Riposte,'" in *Petrus Venerabilis, 1156–1956* (Studia Anselmiana 40, Rome 1956) 72–80.

81. *Letter* 28: ed. Constable 1.52–101, with commentary, 2.115–20.

ing a letter and a nasty text by Peter Abelard;[82] but most of it
arose out of local disputes. Rupert's work is of interest on this
score too, for it represented a direct response to the first Cistercian entrance into the Empire. Moreover, by the early 1130's
Benedictines themselves had begun to institute numerous reforms, moving noticeably closer to the Cistercians in many
ways. Much of the argument came then to turn on just how poor
and how isolated monks should be and just how large an office
they should maintain. Rupert by contrast still fully espoused and
defended traditional Benedictine monasticism as the intercession
of monk-priests for the rest of Christian society, the highest and
most important task in Christendom. Yet at the same time, he
sought to reform or to intensify monastic life by helping monk-
priests to understand, and as contemplatives more fully and personally to appropriate, the mysteries of the divine office. That is,
he sought to bring a new sense of awareness and of personal commitment to traditional Benedictine life and practice.

4

The Right to Preach: Rupert
against the Canons Regular

Rupert thought the canons regular posed a far greater challenge to traditional Benedictine life than the new monks.[83] He
knew little still about the Cistercians, but he encountered canons regular all around him. Quite apart from his debate with
Bishop John and his knowledge of Springiersbach, there had

82. *Letter* 10: PL 178.335–40; and see L. J. Engels, "*Adtendite a falsis pro-
phetis*: Un texte de Pierre Abélard contre les Cisterciens retrouvé?" in *Corona
gratiarum: Festschrift E. Dekkers* (Brugge 1975) 2.195–228.

83. On the canons regular, see C. Dereine, "Chanoines," in *Dictionnaire
d'histoire et de géographie ecclésiastique* 12 (Paris 1953) 353–405; S. Weinfurter,
"Neuere Forschungen zu den Regularkanonikern im deutschen Reich des 11.
und 12. Jahrhunderts," *Historische Zeitschrift* 224 (1977) 379–97; Jean Châ-
tillon, "La crise de l'Eglise aux XIe et XIIe siècles et les origines des grandes
fédérations canoniales," *Revue d'histoire de la spiritualité* 53 (1977) 3–45; Bynum
(n. 3 above) passim; and Little (n. 1 above) 87–90, 99–112.

been six houses founded in the diocese of Liège prior to 1119, one of them (St. Gilles) very near and jurisdictionally subject to St. Lawrence.[84] In Cologne he had experienced at least one bitter confrontation with Norbert, who in 1122 founded his second house at Floreffe in the diocese of Liège and that same year helped with a new foundation at Cappenberg outside Cologne.[85] But most important, Archbishop Frederick also lent his support to this movement with a new foundation at Steinfeld. Originally a proprietary convent of Benedictine nuns, now fallen on evil days, the house of Steinfeld, located in the Eifel southwest of Cologne, was obtained by the archbishop, who resolved to found there in 1121 the first house of Augustinian canons in the archdiocese. His language echoed that of the foundation charter for Camp: the canons observed the "apostolic, Augustinian" *Rule*, they were now vigorously active (*pullulantem*) in the modern Church, and Frederick wished to pluck spiritual benefits from this new plant. Richard of Springiersbach played a role in organizing and establishing this house, before it was joined (between 1126 and 1135) to Norbert's Premonstratensian Order.[86] The first provost, Eberwin (1121–ca. 1150), became closely acquainted with St. Bernard: Steinfeld possessed an early copy (still extant) of Bernard's *Apologia*, and Eberwin later asked Bernard to preach against heretics active in Cologne.

Because Rupert's dealings with Augustinian canons were numerous and varied, his comments in Book IV take up a series of problems rather than a single theme. The general setting is the "grievous contention" between canons and monks: the followers of St. Augustine claim to be greater (*maior, altior*) because he was a bishop, and so they not only forbid their people to

84. Dereine (n. 2 above) 105–220.

85. Niemeyer (n. 41 above) 422–25.

86. I. Joester, *Urkundenbuch der Abtei Steinfeld* (Publikationen der Gesellschaft für Rheinische Geschichtskunde 60, Cologne and Bonn 1976) 1–2. See F. Oediger, "Steinfeld: Zur Gründung des ersten Klosters," in *Aus Geschichte und Landeskunde* (Bonn 1960) 37–49; Weinfurter (n. 28 above) ix; and idem, "Reformkanoniker und Reichsepiskopat," *Historisches Jahrbuch* 97/98 (1978) 170–72.

become monks but actually claim that a monk can move up to join them, an unheard-of reversal in the traditional ranking of monks, clerics, and laymen. The new canons were attempting to have it both ways. They were obviously clerics, but a rigorous common life, especially for those following the *ordo nouus* or *ordo monasterii*, gave them the appearance of monks. All this must be dealt with openly and in a spirit of charity, Rupert declares, lest the two groups "come to blows" and one group—he meant those self-righteous new canons—become "puffed up" toward the other.[87]

The first problem (cc. 2–5) had originated lately in northern France and spread into the diocese of Liège. The heads of houses of canons regular had begun to assume the title "abbot" (rather than provost) and to receive staffs at their investment into office. This was particularly alarming to Rupert, for it had now occurred at St. Gilles in Liège. Around 1115, when Rupert was still there, Berengar had carefully arranged that its provosts should be freely elected, then "corporally invested" by the abbot of St. Lawrence, and finally presented by the abbot to the bishop of Liège for consecration.[88] But Bishop Albero I of Liège (1123–28) favored the canons regular—he was later buried at St. Gilles—and granted them many privileges, including the right to have their own "abbots."[89] Archbishop Frederick of Cologne sent a letter of reprimand to his suffragan, instructing him to maintain the good old tradition whereby monks were subject to abbots and clerics to bishops. Just "a few days later" Rupert set to work on the present Book IV, and after quoting

87. *RegBen.* 4.1: PL 170.525–26. J. Leclercq has argued that all "cloistered" groups should be taken together: "La spiritualité des chanoines réguliers," in *La vita comune del clero nei secoli XI e XII* (Milan 1962) 1.117–35; but compare C. W. Bynum, "The Spirituality of Regular Canons in the Twelfth Century: A New Approach," *Medievalia et Humanistica* 4 (1973) 3–24.

88. *Wibaldi Epistola* 395: ed. P. Jaffé, *Bibliotheca rerum germanicarum* 5.527. Dereine (n. 2 above) 121–37; Weinfurter (n. 28 above) xii, and the reference there to an unpublished dissertation, W. Gartner, "Das Chorherrenstift Klosterrath [Rolduc] in der Kanonikerreform des 12. Jahrhunderts" (Cologne).

89. Dereine (n. 2 above) 127ff (St. Gilles), 196 (Rolduc).

his "revered" (*reuerendus*) archbishop (c. 2) he discussed the authority of the abbatial office by way of its insignia.

Only two staffs possessed the authority of the Holy Spirit: that of bishops, which went back to Moses and Aaron, the head of the Old Testament priesthood,[90] and that of abbots, which originatd with Elisha (II Kings 4:29), who Jerome had taught (*Epist.* 58.5) was the biblical father of monasticism. Both staffs conferred the same divine authority over their respective flocks, and they were, Rupert contended, independent of one another. Even before abbots were ordained as they normally are "today," they were already charged with the responsibilities and authority of a pastoral office, though not with the right to preach, something reserved for the priesthood.[91] As proof Rupert cited the first biblical abbot, Elisha, who was not a priest but had charge over a company of prophets (later, Rupert says, called the Essenes), and the abbot Equitius in Gregory's *Dialogi* 1.4. In short, each order in Christendom, of which the first two were monks and clerics, had its own divinely appointed superior[92]— laymen too, though Rupert did not say it here, had kings who carried sceptres—and to confuse the two, to have provosts called abbots and to confer staffs upon them, was simply to controvert the sacred order established by Scripture and tradition. With the archbishop on his side Rupert felt confident this abuse would soon be stopped, but the Customary of Springiersbach, written just after Rupert's polemic, explicitly defended both the abbatial title and the right to bear a staff,[93] and the custom soon spread everywhere.

The most important issue in Rupert's dispute with the canons regular, however, concerned the right of ordained monks to

90. Rupert opines that Moses, the beneficiary of Egyptian wealth and learning, had a curved staff as beautiful as that of modern bishops (*RegBen.* 4.4: PL 170.528)—probably a flattering allusion to Archbishop Frederick's own staff.

91. *RegBen.* 4.10, 12: PL 170.533–35. For background, see R. Bauerreis, "Abtsstab und Bischofsstab," *SMBO* 68 (1957) 215–26.

92. "Ergo utramque . . . eadem auctoritas diuina sacrauit. . . ." *RegBen.* 4.5: PL 170.529.

93. *Consuetudines* 298: CM 48.156–58.

the cure of souls, the incomes attached thereto, and the office of preaching and teaching. Questions of "superiority," "abbots," and manual labor paled, compared to this attempt by canons, both secular and regular, to deny to monks the rights and privileges of the priesthood. From roughly the ninth century on, monks had looked in practice ever more like clerics: large numbers were ordained and many performed pastoral functions in subject churches. This development was never clarified legally. Individual privileges often conceded the right to exercise cure of souls, but conciliar and papal legislation in general continued to oppose it.[94] Indeed, the first Lateran Council had just (1123) reiterated a general prohibition (c. 18). Most religious reformers also disputed Benedictine practice. John of Gualbert (founder of the Vallombrosians), the early Cistercians, the Carthusians, and even the more cloistered groups of canons regular voluntarily rejected both pastoral duties and their attached tithes and oblations as distractions from the contemplative life.[95] Secular canons meanwhile resented ever more deeply monastic involvement in ecclesiastical business and the consequent loss of revenues to monks performing pastoral service. Monks, after all, had voluntarily damned themselves and died to this world; they ought, therefore, to give up secular obligations and return to their cloisters.[96] This challenge troubled Abbot Eberhard of Brauweiler. Siegburg took a positive attitude toward pastoral

94. See U. Berlière, "L'exercice du ministère paroissial par les moines dans le haut moyen-âge" and "L'exercice du ministère paroissial par les moines du XIIe au XVIIe siècle," *RB* 39 (1927) 227–50, 340–64; G. Schreiber, "Gregor VII., Citeaux, Prémontré zu Eigenkirche, Parochie, Seelsorge," *Zeitschrift der Savigny-Stiftung*, Kan. Abt. 34 (1947) 31–171; P. Hofmeister, "Mönchtum und Seelsorge bis zum 13. Jahrhundert," *SMBO* 65 (1953–54) 209–73; Constable (n. 40 above) passim but esp. 136–85; and idem, "The Treatise 'Hortatur nos' and Accompanying Canonical Texts on the Performance of Pastoral Work by Monks," *Speculum Historiale*, ed. Clemens Bauer et al. (Munich 1966) 567–77.

95. Constable (n. 40 above) 137–44, 153–60.

96. See Peter Crassus, *Ad Henricum IV. imperatorem libri VII*: MGH SS 7.672; and especially the canon Thibault d'Etampes, published by R. Foreville and J. Leclercq, "Un débat sur le sacerdoce des moines au XIIe siècle," *Analecta Monastica* IV (Studia Anselmiana 41, Rome 1957) 52, 53.

work, but met resistance from its archbishop and later actually forged charters in his name to assure its right to the *cura animarum*.[97] The abbey of Deutz possessed an extraordinarily large number of parish churches (about forty), but it is not known whether Rupert practiced what he taught by assigning monks to these churches. The parish church at Deutz, subject to the abbey and only a few yards away, was served in Rupert's time by a secular priest named Stephen.[98]

Rupert's argument was for the most part defensive, an attempt to maintain the Black Monks' ancient practice and their right to preach, baptize, say public masses, give absolution, and so forth.[99] Rupert argued that all Christians, not just monks, should have died to this world through baptism, and he cited historical examples of monks active in the Church (Jerome, Gregory).[100] But—most important—he drew a sharp distinction between ordained and unordained monks. Clerical status, Rupert insisted, referred neither to learning nor to tonsure but only and always to service at the altar, that is, to the priestly office.[101] In so far as they both served the altar secular clerics and monks were the same, and therefore shared fully in the same privileges.[102] Rupert had simply formulated rather more sharply a view held by several other contemporary Benedictines for whom traditional Benedictine monasticism also turned on the role and ideal of the monk-priest.[103]

97. Semmler (n. 3 above) 275–81.
98. *Incendio* 5: ed. Grundmann 446.
99. *Epistola*: PL 170.542–43; *Quaestio*: ed. Endres 146.
100. *Alt.*: PL 170.538–39.
101. *RegBen.* 4.8, 10: PL 170.532, 533–34; *Quaestio*: ed. Endres 146; *Epistola*: PL 170.543–44; *Alt.*: PL 170.538–40.
102. "Igitur sicut omnibus presbyteris indifferenter licet missas celebrare, ita omnibus presbyteris cuiuscumque professionis licet predicare et baptizare et cetera ecclesiastici ordinis officia peragere." *Quaestio*: ed. Endres 146. Cf. *Alt.*: PL 170.542; *Epistola*: PL 170.544.
103. Bernold, *Apologeticae rationes contra scismaticorum obiectiones*: MGH LdL 2.98; Ordericus Vitalis, *Hist. eccles.* 8.26: ed. Chibnall 4.315–23; Hugh of Reading, *Dialogi*: ed. Martène-Durand, *Thesaurus novus anecdotorum* 5.972–73. See in general J. Winandy, "Les moines et le sacerdoce," *La Vie Spirituelle* 336 (Jan. 1949) 23–36 and Constable (n. 40 above) 147–48.

Had monks been content to stay inside their cloisters and say mass privately this issue would not have arisen, but their service in parochial churches had made them competitors of the secular clergy. In the only extant administrative document from his reign, Rupert showed a genuine concern for the proper cure of souls, though he rarely alluded to this matter in his commentaries. He was insistent, however, upon the right of monks to receive parochial incomes. He seems not to have distinguished clearly between the oblations of the faithful, which clerics may have resented but could hardly contest, and tithes owing to parish churches "possessed" by monasteries. He refers repeatedly to living from the altar or the Gospel: monk-priests, freed from all secular concerns and pledged to the common life, who continually intercede before God for the people and who minister to them by preaching the spiritual sense of Scripture publicly (*in publica ecclesia*), are workmen worthy of their hire (Luke 10:7) who can expect, as Scripture teaches (I Cor. 9:7–14), to have their material needs provided for.[104] Again and again he stressed that this was only right and proper (*legitime, iure, iusta et antiqua lege*).[105] Though manifestly on the defensive, he yielded nothing; and on this point Black Monks were eventually to prevail, owing to long-established custom, to the undeniable service they rendered in the secular church (as the *Libellus de diuersis ordinibus* also pointed out),[106] and not least to the monastic master who authored the basic textbook in canon law and defended it there.

Of still greater importance to Rupert personally was the right of monks to preach. Rupert's clerical adversary in the *Altercatio* had specifically contested his right to teach and preach publicly. Rupert agreed that only those properly "sent" could preach, but since (drawing upon Rom. 10:15, *Quomodo enim praedicabunt nisi mittantur?*) ordination constituted that sending

104. *Deut.* 1.35: CM 22.1056. Cf. *Reg.* 1.8: CM 22.1210; *John* 4, 5: CM 9.223, 249; *Levit.* 1.38: CM 22.853; *Is.* 2.25: CM 23.1555.
105. *Gen.* 8.25: CM 21.460; *Levit.* 1.34: CM 22.846; *Num.* 1.21: CM 22.941.
106. *Libellus* 2: ed. Constable and Smith 26 (citing arguments and texts remarkably similar to Rupert's).

(*Mitti autem ordinari est*), ordained monks could not be denied the right to preach and teach.[107] Whether or not Rupert preached publicly is not known (see n. 104 above), but certainly his scriptural commentaries, his life's work, represented a form of preaching and teaching. The cleric's challenge in effect threatened his very vocation.

Whatever the circumstances behind the *Altercatio* and whatever general pressures the archdiocese felt against the monastic exercise of pastoral care, another direct challenge inspired Rupert to write the second half of Book IV. An outspoken Augustinian canon had said either to Rupert or in his hearing that clerics might not become monks but monks clerics—an exact reversal, in other words, of the religious world-order which had prevailed for almost five hundred years. The vigor of this Augustinian's critique, his strong animosity to Benedictine monasticism, shocked Rupert (*Res enim noua est*), who had, he said, heard Augustinian canons inveigh against Benedictines before, but never like this person (*non tamen ita uehementer*):[108] he never said a single good thing about the Cluniacs and once compared the rise and fall of the four world-empires, the beasts in the vision recorded in Daniel, to the rise and fall of religious orders— a truly scandalous comparison, in Rupert's view, and in addition an altogether misguided attempt to interpret Scripture (Rupert's own bailiwick).[109] Unfortunately, this zealous Augustinian cannot be identified with absolute certainty. Dereine believed it was Richard of Springiersbach, but Bischoff has now argued for Eberwin of Steinfeld.[110] Rupert provides only two pieces of evidence: his adversary adhered to the much stricter *ordo nouus*, which would apply equally to Richard, Eberwin, and Norbert, and he was a relatively recent convert thereto,[111] which would be

107. *Alt.*: PL 170.541–42; *Epistola*: PL 170.544; *RegBen.* 4.10: PL 170.533–34; *Quaestio*: ed. Endres 146. Cf. already *Off.* 1.12: CM 7.12.

108. *RegBen.* 4.9: PL 170.532.

109. *RegBen.* 4.13: PL 170.535–36.

110. Dereine (n. 2 above) 98. G. Bischoff, "Early Premonstratensian Eschatology: The Apocalyptic Myth," in *The Spirituality of Western Christendom*, ed. E. Rozanne Elder (Kalamazoo 1976) 41–71, esp. 47–50.

111. "Si de austeritate conuersationis quam nouiter assumpsisti auctoritatem assumere uis. . . ." *RegBen.* 4.13: PL 170.536.

true particularly of Eberwin at Steinfeld (1121) and of Norbert at
Prémontré (ca. 1120). Given the personal contact Rupert's language and remarks presuppose and also his purpose in writing
this commentary for Cuno and—indirectly—the archbishop,
Eberwin seems the more likely candidate. Thus, just as the earlier part of his polemic (Book III) was directed at the first Cistercian foundation in the Empire, so the latter part of Book IV addressed the first Augustinian house in the archdiocese.

The Augustinians had turned the tables and claimed for
themselves precisely the place and role Benedictines had traditionally assumed. This Augustinian adversary distinguished the
monastic from the clerical state, as Rupert had, and also argued
that the clerical was clearly superior. Rupert reiterated at greater
length his argument that ordained monks were also clerics
(whence the title in the manuscript: *quod monachi ordinati sint
etiam clerici*), and recalled that both of them had been invested
with the same insignia at ordination.[112] But the canon went on
to vilify the monastic state, thus forcing Rupert to defend something he had always considered quite beyond question. He produced two arguments for the special status of monks: consecrated lay monks were equal to ordained clerics in canon law,
and the former elevation of lay monks to abbatial posts proved
the monastic state as such conferred a special grace—he believed
it a second baptism—which made the care of souls and the bearing of staffs possible.[113] Behind the canon's critique, however,
lay his conviction that Augustinian canons who followed the
strict *ordo nouus* were more regular and austere than Benedictine
monks. For instance, they refused to eat meat at certain times.
Rupert responded that monks too were forbidden to eat meat,
though a council of the Church had permitted the use of animal
fat.[114] But such one-upmanship in ascesis confounded all of
Rupert's traditional categories, and he frankly admitted it. Before canons came to adopt such an austere rule, he explains, he
had used this same argument himself against Bishop John to

112. *RegBen.* 4.6–9: PL 170.529–33.
113. *RegBen.* 4.9, 11: PL 170.533, 534.
114. *RegBen.* 4.13: PL 170.536–37. See *Consuetudines Springirsbacenses* 199:
CM 48.106–08, and Semmler (n. 3 above) 361 n. 63.

prove the superiority of the monastic life. But it is now plain to see that by such an argument a very austere layman could consider himself superior to a cleric.

Rupert understood very well that canons regular who were by definition "clerics" and who also excelled in religious discipline seemed to fit perfectly his own definition of the "apostolic life." His last chapter signaled a partial retreat. He recalled that his Augustinian critic had once used another image much more to his liking than that of the "four beasts": just as the moon waxes and wanes but never wholly disappears, so also religious orders in the Church, through the inspiration of the Holy Spirit, prosper and decline but never wholly fail. Which is to say, the religious life may be more varied in expression and in its historical course than an older generation of Benedictines had ever imagined. Rupert concluded: each is blessed in his own state of life; a simple monk may excel over a monk-priest in certain graces, and a simple priest over a priest-monk, but neither still can equal him who excels in both (n. 109 above). This is not much of a concession, but it does take account of the "simple monk" (probably the austere new monks) and of the "simple priest" who happened also to excel in certain virtues of the religious life (probably the Augustinians). Rupert never for a moment yielded in his conviction that Benedictine monk-priests dedicated to intercession and contemplation represented the highest form of the religious life.[115] But the canons regular, in their claims on the priestly office, in their degree of ascesis, and soon in their preaching and teaching, challenged the Benedictines more fundamentally than any of the other religious reformers, and they manifestly had a sobering impact upon Rupert.

Very reluctantly he had to concede that monks did not have a monopoly on the virtues and privileges of the religious life. Many religious leaders and thinkers reacted quickly to this new situation, and beginning in the mid-1120's several came to accept and even applaud such diversity.[116] The *Libellus de diuersis ordinibus* reviewed the various groups in an evenhanded way,

115. Thus a monk, in Rupert's view, still could not leave a monastery to join cloistered canons: *RegBen.* 4.7: PL 170.530–31.
116. See G. Constable, "Cluny, Citeaux, La Chartreuse: San Bernardo e la

and Anselm of Havelbert interpreted the apocalyptic image of the seven seals to prophesy increasing diversity in the Church. But Rupert was too much a product of the old order ever to embrace such diversity fully and warmly. Quite unlike his usual penchant for overturning received traditions, he argued here from Scripture (Prov. 22:28: *Ne transgrediaris terminos antiquos quos posuerunt patres tui*) that the traditions of the Fathers were not to be violated.[117] But neither was he a complete reactionary; he yielded as much as he could without giving up the superiority of the Benedictine ideal of monk-priests.

Disputes between Benedictines and canons regular developed all across Latin Christendom, producing a literature multifarious in expression though generally local in its circumstances and orientation.[118] Rupert's work was comparatively early and weighty, though by no means singular. It also exercised some influence. In the area of Cologne, Abbot Egbert of Huysburg (1135–53) used Rupert's arguments in the 1130's to call for the return of a monk named Peter of Hamersleben who had joined a house of canons regular.[119] Anselm of Havelberg, a disciple of Norbert's, responded to Abbot Egbert with depreciatory remarks about Rupert and a refutation of "Rupertian" arguments. He contended that "cleric" was not a name common to monks and secular or regular clerics alike, as Rupert had persistently maintained, and he protested vociferously against any notion that monks alone were true contemplatives, thus challenging precisely the constituent parts of the traditional Benedictine ideal.[120] Rupert's work would also become known in Bavaria, doubtless by way of Cuno; there it may have influenced Honorius Augustodunensis and Idung of Prüfening.

---

diversità delle forme di vita religiosa nel XII secolo," in *Studi su S. Bernardo di Chiaravalle* (Bibliotheca Cisterciensis 6, Rome 1975) 93–114.

117. *RegBen.* 4.7: PL 170.530–31 (also cited by Archbishop Frederick in his letter 4.2: 527).

118. See Constable (n. 40 above) 136–85 for the major treatises.

119. See Semmler (n. 3 above) 362 and Constable (n. 40 above) 145. An attempt to reconstruct Egbert's letter was made by K. Fina, "Anselm von Havelberg: Untersuchungen zur Kirchen- und Geistesgeschichte des 12. Jahrhunderts," *Analecta Praemonstratensia* 32 (1956) 87–93.

120. *Epistola*: PL 188.1120, 1123, 1129.

Rupert's defense of Benedictine monasticism was not its dying gasp. Black Monks were to persist in goodly numbers and in relative prosperity throughout the middle ages and beyond. But just about the time of Rupert's death (1129) they clearly lost that leadership role they had enjoyed for almost two centuries.[121] New monks, especially the Cistercians, seized the initiative as the foremost representatives of the communal religious life, and canons regular assumed leadership in many of the pastoral and intellectual functions Benedictines had taken upon themselves originally almost by default. It was not until seventy-five years later, and then in the very different social and intellectual milieu of cities and universities, that the mendicants reunited these two aspects, not just in practice as the Benedictines who had always remained contemplatives in theory, but also in principle, through the mixed life. The great interest of Rupert's work lies in his open defense of both the contemplative and the pastoral or intellectual facets of the religious life as required together to make up the truly apostolic ideal.

121. There is a tendency among recent historians to anticipate the triumph of the new orders, but G. Duby, *Saint Bernard: L'art cistercien* (Paris 1976) 14 has argued for 1134 as marking roughly the time Cistercians came clearly into prominence.

IX

The
Benedictine
Theologian

REFORM OF THE CHURCH and defense of Benedictine monasticism shaped and informed much of Rupert's work. But through it all, as monk, exile, or abbot, Rupert continued to focus steadily upon the interpretation of Holy Scripture as his chief task or, to put it in his own terms, his divine calling. It is altogether appropriate, therefore, to conclude with a review of his life and work as the most highly regarded theologian (*praeclaram . . . famam in sanctarum Scripturarum scientia*) in the archdiocese and probably the province of Cologne. Already in Liège, as a monastic teacher and preacher, Rupert had undertaken the interpretation of Scripture. At Deutz he continued to comment prodigiously on Scripture, now as an abbot in command of his own scriptorium and a public figure regularly consulted on theological and religious questions. When difficulties arose at Deutz too, Rupert defended his teachings and especially his status as a theologian in a way that deserves attention for its relative novelty. He also put to rest at long last, with an original theological position, the schoolmen's questions regarding Christ's incarnation, and went on to recapitulate most of his distinctive views in a kind of *summa*, the last of his completed works. But to the very end of his life Rupert suffered under charges of novelty and heresy.

1

Heresy Charged Again

From 1120 until about 1124 Rupert interpreted Scripture without hindrance, secure in the patronage of Archbishop Frederick and Abbot Cuno and far removed from the sniping criticism of adversaries in Liège. The works produced in those years, his *Commentary on the Apocalypse, Commentary on the Minor Prophets*, and *De uictoria Verbi Dei*, radiated self-confidence. He remained sensitive still to charges of pride and novelty, but dealt with them in a relatively noncombative way, as, for instance, in his prologue to the second half of the Minor Prophets commentary. Quoting St. Paul (I Cor. 3:11ff), he noted that those whose work served to build up gold, silver, and precious stones upon the foundation of Jesus Christ would receive their just reward. But, queried an "envious" opponent, is this not to liken your interpretations (*sensus tui*) and commentaries (*sermones tui*) to gold and silver? Such, Rupert replied, is not my own but many others' judgement, whereupon he cited laudatory letters just received from Abbot Erkenbert of Corvey and Prior Reginhard of Helmarshausen.[1] Just a few months later, however, he confronted charges not so lightly dismissed. First responding to them at the beginning of his *Commentary on Matthew* written early in 1125, he described the incident itself in his apologia written later that same year.[2] In combination with other troubling developments—his protector's departure for Regensburg in 1126, his strife with Archbishop Frederick during the years 1126–28, another charge of false teaching in 1126 or 1127 (see below), and the fire at Deutz in 1128—it was to have a devastating impact upon him. Though favorable in its outcome, this encounter threw Rupert severely off-balance, so much so that he

1. PL 168.527–28. See J. Van Engen, "Theophilis Presbyter and Rupert of Deutz: The Manual Arts and Benedictine Theology in the Early Twelfth Century," *Viator* 11 (1980) 161.
2. *RegBen.* 1: PL 170.490–92. (This is the source for what follows.)

was never quite able to regain that serenity of spirit evident in the earlier 1120's.

Rupert's adversary this time was none other than Norbert of Xanten, and the incident should be dated to the end of the year 1124.[3] Rupert described his accuser twice as someone well known (*bene nosti*) to Abbot Cuno (Norbert spent several months at Siegburg following his conversion), as recently converted and promoted too rapidly to the priesthood (charged against Norbert at the Council of Fritzlar in 1118), as a prelate without hardly ever having been a subject (except at Siegburg Norbert never lived as a monk before he became head of the new house of canons regular at Prémontré), and as an extremely critical wandering preacher who claimed to enjoy a papal sanction (granted by Gelasius II in 1119).[4] Rupert ascribed Norbert's attack upon him to "secret envy and malice," possibly because he had once criticized Norbert for his uncanonical promotion to the priesthood and his audacious preaching tours. Norbert and Rupert may indeed already have squared off over the monastic right to preach, if, as seems likely, he was the original "*clericus*" in Rupert's *Altercatio*. Rupert apparently came off better in that debate, and he also enjoyed a greater reputation in Cologne as a theologian. Just as Anselm of Havelberg, one of Norbert's disciples, once met Rupert and read some of his works "out of curiosity,"[5] so now Norbert as a personal acquaintance (*familiariter a me*) asked to read something, and Rupert lent him a copy of *De*

3. The identification was first argued by M. Van den Elsen, "De H. Norbertus en Rupertus," *De Katholiek* 89 (1886) 223–37, 93 (1888) 148–63, and 95 (1889) 351–66; further explored by M. L. Arduini, "Contributo alla biografia di Ruperto di Deutz," *Studi Medievali* 3rd ser. 16 (1975) 569–70; and accepted by J. Semmler, *Die Klosterreform von Siegburg* (Bonn 1959) 47, 452–57; Magrassi, *Teologia* 19–20; and H. Silvestre, "La répartition des citations nominatives des Pères dans l'oeuvre de Rupert de Deutz," in *Sapientiae Doctrina: Mélanges H. Bascour O.S.B.* (Louvain 1980) 291–93. Objections raised by U. Berlière, "Rupert de Deutz et Saint Norbert," *RB* 7 (1890) 452–57 are well taken with regard to some of Van den Elsen's exaggerated claims but represent no more than unsubstantiated general doubts about this particular incident.

4. *RegBen.* 1: PL 170.490; cf. CM 29.3–4.

5. PL 188.1120.

diuinis officiis, a work much favored by Abbot Cuno. That Norbert traveled through Cologne in 1124 cannot be proved, but it is at least possible since the death of Godfrey of Cappenberg's father-in-law early that year brought additional complications for the new foundation at Cappenberg.[6]

The ensuing controversy, though known only from Rupert's account, took on a distinctly public dimension: Abbot Cuno, says Rupert about 1127 in the preface to his Matthew commentary, not only learned of but also "heard and saw" what evil things were whipped up against him by those who read his works only in order to plot against him. And in the 1150's Philip of Harvengt referred to theirs as a serious falling-out (*grauiter disceptaret*).[7] Thus Rupert's account, written soon afterwards and addressed to Cuno who knew the facts, cannot be too far amiss.

As Rupert tells it, Norbert took the book with him so he could read as much as he liked and eventually sent it back without question or comment. Many days later, rumors reached the abbot of Deutz from various persons that he had taught heresy; indeed, so widespread were they to become that learned brothers were sent from other cities to determine the truth. Rupert was horrified and diligently sought out the source of the rumors. Certain fellow monks revealed that Norbert was his incriminator and that he based the charge on a sentence culled from *De diuinis officiis*. Worse still, he had made those charges publicly before the "band of ignorant folk that followed his preaching." Pointing to the offending passage, he had cried out that such an heretical book ought to be burnt (*flammis exurendum*). His followers, as Rupert put it, "showing greater zeal for the profundities of the faith in their untutored ignorance than do many of the learned," demanded the book be handed over so they could burn it at once. Apparently they did not get it, for it was sent back to Rupert, but the outrage stirred up in him by this latest assault upon his theological orthodoxy was beyond description.

6. See G. Niemeyer, "Die Vitae Godefridi Cappenbergensis," DA 23 (1967) 444–47.

7. Philip of Harvengt, *De continentia* 103: PL 203.807.

This time, however, Rupert had the better of his adversary, who, he declared, had shown himself not only "envious" but also "very ignorant" (*satis imperitum*). For Norbert had made a most unlucky choice of sentences to indict: the text was an unmarked direct quotation from a homily by St. Gregory the Great.[8] Tongue in cheek, Rupert assumed a measure of responsibility himself for Norbert's mistake since he had not originally marked the quotation with "*ut Gregorius ait.*" As the Old Testament law teaches (Exod. 21:33–34), if someone digs a well (a familiar image for investigating Scripture) and fails to cover it so that an ox or an ass falls in, he shall be made responsible for the loss. Norbert quickly withdrew his charge once Gregory's authorship was established and his own mistake revealed. Rupert only "heard" about this—Norbert was presumably then at Prémontré—and had in the meantime initiated a suit in Cologne charging that famous preacher with false incrimination. He was persuaded to give it up following Norbert's "correction," but with great reluctance. About two years later, Rupert conceded in the prologue to his *Commentary on Matthew* that vengeance belonged to the Lord.

Norbert had charged Rupert with teaching that "the Holy Spirit became incarnate in the Virgin Mary." The charge as such, if Rupert reported it accurately, was preposterous and represented an egregious misreading of Rupert's chapter and Gregory's sentence, particularly the word "*animatur.*"[9] But there must have been more to it than Rupert chose to relate. According to Philip of Harvengt, Norbert consulted with the masters in nearby Laon, and they found in his favor (*saniorem eius sententiam indicaret,* n. 7 above), which they could hardly have done if the matter hinged wholly on the reading of this Gregorian sen-

8. The suspect sentence in *Off.* 3.11: CM 7.77 (quoted in n. 9 below) is taken verbatim from Gregory, *Hom. Evang.* 7.3: PL 76.1101. I am not persuaded by the recent argument of Silvestre (n. 3 above) 290 that Rupert purposely inserted such unmarked quotations in order to trip up potential adversaries.

9. The misunderstood sentence of Gregory quoted by Rupert (n. 8 above) was: "Inuestigare enim quis potest quomodo incorporatur Verbum, *quomodo summus et uiuificator Spiritus intra uterum Virginis matris animatur,* quomodo is, qui initium non habet, et exstitit et concipitur?" (my italics).

tence. In fact Norbert—whether perceptively or sheerly by accident—had touched upon a very sensitive area of Rupert's theology, his tendency to blur the distinction between the person and the work of the Holy Spirit. Once this point had been questioned, Rupert returned to Scripture and developed an even more radical version of his original thesis.

In earlier commentaries Rupert had argued that the Holy Spirit as sanctifying grace (the "remission of sins") could be said to have proceeded from Christ's incarnation, or more particularly, from His passion, and that the sign of the Spirit's new role or presence was the new name Christ had conferred on Him, that of Paraclete or comforter (chapter III, part 3). The controversy with Norbert inspired Rupert to defend this same idea in a new and more striking way.[10] Prior to the incarnation of Christ, which made the grace of God manifest and available, there was no sanctifying or reconciling grace as such. Hence it is that in the Old Testament, with the exception of a single verse (Ps. 50[51]:13), the Spirit is always referred to as the "Spirit of God" or the "Spirit of the Lord" and that only in the New Testament, at the moment of Christ's and John's conception, is the *Holy* (*sanctus*) Spirit first said to operate. That is, Holy Scripture conferred a new name on the Spirit (*Spiritus sanctus*) at the point when He took up His new task as the effecter or bearer of saving grace. Thus, while it is sheer foolishness to say, as Norbert charged, that the Spirit was incarnate or brought to life (*animatur*) in the Blessed Virgin's miraculous conception, it is scripturally sound to argue that the Holy Spirit then assumed a new task and a new name! Rupert's argument here identified almost totally the person and work of the Holy Spirit with what later scholastic theologians would call sanctifying grace, and Norbert or another of Rupert's critics seems to have spotted that. Why, they asked, since the Father and the Son are also holy should the term "Holy Spirit" be assigned to the third person of the Trinity alone? Rupert's answer was simple and consistent with his general emphasis upon God's work in salvation-history: the whole

10. Rupert first argued it in *Matt.* 1: CM 29.22–28, and recapitulated it in *RegBen.* 1: PL 170.491 and again in *Glor.* 1.11–19: PL 169.23–32.

and proper work of the third Person is the sanctification of men
and angels, whence He alone is rightly called the Holy Spirit.
Norbert's challenge, in short, brought no apologies or retreat,
but rather an even more explicit statement of what had been implicit in Rupert's thought all along.

Sometime between late 1125 and early 1128 Rupert faced
criticism again, this time for his innovative Marian interpretation of the Song of Songs. This might have been surmised from
an oblique reference in Rupert's last work, but the recent discovery of a letter defending his interpretation against attack has
confirmed it.[11] Because the letter was included in an elementary
twelfth-century schoolbook as an example of *dictamen*, the names
were dropped and the circumstances are no longer discoverable.
The monks of a certain abbey criticized Rupert's interpretation
for ascribing to the Virgin Mary in particular (*specialitati*) what
was said generally (*generalitati*) of the whole Church—an accurate reading of what he had done. A friend of Rupert's in that
abbey known only by the initial "F" (*fratri et amico F, frater ka-
rissime*), who, to judge from hints in Rupert's letter, may well
have been the teacher there, asked him to respond in defense of
his interpretation. As so often when he faced criticism, Rupert
began on a petulant note: what kind of pseudo-learning is this,
he asked, which likens Mary to a "*species*" and the Church to a
"*genus*"? Indeed, if they wish to use such language they stand
refuted on their own terms since what is said of a "*genus*" can
logically also be said of the "*species*." But, he continued rather
haughtily, he would not exchange words with them on this
matter since they were not prepared to see that Jerome had already anticipated this interpretation in one of his letters.[12] For
his friend (*tibi autem familiariter*), however, he developed this interpretation further by way of the liturgical usages to which

11. *Glor.* 7.13: PL 169.155. See L. Csoka, "Ein unbekannter Brief des
Abtes Rupert von Deutz," *SMBO* 84 (1973) 383–93.
12. Rupert referred to a letter-treatise which went under Jerome's name,
in fact written by Paschasius Radbertus: A. Ripberger, *Der Pseudo-Hieronymus–
Brief IX "Cogitis me"* (Spicilegium Friburgense 9, Freiburg 1962).

texts regarding the Shulamite woman had been put. He concluded on a familiar but bold note: he had never intended to contradict the Fathers, but only to "add a little something" (*aliquid supererogare*), on grounds that the field of Holy Scripture in which the treasures of the Kingdom are hidden is open to all those (*nobis omnibus communis est*) upon whom God has conferred the desire and ability (*uoluntas siue facultas*) to seek them out. Beyond particular theological or exegetical points, in other words, Rupert now defended himself, or rather his right to interpret Scripture in sometimes novel ways.

2

Rupert's Apologia

From the very beginning of his career, Rupert was quick to defend both his teachings and his right to teach. The dedicatory epistle to *De sancta Trinitate* and the prefatory letter to his *Commentary on John*, both written from exile, comprised miniature apologias, and soon after leaving Liège Rupert penned that bold prologue to his *Commentary on the Apocalypse*, claiming for himself the "right to turn over the field of Scripture with the ploughshare of his own genius."[13] After four years of relative peace Norbert's attack compelled him to undertake a still more forceful defense of himself and his work. In the space of the next four years (mid-1125, mid-1126, and late 1128) Rupert drew up three separate lists of his works, seeking for them the approval or blessing of Abbot (then Bishop) Cuno, and finally Pope Honorius II.[14] Though several other Black Monks, Sigebert of Gembloux and Honorius Augustodunensis, for instance, listed their own writings at the end of literary histories, Rupert's appears to be an unprecedented attempt to defend—and also to promote—his own work.

The first list appeared in a full-fledged apologia treated below. About a year later (after May 1126) Rupert dedicated *De*

13. PL 169.827.
14. See Dinter, *Heribert* 100; and chapter VI above, nn. 55–57.

diuinis officiis to Cuno upon his elevation to the bishopric of Regensburg. In the dedicatory epistle he listed all his scriptural commentaries, the works he considered direct products of his divine calling, and requested that Cuno bestow an episcopal blessing upon them. Without recounting the details, Rupert reiterated the importance of Cuno's patronage in protecting him from enemies past and present, including those who still carped at his work as "superfluous and offensive to the authority of the Fathers," mere products of "his own ignorant heart."[15] Just months earlier, Rupert had spent the first half of another prologue complaining about such critics who gave him no peace, while thanking others, in this case Abbot Rudolph of St. Trond, who generously recognized the Spirit of God at work in him.[16] Then in the prologue to his *Commentary on Matthew* Rupert compared himself to Zacchaeus, the man who succeeded in seeing Christ and gaining His recognition despite turbulent crowds, meaning, the pressing burden of his office (especially strife with the archbishop) and disparaging remarks by the envious.[17] Halfway through that work he groaned aloud again about all those who took offense at his reflections on the mysteries of Holy Scripture, ascribing them to "sheer vainglory" and "asking in hushed whispers" (*subsannando quaeritans*) what business he had writing on such matters when the Fathers had already written more than enough.[18]

Late in the year 1128, just weeks or months before his death, Rupert sent a copy of his newest work, the *De glorificatione Trinitatis*, to Pope Honorius II, and in the accompanying letter rehearsed all these themes in a manner suitable to the papal office.[19] Rupert approached seeking recognition (*spatium habere nostra paruitas deposcit*) from the Blessed Peter, prince of the apostles, and from his vicar the pope. He came therefore bearing a gift, but not one made of corruptible gold and silver such as delighted the princes of this world, but rather one effected by

15. CM 7.2.
16. *Anulus prologus*: ed. Haacke 183–84.
17. CM 29.4.   18. *Matt.* 7: CM 29.196.
19. PL 169.9–12.

the grace of God (*opus ex gratia Dei*) such as pleased holy princes. And to those who protested that the Church had already received enough such gifts, Rupert asked the Holy Father rhetorically whether indeed gifts of the Holy Spirit, who blows where He will, could ever be turned back or restrained. He insisted (*Fateor tibi, magne sacerdos*) that his works were never prepared as items of gold and silver (that is, out of vainglory) but rather as wood to fuel the fire of God's love on the altar of each reader's heart. Those envious readers who considered his works burdensome and superfluous need not read them (*nolentem autem nostra nemo compellit*); but he begged the pope to accept and bless them now as the first fruits God had commanded to be brought to the priests. Few if any contemporary religious writers are known to have sought so openly the Roman pope's recognition for themselves, their writings, and their God-given talents.

More than a generation ago, historians of spirituality first pointed out a new concern with the self in twelfth-century devotional and mystical writings, especially with the soul's inner movement toward God. Other historians extended this theme to additional spheres of twelfth-century life and thought, to a new "discovery of the individual."[20] Rupert, however, rarely spoke directly about his own life, his birthplace, family, social standing, or tasks, quite unlike (for instance) Guibert of Nogent in his *De uita sua*. Beyond an aside suggesting that he was portly as an adult, there is just one exception: more than once, Rupert reports, Cuno referred to him as "lazy."[21] Given his stupendous production, this reproach hardly seems deserved. It means, in my view, that in the face of "envious critics" Rupert required almost constant encouragement, and Abbot Cuno, spiritual father to one hundred twenty monks, understood the psychologi-

20. See C. Morris, *The Discovery of the Individual 1050–1200* (New York 1973), building upon the work of R. W. Southern, A. Wilmart, and others; and the critical analysis by C. W. Bynum, "Did the Twelfth Century Discover the Individual?" *Journal of Ecclesiastical History* 31 (1980) 1–17 (with further bibliography), with Morris's response, "Individualism in Twelfth-Century Religion: Some Further Reflections," ibid. 195–206.

21. PL 168.12.

cal dynamics at work here and provided just such steady support and stimulus even while teasing him about "sloth."

Rupert also spent little time describing or reflecting upon inner states of being. Though he sought to have his readers appropriate personally the great mysteries of the Christian faith recorded in Scripture and commemorated in the divine office, and he did on occasion (chapter VIII, n. 21) describe the soul's experience in choir, Rupert continued to focus upon the mysteries themselves as revelatory of God and not primarily upon the means or experience as such of knowing God. Faculties of the soul and various states of mystical encounter receive little treatment in his commentaries, quite unlike what is found in a whole host of Cistercian, Carthusian, and other twelfth-century devotional writers. So also he considered his own mystical experiences, though essential to his divine calling, an altogether extraordinary event. To discuss them, indeed even to reveal them, was to risk profaning or demeaning the Spirit's personal, extraordinary visitation.[22]

And yet, Rupert's "self-assertiveness" set him quite distinctly apart from most early medieval predecessors. From his first prologue published anonymously around 1111 to his last addressed in 1128/29 to Pope Honorius II, Rupert consistently made the same claim, expressed in a phrase borrowed partly from Horace, that "it always was and would be permitted for anyone to say, within the bounds of the faith, whatever he himself thought or perceived in interpreting Scripture,"[23] or, as in his *Commentary on the Apocalypse*, "to turn over the field of Scripture with the ploughshare of his own genius." Few authors before or even during the twelfth century dared assert such a remarkable sense of freedom from the constraints imposed by the received tradition of scriptural exegesis. Indeed, Rupert was often made to feel the heat of his more conservative critics' wrath, those who charged him with presumptuousness, vain-

22. *Matt.* 12: CM 29.366–67.
23. Thus to Pope Honorius: "semper licuit semperque licebit unicuique dicere salua fide quod sentit." PL 168.11. For the phrase "licuit semperque licebit," see P. Classen, *DA* 26 (1970) 514.

glory, and superfluity. Moreover, whenever he was about to disagree with such a received opinion or to respond to an adversary's criticism, he would begin with the words, "But to this I say" (*Ad haec inquam*).[24] This phrase served a simple stylistic function, but it bespoke as well his conviction of an undeniable right to address such matters himself. And whenever one of his new interpretations was challenged, Rupert would declare that he had aimed "not to contradict the Fathers" but simply "to add a little something of his own" (*supererogare*). Taken together these three phrases reveal a man persuaded he could speak with the Fathers and to other theologians as a peer. Hence he copied out and elaborated upon a remarkable passage from Jerome to the effect that future readers, long after he and his critics were dead and forgotten, would read his works and judge them only on their quality (*operum merito*), not on the person, power, or rank of their author[25]—and clearly he, a commoner now under attack, expected favorable judgement in the future.

Rupert's assertion of his own theological rights and gifts, together with his concern that readers understand inwardly the mysteries they read and celebrated each day, made up an important part of that new world of the early twelfth century, whether or not such phenomena should rightly be dubbed a "new individualism." The numerous remarks made in his prologues—remarks which have made this study possible—were aimed essentially, however, at justifying and explaining his many and sometimes innovative commentaries to "envious" readers. For his critics incessantly demanded to know on what authority he dared so multiply books beyond the work of the Fathers and offer his own interpretations of Holy Scripture. Toward the end of his life Rupert finally was compelled to answer them directly, first (1125) by composing a formal apologia and then (1127), very reluctantly, by revealing the source of his vocation, his mystical visions.

Not long after Norbert's attack upon him, Rupert yielded

24. For instance, in his first statement on eucharistic theology (*Off.* 2.9), and his response to Norbert on the Holy Spirit (*Matt.* 1: CM 29.24).
25. *Matt.* 7: CM 29.197; cf. Jerome, *In Osee* 2: CC 76.55–56.

to Abbot Cuno's request for a treatise on those disputed religious questions. Because the resultant *Commentary on the Benedictine Rule*, which in manuscript bears the title *Liber de apollogeticis suis*, dealt first with this pressing personal matter, Book I is here called simply his apologia. Following a prefatory letter, Rupert turned directly to the question of authority: I have spoken, he says, and because I have spoken people say, Who is this? The time had come to set forth publicly why he still seemed such a "poor fool" in their eyes.[26] But Rupert's apologia comprised much more than the spontaneously composed list of complaints (*quodcumque mihi mens suggesserit*) his prefatory letter suggests. He was a skillful writer, and his apologia presented a carefully structured defense of his teachings and actions in past disputes together with a heartfelt expression of gratitude to his major patron, Abbot Cuno. Rupert recounted four incidents (all treated already in this study), each containing three elements: a narration of the events from his (consistently triumphalist) point of view, a reassertion with additional evidence of his theological position, and the establishment of what might be called a methodological point critical to his own defense.

In Rupert's view his critics despised him because he had never left the cloister to study arts and Scripture with one of their famous new masters. But (Rupert went on, launching into his first account) what did these new masters teach? Heresy, of course, by twisting out of Scripture the view that "God willed evil," an ancient heresy in fact, once taught by Florinus and Colitianus and refuted already by Jerome and Augustine![27] After recounting his brave and persistent rebuttal of this heresy at Liège, Laon, and Châlons-sur-Marne, Rupert reviewed at length the proper interpretation of those four key scriptural texts and that crucial passage in St. Augustine, thereby restating even more strongly his own position while also making the point that he, an untutored monk, understood Holy Scripture and the Fathers far better than any of those learned masters. It was this

26. *RegBen.* 1: PL 170.480. Cf. *John* 7: CM 9.394–96.
27. See Jerome, *In Isaiam* 12.45.7: CC 73A.505, which Rupert referred to directly; and Augustine, *De haeresibus* 65–66: CC 46.330.

last point, Rupert says here and elsewhere, which so aroused their ire against him; but he persevered in speaking the truth, and so that others might know what he had said Rupert now listed for the first time all of his scriptural commentaries to date.

Next Rupert provided examples of how these people had scrutinized his works in a continuing effort to ruin him—never, of course, successfully. He introduced the first with a line from Vergil's *Aeneid: "Et crimine ab uno disce omnes"* (2.65–66). This was the most recent and therefore the most pressing on his mind, the dispute with Norbert. Once again he recounted his triumph despite Norbert's ill treatment of him, forcefully restated his position on the Holy Spirit as the effecter of sanctifying grace, and proved himself an ingenious interpreter of Scripture with his observations on the Spirit's new title in the New Testament. As another example of such malicious reading of his works, he then went back to the dispute over the creation of angels, provoked by his interpretation of Genesis, which had taken place in Liège after his return from France. As before, he defended his interpretation, cited additional patristic evidence for some elements of it, and demanded that his adversaries produce something better if they did not like his reading. Here he declared explicitly that he had "no fear of their accusations so long as they could not prove him contrary to canonical Holy Scripture."

This remark introduced the last episode, which was in fact the first chronologically. The "Judas question" in the eucharistic controversy had come closest to destroying him on both theological and methodological grounds and had also occasioned Cuno's saving intervention. He reviewed the circumstances as briefly and positively as he could, but this time prefaced the narrative portion with a passionate argument to the effect that where the Fathers had contradicted themselves—quoting in full Augustine's and Hilary's respective positions—that one is to be followed who came closest to the testimony of canonical Scripture. Rupert went on to argue that Hilary's was in this case the better reading of the Gospels. He concluded by recalling Cuno's "miraculous" discovery of the Hilary text and his "providential" offer of refuge in 1119 during the schism at Liège.

Rupert's straightforward defense of his theological career and teachings had virtually no precedent in the early twelfth century, even among those new masters of the Sacred Page to whom the term "theological career" might be applied more appropriately. Peter Abelard's much more famous and nearly contemporaneous *Historia calamitatum* has still not received a wholly convincing interpretation of its circumstances and purposes, though it might well be said, among other things, to set forth and defend the career of a philosopher.[28] The closest parallels are to be found in the works of two Black Monks: Otloh of St. Emmeran's *Liber de tentatione cuiusdam monachi* (about 1070) described his work as a scribe and writer even as it defended the appropriateness of such activity to the monastic life; and Suger of St. Denis's *Liber de rebus in administratione sua gestis* commemorated and defended his accomplishments, administrative rather than literary or theological, as abbot of the royal abbey in the kingdom of France. On reflection it may not be so surprising that Black Monks were the first to compose such apologias. New monks and new masters had still to make their way, and they did so in good part by attacking what had gone wrong in the recent past. Black Monks were compelled thus to defend either the appropriateness or the quality of their work as scribes, teachers, administrators, and theologians, tasks in which they had often led the way for almost two centuries.

Bold and forthright as Rupert's apologia was, it did not address directly what he too perceived to be the central issue, the question of his authority to speak at such length and sometimes with such novelty on the meaning of Holy Scripture. In his apologia Rupert reverted to this point three times: in his second paragraph (right after setting forth his adversaries' view of him: *Quis est hic?*), then upon listing his commentaries, and again at the very end. His answer rested ultimately on a conviction born of his deepest spiritual experience, a mystical and visionary call from God Himself whereby he had sensibly received the spiri-

28. Thus Bynum (n. 20 above) 9; but cf. Mary McLaughlin, "Abelard as Autobiographer: The Motives and Meaning of his 'Story of Calamities,'" *Speculum* 42 (1967) 463–88.

tual gift of interpretation. Such an intimate matter he flatly refused to chatter about publicly in his prefaces and commentaries. In growing desperation, though, he broadly hinted at it
in the last lines of his apologia, comparing himself to the prophets of old who were compelled to say what God the Father had
enjoined upon them; and in his Canticles commentary, also
written in 1125, he even described one of his visions as the experience of a "certain adolescent."[29] But Abbot Cuno had also begun to wonder about the source of Rupert's prodigious talent,
this ability to comment on Scripture even "more usefully" sometimes than the Catholic Fathers, and in an unguarded moment
of intimacy and friendship Rupert disclosed to him the secret of
his visions. Abbot Cuno, an enthusiastic patron knowledgeable
in the ways of the world, immediately ordered him to write this
down so as "to commend his works still more," and when Rupert resisted Cuno commanded him to do so in the name of the
Triune God. Rupert hesitated, as he tells us more than once, because he feared others would scoff at his visions or dismiss them
as vainglorious presumption.[30] But finally, almost three years
after his conversation with Cuno and perhaps two after Norbert's attack, Rupert carried out his patron's order in the twelfth
book of his *Commentary on Matthew*.

There Rupert described his visionary experiences as part of
a lengthy vocational crisis which culminated in his ordination
and his irresistible compulsion to write (chapter I, part 5). Other
works suggest that he was visited throughout his life with extraordinary experiences, probably now mystical rather than visionary. When he was about to resign his abbatial post and give
up the fight with Archbishop Frederick, for instance, such an
experience inspired him to hold fast, largely on grounds, it
seems, that with his patron now in Regensburg he could not be
sure of gaining another secure base from which to continue the
writing he felt constrained to do. So also whenever the abusive
criticism of his adversaries threatened to overwhelm him, Christ
would touch him anew, an experience Rupert described by con-

29. *RegBen.* 1: PL 170.497–98; *Cant.* 5: CM 26.110–11.
30. *Matt.* 12: CM 29.366–67, 394–96; *RegBen.* 1: PL 170.481.

THE BENEDICTINE THEOLOGIAN

flating two images, that of the bridegroom touching the intimate parts of his beloved and of the master wielding a stick over
his pupil.[31] Rupert insisted this experience was so powerful he
could not have stopped writing even if he had wanted to.[32] He
also believed it brought him that deeper understanding of Scripture which "authorized" his own writing.

Rupert made the point explicitly in remarks appended to his
account of these visions.[33] He recalled how his adversaries had
espoused certain erroneous views on the supposed authority of
their renowned teachers, whom they considered their "fathers,"
and how when he had dared to contradict those masters on the
authority of Holy Scripture, they had reproached him, not just
for days but for years, and had demanded to know who his own
masters (= fathers) were. Finally, Rupert claimed, canonical
Scripture was his authority, and his victory against the masters
came in good part because, as Cuno testified too, his interpretation of Scripture was born neither of pride nor presumption but
rather of the grace of God. Indeed, Rupert went on, even though
he too had had several teachers (*patres*) and had once diligently
studied the liberal arts, he preferred just one "visit from on
high" to ten of their masters (*patres*), and in fact the "master's
cane" of the Spirit had struck him more than once, not just on
the lips but over the whole body, so that he now followed Him
as his guide (*monitor*) in all his writings!

Truth resides in Holy Scripture; thus far all agreed. At issue
remained the question of authoritative interpretation. Rupert's
adversaries stood upon the teaching authority of the Fathers and
their new masters, several of whose opinions were just then
coming to be listed alongside those of the ancient Fathers (in the
Liber Pancrisis, for instance). Though he knew the Fathers as
well as his critics did, or better, and often quoted or echoed
them, Rupert stood finally upon the authority of his own extraordinary call to interpret Scripture. Over against these new

31. *Incendio* 15: ed. Grundmann 459–60.
32. ". . . cessare quin scriberem nequaquam potui, et usque nunc, etiam si
uelim, tacere non possum." *Matt.* 12: CM 29.384.
33. CM 29.385–86.

"fathers," Rupert's claim betrayed a more traditional perspective, here present in a greatly heightened intensity: the talent to interpret Scripture profoundly or edifyingly (*utiliter*) was still considered a God-given grace rather than the necessary or at least expected product of an institutionalized education culminating in a license. The reception of Rupert's claim confirmed Abbot Cuno's instinct on this point: in the generation after his death four of the five persons who commented on or listed Rupert's works referred directly to the special, divine grace he had received to interpret the mysteries of Holy Scripture so profoundly. Rupert, moreover, could not conceive of any genuine understanding of those scriptural mysteries apart from their celebration. The life of the schools was notorious. So-called wisdom was sold for cold cash, subjects studied with a view to preferment, and ancient heresies taught by new masters. In short, Rupert's apologia, though unprecedented for its self-assertiveness, finally presupposed a more traditional setting in which gifted monks had at least as good a claim to treat theological or scriptural matters as did educated schoolmen.

3

Christ's Incarnation
and Man's Redemption

Soon after Rupert completed his book *On the Victory of the Word of God* Abbot Cuno asked him to write another *On the Glory and Honor of the Son of Man*, this one to be based upon the Gospel of St. Matthew. Rupert agreed and adopted as his principle of organization the four mysteries which "every Christian ought to know," namely, Christ's incarnation, passion, resurrection, and ascension. He had borrowed here from an influential sermon of St. Gregory which linked these four mysteries to the four beings in Ezechiel's vision, and he intended originally to treat only those verses of the Gospel pertinent to this scheme.[34]

34. Gregory, *Hom. Ezech.* 1.4.1–3; cf. Jerome's *Comm. in Matthaeum*: CC 77.3. See Rupert's own statements in *Matt.* 1, 2, and esp. 10: CM 29.7–8, 39, 299; and my review of Pater Haacke's new edition in *Speculum* 57 (1982) 426–28.

But the writing of this work, more so perhaps than any of his others save the lengthy *De sancta Trinitate*, was interrupted repeatedly. He took time to repel Norbert's attack in Book I, but then treated most of the verses of Matt. 1–4 in Books I–III, highlighting ways in which Christ's glory and honor became manifest in His incarnation. After completing commentaries on the Benedictine *Rule* and the Song of Songs, he transformed Books IV–VII (the Sermon on the Mount) into a miniature treatise on the religious life (chapter VIII, part 1), and in Book IX, probably after writing the *Anulus*, gave considerable attention to the Jews. Books X and XI finally take up the second of the mysteries, Christ's passion, but various remarks suggest that his struggle with Archbishop Frederick over the castle was underway. Book XII is devoted almost entirely to the narrative of his visionary experiences, and Book XIII to the question of the cause and necessity of Christ's incarnation.

The question of God's predestinating will was traditionally framed in such a way that it dealt not only with the origins of evil, a matter Rupert regarded now as essentially settled, but also with the cause and necessity of the incarnation. As Rupert reported already in his first work and now repeated sharply here, certain theologians argued that God must have lacked either the omnipotence or the wisdom to prevent evil, but in either case He had thus made it necessary for His own Son to suffer the humiliation of incarnation and death. And those same "pesty moderns" claimed they could scarcely harmonize God's will for man's salvation (I Tim. 2:4) with Christ's cursing of unrepentant Hebrew cities (Matt. 11:20–24).[35] Still others, Rupert had "learned by experience," wondered why Christ's incarnation was delayed so long.[36] In short, the question of Christ's incarnation, the central focus of Rupert's own thought and devotion, still required definitive exposition. This he now undertook in the final book of his work on the "glory and honor of the Son of Man."

Beyond the theologians' importunate questions, the Jews too, with whom Rupert now had much more frequent contact

35. *Matt.* 13, 9: CM 29.413, 281–84.
36. *Matt.* 1: CM 29.16.

and against whom he had just (1126) written his *Anulus*, directed their sharpest attacks against any notion that God had become flesh and suffered death. As St. Paul said long before (I Cor. 1:23), this was a "scandal" to them: the Jews charged in particular that this "new covenant" with its "new plan of salvation" represented a change of mind and therefore fickleness or unreliability in the will of a supposedly immutable God.[37] This criticism struck deeply into the hearts and minds of Christians, who also professed belief in God's immutability, and several of Rupert's contemporaries, all of them Black Monks, attempted to refute it.[38] Rupert himself argued that Jewish cultic and ceremonial law were formerly only "permitted," not "mandated," revealing therefore no change in God's position here.[39] But Jews questioned outright the "necessity" of an incarnation, since God had already made covenant with his Chosen People and those promises presumably still held if God was indeed reliable. Hence, as recent scholars have come increasingly to see, several treatises written at this time bore titles such as "*De incarnatione contra Judaeos*" and "*Cur Deus homo*" not only in order to describe Jesus as God become flesh but, even more important, to establish or "prove" the necessity and rationale of that event.[40] In fact Rupert was asked to take up exactly this problem. In 1127 Rudolph of St. Trond thanked him profusely for the *Anulus* (composed at his request), but begged him to complete (*ad perficiendum*) his review of disputed questions with further remarks on the Trinity, the right interpretation of Gen. 49:10, and the necessity of the incarnation.[41] Rupert would refer to this letter and deal with

37. For this issue cf. Honorius, *Elucidarius* 1.18; *Sent. divinae paginae*, ed. Bliemetzrieder (BGPT 18) 37.

38. See B. Smalley, "Ralph of Flaix on Leviticus," *RTAM* 35 (1968) 54–55 for the frequency of this criticism; as an example of Christian rejoinder, see Guibert, *De incarnatione contra Iudaeos*: PL 156.517.

39. *Spir.* 5.8–12: CM 24.1984–91.

40. See R. W. Southern, *St. Anselm and His Biographer* (Cambridge 1963) 88–91; Odo of Cambrai, *Disputatio contra Iudaeum de adventu Christi Filii Dei* (PL 160.1103–12); and Herman of Tournai, *Tractatus de incarnatione Jesu Christi* (PL 180.9–38) and Guibert (n. 38 above).

41. "Et rationem redderes, cuius multam copiam tum ex diuina in te effusa gratia tum ex sanctorum patrum scriptis habes, quomodo ad solum fi-

these questions explicitly in his next work, the *De glorificatione Trinitatis*, but it seems likely that Rudolph's letter influenced him now to devote the entire last book of his *De gloria et honore Filii hominis* to a reconsideration of the cause and necessity of Christ's incarnation.

Rupert was annoyed that "even certain churchmen" (*nonnullis etiam ecclesiasticis*) thought the only way to show the necessity of Christ's incarnation and passion was to have God "will evil."[42] For if God did not will evil and set the whole plan in motion, then Christ's incarnation represented a "new plan" (*nouum concilium*), a change of untold magnitude in the divine operation which would seem contrary to the nature of a truly omnipotent and immutable God.[43] From Rupert's earliest work, it becomes clear that the question also involved the nature of God's foreknowledge. God foreknew that man would fall and be restored by His own omnipotent intervention, but while the first He "foreknew and permitted" in order to heap further damnation on the Devil, the second He "foreknew and foreordained" (*praeordinauit*) in order to "make known to the principalities and powers in high places through the Church the manifold wisdom of God" (Eph. 3:10). Rupert truly meant "foreordained." In the first chapter of his *Commentary on Genesis* and in the opening pages of his *Commentary on John* Rupert stated clearly that God planned from the very beginning to have His son assume flesh and dwell among us.[44] But he took this position largely in reaction to his first encounter with those who claimed that unless God had willed evil and the atoning incarnation it necessitated He was not truly omnipotent and immutable. The central theme of his commentary on Matthew (*De gloria et honore Filii hominis*), a felt need still to answer these old adversaries, and the Jewish question raised anew by Rudolph impelled Rupert in 1127 to formulate the question much more pointedly.[45]

---

lium pertinet incarnatio, et quod necesse fuerit eum incarnari." Ed. F. W. E. Roth, *Neues Archiv* 17 (1892) 617–18.

42. *Matt.* 13: CM 29.412.   43. *John* 1: CM 9.13.

44. *Off.* 6:2: CM 7.188–89 (referring to Jerome's commentary on Ephesians, PL 26.515); *Gen.* 1.1: CM 21.169; John 1: CM 9.14–15.

45. "Hic primum illud quaerere libet utrum iste Filius Dei, de quo hic

Scholars have long recognized that Rupert adopted a position comparable in certain respects to the Scotist argument for an "unconditional incarnation." More recent studies have investigated the degree to which Rupert held this view uniformly (Haacke) or arrived at it only toward the end of his life (Magrassi).[46] It is important to bear in mind the positions Rupert sought to rebut, namely, the Jewish denial of the incarnation as either fact or necessity and the theologians' claim that God permitted or even willed evil in order to bring about the incarnation of His son. Rupert held in response that God intended all along to have the second person of the Trinity assume a concrete, earthly role in the divine plan for His chosen people. Indeed, Christ was meant from all eternity to reign as the King of creation and of His elect, a view expounded by way of Eph. 3:8–11 and Hebr. 2:9–10 (used earlier for his christology).[47] The world was created not only in Him but also for Him (*propter quod*), and so His assumption of the flesh constituted no "new plan" on God's part. Rupert took as a basic description of God's intent the concluding verse from a passage in Proverbs (8:31) traditionally applied to Christ: *Quando appendebat fundamenta terrae cum eo eram cuncta componens, et delectabar per singulos dies, ludens coram eo omni tempore, ludens in orbe terrarum, et deliciae meae cum filiis hominum.* The Wisdom of God, in other words, was foreordained by God's eternal plan to rejoice among men as their incarnate King. All that was "new" had rather to be attributed to man and the Devil, namely, the fall required that the Son suffer sacrificial death in order to requite God's righteousness and preserve His people. Should we not then be fearful of God's wrath, Rupert continued, since our sin caused the incarnate King also to suffer such humiliation? He put his answer in

---

sermo est, etiam si peccatum propter quod omnes morimur non intercessisset homo fieret, an non." *Matt.* 13: CM 29.415.

46. The basic studies (with further literature) are Séjourné, in *DTC* 14.192–94; Magrassi, *Teologia* 219–55; and R. Haacke, "Rupert von Deutz zur Frage: Cur Deus Homo?" in *Corona Gratiarum: Festschrift E. Dekkers* (Brugge 1975) 2.143–59.

47. *Matt.* 13: CM 29.408–16.

Christ's own mouth: "I would not have been crowned with such glory and honor as I now have were it not for my sacrificial intercession."[48] Thus Christ in fact owes much to the impious (*Multum igitur debet impiis*), whence man gains the confidence (*Hinc iure nobis fiducia*) to approach His throne of grace (see Hebr. 4:16). In sum, Christ's incarnate kingship, the chief revelation of Himself to man, was planned from all eternity, but His sacrificial atonement, God's response to man's fall, only raised Him to new heights of glory and honor.

Rupert had managed to combine two essential components of his devotion and theology, Christ's incarnation as the absolute focal point of God's plan (best seen in the *De uictoria Verbi Dei*) and Christ's sacrifice as the source now of His glory and honor. But if Christ was indeed predestined from all eternity to become the incarnate King not only of creation but also of His chosen creatures, then the elect necessarily also had an earthly existence foreseen from the very beginning of God's plan. Rupert said as much when he consistently and insistently interpreted the command "to be fruitful and multiply" (Gen. 1:28), given before the fall, as a direct reference to the bearing of God's elect. After man's fall, the terrible grief of Eve and all mothers is that they bear not only the elect but also those whom the Devil will claim (Gen. 3:16: *Multiplicabo . . . conceptos tuos*).[49] Rupert's view required that Adam and Eve produce children (all elect) irrespective of the fall, a position for which he had argued first in his *Commentary on Genesis* when he severely criticized an asexual view of the proto-parents, and again in his *Commentary on Matthew*, this time citing a lengthy passage from St. Augustine in his behalf.[50] That is, the elect were to be born irrespective

48. "Nec ergo talis ac tantus nunc existerem, nisi causa tui, nisi propter peccata generis humani. . . . *Videmus* autem, ait idem apostolus, *Dominum Iesum Christum propter passionem mortis gloria et honore coronatum* (Hebr. 2:9). Ergo pro impiis gloria et honore coronatus est. Ergo impii et scelerati causa fuerunt ei ut coronaretur et sederet a dextris Dei, coronatus gloria regni, honore pontificii." Ibid. 417.

49. See *Gen.* 3.22–23: CM 21.259–61.

50. *Gen.* 3.10–11: CM 21.245–47; *Matt.* 13: CM 29.415. See Augustine, *De civitate Dei* 14.23: CM 48.444–45.

of the fall, according to God's predestined plan for them to rejoice with their incarnate King.

But Rupert's view cut against the grain of early medieval
theology in still another way. His vision of God's eternal plan
contradicted the prevailing Gregorian view that man was created essentially to replace fallen angels.[51] This view was deeply
grounded in early medieval spirituality, which considered the
life of monks to prefigure the ultimate "angelic" state of the
blessed. St. Anselm held to this view, and Hugh of St. Victor
and Peter Lombard still wondered about correspondences between fallen angels and elect men.[52] They often cited a text from
St. Augustine's *Enchiridion* (c. 29), but the major supporting
text for the received view came from Gregory's *Homilies on the
Gospel* (34.11), and Rupert apparently was the first to challenge
it.[53] He contended that Gregory's version of the key verse (Deut.
32:8) read contrary to the "*Hebraica ueritas*" (Jerome)—Gregory's was in fact an older Latin rendering—and that he had in
any case falsely interpreted it. Angels did not fall from their
various orders, since that would be to suggest that Seraphim
and Cherubim, for instance, fell from their burning love of
God; rather, following their time of testing—for which Rupert
had argued long ago—the angels were fixed as a reward and by
grace in the nine orders mentioned in Scripture.[54] But men also
receive varieties of spiritual graces exactly comparable to the
nine orders of angels, and in so far they are the equals of angels,
just as Holy Scripture teaches (Luke 20:36: *Aequales enim sunt*

51. See the important essay of M.-D. Chenu, "Cur homo? Le sous-sol
d'une controverse théologique au XIIe siècle," in his *Théologie* 52–59; however, he overlooked Rupert's contribution. On Rupert, see Magrassi, *Teologia*
256–80.

52. Anselm, *Cur Deus homo* 1.16–18: ed. Schmitt 2.74–84; Hugh, *De sacramentis* 1.5.31–34: PL 176.261–64; Peter Lombard, *Sent.* 2.9.6–7. See L. Ott,
Theologischen Briefliteratur der Frühscholastik (BGPT 34, Münster 1937) 480–82.

53. *Glor.* 3.16–22: PL 169.67–74.

54. "Nunc autem non ita est. Nulla enim Scriptura canonica opinioni illi
[Gregory's] suffragatur. . . . Verius ergo et rationabilius hoc dicimus quia in
remuneratione pro eo quod non peccauerunt et creatori suo subici maluerunt,
ordines illos acceperunt quos habent nunc. . . ." *Glor.* 3.17: PL 169.69.

angelis cum sint filii resurrectionis). Indeed, since men receive not only "graces" but also "remission of sins," the Spirit's second gift, men owe God more than angels do, and men's hearts correspondingly ought to burn with a more ardent love.[55] Nor should we be so "childish" (*ne ita pueri simus*) as to think God had no plan (*nullum propositum*) to create mankind until after the angels fell. It is far better to say that the angels were created because of the One Man for whom and through whom all things were created, and that men too were created as a part of the predestined plan which had the incarnate King as its center and purpose.[56]

The central image here is that of a king (*rex*) or a lord (*dominus*) ruling in his household (*familia*). This, Rupert held, was necessarily to be as the result of an absolute, immutable plan which God carried out despite the Devil and man's evil. The execution of that plan, the victory of the Word of God, he had just traced through Scripture in another work. To suggest that the key elements in this epic story, Christ's incarnate kingship and man's creation for bliss, were the product of mere contingencies, the fall of the angels and of man, would be grievously to offend against almighty God's majestic plan (*propositum*). Rupert's image deserves attention, for it would have had a striking impact upon contemporary readers. Just as he had depicted the story of salvation as an epic battle, so now incarnation and predestination have become the predetermined and joyous reign of a lord in His household, a king among his people. That the King had, moreover, to suffer in order to save His people served only to crown Him with still greater glory and honor and to

55. *Glor.* 3.19: PL 169.71. Cf. the closely parallel last paragraph of *Matt.* 13: CM 29.421.

56. "Igitur probabilius hoc dicimus, quod non tam homo propter supplendum angelorum numerum quam et angeli et homines propter unum hominem Iesum Christum facti sunt, ut quoniam unus idemque et Deus ex Deo erat et homo nasciturus erat, haberet praeparatam ex utroque latere familiam, hinc angelorum, hinc hominum; et ipse Deus et homo, Dominus et Creator angelorum, Dominus et Creator atque Saluator emineret hominum sanctorum, Dominus, inquam, in eis sicut in domo sua, Rex in gente sua, Deus in maiestate sua!" *Glor.* 3.21: PL 169.72–73.

render His subjects so much the more indebted to him in love and fidelity.

Rupert's was an ingenious, even poetic, transformation of theological concepts into images drawn from his own social setting. This should not be misconstrued as the inability to handle theological issues abstractly.[57] It was rather the choice to deal with them concretely, in images molded by his society but equally or even more, I think, by the divine office. The focus of Rupert's entire life was to celebrate all day long the advent and saving work of Christ. Such worship had so shaped his life and thought as to make it practically inconceivable that the events celebrated were not themselves predetermined from all eternity for both Christ and mankind. Only the blindness of Jews and the foolishness of new theologians could fail to grasp such a glorious vision of God's plan.

4

Rupert's *Summa*: The Works of God and the Work of God

Sometime during the year 1127 Rupert completed his *Commentary on Matthew* for Bishop Cuno and his *Commentary on Kings* for Archbishop Frederick. Of the first work there are four extant copies, and of the second none. In the midst still of his struggle with Archbishop Frederick and Count Adolph, Rupert took up another work, which proved to be his last, the *De glorificatione Trinitatis et processione Spiritus sancti*, completed just before the fire at Deutz on 28 August 1128.[58] After the fire but before his death on 4 March 1129, Rupert sent copies to Bishop Cuno in Regensburg and Pope Honorius II in Rome. Of this work there are still five extant manuscripts, one each from Cologne and the diocese of Liège (his two homebases), one from Bavaria (doubtless via Bishop Cuno), one in Rome, and a late copy in Paris.[59]

57. Thus R. Haacke, CM 29.xii.
58. *Incendio* 19: ed. Grundmann 465.
59. R. Haacke, *DA* 26 (1970) 539.

This last work was begun originally to meet two specific requests. In response to Abbot Rudolph, whose letter Rupert paraphrased in his prologue,[60] he gathered testimony from the Law and the prophets to demonstrate against the perfidy of Jews the triune nature of God and the necessity of the incarnation. While mulling over this difficult task Rupert recalled an earlier request from the papal legate William of Palestrina, who had urged him to write something useful for the Roman See on the double procession of the Holy Spirit.[61] Twenty years earlier Pope Urban had made a similar request of St. Anselm.[62] In a moment of inspiration, possibly from the Spirit Himself (*quae utinam ipsius sit Paracleti*), Rupert realized he could treat both subjects at once. So he abandoned both the dialogue form Rudolph had requested earlier and the Jews' "annoying questions" and proceeded with a meditation on the central mysteries of the Christian faith as they stood revealed in Holy Scripture (*sola cum quieto et tranquillo otio sacras perageret paginas Christiana fides*). Hence Rupert's title: *The Glorification of the Trinity and Procession of the Holy Spirit*.

The mysteries of the Christian faith, Rupert began, are treasures hidden in the field of Scripture (Matt. 13:44) from the envious and the blind. But unlike the works of Plato and Aristotle Holy Scripture makes its teachings, at least in its literal and moral senses, open to all believers of a simple and upright faith (1.1–2). All Scripture, moreover, is a single book, the one canonical authority authored by God Himself; in this it is sharply differentiated from the numerous books written by men not inspired with the Spirit of Truth (1.5). And the primary content of Scripture is the "work of God, all those beneficial deeds which God has wrought from creation through the incarnation to the present." Thus, in good systematic fashion Rupert set out

---

60. PL 169.11–13; for Rudolph's letter, see n. 41 above.

61. PL 169.13–14. William of Palestrina was in Cologne during the fall of 1124, read the first half of the Minor Prophets commentary with enthusiasm, and took a copy back with him to Rome. See O. Schumann, *Die päpstlichen Legaten in Deutschland zur Zeit Heinrich IV. und Heinrich V.* (diss. Marburg 1912) 119–22.

62. See G. R. Evans, *Anselm and a New Generation* (Oxford 1980) 41–59.

as his foundation that distinctive position on scriptural authority he had worked out in years gone by against those who relied too much upon either the Fathers or dialectics. The premise for nearly all Rupert's theological endeavors was that God stands revealed in His works (*cognoscitur ex operibus*). Proceeding in the order of Scripture (*secundum ordinem Scripturarum procedere nobis propositum est*), he now set forth those works, the mysteries of the Trinity and the incarnation for the Jews and of the Spirit's double procession for the Greeks. As it unfolded, this last work thus became a summary of all Rupert's major themes.

The Son, the second person of the Trinity, is the *principium* of Gen. 1:1 in three senses: He is the one through whom and for whom all things were created, especially men and angels, and He was also to become the prince and the first principle of man's salvation (1.6–9). This last point proved manifestly that "Christ existed before Mary" (1.10). Moreover, He was revealed in Holy Scripture not so much as the second person of the Three-in-One, but rather as the incarnate King of creation predestined from all eternity to reign over His elect.[63] Just as woman was created for man, so the Church was made for (*propter*) Christ but not, Rupert insists, out of Christ (*non de Filio*), for participation in His divine being is attained only through the eating and drinking of His body and blood.[64] It may be slightly exaggerated to say that the "unconditional incarnation" is the chief theme of *De glorificatione*.[65] Yet Christ's predestined reign as the incarnate King of creation certainly looms over and to some degree structures the entire work.

The remainder of Book I and all of Book II treat the procession of the Holy Spirit in a discussion aimed mostly at the Greeks, though partly still at Norbert. Rupert employed an argument similar in method to that used for the second person of the Trinity and the rationale for His incarnation. Liturgical "processions," this Black Monk begins, involve the splendid marching out of notables so that the people (*plebs*) may see them and rejoice. So also the procession of the divine Persons, though not

63. *Glor.* 3.7, 20–21; 4.2: PL 169.58, 72–73, 75–76.
64. *Glor.* 1.8–9: PL 169.20–21.
65. Thus Magrassi, *Teologia* 242–43.

a local phenomenon, involves a manifest deed (*effectus mirandi operis*) whereby the majesty of God Himself is revealed to us. Thus the Son, using the past tense (John 8:42, *ego enim ex Deo processi et ueni*), spoke of His procession from the Father as already accomplished, in His incarnation; but the procession of the Spirit, which began at creation in His brooding over the waters (Gen. 1:2), will continue to the end of time.[66] In particular, the Spirit proceeds in three ways (*modis*): His cooperation at creation, His bestowal of spiritual gifts, especially upon the prophets, and His remission of sins or sanctifying grace, first conferred after Christ's advent.[67] Against the Jews Rupert made it clear that the third person of the Trinity "began to proceed already at the moment of creation,"[68] and against Norbert and the Greeks that the Spirit as sanctifying grace proceeded from the Son in His advent and passion. It was this latter mode of procession which Rupert then treated in a lengthy discussion of the "*filioque*," replete with scriptural references and mostly complementary to what he had already argued in his *Commentary on John*.[69]

Moreover, the Spirit's "procession" was manifest still today, something Rupert illustrated near the end of his discussion. The bestowal of special graces is an experience never granted to the proud or avaricious but only to pilgrims and contemplatives, and Rupert gave two examples of such visitations in his own day.[70] The first concerned a female recluse named Waldrada; the second (*alius quidam*) was none other than Rupert himself, who recalled almost verbatim the ineffable mystical experience described in his recent *Commentary on Matthew*, the one which had finally impelled him to ordination and his writing.[71] The procession of the Holy Spirit, in other words, Rupert grounded not

66. *Spir.* 1.14–16: PL 169.26–29.
67. *Glor.* 1.11: PL 169.23. Cf. 1.18: 30.
68. "Magna res et processio Spiritus sancti, cuius uidelicet processionis illud initium erat quod ferebatur super aquas." *Glor.* 1.13; PL 169.25.
69. *Glor.* 1.18, 19: PL 169.30, 32. Cf. *Spir.* 1.28: CM 24.1855–56; and chapter III, part 3.
70. *Glor.* 2.13–17, 3.9–12: PL 169.44–48, 60, 63.
71. *Glor.* 2.18: PL 169.49 is in part identical to Rupert's narration of his culminating mystical experience in *Matt.* 12: CM 29.379.

only in those deeds recorded in Scripture and celebrated in the office but also in his own extraordinary experience.

In Book III Rupert took up the creation and fall of the angels (= light). He reiterated his earlier stand against their instantaneous creation and fall, pointing out again that this widely held Augustinian "opinion" had no scriptural support.[72] He then (3.16–22) rebutted Gregory's view that man was created to replace fallen angels, arguing instead that man should burn with an even greater love because he had received two gifts from the Holy Spirit. Book IV treats the creation and fall of man in so far as it is revelatory of the glory of Triune God.[73] With that flair for exegetical novelty which had always been his, Rupert next (midway in Books IV–VI) commented upon events selected from the Old Testament to illustrate either of his two themes, choosing mostly the unusual rather than the received image: the three sons of Noah or the three patriarchs rather than Abraham's three visitors, for instance, as figures of the Trinity. By Pentecost 1128 (June 10) he had completed the first six books.[74] Book VII interprets the three books of Solomon as teaching respectively the faith, hope, and charity required to reform man toward his original image-likeness to God, and this book closes with a suitable prayer.[75] (Here Rupert defended his Marian interpretation of the Song of Songs, referring indirectly to the critical letter he had received; see above, at n. 11.) Book VIII takes up Trinitarian images found in the Book of Daniel, and soon digresses

72. *Glor.* 3.17: PL 169.68–69. Cf. *Vict.* 1.28: ed. Haacke 41–43, and the reaction still of Meingoz of St. Martin in Liège: ed. H. Grundmann, *DA* 21 (1965) 274–75.

73. By way of introduction Rupert restated his theme: "Igitur de humana creatura iam dicturi aliquid ad gloriam et laudem sanctae Trinitatis, ad honorem Spiritus sancti de Patre et Filio precedentis cuius in ista creatura ualde clara rutilant dona. . . ." *Glor.* 4.1: PL 169.75.

74. *Glor.* 6.21: PL 169.140. Since Rupert almost certainly spent January–February 1128 at Münster, where he debated Hermannus (chapter VI, part 3), the first six books were probably written between March and June and the last three between June and late August.

75. "Quoniam igitur per haec ad similitudinem tui reformamur, auge in nobis fidem, auge spem, auge charitatem, O beata Trinitas." *Glor.* 7.18: PL 169.160.

into another summary of the negative role played by the four beasts (=world-empires) in salvation-history. The culminating work of Triune God was the incarnation of Christ (Book IX), who possessed the fullness of the Spirit and from whose crucified body the Spirit proceeded in remission of sin for the whole Church, a gift carried abroad by the apostles.

Systematization requires a methodological instrument through which to approach and organize Christian truth. When theologians began to systematize the Christian faith early in the twelfth century, they generally followed one of two models: the biblical order of topics in the history of salvation (creation, fall, redemption, and so forth), or a more abstract dialectical presentation of Christian truth.[76] Teachers of Scripture (the so-called School of Laon and Hugh of St. Victor) gathered, organized, and attempted to harmonize the teachings of the Fathers on particular scriptural verses, and then summarized or abbreviated those biblical teachings in topical handbooks. Peter Abelard and other dialecticians sought rather to unravel the truths of the Christian faith step by step as a logical exposition; Abelard's *Theologia Christiana*, for instance, written in the 1120's, attempted to set forth the Christian faith by way of a philosophical analysis of the Three-in-One.[77] Critics complained that logic and philosophy too often distorted the exposition, as when Abelard identified the Holy Spirit with Plato's world-soul and Gilbert seemed to have found a fourth entity in the Holy Trinity. Peter Lombard's authoritative textbook finally used something of both methods while remaining closer to the first.

Historians have studied representatives of both the scriptural and the dialectical methods, but they have paid virtually

76. H. Cloes, "La systématisation théologique pendant la première moitié du XIIᵉ siècle," *Ephemerides theologicae Lovanienses* 34 (1958) 277–329.

77. Note Abelard's own description (which is not without reference to Scripture): "Primus liber continet quid uelit distinctio trium personarum in Deo uel quid sonent in haec nomina personarum 'Pater,' 'Filius,' 'Spiritus Sanctus,' et testimonia tam prophetarum quam philosophorum de sancta Trinitate, necnon et quare sapientia Dei uocetur Verbum aut benignitas ipsius dicatur Spiritus sanctus. In quo etiam ea quae de anima mundi a philosophis dicta sunt recte de Spiritus sancto intelligi monstrantur." CM 12.71.

no attention to the systematic efforts of the Benedictine theologian Rupert of Deutz. The shaping instrument of Rupert's theological vision was the divine office, and that an office peculiar to Benedictine monk-priests, one in which elaborate prayers absorbed nearly all of a monk's time and devotion, and daily mass, whether public or private, marked the high point of each day. Meditation on Scripture loomed large too, so large that Rupert virtually identified it with the religious life; but the office shaped the reading and understanding of Scripture. Benedictines had made this office their all-encompassing task. Its ever greater elaboration justified the whole of their existence, their freedom from manual labor, their outstanding education, their magnificent churches. For their work—the prayers sung, intercession made, and masses said for all other Christians including secular clerics—was the most important work of all, the Work of God (*Opus Dei*).

Their absorption in the Work of God also represented, contrary to the new religious with their ascesis and manual labor, the best available means for personal sanctification and communion with God. The office opened one's heart to the grace of the Spirit. Beyond that, daily and total participation in the office brought to life the "glorification of Triune God," "the honor and glory of the Son of Man," "the very procession of the Holy Spirit," and above all—something stressed to the new Benedictines—the daily incarnational presence of Christ's sacrificial atonement.[78] The mysteries of Christ and of salvation-history, in sum, were to be approached primarily through their daily celebration in the office and at the altar. Doing the Work of God since childhood had clearly shaped Rupert's vision of the "works of God" he came to consider the essential contents of Holy Scripture (*opera utilia de quibus omnis Scriptura sancta consistit*).

But there is something more, something directly pertinent

---

78. "Ubi enim sunt pedes eius [Christ's, this put to the new monks], nisi sacramento altaris eius? Ibi enim sunt uestigia passionis eius, uestigia resurrectionis et ascensionis eius. Ergo sacramento altaris inseruire et ob hoc omnibus negotiis expeditum esse, ut uacet tibi meditari sacramenta salutis nostrae, quam ille *est in medio terrae operatus* (Ps. 73 : 12), hoc sedere est ad pedes Domini et audire uerba oris eius." *RegBen.* 3.8: PL 170.515. Cf. ibid. 10.5–18.

to the question of methodology and insofar fully comparable
to the problems raised for Abelard and later scholastic theologians by their dialectical approach. For those same works celebrated in the office not only revealed God but also came close to
defining His very being. Thus the second person of the Trinity
becomes almost literally inconceivable apart from His incarnate
kingship, like His glory and honor apart from His victory on
the cross; so also the third person of the Trinity "proceeds" in
His bestowal of spiritual gifts and the remission of sin. This is
not just pious hyperbole, any more than the notion that God
cannot contradict Himself was a playful jest on the schoolmen's
part. Each betrays a frame of mind which shaped the exposition
of the Christian faith to an extraordinary degree. Each also pre-
supposes a certain foundation required for the satisfactory treatment of divine matters. For the new teachers of Scripture and
dialectic it was thorough grounding in their respective disciplines. For Rupert it was total commitment to the Work of God
and the possession of an extraordinary gift of spiritual understanding. Those who had such a gift Rupert ranked directly
after the apostles and charged with the instruction and edification of God's people even in the face of criticism from "envious"
new masters and conservative brother-monks.[79]

Such large shaping structures cannot be adequately explained
simply by referring to "schools" or "cloisters," as has become
rather fashionable in the past twenty-five years. In the schools,
for instance, quite apart from individual differences, it mattered
much in a theologian's understanding of the world and the Christian faith whether his spiritual formation was secular, Franciscan, Dominican, Augustinian, or Carthusian. So also there is no
single "monastic theology," even though there may well have
been concerns and methods common to those in cloisters as
there were to those in schools. Apart again from individual differences, the character of the religious life shaped by rules and
customaries and the nature of the spirituality fostered therein
greatly influenced individual perceptions of the Scriptures and
of Christian truth. Too much of what has recently been called

79. *Matt.* 4: CM 29.115–19.

"monastic theology" is in fact peculiar to Cistercian monasteries, where grown men sought refuge from the world, the secular Church, and the schools, and where they also gave relatively less attention to the priesthood and the divine office. Benedictines, who had lived and moved easily in an aristocratic world for almost two centuries and who had at the same time upheld the highest standards anywhere in the priesthood and the divine office, took an entirely different approach. Rupert insisted on his right to preach, and presupposed that he had at least as much ability to speak to questions arising from Holy Scripture as any of the secular schoolmen. The structure he gave his theological exposition grew directly out of his celebration every day all day long of God's deeds in the history of salvation. His work gave expression to the theological vision implicit in almost two hundred years of traditional Benedictine monasticism.

5

Meditation on Death

Shortly after Rupert finished *De glorificatione Trinitatis* fire destroyed parts of the castle and parish church at Deutz and for a time also threatened the monastic church and its cloister. This struck the final blow in Rupert's exhausting two-year struggle against Archbishop Frederick, Count Adolph, and certain local lords. Whether or not his health had already begun to fail, his spirits certainly were brought low. He saw to the most pressing necessities with regard to his writing and his abbey. He apparently had copies made of *De glorificatione* and sent to Bishop Cuno in Regensburg and Pope Honorius II in Rome; and he composed his finely wrought little work *De incendio*, interpreting the fire as a divine judgement and putting on parchment his claims to full control over the castle at Deutz. Then, in the immediate aftermath of the fire and right after completing *De incendio*,[80] he set to work on a *Meditation on Death*.[80] The opening

80. ". . . in hoc opusculo, quod nuncupare placet meditationem mortis, cuius uidelicet opusculi scribendi mihi occasio fuit periculum ignis, quod praecedente libello denarraui. . . ." *Medit.* 1.2: PL 170.359.

lines make clear his mood: "What more, O my soul? Henceforth be wiser, and in the time that remains (*quod reliquum est temporis*), live the life of wisdom, which is to meditate upon death."[81]

Selecting texts from the Book of Job probably suggested by readings prescribed for the Office of the Dead, Rupert attempted to show the necessity, even good fortune, of death as a prelude to the glorified state, especially since it also served to discipline man's pride in the flesh and the things of this world. A gifted writer to the end, Rupert marveled at how much there was to say about this topic as he concluded one book and launched into a second.[82] He also remained a theologian to the end. He condemned anew the view which held that "God willed evil."[83] Several chapters later he asserted that truly wise (*sapiens*) souls could never fail to rise up in defense of truth when they heard false teaching in the Church. Such persons could die but they could not keep silent (*mori potest, silere non potest*).[84]

Those, strikingly, were virtually his last written words, a very fitting epitaph for a man so tireless in expounding Holy Scripture and combatting error. On 4 March 1129 he died, taken away suddenly (according to a slightly later report) by a high fever.[85] He was buried in the St. Michael's chapel at Deutz. A generation later Reiner of St. Lawrence (ca. 1160) and Thiodericus of Deutz (ca. 1164) celebrated him as the greatest writer and master ever to have come out of their respective houses.

81. *Medit.* 1.1: PL 170.357.

82. Until a critical edition has been prepared, it will not be clear how far Rupert actually got into Book II, since someone early on completed this book with excerpts from his earlier works: see Grundmann, *DA* 22 (1966) 388. There are six extant MSS of this work: R. Haacke, *DA* 26 (1970) 540.

83. *Medit.* 1.19: PL 170.377–78.

84. *Medit.* 2.6: PL 170.384.

85. Reiner, *De ineptiis* 1: MGH SS 20.597. It is worth noting that Rupert himself described at length the debilitating effects of a high fever: *Medit.* 1.5: PL 170.361–62.

Conclusion

BENEDICTINE MONK-PRIESTS had been at work for nearly two centuries shaping the religious world which Rupert entered as a child around 1082 and within which he grew to maturity. As contemplatives, Benedictines ranked still as the highest *ordo* in Christendom, the closest approximation here on earth to angels singing God's praise eternally in heaven. As intercessors, their daily prayers and masses were thought to avail more than all others, and so justified the magnificence of their liturgy and churches and the opulent support of kings, bishops, and peasants alike. As efficient administrators of this landed wealth, their abbots and priors had few equals, and the parochial churches on their lands generally benefitted from higher standards of pastoral care. As learned churchmen, finally, they rendered frequent and invaluable service to the secular Church on all manner of educational, canonistic, and theological issues. It comes as no surprise that virtually all the reforming popes down to about 1120 had ties of some kind to Benedictine monasticism. So also Rupert, when confronted with startling ecclesiastical, educational, and religious reforms, endeavored to deal with them by creatively applying the venerable Benedictine tradition he had inherited; and he never quite comprehended why religious and educational reformers in particular presumed to rebuff his work as old-fashioned, if not indeed corrupt and simple-minded.

Three distinct instances of reform or renewal deeply affected Rupert's early life. Though an oblate, he underwent an extended vocational crisis accompanied by visionary and mystical experiences. Rather than driving him out of an established house into a new order, as it did so many of his contemporaries, this experience "called" him to undertake with an "apostolic" zeal and truly extraordinary talent something Benedictines had always done, namely, to uncover and to preach the mysteries of Holy Scripture. At the same time, in a region dominated by imperial loyalists, he pledged himself to the radical reform party in the Church, a choice that caused him to suffer three years' exile in France, to postpone his ordination, and finally to remain permanently at odds with the imperial prince-bishop of Liège and much of its secular clergy. This experience instilled in him a lasting concern for the nature and course of the Church, the quality of her ministers, and the valid functioning of her sacraments. Between his return from exile (1095) and his ordination (ca. 1108) Rupert participated as well in the renewal of the monastic office and customary at St. Lawrence, and this may well have inspired him to undertake as his first major work a commentary on the divine office. The combined effect of these reform movements was to generate in him a fervor he felt called to communicate to his readers, first of all to his fellow Benedictine monk-priests, especially all those inclined to carry out their daily intercessory tasks far too perfunctorily, but then also to priests and prelates in the Church at large.

Rupert's interpretation of Holy Scripture was at once traditional and innovative. Thoroughly grounded in the received tradition, he took constant delight in finding new and "more useful" meanings. The Word of God read endlessly in the monastic office he considered as inexhaustible as the mysteries of Christ Himself; and any new understanding of that Word which opened the way to a fresh perception of, even direct communion with, the Lord Christ deserved only grateful praise to the Spirit who had provided it. Pedantic masters devoted to gathering and harmonizing the Fathers and conservative monks wary of going beyond the received tradition accused Rupert repeatedly of "showing off" and "burdening readers" with all these new commentaries. Just like Abelard, similarly accused for his

371

dialectical innovations, Rupert charged them in turn with "envy." Sometimes such criticism dampened his spirits and once it silenced him for almost two years, but ultimately his "apostolic" zeal to preach Scripture proved irrepressible. The first work ever on the whole of Scripture under a single theme (the work of Triune God), the first new commentary on John's Gospel since Augustine, the first new commentary on the twelve Minor Prophets since Jerome, the story of salvation narrated as an epic battle, the most innovative commentary on the Apocalypse before Joachim, and the first consistently Marian interpretation of the Song of Songs—such were a few of Rupert's exegetical achievements.

They make him one of the first and greatest representatives of a new kind of "Figural Thought." Almost poetic in style and imagination, though scriptural in base, this form of thought eventually came to saturate later medieval culture. But where later authors recognized almost no limits to such imaginative allegorizing (and so came to be judged degenerate by moderns), Rupert never strayed far in his interpretations from the experiential center of his own religious life: the history of salvation recorded in Holy Scripture and celebrated in the divine office, or, differently put, the gracious "work of God" commemorated in the monastic Work of God. Rupert insisted that each day monk-priests encountered Christ the Lord and Savior Himself in their ministry at the altar, and brought to life the mysteries of Scripture and the way of salvation in their performance of the liturgical office.

Rupert's zeal could come to fine literary expression because he had received a good education in the liberal arts, made possible indirectly by the excellent schools in eleventh-century Liège. He never attended one of the flourishing new cathedral schools, nor heard one of the new masters lecture, but he followed their discussions with interest from the confines of his cloister. When masters of dialectic challenged the real bodily presence of Christ in the Blessed Sacrament, when they also insisted that God's omnipotence could be saved and the process of salvation set in motion only if God were said to have "willed evil," when new masters of the Sacred Page uncovered biblical and patristic texts which seemed to make the suffering Son of Man something less than the eternal Son of God, and when churchmen struggled to explain the validity of sacraments only within Holy Church, Rupert intervened boldly and aggressively. On each point he put forth a new and distinctive theological position—grounded, however, in traditional Benedictine piety. For it was not in rational arguments, he declared, that God had revealed Himself, but rather in deeds, the deeds recorded in Holy Scripture, celebrated daily in the divine office, and interpreted by those (like himself) endowed with an extraordinary spiritual gift of understanding. His understanding of Holy Scripture, the divinely authoritative record of those deeds, stood supreme therefore over against all human argumentation and, if necessary, also over against particular teachings of the Fathers. In rising to defend the truth Rupert never feared to differ with received interpretations, to argue his views in the marketplace, and even, like a knight-errant, to carry his campaign into the land of the enemy in single combat. He rejected out of hand any notion that as a mere monk he was unqualified and untrained to speak as a theologian.

But new religious as well as new masters now attacked the Benedictine tradition which had nurtured and protected him since childhood. New monks called on Black Monks to give up their absorption in liturgical performance, their wealth in lands, their pastoral work in the secular Church, and their intellectual pursuits. It was better, they said, to withdraw wholly from the world, to live off the labor of their own hands, and to concentrate entirely on their own salvation in strict personal ascesis. Rupert was horrified that they would thus neglect the ministry at the altar, this daily encounter with Christ Himself, and voluntarily give up the work of intercession for all souls committed to their care—the very focal-point of his own life, piety, and work. To make matters worse, canons demanded that Benedictines give up their pastoral and intellectual functions, and with their new-found devotion to ascesis and the common life canons regular even challenged the monks' five-hundred-year reign as the supreme *ordo* in Christendom. Rupert refused to acknowledge Augustinians as "fellow monks" and argued back that Benedictine monk-priests also possessed all the rights and privileges of the priesthood, including the right to certain incomes and the duty to teach and preach in the Church. Failure to combine religious practice with scriptural learning, as the Benedictines had now done for generations, could only produce learning without piety (the new schoolmen) or piety without learning (the new monks). Yet the real successor to Rupert, Benedictine monk and scriptural preacher in Liège and Cologne, was in fact to be Hugh of St. Victor, canon regular and scriptural teacher in Paris.

Rupert always presumed that Benedictine monk-priests represented the apostolic ideal, the highest position in the Christian world-order and closest thing here on earth to that future "third status" of the Kingdom of God; and likewise he consistently placed those divinely gifted with the understanding of Scripture directly after the apostles. The new educational and religious reformers rattled his self-confidence at times, but never his convictions. By rising to defend his religious and theological calling in a personal apologia he anticipated some aspects of that twelfth-century phenomenon sometimes called the "discovery of the individual." But the time was nearly gone when the Benedictine tradition could accommodate the first theologians systematically to apply dialectic to revealed truth, the first craftsman to teach in writing the skills of his trade, the learned abbot who first took the intellectual challenge of Islam seriously, numerous great chroniclers, and the patron of a new art and regent of a Christian land. Benedictine monks had played a crucial role in putting Christian Europe back together again in the dismal days of the early tenth century. In the early twelfth century, a new age which their own work had in good part made possible, they creatively adapted and defended that tradition of piety, learning, and intercession founded two hundred years earlier. When in the 1110's and 1120's Rupert took it upon himself to teach the mysteries of salvation, to preach reform in the Church at large, to uphold Scripture in the midst of false teaching, and to proclaim Benedictine monk-priests the true apostolic ideal, he did so with an energy and a genius all his own, but as spokesman for a tradition generations older now come to fruition.

Select Bibliography
of Works Pertaining
to Rupert of Deutz

ALBERS, BRUNO. "Das Verbrüderungsbuch der Abtei Deutz," *SMBO* 16 (1895) 96–104

ALGER. *De sacramentis corporis et sanguinis dominici*, PL 180.739–854

———. *Liber de misericordia et iustitia*, PL 180.857–968

ARANCIBIA, JOSÉ M. "Ruperto de Deutz y la crisis sacerdotal del siglo XII," *Scriptorium Victoriense* 17 (1970) 34–64

———. "Las virtudes de los prelados según Ruperto de Deutz," ibid. 241–82

ARDUINI, MARIA L. "Contributo alla biografia di Ruperto di Deutz," *Studi Medievali* 3rd ser. 16 (1975) 537–82

———. "Il problema della *paupertas* nella *Vita sancti Heriberti archiepiscopi Coloniensis* di Ruperto di Deutz," *Studi Medievali* 3rd ser. 20 (1979) 87–138

———. *Ruperto di Deutz e la controversia tra Cristiani ed Ebrei nel secolo XII*, con testo critico dell'*Anulus seu dialogus inter Christianum et Iudaeum*, a cura di Rhabanus Haacke, OSB (Studi Storici 119–121, Rome 1979)

BACH, JOSEF. *Die Dogmengeschichte des Mittelalters vom christologischen Standpunkte* (2 vols. Vienna 1873–75)

BALAU, SYLVESTRE. *Les sources de l'histoire du pays de Liège au moyen âge: Étude critique* (Académie royale des sciences, des lettres et des beaux-arts de Belgique, Mémoires couronnés 61, Brussels 1902–03)

BEINERT, WOLFGANG. *Die Kirche–Gottes Heil in der Welt: Die Lehre von der Kirche nach den Schriften des Rupert von Deutz, Honorius Au-*

gustodunensis und Gerhoch von Reichersberg (BGPT neue Folge 13, Münster 1973)

BEITZ, EGID. *Rupertus von Deutz: Seine Werke und die bildende Kunst* (Veröffentlichungen des kölnischen Geschichtsvereins 4, Cologne 1930)

BERLIÈRE, URSMER. *L'ascèse bénédictine des origines à la fin du XIIe siècle: essai historique* (Paris and Maredsous 1927)

————. *Monasticon Belge* II (Maredsous 1928)

————. "Rupert de Deutz et Saint Norbert," *RB* 7 (1890) 452–57

BERNARDS, MATTHÄUS. "Geschichtsperiodisches Denken in der Theologie des 12. Jahrhunderts," *Kölner Domblatt* 27 (1967) 115–24

————. "Die Welt der Laien in der kölnischen Theologie des 12. Jahrhunderts: Beobachtungen zur Ekklesiologie Ruperts von Deutz," in *Die Kirche und ihre Ämter und Stände: Festgabe für Josef Kardinal Frings* (Cologne 1960) 391–416

BEUMER, JOHANNES. "Die lateinische Messe zu Beginn des 12. Jahrhunderts nach Rupert von Deutz: *De diuinis officiis*," *Münchener Theologische Zeitschrift* 25 (1974) 34–50

————. "Rupert von Deutz und sein Einfluss auf die Kontroverstheologie der Reformationszeit," *Catholica* 22 (1968) 207–16

————. "Rupert von Deutz und seine 'Vermittlungstheologie,'" *Münchener Theologische Zeitschrift* 4 (1953) 255–70

BISCHOFF, GUNTRAM. "Early Premonstratensian Eschatology: The Apocalyptic Myth," in *The Spirituality of Western Christendom*, ed. E. Rozanne Elder (Cistercian Studies Series 30, Kalamazoo 1976) 41–71

————. "The Eucharistic Controversy between Rupert of Deutz and His Anonymous Adversary: Studies in the Theology and Chronology of Rupert of Deutz (c. 1076–c. 1129) and His Earlier Literary Work" (diss. Princeton Theological Seminary 1965)

BOEHMER, HEINRICH, ed. *Monachi cuiusdam exulis s. Laurentii de calamitatibus ecclesiae Leodiensis opusculum*, in MGH LdL 3 (Hannover 1897) 622–41

BRUYNE, DONATIEN DE. "Un traité inédit contre le mariage des prêtres," *RB* 35 (1923) 246–54

BYNUM, CAROLINE WALKER. *Docere verbo et exemplo: An Aspect of Twelfth-Century Spirituality* (Harvard Theological Studies 31, Missoula, Mont. 1979)

Catalogus codicum hagiographicorum bibliothecae regiae bruxellensis: codices latini (2 vols. Brussels 1886–89)

CAUCHIE, ALFRED. *Le querelle des investitures dans les diocèses de Liège et de Cambrai* (2 vols. Louvain 1890)

———. "Rupert de Saint-Laurent ou de Deutz," in *Biographie Nationale* 20 (Brussels 1910) 426–58

CHENU, MARIE-DOMINIQUE. "Histoire et allégorie au douzième siècle," in *Festgabe Joseph Lortz*, ed. E. Iserloh and P. Manns (Baden-Baden 1958) 2.59–71

———. *La théologie au douzième siècle* (Etudes de philosophie médiévale 45, Paris 1957)

CHRONICON BRUNWYLRENSE. Ed. G. Eckertz, in *Annalen des historischen Vereins für den Niederrhein* 17 (1866) 119–91

CLASSEN, PETER. "Codex latinus monacensis 14355 und die Revision der Eucharistielehre Ruperts von Deutz," *Studi Medievali* 3rd ser. 1 (1960) 99–106

———. *Gerhoch von Reichersberg: Eine Biographie* (Wiesbaden 1960)

———. "*Res Gestae*, Universal History, Apocalypse: Visions of Past and Future," in *Renaissance and Renewal in the Twelfth Century*, ed. R. L. Benson, G. Constable, and C. D. Lanham (Cambridge, Mass. 1982)

———. "Zur kritischen Edition der Schriften Ruperts von Deutz," *DA* 26 (1970) 513–27

COENS, MAURICE. "Un sermon inconnu de Rupert, abbé de Deutz, sur s. Pantaleón," *Analecta Bollandiana* 55 (1937) 244–67

CONGAR, YVES. *L'église de Saint Augustin à l'époque moderne* (Paris 1970)

CSOKA, LAJOS. "Ein unbekannter Brief des Abtes Rupert von Deutz," *SMBO* 84 (1973) 383–93

DEMPF, ALOIS. *Sacrum Imperium* (Munich 1929)

DEREINE, CHARLES. *Les chanoines réguliers au diocèse de Liège avant Saint Norbert* (Mémoires de l'Académie Belge, Classe des lettres 47, Brussels 1952)

DINTER, PETER. *Rupert von Deutz, Vita Heriberti: Kritische Edition mit Kommentar und Untersuchungen* (Veröffentlichungen des historischen Vereins für den Niederrhein insbesondere das alte Erzbistum Köln 13, Bonn 1976)

DÜMMLER, ERNST. "Zur Geschichte des Investiturstreites im Bisthum Lüttich," *Neues Archiv* 11 (1886) 175–94

ENDRES, JOSEPH. *Honorius Augustodunensis: Beitrag zur Geschichte des geistigen Lebens im 12. Jahrhundert* (Kempten and Munich 1906)

EVANS, GILLIAN R. *Anselm and a New Generation* (Oxford 1980)

————. *Old Arts and New Theology: The Beginnings of Theology as an Academic Discipline* (Oxford 1980)

FLINT, VALERIE I. J. "The Date of the Arrival of Rupert of Deutz at Siegburg," *RB* 81 (1971) 317–19

GERBERON, GABRIEL. *Apologia pro Ruperto abbate Tuitiensi* (Paris 1669 = PL 170.23–194)

GESSLER, JEAN. "La bibliothèque de l'abbaye de Saint-Laurent à Liège au XIIe et XIIIe siècles," *Bulletin de la société des bibliophiles liégeois* 12 (1927) 91–135

GHELLINCK, JOSEPH DE. *Le mouvement théologique du XIIe siècle* (2nd ed. Brussels 1948)

GRABMANN, MARTIN. *Die Geschichte der scholastischen Methode* (2 vols. Freiburg 1909–11)

GRIBOMONT, JEAN. *Rupert de Deutz, Les oeuvres du Saint-Esprit* (2 vols. Sources chrétiennes 131 and 165, Paris 1967 and 1970)

GRUNDMANN, HERBERT. "Der Brand von Deutz 1128 in der Darstellung Abt Ruperts von Deutz: Interpretation und Text-Ausgabe," *DA* 22 (1966) 385–471

————. "Zwei Briefe des Kanonikers Meingoz von St. Martin an Abt Rupert von Deutz (nach 1124–Anfang 1128)," *DA* 21 (1965) 264–76

HAACKE, RHABANUS. "Die mystischen Visionen Ruperts von Deutz," in *Sapientiae Doctrina: Mélanges de théologie et de littérature médiévales offerts à Dom Hildebrand Bascour O.S.B.* (Louvain 1980) 68–90

————. "Nachlese zur Ueberlieferung Ruperts von Deutz," *DA* 26 (1970) 528–40

————. *Programme zur bildenden Kunst in den Schriften Ruperts von Deutz* (Siegburger Studien 9, Siegburg 1974)

————. "Rupert von Deutz zur Frage: *Cur Deus Homo*," in *Corona Gratiarum: Miscellanea Eligio Dekkers O.S.B. Oblata* (Brugge 1975) 2.143–59

————. "Die Ueberlieferung der Schriften Ruperts von Deutz," *DA* 16 (1960) 397–436

HAUCK, ALBERT. *Kirchengeschichte Deutschlands*, vol. 4 (Leipzig 1913)

HAURÉAU, BARTHÉLEMY. "Notice sur un poème contenu dans le numéro 386 [410] des manuscrits de Cambrai," *Notices et extraits des manuscrits de la bibliothèque nationale et autres bibliothèques* 31.2 (1886) 165–94

JAFFÉ, PHILLIP. *Rupertus de incendio Tuitiensi et de Cunone episcopo Ratisponensi*, in MGH SS 12 (Hannover 1856) 624–38

KAHLES, WILHELM. *Geschichte als Liturgie: Die Geschichtstheologie des Rupertus von Deutz* (Münster 1960)

KAMLAH, WILHELM. *Apokalypse und Geschichtstheologie: Die mittelalterliche Auslegung der Apokalypse von Joachim von Fiore* (Historische Studien 285, Berlin 1935)

LECLERCQ, JEAN. *The Love of Learning and the Desire for God*, trans. C. Misrahi (2nd paperback ed. New York 1974)

LUBAC, HENRI DE. *Exégèse médiévale: Les quatre sens de l'Ecriture* (2 vols. in 4, Théologie 41.1–2, 42, 59, Paris 1959–64)

McGINN, BERNARD. *Visions of the End* (New York 1979)

MAGRASSI, MARIO. *Teologia e storia nel pensiero di Ruperto di Deutz* (Studia Urbaniana 2, Rome 1959)

MERING, FRIEDRICH. *Geschichte der Burgen, Rittergüter, Abteien und Klöster in den Rheinlanden*, vol. 10 (Cologne 1855)

MEUTHEN, ERICH. "Ruperts von Deutz *De victoria Verbi Dei* nach Clm 14055," *DA* 28 (1972) 542–57

MILZ, JOSEPH. *Studien zur mittelalterlichen Wirtschafts- und Verfassungsgeschichte der Abtei Deutz* (Veröffentlichungen des Kölnischen Geschichtsvereins 30, Cologne 1970)

MOREAU, EDOUARD DE. *Histoire de l'église en Belgique* (2nd ed. 5 vols. Brussels 1945–52)

NEUSS, WILHELM. *Das Buch Ezechiel in Theologie und Kunst bis zum Ende des 12. Jahrhunderts* (Beiträge zur Geschichte des alten Mönchtums und des Benediktinerordens 1–2, Münster 1912)

OHLY, FRIEDRICH. *Hohelied-Studien: Grundzüge einer Geschichte der Hoheliedauslegung des Abendlandes bis um 1200* (Wiesbaden 1958)

OTT, LUDWIG. *Untersuchungen zur theologischen Briefliteratur der Frühscholastik* (BGPT 34, Münster 1937)

PEINADOR, MAXIMO. "La actitud negativa de Ruperto de Deutz ante la Immaculada Concepción de la Virgen: Ambiente doctrinal y motivación de la misma," *Marianum* 30 (1968) 192–217

———. "El comentario de Ruperto de Deutz al Cantar de los cantares:

Introducción, análisis critico, temas principales," *Marianum* 31 (1969) 1–58

———. "Maria y la Iglesia en la historia de la salvación según Ruperto de Deutz," *Ephemerides Mariologicae* 18 (1968) 337–81

———. "La mariologia de Ruperto de Deutz," *Ephemerides Mariologicae* 17 (1967) 121–48

PELIKAN, JAROSLAV. *The Growth of Medieval Theology* (The Christian Tradition 3, Chicago 1978)

PERI, ISRAEL. "Das Hexaemeron Arnos von Reichersberg: Eine Exegese aus dem 12. Jahrhundert," *Jahrbuch des Stiftes Klosterneuberg,* neue Folge 10 (1976) 9–115

PICKERING, FREDERICK. "Exegesis and Imagination," in his *Essays on Medieval German Literature and Iconography* (Cambridge 1980) 31–45

RATZINGER, JOSEPH. *The Theology of History in St. Bonaventure* (Chicago 1971)

RAUH, HORST D. *Das Bild des Antichrist im Mittelalter: Von Tyconius zum deutschen Symbolismus* (BGPT neue Folge 9, Münster 1972)

REINER OF ST. LAWRENCE, *De ineptiis cuiusdam idiotae libellus ad amicum,* ed. W. Arndt, in MGH SS 20 (Hannover 1868) 593–603

RENARDY, CHRISTINE. "Les écoles liégeoises du IXe au XIIe siècle: grandes lignes de leur évolution," *RBPH* 57 (1979) 309–28

Rhein und Maas: Kunst und Kultur (800–1400) (2 vols. Cologne 1972–73)

ROCHOLL, RUDOLF. *Rupert von Deutz: Ein Beitrag zur Geschichte der Kirche im 12. Jahrhundert* (Gütersloh 1886)

———. "Rupert von Deutz," in *Realenzyklopädie für protestantische Theologie und Kirche* 3rd ed. 17 (Leipzig 1906) 229–43

RODULPHUS, *Gesta abbatum Trudonensium,* ed. R. Koepke, in MGH SS 10 (Hannover 1852) 213–332

ROTH, FRIEDRICH. "Ein Brief des Chronisten Rudolf von St. Trond an Rupert von Deutz," *Neues Archiv* 17 (1892) 617–18

RUPERTUS TUITIENSIS, *Commentaria in Canticum Canticorum De incarnatione Domini,* ed. R. Haacke (CM 26, Turnhout 1974)

———. *Commentaria in euangelium sancti Iohannis,* ed. R. Haacke (CM 9, Turnhout 1969)

———. *De gloria et honore Filii hominis super Matthaeum,* ed. R. Haacke (CM 29, Turnhout 1979)

————. *Liber de diuinis officiis*, ed. R. Haacke (CM 7, Turnhout 1967)

————. *Opera omnia (iuxta editionem Venetam anni 1748)*, ed. J. P. Migne, in PL 167–70 (Paris 1894)

————. *De sancta Trinitate et operibus eius*, ed. R. Haacke (CM 21–24, Turnhout 1971–72)

————. *De uictoria Verbi Dei*, ed. R. Haacke (MGH Geistesgeschichte 5, Weimar 1970)

Saint-Laurent de Liège: Eglise, abbaye et hôpital. Mille ans d'histoire, ed. R. Lejeune (Liège 1968)

SCHEFFCZYK, LEO. "Die heilsökonomische Trinitätslehre des Rupert von Deutz und ihre dogmatische Bedeutung," in *Kirche und Ueberlieferung*, ed. J. Betz and H. Fries (Freiburg 1960) 90–118

SÉJOURNÉ, PAUL. "Rupert de Deutz," in *DTC* 14 (Paris 1939) 169–205

SEMMLER, JOSEF. *Die Klosterreform von Siegburg: Ihre Ausbreitung und ihr Reformprogramm im 11. und 12. Jahrhundert* (Rheinisches Archiv 53, Bonn 1959)

SILVESTRE, HUBERT. "A propos de la lettre d'Anselme de Laon à Heribrand de Saint-Laurent," *RTAM* 28 (1961) 5–25

————. "A propos du Bruxellensis 10066–77 et de son noyau primitif," in *Miscellanea codicologica F. Masai dicata*, ed. P. Cockshaw, M. Garand, and P. Jodogne (Ghent 1979) 131–56

————. *Le Chronicon sancti Laurentii Leodiensis dit de Rupert de Deutz* (Recueil de travaux d'histoire et de philologie 43, Louvain 1952)

————. "Les citations et réminiscences classiques dans l'oeuvre de Rupert de Deutz," *RHE* 45 (1950) 140–74

————. "La date de la naissance de Rupert et la date de son départ pour Siegburg," *Scriptorium* 16 (1962) 345–48

————. "Le *De concordia et expositione quattuor evangeliorum* inédit de Wazelin II, abbé de Saint-Laurent à Liège (ca. 1150–ca. 1157)," *RB* 63 (1953) 310–25

————. "*Diuersi sed non aduersi*," *RTAM* 31 (1964) 124–32

————. "L'édition Rh. Haacke du *De Trinitate* de Rupert de Deutz," *Sacris Erudiri* 22 (1974–75) 377–99

————. "Emprunts non répéres à Jérome et à Bède dans l'*In Iohannem* de Rupert de Deutz," *RB* 84 (1974) 372–82

————. "Macrobe utilisé par un Pseudo-Erigène et par Rupert de Deutz," *Classica et Mediaevalia* 19 (1958) 129–32

————. "Notes sur la controverse de Rupert de Saint-Laurent avec Anselme de Laon et Guillaume de Champeaux," in *Saint-Laurent* 63–80

————. "Du nouveau sur Rupert de Deutz," *RHE* 63 (1968) 54–58

————. "La répartition des citations nominatives des Pères dans l'oeuvre de Rupert de Deutz," in *Sapientiae Doctrina: Mélanges de théologie et de littérature médiévales offerts à Dom Hildebrand Bascour O.S.B.* (Louvain 1980) 271–98

————. "Le retable de l'agneau mystique et Rupert de Deutz," *RB* 88 (1978) 274–89

————. "Rupert de Saint-Laurent et les auteurs classiques," in *Mélanges Felix Rousseau* (Brussels 1958) 541–51

————. "La tradition manuscrite des oeuvres de Rupert de Deutz," *Scriptorium* 16 (1962) 336–45

————. "Trois témoignages mosans du début du XIIe siècle sur le crucifix de l'arc triomphal," *Revue des archéologues et historiens d'art de Louvain* 9 (1976) 225–31

SPICQ, CESLAUS. *Esquisse d'une histoire de l'exégèse latine au moyen âge* (Bibliothèque Thomiste 26, Paris 1944)

SPILKER, REGINHARD. "Maria-Kirche nach dem Hoheliedkommentar des Rupertus von Deutz," in *Maria et ecclesia, Acta congressus Mariologici-Mariani in Lourdes 1958* (Rome 1959) 3.291–317

SPITZ, HANS. *Die Metaphorik des geistigen Schriftsinns* (Münstersche Mittelalter-Schriften 12, Münster 1972)

SPÖRL, JOHANNES. *Grundformen hochmittelalterlicher Geschichtsanschauung* (Munich 1935)

STIENNON, JACQUES. "La Vierge de Dom Rupert," in *Saint-Laurent* 81–92

THIODERICUS AEDITUI TUITIENSIS, *Opuscula*, in MGH SS 14 (Hannover 1883) 560–77

TRITHEMIUS, JOHANNES. *Opera historica* (Frankfurt 1601; repr. Frankfurt 1966)

VAN DEN ELSEN, MATHIAS. "De H. Norbertus en Rupertus," *De Katholiek* 89 (1886) 223–37, 93 (1888) 148–63, 95 (1889) 351–66

VAN ENGEN, JOHN. "Rupert von Deutz und das sogennannte Chronicon sancti Laurentii Leodiensis: Zur Geschichte des Investiturstreites in Lüttich," *DA* 35 (1979) 33–81

————. "Theophilus Presbyter and Rupert of Deutz: The Manual Arts and Benedictine Theology in the Early Twelfth Century," *Viator* 11 (1980) 147–63

WASSELYNCK, RENÉ. "L'influence de l'exégèse de S. Grégoire le Grand sur les commentaires bibliques médiévaux (VIIe–XIIe s.)," *RTAM* 32 (1965) 157–204

WOLFF, ODO. *Mein Meister Rupertus: Ein Mönchsleben aus dem zwölften Jahrhundert* (Freiburg 1920)

General Index

Designer: Wolfgang Lederer
Compositor: G & S Typesetters, Inc.
Printer: Braun-Brumfield, Inc.
Binder: Braun-Brumfield, Inc.
Text: 11/13 Bembo
Display: Bembo